TRADE IMBALANCE: THE STRUGGLE TO WEIGH HUMAN RIGHTS CONCERNS IN TRADE POLICYMAKING

Trade is controversial; around the world many people believe that trade agreements, even trade per se, undermine particular human rights such as labor rights or access to affordable medicine (the right to health). But trade and trade agreements can also advance human rights, directly or indirectly. In fact, some countries use trade policies to advance specific human rights such as labor rights or property rights. But in almost every country policymakers struggle to achieve both goals. Trade and human rights are out of balance.

Although scholars, policymakers, and activists have long debated the relationship between trade and human rights, in truth we know very little about this relationship. This book aims to provide readers with greater insights into the relationship between human rights and trade. The authors use stories about AIDS, frogs, slavery, and other topics to discuss what policymakers do to promote human rights as they seek to expand trade. Second, the book includes the first study of how South Africa, Brazil, the United States, and the European Union coordinate trade and human rights objectives and resolve conflicts. It also looks at how human rights issues are seeping into the WTO. Finally, it provides suggestions to policymakers for making their trade and human rights policies more coherent and balanced.

Susan Ariel Aaronson is Research Associate Professor of International Affairs at the Elliott School of International Affairs and Adjunct Associate Professor at the Business School, George Washington University. She also works as a consultant for various organizations including the ILO, the Extractive Industries Transparency Initiative, Free the Slaves, and the U.S. government and private companies. Aaronson is the author of five books and numerous articles on trade, investment, development, human rights, and global corporate social responsibility issues. She has received numerous grants for her research from foundations such as the Ford, UN, Rockefeller, and Levi-Strauss Foundations. Aaronson is a frequent speaker on globalization issues and has appeared on CNN, the BBC, and PBS. From 1995 to 1999, she was a commentator for *All Things Considered*, *Marketplace*, and *Morning Edition*. Aaronson is a pro bono consultant to John Ruggie, the UN Special Representative on the issue of human rights and transnational corporations, and she serves on the advisory board of business-humanrights.org.

Jamie M. Zimmerman is the Associate Director of the Global Assets Project, part of the Asset Building Program at the New America Foundation, which is working to develop vision and direction for the advancement of savings and asset-building in the developed and developing world. She previously worked with Dr. Aaronson as the Associate Director of Globalization Studies at the Kenan Institute of Private Enterprise of the University of North Carolina. She managed the field research for the developing country case studies for the book (Brazil, India, and South Africa). With Dr. Aaronson, she published a number of articles and op-eds in such publications as *YaleGlobal* and *Human Rights Quarterly*. Zimmerman completed her master's degree in international political economy and international development from the Patterson School at the University of Kentucky in 2003. She also holds a B.A. in foreign languages and international economics from the same university.

Trade Imbalance: The Struggle to Weigh Human Rights Concerns in Trade Policymaking

SUSAN ARIEL AARONSON, PH.D.

Business School,
George Washington University
Elliott School of International Affairs

JAMIE M. ZIMMERMAN

Senior Advisor, Global Assets Program,
New America Foundation

CAMBRIDGE
UNIVERSITY PRESS

CAMBRIDGE UNIVERSITY PRESS
Cambridge, New York, Melbourne, Madrid, Cape Town, Singapore, São Paulo, Delhi

Cambridge University Press
32 Avenue of the Americas, New York, NY 10013-2473, USA

www.cambridge.org
Information on this title: www.cambridge.org/9780521872560

First published 2008

Printed in the United States of America

A catalog record for this publication is available from the British Library.

Library of Congress Cataloging in Publication Data
Aaronson, Susan A.
Trade imbalance : the struggle to weigh human rights concerns in trade policymaking /
Susan Ariel Aaronson, Jamie M. Zimmerman.
p.   cm.
Includes bibliographical references and index.
ISBN 978-0-521-87256-0 (hardback) – ISBN 978-0-521-69420-9 (pbk.)
1. Human rights – Economic aspects.   2. International trade – Social aspects
3. Foreign trade regulation – Social aspects.   4. Social responsibility of business.
I. Zimmerman, Jamie M.   II. Title.
K3240.A27   2007
330–dc22   2007007719

ISBN   978-0-521-87256-0 hardback
ISBN   978-0-521-69420-9 paperback

Contents

Abbreviations

ACP	Africa, Caribbean, and Pacific Countries (EU)
AFL–CIO	American Federation of Labor, Congress of Industrial Organizations
ANC	African National Congress (South Africa)
BEE	Black Economic Empowerment Act (South Africa)
CAP	Common Agricultural Policy (EU)
CBD	Convention on Biodiversity
COSATU	Congress of South African Trade Unions
CIRI	Cingranelli–Richards Human Rights Data Set
CSR	Corporate Social Responsibility
DR–CAFTA	Dominican Republic/Central American Free Trade Agreement (also known as CAFTA-DR)
EC	European Community
EPZ	Export processing zones
EU	European Union
FTA	Free Trade Agreement
FTAA	Free Trade Agreement of the Americas
GATT	General Agreement on Tariffs and Trade
GDP	Gross domestic product
GSP	Generalized System of Preferences
IPR	Intellectual property rights
ITO	International Trade Organization
LDC	Least developed country
MERCOSUR	Common Market of the South; a trade agreement among Argentina, Brazil, Paraguay, Uruguay, and Venezuela
MFN	Most favored nation (also known as normal trade relations in the United States)
NAFTA	North American Free Trade Agreement (Canada, Mexico, and the United States)
NEDLAC	National Economic Development and Labor Council (South Africa)
NGO	Nongovernmental organization

SACU	Southern African Customs Union (South Africa, Botswana, Lesotho, Namibia, and Swaziland)
TEPAC	Trade and Environment Policy Advisory Committee (US)
TPA	Trade Promotion Authority (also known as fast track – US)
TRIPS	Trade-Related Intellectual Property Agreement of the WTO
UDHR	Universal Declaration of Human Rights
UN	United Nations
UNDP	United Nations Development Programme
UNESCO	United Nations Educational, Scientific, and Cultural Organization
UNESCR	International Covenant on Economic, Social, and Cultural Rights
UNICCPR	International Covenant on Civil and Political Rights
USTR	U.S. Trade Representative
WIPO	World Intellectual Property Organization
WTO	World Trade Organization

Acknowledgments

Gandhi said, "You must be the change you wish to see in the world." With this book, we hope to encourage other scholars, citizens, and policymakers to think about the relationship between trade and human rights goals. We could not have written this book without the encouragement, assistance, and support of a wide range of individuals around the world.

Theresa Fay Bustillos, Cindy Pierson, and Bruce Moats of the Levi-Strauss Foundation and the Levi-Strauss Corporation were our earliest donors. Theresa and Bruce forced us to defend our ideas and to explain how they would help make the world a better place. They helped make this project viable. Peggy Foran of the Pfizer Corporation also provided much needed early financial support. She was always ready to give feedback and encouragement. We were also supported by grants from Starbucks, Unilever, and other companies. Susan Aaronson also received a research grant from the University of North Carolina Center for International Studies for travel.

Our distinguished advisory board gave us critical feedback throughout the research and writing process. These advisors came from around the world and from different academic and work backgrounds. We are particularly thankful for the insights of Welber Barral, David Cingranelli, Caroline Dommen, Kimberley Ann Elliott, Maria Green, Emily Hafner Burton, Robert Howse, Andre Growenewald, Scott Jerbi, Hoe Lim, John Morijin, Sylvia Ostry, Carol Pier, Chip Pitts, Aaron Rosenberg, Debora Spar, Joel Trachtman, Margriet Vonno, Jochem Wiers, and other members of our advisory committee who patiently reviewed and improved our early drafts. Rod Adoubhab, Eric Biel, Iren Borissova, Jennifer Bremer, Mara Burr, Claes Hammar, Shareen Hertel, Adeline Hinderer, Thea Lee, Stephen J. Norton, Miguel Pestana, Robert Stumberg, Kay Wilkie, and Nicolais Zaimos also provided significant comments on the drafts. Officials at the WTO, the European Commission, the Office of the U.S. Trade Representative, and the U.S. State Department went out of their way to help us. Debashis Chakraborty at the Indian Institute of Foreign Trade helped Jamie conduct her research in India, although in the end we decided not to include a chapter on India. We are also grateful to anonymous reviewers at Cambridge University Press and *World Trade Review*. Our editor, John Berger, helped us with the title and provided us with early encouragement and advice. Finally, many policymakers, business executives, civil society and labor leaders, and academics provided us with country-specific insights. They are listed in the List of Interviews.

Graduate and undergraduate students frequently assisted us in our research and designed many of the tables/charts in the book. We are especially grateful to Julie Maupin, Philip Van der Celen, and Carla Winston. Julie assisted field research in South Africa and prepared an early draft of the South Africa chapter. Philip Van der Celen worked with Jamie in Brazil; he researched and prepared an initial draft of the European Union chapter. Carla Winston indexed the book and gave us advice on human rights issues.

We also benefited from the research and programmatic support of several wonderful interns throughout the course of the research: Nick Alexsovich, Jillian Bohinc, Jan Cartwright, Matt Daly, Amanda Dixon, and Eric Lundgren.

Our friends and family were extraordinarily patient as we spent many days and nights researching and writing this book. Thus, this book is dedicated to Doug, Ethan, and Allegra Wham and to Robert and Dorothy Zimmerman. We hope our readers will find this complex topic as interesting and as important as we do.

1

Introduction

The Struggle to Weigh Human Rights in Trade Policymaking

Overview

If birth and geography are destiny, the citizens of Cochabamba, Bolivia, were determined to change their fate.[1] Although the city lies in a fertile valley near the Rocha River and the Alalay Lagoon, Cochabamba has long had a chronic water shortage.[2] For many years, the people of Cochabamba struggled to obtain enough water to meet their basic needs. The local water utility was poorly managed and barely provided adequate services for the city proper. Moreover, the city was ringed by slums where the government did not provide such basic services as electricity or water.

In 1994, citizens in some of the slums surrounding the city decided to solve their chronic water problem on their own. They dug a well and organized a cooperative that provided clean, plentiful water at a reasonable price to many of the citizens living outside the city proper. Soon, other groups inside and outside the city were emulating this approach.

But, in 1999, the Bolivian government auctioned off the city's water utility as part of a broad-based effort to privatize the state utilities and transportation infrastructure. The government opened up the bidding to all investors, foreign and domestic. A U.S./Italian consortium (controlled by the U.S. company Bechtel) acquired the utility. That utility was granted the rights to neighborhood wells and water cooperatives, even though the cooperatives were not part of the original utility's purview. Moreover, the new water services provider decided the company must invest in a more effective water infrastructure. To pay for these costs, the company raised prices some 35%. But many of Cochabamba's citizens could not afford these prices, including those citizens who had created the cooperatives. Thus, they organized to defend the cooperatives they had set up. In January 2000, they took to the streets in protest, claiming that water would become less affordable.[3] Citizens battled police and soldiers in what journalists called "*la Guerra del Agua*" – the Water War.

The protests provided a preview of a problem surfacing around the world. Water is essential to survival, sanitation, public health, and numerous activities that sustain human life and ensure human dignity.[4] Yet the global supply of water is declining at the same time that the demand for and competition for water are rising.[5]

Water became the "poster child" – an archetype for public concern that trade policies and trade in general could undermine access to resources and in so doing, human rights. Under the Universal Declaration of Human Rights (UDHR), the basic code of human rights outlined by the members of the United Nations, there is no "right to water." However, as no one can survive without access to water, human rights bodies as well as the World Health Organization have delineated what governments should do to ensure that all of their people can enjoy sufficient, safe, acceptable, accessible, and affordable water without discrimination.[6] Alas, in many countries, government officials do not have the skill, expertise, or funds to regulate the provision of water. In the belief that outside companies may more efficiently provide access to safe, affordable drinking water, some policymakers have privatized water services, often permitting foreign companies to operate and manage water delivery systems.[7] In these instances, water services are traded.

Fairly or unfairly, many people perceived that trade in water services had undermined the right to water of the people of Cochabamba. Trade policies and trade agreements did not directly *cause* Cochabamba's water problem. Nonetheless, trade in water services (opening up the water supplier to foreign investment) *contributed* to making water less accessible and affordable.

The Bolivian experience has convinced some officials in other governments that they should neither open their water services to trade nor treat water as a commodity for trade.[8] For example, in May 2005, the Australian government made a public commitment to exclude water for human use from its World Trade Organization (WTO) trade negotiations agenda.[9] The government of Canada has banned bulk exports of water.[10] Members of the WTO have become so concerned about trade in water issues that they waded into the debate with a fact sheet – "The WTO is not after Your Water."[11]

But trade in water and water services can also *improve* peoples' access to water. For example, foreign investment in water services may lead to a more efficient and cheaper supply of water. Thus, trade may indeed promote access to clean, affordable water.[12] Clearly, the effect of trade on the public's right to water is not black-and-white.[13]

✳   ✳   ✳

In many countries, citizens and policymakers have alleged that trade policies and agreements can undermine specific rights such as the right to food, labor rights, the right to education, or the right to health (through access to affordable medicines). To some degree, the perception that trade and human rights may conflict stems from an imbalance in the international rule-based system. The WTO stipulates a set of rules that limit how and when nations may apply protectionist tools. It is also a forum for negotiating trade and has an effective and enforceable dispute settlement body. If any of the WTO's 150 members believes that another member nation's trade policies impede trade in violation of WTO rules, that nation can challenge those policies under the WTO's binding system of dispute resolution.[14]

However, there is no equally influential and binding international system to promote human rights globally. The United Nation's International Bill of Human Rights, (which includes the UDHR and its subsequent covenants), global public support, and governmental and civil society activism demonstrate an international commitment to fulfilling human rights obligations. Yet nations have not agreed on an effective universal mechanism to ensure the implementation of human rights norms and principles, to assess violations, or to punish violators. Moreover, because countries act differently at the intersection of trade and human rights, there is also an imbalance in behavior among countries. When confronted with a potential conflict between their human rights and trade objectives, some countries develop long-term strategies and mechanisms, other countries respond in an ad hoc manner, and still other countries do nothing.

Although scholars, policymakers, and activists have long debated the relationship between trade and human rights, in fact we still know very little about that relationship. Scholars are only beginning to study empirically the effects of trade or particular trade agreements on individual rights, and they have just started to examine which rights (such as property rights or the right to equality before the law) must be protected by governments for trade to flourish Nonetheless, current studies seem to indicate that, over time, trade policies and agreements – and the trade they stimulate – could (even simultaneously) undermine some rights and enhance others.

Policymakers may find it difficult to evaluate the impact of a particular trade agreement or policy on each one of thirty-some rights delineated in the UDHR. Moreover, the effect of trade policies upon a particular human right may change over time. There is no one set way that trade affects a basket of rights or a particular human right.[15]

Despite this lack of insight into the relationship between trade and human rights, policymakers around the world frequently use their trade policies to achieve human rights objectives. Sometimes they use incentives, such as increasing market access for countries that improve human rights. But government officials must be careful that when they use such incentives they do not violate international trade rules. At other times, government officials use disincentives, such as trade sanctions, to get other states to change their human rights behavior.[16] But a sanctions-based approach cannot build the capacity of state actors to protect internationally accepted human rights standards, such as those delineated by the International Labor Organization (ILO) or the UDHR. Some governments have tried to link trade and human rights by obtaining a waiver from their trade obligations. And, finally, some governments have tried to address specific areas where trade and human rights may conflict outside of the WTO system. For example, under the aegis of the United Nations Educational, Scientific and Cultural Organization (UNESCO) in Paris, a wide range of nations agreed to a Convention on the Protection of the Diversity of Cultural Contents and Artistic Expression. France and Canada led a bloc of countries that argued that cultural rights (and industries) should be shielded from international trade rules under the WTO.[17]

The WTO, the international system of rules governing trade, provides very little guidance to its member governments on what they should do if a fellow member undermines particular human rights. Nor does it provide guidance as to how WTO members can promote human rights without distorting trade. The WTO system stipulates what governments *cannot* do, not what they can do. Yet, when policymakers fail to coordinate trade and human rights objectives, they risk perpetuating human rights problems both at home and abroad.

This book enters this murky territory with three goals. First, we aim to provide readers with greater insights into the relationship between human rights and trade. We will present readers with an overview of the international systems governing trade and human rights and background on some of the research on the relationship among trade, trade policies and agreements, and human rights. We believe that, with such background, policymakers will have additional tools and insights to help them develop more effective approaches to achieving expanded trade as well as to progressively realize human rights over time.

Second, we have prepared the first in-depth comparative analysis of how four case studies (South Africa, Brazil, the European Union [EU], and the United States) try to coordinate trade and human rights objectives and resolve conflicts at both the domestic and international levels. In an additional chapter, we also discuss how governments have introduced and discussed human rights concerns at the WTO. We hope these chapters will give our readers a better understanding of how these very different nations and the EU juggle the important goals of advancing human rights and expanding trade. We will show that none of our case studies have found a direct path or "right way" to protect and advance human rights as they seek to expand trade. We believe that greater knowledge of what other countries are doing may help policymakers achieve a more coordinated approach to these important objectives.

Our third goal is to help policymakers do a better job of governing globalization. As noted previously, because trade and human rights exist in separate governance spheres, scholars, advocates, and officials working in these areas often rely on bureaucratic jargon, use different policy tools, and do not often work collaboratively. Thus, in each of our country chapters, we examine how policymakers make trade policy and discuss how and when human rights concerns can enter the discussion about trade. We will make suggestions to foster greater dialogue and coordination *within* governments, because we believe a more coordinated approach will help make policy more coherent and more effective. In addition, we will also make some suggestions on how to foster a dialogue *between* countries that seek to promote human rights abroad with trade policies.[18]

What Do We Know about the Relationships among Human Rights, Trade, and Development?

As long as men and women have traded, they have wrestled with questions of human rights. Archaeological evidence shows that ancient civilizations traded at great risk to their freedoms. According to economist Peter Temin, the ancients shipped a wide range of goods from wheat to wine.[19] But these traders often lived in fear; when they engaged in trade they risked being captured, sold as slaves, or enslaved by pirates.[20] Not surprisingly, the ancients had a bifurcated view of trade. The sea could bring contact with strangers who could enhance national prosperity, but these same strangers might threaten the security of the nation and its people.[21] The first trade sanction, the Pericles Megarian decree, was developed in 432 B.C. in response to the kidnapping of three Aspasian women.[22]

Many years later, during the Age of Exploration, theologians, scholars, and royal advisors debated whether they had the right to exploit the land and wealth of indigenous populations. The economic historian Douglas Irwin notes that Vitoria, one of the "founders of international law," contended that the right to trade is "derived from the law of nations.... Foreigners may carry on trade, provided they do no hurt to citizens."[23]

In the centuries that followed, policymakers around the globe developed a wide range of approaches to govern the behavior of states and citizens at the intersection of trade and human rights. Often one state would act and challenge (or inspire) others to follow. For example, after England banned the slave trade in 1807, it signed treaties with Portugal, Denmark, and Sweden to supplement its own ban. After the United States banned goods manufactured by convict labor in the Tariff Act of 1890 (section 51), Great Britain, Australia, and Canada adopted similar bans. Ever so gradually, these national laws inspired international cooperation.[24]

Recent Scholarship on Trade and Human Rights

Today, citizens and policymakers increasingly debate the relationship between trade and human rights. Many policymakers and scholars of trade argue that trade per se (and the agreements governing trade) inherently enhances human rights. They claim that trade stimulates an export-oriented middle class, which will use its increasing economic clout to demand political freedoms and to press for openness and good governance.[25] Thus, they are asserting that trade, in effect, may help to encourage guarantees of civil and political liberties. In this regard, law professor Joel Paul cites the example of Mexico, where greater trade with Canada and the United States helped Mexico mature into a "multi-party democracy."[26] Policymakers and scholars also argue that trade improves human welfare. They note that, over time, the General Agreement on Tariffs and Trade (GATT) and the WTO (as well as bilateral trade agreements) have effectively stimulated and regulated trade. These agreements have thus contributed to economic activity, which, in turn, has helped more people improve their quality of life.[27]

Other analysts acknowledge the benefits of trade to economic growth and political liberalization, but they have a more nuanced view of how trade affects particular human rights. For example, according to economists Kimberley Ann Elliott and Richard B. Freeman, trade does not necessarily improve labor rights. They concluded that the impact of trade on labor standards depends on the quality of country-specific institutions and conditions.[28]

Although people have been debating the relationship between human rights and trade for centuries, the truth is that we know very little about how the two interact. Some scholars are testing how trade and foreign investment affect human rights.[29] The more rigorous studies are finding a complex relationship. For example, some studies have found that some types of foreign economic penetration (investment, trade, and aid) are reliably associated with increased levels of government respect for some – but not all – human rights. Several studies indicate that as citizens engage in trade, some rights seem to advance, whereas others seem to decline.[30]

Some scholars have begun to rely on a comprehensive data set, the Cingranelli and Richards (CIRI) Human Rights Data Set, that provides a country-by-country summary of each nation's human rights behavior (see http://ciri.binghamton.edu/.) Working with this data set, scholars have found that higher levels of foreign investment and trade increase governmental respect for personal integrity rights (such as freedom from torture or arbitrary imprisonment). Thus far, studies reveal that states with better human rights records receive more investment.[31] But none of these studies examine how trade flows per se affect particular human rights or how membership in the GATT/WTO over time affects particular human rights.

Scholars also don't know if promoting *certain* human rights could be trade enhancing or if increased trade inspires policymakers to do more to protect *specific* human rights. Moreover, researchers know little about the lines of causality. Do enhanced human rights protections lead to increased trade? Or does increased trade lead to improved human rights? Finally, we have little insight as to how trade policies and agreements will influence the realization of human rights *over time*.

To some extent, this knowledge gap is part of a larger hole in knowledge: scholars know very little about the relationship between economic development and human rights. Economists find it difficult to tease out the many variables that can stimulate or undermine economic or social development. In recent years, one scholar has stimulated a forceful rethinking about the relationship between human rights and development: the Nobel Prize winner Amartya Sen. Sen's insights have greatly influenced practitioners as well as scholars, including the authors of this book (Figure 1.1).

Sen's Insights

In the post–World War II period, development officials and scholars generally thought that public policies could facilitate economic growth and development if these policies could simply raise the income of the poor. They thought the problems of poverty could be solved by increasing the supply of money available for development. With foreign aid, they hoped, the poor and middle classes in the developing world would get jobs and use their earnings to save, consume, or invest. The economy could then "take off." But Sen believed countries and individuals are poor because, in many countries, citizens (a nation's most valuable resource) lack access to other productive resources such as education, land, health, justice, and credit. He argued that governments must actively provide these public goods to ensure that all citizens can obtain the services and resources they need to achieve sustainable development.

Sen also provided a normative framework for how human rights could guide the development process and, in turn, the international institutions designed to foster development. In *Development as Freedom* (1999), he explores the ways in which freedom is both a constituent of and a means to foster development. The

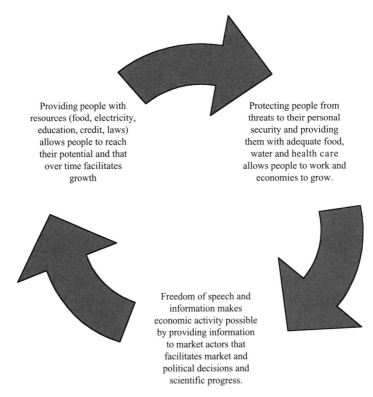

Providing people with resources (food, electricity, education, credit, laws) allows people to reach their potential and that over time facilitates growth

Protecting people from threats to their personal security and providing them with adequate food, water and health care allows people to work and economies to grow.

Freedom of speech and information makes economic activity possible by providing information to market actors that facilitates market and political decisions and scientific progress.

FIGURE 1.1. Sen's ideas on human rights and development.

book focuses on political freedoms and democracy, in particular, as democracy gives people a voice and a constructive role in shaping values, norms, and, ultimately, policy responses.[32]

Sen is not the only modern economist to present ideas about the relationship between human rights and development. Nobel Prize–winning economist Robert Barro has shown that per capita gross domestic product (GDP), education level, and life expectancy are highly significant predictors of democracy and civil liberties, "firmly establishing the general link between democracy and the standard of living."[33]

Sen's insights have greatly influenced how economists think about development. For example, in 2000, the United Nations Development Programme (UNDP) declared, "rights make human beings better economic actors."[34] In 2004, the WTO's Consultative Board noted, "the case for trade is made very definitely in terms of enhancing human welfare. Trade is a means to an end, not an end in itself."[35] In its 2005 report, the UNDP noted, "eradicating poverty is more than a major development challenge; it is a human rights challenge."[36]

Sen's ideas have also inspired scholars to test the relationship between human rights and development. In a wide range of studies, for example, World Bank scholars have found that governance matters for growth. Scholars have found an important link between the quality of institutions (such as courts, government agencies, and schools) and economic growth.[37] They have also discovered that protecting certain human rights is important for growth. Dani Kaufman of the World Bank Institute found that nations with greater civil liberties tend to have greater economic growth.[38] In another study, Kaufman and his team compared Bolivia's development and business environment with that of some eighty other countries. This study found that the lack of political freedoms as well as governance factors, such as corruption, limited Bolivia's economic performance.[39]

Although these studies on human rights and development are thought-provoking, additional research is necessary to fully understand the relationship between human rights and development. We hope that in the future scholars will examine questions such as: What rights are the building blocks for growth to occur? Are there certain human rights that are a precondition for the protection of other types of rights? For example, are political rights a precursor to economic rights or are they mutually exclusive?[40]

In sum, policymakers need more information to develop appropriate and effective policies at the intersection of trade and human rights. But that is not the only hurdle for scholars and policymakers seeking to examine this relationship. Human rights may be universal, but human rights are not universally accepted by all the world's peoples.

What Do We Mean by "Human Rights"?

Although policymakers have established internationally accepted human rights standards, the words *human rights* have different meanings to different people around the world. Every country has its own particular human rights objectives, priorities, policies, and experience. Thus, we believe we need to delineate what human rights we are talking about, so that we could have a consistent definition to use throughout the book. However, to understand what definition we adopted, we first discuss why human rights are important.

Human rights protection may be a precondition for capitalism as well as democracy. Without rights, people could not articulate or defend their freedom, ideas, or property. Technological and scientific progress could not occur without the protection of some human rights. Almost every culture and government recognizes the existence of certain rights or claims to specific freedoms and goods. For citizens to realize these rights, governments have a responsibility to put such rights into law as well as into effect.[41]

Today's notion of human rights is derived from the notion of "natural" rights articulated by John Locke and other philosophers from the European Enlightenment. An ideology of rights was maintained in England by the common law and in the United States by the Constitution and the Bill of Rights. In revolutionary France, human rights were embodied in the Declaration of the Rights of Man and of the Citizen. But writing these rights into law did not guarantee their realization. For example, the United States allowed slavery and denied minorities and women the right to vote. The French government abandoned the Declaration during the Reign of Terror. Nor did these governments seek to disperse their vision of rights. The ideology of rights did not spread to the colonies of the British and French empires.[42]

In the 20th century, policymakers began to recognize the need to root protection for human rights in international law. For example, the signatories of the Versailles Treaty tried to engineer a peace that would both stabilize Europe and protect various minority groups. They created an international organization to cooperate on the peace – the League of Nations. They also pledged to "endeavor to secure and maintain fair and humane conditions of labour . . . in all countries in which their commercial and industrial relations extend." To meet that goal, they created an ILO. Although the ILO has endured, the League of Nations was unable to prevent aggression by Germany, Italy, Japan, and Russia in the 1930s. By 1939, the League of Nations had collapsed.[43] Some policymakers were determined to learn from this failure and they planned a more comprehensive approach to global governance.

During the dark days of World War II, U.S. President Franklin D. Roosevelt outlined a vision of how human rights might be protected in international law. On January 6, 1941, he addressed the U.S. Congress about his hopes for a future world. Roosevelt said, "In the future . . . we look forward to a world founded upon four essential human freedoms: freedom of speech, freedom of religion, freedom from want, and freedom from fear."[44] Roosevelt and British Prime Minister Winston Churchill worked to ensure that advancing these four freedoms would become a central tenet of the planned United Nations.[45] After Roosevelt's death, his wife, Eleanor, became the driving force behind the adoption of the UDHR.[46]

The architects of the United Nations were the first to apply the term *human rights*, in Articles 55 and 45 of the UN Charter. All members of the United Nations pledged to take action for the achievement of "universal respect for, and observance of, human rights and fundamental freedoms for all without distinction as to race, sex, language, or religion." But human rights were not clearly defined in the UN Charter. Thus, when the UN General Assembly met for the first time in 1946, the members called for an international bill of rights. The Commission on Human Rights tried to formulate such a document in both a declaration and a convention. After difficult negotiations, in 1948, member nations developed a more detailed code of human rights, the UDHR.[47] The Declaration delineated more than thirty rights that member states were supposed to promote and protect. However, although the Declaration limits the behavior of the state, it is not legally binding upon member states.[48]

In the years that followed, government officials struggled to write the UDHR into legally binding conventions. They eventually developed two covenants, the International Covenant on Civil and Political Rights (ICCPR) and the International Covenant on Economic, Social and Cultural Rights (ICESCR). The ICCPR delineates rights that a state may not take away from its citizens (such as freedom of speech or freedom of movement). In general, the ICESCR delineates rights (often necessities) that a state – *insofar as it is able* – should provide for its citizens, such as basic education or health care.[49]

The Declaration and the Covenants have different standing in international law. The Universal Declaration is truly universal in scope; it applies to everyone, regardless of whether individual governments have formally accepted its principles or ratified the Covenants. However, the Covenants, by their nature as multilateral conventions, are legally binding only on those states that have accepted them by ratification or accession. These conventions did not go into force until 1976, when 35 member states of the UN ratified them.[50]

Since the covenants went into force, human rights objectives and laws have continued to evolve, reflecting changes in technology, politics, resources, and human understanding. Today many human rights activists have identified new human rights such as the right to development, the right to a healthy environment, or intergenerational rights. These newer rights, however, are not embodied in the Covenants and in general are thus far not binding on states.[51] Thus, in this book, we generally limit our study to the most widely accepted and legally enforceable listing of human rights, those delineated in the International Bill of Human Rights. It includes the rights enumerated in the UDHR and subsequently made enforceable under the two covenants.[52] Table 1.1 delineates these rights.

Although we limit our analysis to these human rights, in both the chapters on the EU and United States, when we discuss the right to political participation, we also touch on the right to information. In a democracy, individuals cannot effectively participate if they do not have access to the information they need to make decisions. In the chapters on South Africa, Brazil, and the United States, we also discuss the right to protection of intellectual property, which is a basic human right in the International Bill. However, many people argue that the system of national and international regulations put in place to protect the right to intellectual property actually undermine human rights because these regulations may limit access to knowledge. They note this is particularly true for citizens in developing countries. The international research body, the Organization for Economic Cooperation and Development (OECD) has stressed that "too broad and rigid intellectual property rules can discourage innovation" and have a "negative effect on diffusion and competition."[53]

The International System of Rules Governing Trade and Its Intersection with Human Rights: A Primer

When policymakers first conceived of a global system of rules to govern trade, human rights were an important part of that vision. But today, the international system of rules that governs trade says very little about human rights. It also limits how and when nations can use trade as a tool to change the human rights behavior of other countries.[54]

In 1939, before the United States entered World War II, Secretary of State Cordell Hull set up an office and staff to devise a system of institutions to "work on problems of the peace." After Japan attacked the U.S. base in Pearl Harbor, Hawaii, twenty-four other nations joined Great Britain and the United States to sign the Declaration of the United Nations. These nations committed to devising multilateral strategies "to further the enjoyment by all States . . . of access, on equal terms, to the trade and to the raw materials of the world which are needed for their economic prosperity; to bring about the fullest collaboration between all nations in the economic field with the object of securing for all, *improved labor standards, economic advancement and social security*; . . . and they hope to see established a peace . . . which will afford assurance that all the men in all the lands may live out their lives *in freedom from fear and want*."[55] Thus, the postwar planners saw labor rights, the right to food and personal integrity rights (freedom from want and fear) as crucial objectives for the peace.

As the war raged in the Pacific and Europe, British and U.S. officials collaborated on strategies and an institutional structure to achieve these goals. They envisioned several international organizations that would meet specific functional needs. One organization, the United Nations, would govern the peace and promote political stability. Another, an International Bank for Reconstruction and Development (IBRD) would help European nations recover from the devastation of World War II. Finally, an International Trade Organization (ITO) would stimulate trade, employment, and international investment. But these officials would soon learn that the world's ever-evolving problems would not neatly fit in these institutional boxes.

TABLE 1.1. *What human rights are we talking about?*

Universal Declaration of Human Rights	
International Covenant on Civil and Political Rights[56]	International Covenant on Economic, Social and Cultural Rights[57]
Right to life (Art. 3)	Right to marriage and found a family (Art. 16)
Right to liberty (Art. 3)	Right to social security (Art. 22)
Right to security (Art. 3)	Right to work, free choice of employment, just and favorable conditions of work, and protection against unemployment (Art. 23.1)
Right to the abolition of slavery and slave trade (Art. 4)	Right to equal pay for equal work (Art. 23.2)
Right to the prevention of torture or cruel, inhuman, or degrading treatment or punishment (Art. 5)	Right to just and favorable remuneration (Art. 23.3)
Right to recognition before the law (Art. 6)	Right to form and join a trade union (Art. 23.4)
Right to equality before the law and equal protection of the law (Art. 7)	Right to rest and leisure, including reasonable limitation of working hours and periodic holidays with pay (Art. 24)
Right to effective judicial remedy (Art. 8)	Right to a sustainable standard of living (including food, clothing, housing, medical care, and necessary social services) and the right to security in the event of unemployment, sickness, disability, widowhood, old age, or other lack of livelihood in circumstances beyond his control (Art. 25.1)
Right to the prevention of arbitrary arrest, detention, or exile (Art. 9)	Right to special care and assistance for motherhood and childhood (Art. 25.2)
Right to fair and public hearing by a neutral tribunal (Art.10)	Right to education (Art. 26)
Right to presumption of innocence (Art. 11.1)	Right to cultural participation (Art. 27.1)
Right to non-retroactive penal code (Art. 11.2)	Right to the protection of intellectual property (Art. 27.2)

(continued)

TABLE 1.1 (*continued*)

Universal Declaration of Human Rights	
International Covenant on Civil and Political Rights	International Covenant on Economic, Social and Cultural Rights
Right to privacy (Art. 12)	
Right to freedom of movement and residence in the country (Art. 13.1)	
Right to leave the country and return (Art. 13.2)	
Right to seek and enjoy asylum from prosecution (Art. 14)	
Right to a nationality (Art. 15)	
Right to freedom of thought, conscience and religion (Art. 18)	
Right to freedom of opinion and expression (Art. 19)	
Right to freedom of peaceful assembly and association (Art. 20)	
Right to governmental participation, directly or through freely chosen representatives (Art. 21.1)	
Right of equal access to public services (Art. 21.2)	
Right to periodic and fair elections (Art. 21.3)	

Note: Prepared by Philip Van der Celen.

The postwar planners took years to achieve common ground on the draft ITO Charter. They redrafted the ITO Charter three times from 1945 to 1948 before fifty-four nations finally signed it in Havana, Cuba, in March 1948. It was the most comprehensive international agreement ever negotiated. The ITO included provisions delineating rules of behavior for the use of import quotas, exchange controls, state trading, and commodity agreements; policies to achieve full employment; and rules to regulate investment and economic development.

The ITO Charter also included significant human rights language. First, many of the delegates at Havana had come to believe that protectionist policies had prolonged the Great Depression by, effectively, allowing nations to export unemployment. (By putting in place protectionist policies, producers were sheltered from market conditions and more efficient producers were not able to increase their market share.) Thus, the delegates made employment issues (the rights of humans to work and to receive a fair wage for such work) a priority of the ITO charter. Moreover, the delegates recognized that unfair conditions of employment could distort trade. Thus, the Charter included Article 7, which stated that the members of the ITO "recognize that unfair labour conditions, particularly in production for export create difficulties in international trade and, accordingly, each Member shall take whatever action may be appropriate and feasible to eliminate such conditions within its territory." The Charter also stated that, in dealing with such potential distortions, the ITO should consult and cooperate with the ILO.[58] Finally, the delegates included an "exception" for measures necessary to protect public morals. Although several earlier commercial treaties and trade policies had established the notion of public morals, the negotiators did not define what "moral" trade practices were, nor did they elaborate a definition of immoral or amoral trade practices. However, the delegates did seem to agree that how people were treated as they made goods and services for export could be a public morals issue.[59]

The ITO Charter was doomed almost as soon as it was signed. Many business leaders in the United States and abroad found it hypocritical because it included rules, as well as exceptions to these rules.[60] The world did not seem ready for such a comprehensive approach to trade. In Europe and Asia, America's allies were struggling to revive their economies and feed their people. Moreover, many policymakers were preoccupied with preventing the spread of communism, which was on the march in Eastern Europe, the Balkans, and Asia.

As the United States and the Soviet bloc became increasingly estranged, the U.S. Congress and the American people were increasingly focused on the battle between "the American assembly line and the Communist party line." The ITO seemed to have little relevance for that struggle. Congress never voted on the ITO. Without the support of the world's healthiest and richest economy, other nations also abandoned it.[61]

The General Agreement on Tariffs and Trade (GATT)

With the collapse of the ITO, trade officials turned to the GATT, the part of the ITO governing solely commercial policy. The GATT was supposed to be

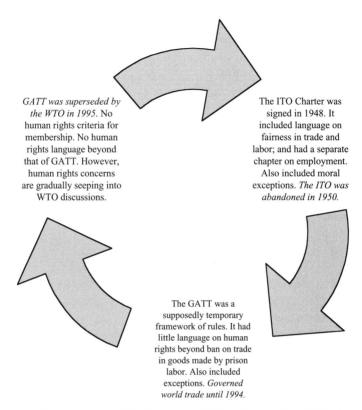

GATT was superseded by the WTO in 1995. No human rights criteria for membership. No human rights language beyond that of GATT. However, human rights concerns are gradually seeping into WTO discussions.

The ITO Charter was signed in 1948. It included language on fairness in trade and labor; and had a separate chapter on employment. Also included moral exceptions. *The ITO was abandoned in 1950.*

The GATT was a supposedly temporary framework of rules. It had little language on human rights beyond ban on trade in goods made by prison labor. Also included exceptions. *Governed world trade until 1994.*

FIGURE 1.2. Human rights and the International Trade Organization (ITO) during the postwar planning process.

a temporary framework of rules, a forum to negotiate trade barrier reductions among nations, and a venue for countries to argue and mediate trade disputes. But with the collapse of the ITO in 1949, the GATT began to govern world trade by default.[62]

Because of the United States' postwar economic and political clout, it had significant influence over the development of the GATT. But the U.S. Congress, which shares authority for trade policies with the Executive, limited the purview of the GATT. From 1948 to 1974, it would allow only the Executive to negotiate reductions in border measures such as tariffs and quotas.[63] As a result, in contrast with the ITO, the GATT said very little about human rights. The GATT (and the WTO, which superseded it) was more concerned with relationships *between* states than those *within* states. Some countries, including the United States and France, repeatedly tried to expand GATT's purview to include labor rights, but each attempt failed. Many contracting partners of the GATT viewed labor standards as de facto trade barriers. As a result, advocates were unable to convince these countries that including labor standards in the GATT was not a subterfuge for protectionism.[64]

The GATT had no human rights qualifications for participating members, nor did it develop any such criteria over time. During the first round of trade talks, all the members of the GATT were stable democracies, so their human rights practices were rarely an issue. But, in 1948, democratic Czechoslovakia, one of the original members of the GATT, was taken over by members of the Czech Communist Party, who were determined to remake the economy along communist lines. The U.S. Congress demanded a withdrawal of GATT concessions to Czechoslovakia in protest, noting that GATT was supposed to consist of like-minded, democratic, capitalist nations. But the United States was unable to convince its allies that they should repudiate Czechoslovakia's membership in the GATT. Consequently, Czechoslovakia remained an original signatory to the GATT.[65] Strangely, the experience did not motivate the contracting parties of the GATT to develop official criteria for membership in the GATT beyond adherence to its guiding principles and the accession requirements of existing members.[66] In the years that followed, many undemocratic countries joined the GATT. A number of countries that lacked the will, funds, or expertise to promote human rights also became signatories to the GATT. But the members of the GATT always made decisions by consensus and the majority of GATT signatories had no interest or will to set human rights conditions for members.

From 1948 to 1974, the number of contracting parties to the GATT expanded dramatically. Many nations recognized that membership in the GATT would help them attract investment and use trade as a means of stimulating growth.[67] As the GATT grew larger, its membership also became more diverse and unruly. Each country was free to decide whether they would adhere to optional side codes, a process that came to be known as "GATT à la carte." Some of these side agreements covered important nontariff barriers to trade such as procurement policies or standards.

Meanwhile, policymakers, business leaders, and academics came to understand that the informal structure of the GATT no longer fit the world's trade liberalization needs. Ever so gradually, members of the GATT decided that the next round (the Uruguay Round) should not only bring new sectors under the GATT's discipline but also strengthen the authority of the GATT. This effort to broaden and strengthen the GATT to govern all types of trade was termed "a single undertaking."[68] The Uruguay Round of trade talks dragged on for some seven years, from 1986 to 1993, as members negotiated both new sectors (agriculture and services) and a new, formal institutional structure to govern world trade. On December 15, 1993, 117 nations finally reached agreement on completion of the round and on the creation of a new organization – the WTO.[69]

The World Trade Organization

The WTO was not a rebirth of the ITO. Nor was it the GATT with a makeover.[70] The WTO was something new and different. It included rules on trade in services, agriculture, and intellectual property. Most (not all) of the GATT's side agreements were made multilateral and part of the WTO. Moreover, the WTO Charter provided legal authority for a secretariat, a director general, and a staff. It also included a strengthened and binding system of dispute settlement.[71]

Although the WTO included thousands of pages of trade agreements – governing trade in goods, services, and trade-related intellectual property among others, the WTO says nothing about the relationship between trade and human rights.[72] Moreover, the WTO provides its members with little advice on how to behave if and when such members seek to link trade and human rights. Like the GATT, the WTO delineates what members cannot do when they link trade policies and human rights policies. Policymakers have little guidance on what they *can* do to promote human rights as they seek to expand trade.

Under GATT/WTO rules, members must adhere to two key principles: the most favored nation principle and the national treatment principle. The most favored nation (MFN) principle requires that the best trade conditions extended to one member by a nation must also be extended automatically to every other nation. The national treatment principle provides that once a product is imported, the importing state may not subject it to regulations less favorable than those that apply to like products produced domestically.[73] The WTO does not in any way prohibit countries from protecting human rights at home or abroad. But its rules constrain the behavior of governments at the intersection of trade and human rights. Taken in sum, these rules require that member governments do not unnecessarily or unduly distort trade when they seek to promote human rights.

However, trade officials also acknowledged that there are times when nations simply cannot adhere to these provisions. They provided two exceptions. Article XX permits nations to restrict trade when necessary to "protect human, animal, or plant life or health" or to conserve exhaustible natural resources. This article also states that governments may restrict imports "relating to the products of prison labor." Although it does not refer explicitly to human rights, per se, the public morals clause allows WTO members to put in place trade bans in the interest of promoting human rights.[74]

The national security exception, Article X, says that WTO rules should not prevent nations from protecting their own security. Members are not permitted to take trade action to protect another member's security or to protect the citizens of another member. But if the UN Security Council authorizes trade sanctions, WTO rules allow nations to use such sanctions to promote human rights (such as those put in place against South Africa's apartheid regime in the 1980s).[75]

The architects of the WTO recognized that nations might disagree about whether a fellow WTO member had fully adhered to WTO rules. If WTO members cannot work bilaterally to negotiate a settlement, they can bring their disputes to the WTO's Dispute Settlement Body, which sets up a panel to issue its findings. These findings can be appealed to the Appellate Body, whose decisions are binding upon member governments. Thus, if a member's trade policies were successfully challenged under that system, they would have to modify their trade-distorting policies, compensate the affected trading partners, or accept potential retaliation from the disputants.

The Dispute Settlement Body has handled many cases since 1995, but not one of them has *directly centered* on how governments can use trade policies to protect human rights. Nor do we know whether and how that body might use human rights law in a trade dispute.[76]

How Human Rights Concerns Are Seeping into the Workings of the WTO

Despite the lack of clarity, human rights issues have seeped into the day-to-day workings of the WTO. As the next chapter will show, members have introduced human rights concerns into discussions over trade waivers, WTO accessions, and even trade negotiations.[77]

Human rights concerns have also penetrated discussions of membership. Human rights issues came to the fore when China, an original GATT member, sought to rejoin the GATT (later the WTO) in the 1990s. The WTO, like the GATT, does not have human rights or democracy criteria for membership. Yet each member must agree on the terms of accession for each country that seeks to join the WTO. These terms differ for each new country. Not surprisingly, concerns about China's human rights practices were central to the debate over accession in the United States and several EU countries.

As China opened to foreign investment, the Chinese people began to gain greater economic freedoms. For example, in the 1980s, the Communist Party gradually allowed some public expression of ideas. But human rights–monitoring organizations such as Amnesty International and Human Rights Watch, as well as the U.S. Department of State, continued to find significant human rights abuses in China. On June 4, 1989, the Chinese government violently suppressed democracy demonstrations in Beijing's Tiananmen Square.[78] The Communist Party made it clear it would not tolerate any challenges to its control of the government. Some policymakers in the United States and Europe concluded that they had to use every means available, including trade policy, to influence human rights conditions in China. These officials hoped to use China's accession to the WTO as leverage to prod China to do more to advance human rights.

Any state or customs territory having full autonomy in the conduct of its trade policies may join ("accede to") the WTO, but WTO members must agree on the terms for accession. If a two-thirds majority of WTO members vote in favor of membership, the applicant is free to sign the protocol and to accede to the organization. In many cases, the country's own parliament or legislature has to ratify the agreement before membership is complete.[79]

The parliaments of many nations held extensive hearings on whether they should grant MFN status to China. But it became a huge political issue in the United States in the late 1990s. The United States had long linked access to the U.S. market (trade privileges) to China's human rights practices. Under the Jackson–Vanik amendment of the Trade Act of 1974, China could achieve MFN benefits in the United States only after a congressional review of its human rights practices.[80] These hearings were often contentious, but in the end, Congress granted such MFN privileges on a yearly basis. But policymakers also recognized that once China entered the WTO, the United States would lose its ability to use trade to press Chinese leaders to make changes. At the hearings, business interests generally argued that including China in the framework of multilateral rules and obligations would ensure improvement in China's adherence to the rule of law and prod China to do more to promote human rights. They stressed that by joining the GATT/WTO, China would learn the skills of good governance, which would spill over into other governance institutions and responsibilities; that greater foreign presence of Western firms within China would expose Chinese workers to ideas about their rights; and that companies would increasingly demand stronger human rights practices of their suppliers, gradually changing China's social and political culture. Union and human rights leaders, however, argued that China would respond only to toughness and would not adhere to WTO rules. They were not keen to grant China MFN status.[81]

In the end, the advocates of greater trade with China triumphed in the United States and around the world. Congressional policymakers were won over by the argument that more trade would improve China's adherence to international human rights norms. China's accession had stimulated a broad discussion of how to use trade to stimulate human rights improvements in China, but it did not inspire the members of the WTO to think about how best to use terms of accession to reap human rights policy changes from members that want to accede to the WTO.

Human rights concerns have also seeped into trade negotiations. The next chapter will delineate how WTO members attempted to reduce agricultural trade barriers while assuring food security, especially in poorer food-importing countries.[82] Members agreed that developing country food importing nations should get special assistance. Food security and issues about access to affordable, safe food became important elements of the Doha Round trade talks (2001–present).[83] WTO members also agreed to negotiate trade in services. Countries can choose which sectors they open to trade. Many developing countries are eager to privatize essential services such as water and electricity. They hope to obtain foreign investment and management of state of the art power, water, transportation, and other services. But these governments are also obligated to ensure that public services such as water, education, health, and transportation are available and affordable for all citizens. Many developing country governments do not have effective regulations to ensure that private sector providers ensure universal access to such services.

Recent Pressure on WTO Members to Discuss Trade and Human Rights

Although the members of the WTO have slowly begun to discuss the relationship between trade and human rights, government officials at other major international organizations were thinking long and hard about how their activities may affect human rights. In 2000, leaders of 191 UN member states agreed to collaborate to reduce global poverty by 50% by 2015. In the Millennium Development Goals, they also promised to improve health, promote peace and gender equality, empower women, and achieve universal primary education.[84]

The Millennium Development Goals also reflected a new approach to global governance and international cooperation. The leaders agreed that poverty is not simply the absence of money, but a lack of access to resources and opportunities. Thus, poverty is a human rights as well as a development problem. To successfully reduce poverty, the leaders committed to coordinate their human rights, development and trade policies at both the national and international levels. In short, they agreed to make policy coherence a priority. For example, the United Nations, the World Bank, and the International Monetary Fund announced that they would work to ensure that their efforts and activities promoted human rights.[85] In July 2006, the International Finance Corporation (IFC), the arm of the World Bank that promotes private sector involvement in development, agreed to develop a global program to prod global industries to adopt better labor standards in global supply chains (the Better Work Program).[86]

Meanwhile, some policymakers and academics also put forth ideas on how the distinct international systems that govern international trade and human rights might be encouraged to work cooperatively.[87] Mary Robinson, the UN high commissioner for human rights from 1997 to 2002, became interested in these issues.[88] Under her direction, the UN Office of the High Commissioner on Human Rights prepared a wide range of papers examining the effects of trade agreements on a broad panoply of rights, ranging from the right to health to gender rights. The high commissioner even advised national trade policymakers that they needed to carefully examine the relationship. The Web site of the Office of the UN High Commissioner on Human Rights urged "states to undertake human rights impact assessments of trade rules and policies both during the process of trade negotiations as well as after."[89]

The American Society of International Law cooperated with the Max Planck Institute at Heidelberg, Germany, and the World Trade Institute at Bern, Switzerland, on a project designed to study the links between trade law and policy, on the one hand, and international human rights law, on the other.[90] Legal scholars such as Joost Pauwelyn, Ernst-Ulrich Petersmann, Steven Charnovitz, Robert Howse, Thomas Cottier, and others began to examine specific WTO provisions and how these provisions affect human rights.[91]

The debate was not limited to academia or the corridors of power. Civil society groups, such as Oxfam, Panos, and Rights and Democracy, began to play a major role in the debate about the relationship between trade and human rights.[92] Many such nongovernmental organizations (NGOs) argued that some trade agreements were undermining the ability of some of the world's people to obtain access to water, education, and food.[93] Other NGOs such as 3DThree worked to educate human rights policymakers about the workings of the WTO and how trade diplomats might be sensitized to human rights law and concerns.[94]

NGOs, Governments, Human Rights, and Trade

Until recently, these NGOs had little direct impact on WTO decisions. However, in the 1990s, their efforts became more visible and more influential. They have used research, naming and shaming, and guilt to pressure WTO members to provide greater clarity at the intersection of WTO rules and human rights. These NGOs, working with developing country governments, prodded the members of the WTO to clarify how developing countries can use the public health exceptions of the WTO's Trade-Related Aspects of Intellectual Property Rights (TRIPS) agreement.

Most industrialized nations have developed national systems to protect intellectual property.[95] Under such systems, individuals can apply for copyrights, patents, and/or trademarks to protect their innovations and creative works.[96] With these copyrights, patents, and trademarks, the creator obtains limited exclusive rights to whatever economic reward the market may provide for their creations and products. These rights are enforceable through government action and the court system.

In the 1980s, as trade in goods and services expanded dramatically, policymakers recognized that they needed to find ways to harmonize these different systems of protecting intellectual property. During the Uruguay Round of trade talks, the members of the GATT agreed to a comprehensive and enforceable system of rules covering intellectual property rights (TRIPS).[97] This agreement helped reduce nontariff trade barriers stemming from different intellectual property rights (IPR) regimes and also established transparency standards that require all members to publish laws, regulations, and decisions on intellectual property.

But academics, policymakers, and development advocates have become increasingly critical of TRIPS. Although that system may promote trade and help developing countries attract investment, it may also undermine access to affordable medicines.[98] For example, many developing countries, such as South Africa, Uganda, and India, face major public health crises, such as epidemics of malaria or AIDS. In these countries, citizens often cannot afford the medications they need. Moreover, public health officials have struggled to provide medicines and to ensure that diseases do not spread. They often find the drugs they need to cure diseases or prevent the spread of disease are too expensive. Thus, many developing country policymakers wanted to use the exceptions to the TRIPS agreement, which would allow them to breach patent rules and create their own versions (*compulsory licensing*) of needed medicines or import the drugs from countries where they may be more affordable (*parallel importing*). However, these policymakers also recognized that if they used these exceptions, foreign investors might be alienated.

Government officials and civil society groups demanded greater clarity as to when nations could use this waiver. In the main Doha Ministerial Declaration of November 14, 2001, WTO member governments adopted a Declaration on the TRIPS Agreement and Public Health, which stressed that the TRIPS agreement does not and should not prevent members from taking measures to protect public health. Members agreed that in times of public health emergencies, policymakers can use the flexibilities that are built into the TRIPS agreement, including allowing governments to issue compulsory licenses and to import drugs from nations where these drugs are cheaper or generics are produced. Moreover, the members of the WTO also stressed that they would allow the least-developed countries more time to put pharmaceutical patent protection laws in place. But members of the WTO could not resolve all these questions at Doha. They asked the TRIPS Council to sort out how countries unable to produce pharmaceuticals domestically can obtain supplies of copies of patented drugs from other countries.[99] On December 5, 2005, in recognition that many countries still needed even greater certainty, policymakers decided to make the waiver a permanent part of the agreements. Two-thirds of the WTO membership must agree to this change by December 2007. The permanent amendment will allow any member country to export pharmaceutical products made under a compulsory license for public health emergencies.[100]

Although that particular issue was resolved, there are many other contentious issues involving human rights and trade that WTO members may need to address. Yet the members of the WTO have not openly discussed the broad relationship between human rights and trade and how the WTO might develop bridges to international human rights institutions. They have dealt with conflict between WTO rules and human rights on a case-by-case basis. Although this strategy comports with WTO rules and procedures, it provides little guidance to policymakers and citizens who want to make globalization more equitable and more coherent. The next chapter, on the WTO, will explore many of these concerns.

Methodology and Organization of This Book: How Do Countries Behave at the Intersection of Trade and Human Rights?

This chapter examined what we know about the relationship among human rights, trade, and development. We presented some historical evidence that people have long perceived conflict between human rights and trade and devised strategies, such as treaties or sanctions, to address this problem. The chapter then moved on to a synopsis of the international systems designed to achieve both human rights and trade expansion. We then provided a brief discussion of some of the rights that trade can affect and how governments have attempted to find their way at the intersection of trade and human rights.

With that background, the bulk of this book focuses on how policymakers in specific countries and varying levels of development *behave* at this intersection when they perceive dissonance between their trade and human rights objectives. We begin with an overview of how countries have behaved at the World Trade Organization when they want to advance human rights at home or abroad. In Chapters 3–6, we examine what South Africa, Brazil, the European Union, and the United States do to promote human rights at home and abroad as they seek to expand trade. We recognize that these countries and the EU are not representative of all trading nations or members of the WTO, but we chose these countries for several reasons. First, all of our case studies are influential players in world trade, yet they are at different levels of development (Table 1.2 illuminates the different levels of development, recent economic growth, recent educational levels, and terms of trade since 1980 of each of the case studies.)

Second, these countries and the EU have different human rights priorities and approaches to progressively realizing human rights at home and abroad. Some of our case study countries think it is perfectly appropriate to use trade policies to intervene in the affairs of other nations; others do not.

In each chapter, we describe how South Africa, Brazil, the United States, and/or the European Union have struggled to expand trade and advance human rights. We begin by describing trade and human rights conditions in each case study and then examine how each country (and the EU) makes trade policy. We then focus on three to five stories that delineate how citizens and policymakers tried to protect human rights at home or to advance human rights abroad through trade. We chose these stories based on information gleaned from both extensive research as well as detailed conversations with those policymakers, negotiators, business leaders, labor rights leaders, NGO activists, and scholars at the forefront of these issues in each country (see Appendix for a list of interviewees in each case study country). We found that several countries

TABLE 1.2. *A statistical snapshot of human development and the terms of trade of our case study countries*

Country	European Union			US	Brazil	South Africa
	Germany joined EU 1951	Spain joined EU 1986	Lithuania joined EU 2004			
Overall human development index ranking	20	21	39	10	63	120
GDP index (on a scale of up to 1.00)	.94	.90	.79	.99	.73	.77
Education index (on a scale of up to 1.00)	.96	.97	.97	.97	.89	.81
Terms of trade (from 1980 scale of 100)	117	132	NA	119	145	86

Source: Table 1, Human Development Index, p. 219 and Table 16, the Structure of Trade, p. 274, UNDP, Human Development Report 2005. We randomly chose older EC member Germany and newer members Lithuania and Spain as proxies for the EU.

experienced similar human rights challenges (e.g., they were determined to ensure that their citizens had access to affordable medicines or trade did not undermine labor rights) and thus, to provide diversity, we did not always choose the most obvious conflicts for each country. In the case of the chapter on the EU, however, we focused on process as well as issues because many of our interviewees told us that although the EU has the most comprehensive strategy to link human rights to market access, the overall process of trade policymaking undermines the right to political participation in the EU. Thus, we examined both in depth.

The table at the end of the chapter summarizes our findings. It shows that many case study governments use *trade* policies to defend human rights at home. In addition, some such as South Africa and Brazil use *other* nontrade policies to maintain trade but defend human rights at home. Some governments have tried to encourage other members of the WTO to agree to negotiate particular human rights concerns as part of the WTO's purview. For example, Brazil has pushed for the inclusion of indigenous rights and the EU has pushed to include labor rights within the purview of the GATT/WTO. Still others such as the United States and the EU use trade agreements as an inducement to prod other governments to protect human rights.

Although we found major differences in behavior, we found several common themes in our discussions within these diverse case studies. Policymakers from South Africa, Brazil, the European Union, and the United States see trade as an engine of growth. In general, they think that trade can help them progressively realize human rights at home. However, policymakers in every case study country also expressed concern that trade could undermine internationally accepted human rights. They stressed that market forces could lead local business leaders to move jobs and investment abroad or demand weaker labor protections. Policymakers were also unsure about how they should try to coordinate policies.

Interestingly, in every country we visited, policymakers consistently stated that human rights and trade, and more specifically the national policies that govern them, exist in separate spheres. Yet, when we finished our discussions we found that many of the individuals whom we interviewed acknowledged that policymakers often have indeed responded to issues at the intersection of trade and human rights, though typically in an ad hoc manner. Finally, they often saw the need for greater coordination of these two important policy objectives but admitted they didn't know how to achieve such coherence.

In the chapters that follow, we will show that policymakers have adopted a wide range of strategies to balance trade and human rights objectives. These strategies may or may not distort trade. And policymakers may not always be moved to act based on altruism or morality. In some circumstances, governments may use the language of human rights to explain their actions, but they may also seek to defend important commercial interests. As we will reveal in the South Africa chapter, some have argued that South African efforts to advance the Kimberley Process (a certification that no human rights abuse occurred in the production of conflict diamonds) really was meant to protect the business interests of the world's largest diamond producer, the South African company De Beers. The United States is not simply motivated by altruism when it includes provisions related to political participation, right to information, and due process rights in its bilateral trade agreements. To some degree, the United States pushes for these provisions in trade agreements to ensure that its exporters and foreign investors can learn about and influence trade policy abroad. But these new regulations may also help citizens in these countries learn how to influence their governments.

When countries (generally developed countries) attempt to promote human rights internationally through trade agreements or policies, recipient governments (generally developing countries) also have a wide range of responses. Some developing country governments use trade agreements as a means of "locking in" improved human rights capabilities. Policymakers from these governments can use the benefits of a trade agreement to increase public support for applying scarce resources to protecting human rights. In other instances, developing country officials may accept limited human rights conditionality in return for the greater benefits of trade. They may perceive the benefits of increased trade are worth the cost of conforming to international human rights expectations (or, in some cases, pretending to conform).[101]

Policymakers also can use trade policies to defend human rights at home. For example, they can use WTO rules such as Article XX exceptions; they can participate or stay out of negotiations (as in services); or they can devise domestic policies (such as social labeling to ensure that in the interests of increasing trade, labor rights do not decline). But, as noted earlier, WTO rules set limits on what these governments can do to advance human rights at home or abroad.

Finally, Chapter 7 summarizes our findings. We found that at the intersection of trade and human rights, trade priorities often prevail. Governments are charged to pursue national interests, not global human rights interests. Although many governments want to advance human rights as they expand trade, we know of no government that is required to ensure that trade does not undermine specific human rights at home or abroad.

But policymakers do not have to rewrite the rules of the road (WTO rules) to accommodate human rights concerns at this intersection. Policymakers can and should do more to make globalization policies more coherent. Thus, we also make recommendations to help policymakers weigh human rights criteria as they make trade policy decisions. We hope that with such information, policymakers can right the current imbalance in policymaking.

TABLE 1.3. *Chapter summary: Case study behavior*

Case	Human rights discussed in chapter
Chapter 2: World Trade Organization	Right to health: Access to affordable medicines
	Human rights in diamond extraction
	Labor rights
	Right to food
Chapter 3: South Africa	Right to work
	Right to equality, promote black economic equity
	Right to health/access to affordable medicines
	Right to basic services
	Human rights in diamond extraction
Chapter 4: Brazil	Right to health/access to affordable medicines
	Right to health/environmental hygiene

Trade issue or strategy	Policy response		
	Trade policy to promote rights *at home*	*Other* policies to promote rights *at home*	*Trade* policy to promote rights *abroad*
TRIPS perceived as making it harder for developing countries to provide affordable medicines. Members of WTO amended TRIPS to clarify.	✔		
Kimberley Process: 50 member states applied for a waiver regarding trade in diamonds to ensure that only certified diamonds are traded.	✔		
Some countries have pushed to include labor rights in the WTO, but some developing countries view such efforts as akin to protectionism. Use trade policy reviews, accessions, and GSP to link labor rights to WTO rules.			✔
Members agree to discuss non-trade concerns such as food security.	✔		✔
Maintain strong labor protections under constitution – will not allow desire for trade and investment to undermine labor protections.		✔	
Develop and maintain investment requirements and policies that may violate WTO norm of non-discrimination and may alienate international investors determined to promote black economic empowerment.		✔	
With other countries, led effort to clarify WTO rules and amend TRIPS to ensure that governments can import and/or produce drugs needed by its citizens in time of public health emergency.	✔		✔
Will not make offers in services negotiations which may jeopardize access to basic services for its poorest citizens.		✔	
Led effort to prevent human rights abuses in the zones where diamonds are produced, at the same time also "protect" diamond key industry: Kimberley Process	✔		✔
Use Article XX, Safeguards to Justify Ban on Imports of Retreaded Tires	✔		✔

(*continued*)

TABLE 1.3 *(continued)*

Case	Human rights discussed in chapter
Chapter 4: Brazil (cont.)	Right to traditional knowledge/indigenous rights
	Slave and forced labor
	Child labor
Chapter 5: European Union	Right to cultural diversity
	Human rights broadly construed
	Right to sustainable livelihood
	Right of political participation and freedom of information
Chapter 6: United States	Right to political participation and administrative due process rights
	Intellectual property rights
	Labor rights

	Policy response		
Trade issue or strategy	*Trade* policy to promote rights *at home*	*Other* policies to promote rights *at home*	*Trade* policy to promote rights *abroad*
To combat biopiracy, press for WTO to include rules similar to Convention on Biodiversity, which protect biodiversity and indigenous rights. Calling for new negotiations on these issues.	✔		✔
Because many sectors may produce goods for export with inputs made with forced labor, policymakers have developed non-trade strategies, including public–private partnerships and naming and shaming.		✔	
Because some exported goods may include inputs made by child labor, business, government and civil society have devised collaborative, non-trade strategies to reduce child labor.		✔	
Because culture is unique and must be defended, devised strategy to govern trade in culture outside of WTO.	✔		✔
Use bilateral trade agreements as an incentive to prod countries to adhere to internationally accepted human rights conventions.	✔		
Use trade policies to protect local farmers (but may undermine right to sustainable livelihood of farmers in developing world.)	✔		
The process of trade policymaking is not transparent and policies are made by a small group of EU officials.		Not applicable	
Use trade to prod other governments to regulate in a transparent manner and encourage involvement, feedback from public.			✔
Includes high property rights standards in bilateral trade agreements, demands enforcement to protect domestic intellectual property rights holders.	✔		✔
Use bilateral trade agreements to prod trade partners to promote and protect labor rights. Also uses trade policy reviews and access to promote labor rights abroad.			✔

2

The World Trade Organization and Human Rights

Providing Some Power to the People Some of the Time

HUMAN RIGHTS DISCUSSED IN THIS CHAPTER

This chapter focuses on (1) the right to political participation, (2) administrative due process rights, (3) labor rights, and (4) the right to food. We also briefly discuss the nexus between IPR protections in the WTO and the right to health.

Right to Political Participation
Under the International Bill of Human Rights, everyone has a right to take part in the government of his country, directly or through freely chosen representatives. The will of the people shall be the basis of the authority of government; this will shall be expressed in periodic and genuine elections which shall be universal and equal suffrage and shall be held by secret vote or by equivalent free voting procedures.

Administrative Due Process Rights
Under the International Bill of Rights, individuals have a right to participate in public affairs. Everyone has a right to recognition everywhere as a person before the law, protection against discrimination, the right to an effective remedy by competent national tribunals, and fair and public hearings by an independent and impartial tribunal, whether in civil, criminal, or administrative proceedings. In recognition that there cannot be democratic participation in decision making if governments do not act in a transparent and open manner, governments are required to take steps to promote the right to information, ensure due process in administrative procedures, and act in a transparent and open manner.

Labor Rights
Under the ILO Declaration on Fundamental Principles and Rights at Work (1998) all members of the ILO, even if they have not ratified the Conventions

in question, are obliged to respect, to promote, and to realize the principles concerning the fundamental rights which are the subject of those Conventions, namely: (a) freedom of association and the effective recognition of the right to collective bargaining; (b) the elimination of all forms of forced or compulsory labor; (c) the effective abolition of child labor; and (d) the elimination of discrimination in employment and occupation.

Intellectual Property Rights
Under the International Bill of Human Rights, authors have a right to protection of the moral and material interests resulting from their scientific, literary, or artistic productions, tempered by the public's right to enjoy the arts and to share in scientific advancement and its benefits. This is not an easy balance to achieve. Governments have tried to protect the rights of authors through copyright, patent, and trademark regimes, but many critics argue that these regimes privilege mass manufacturers and distributors of creative works over both their authors and audiences.

The Right to Food
The International Bill of Human Rights does not explicitly delineate a right to food. However, everyone has the right to life and the right to a standard of living adequate for the health and well-being of himself and his family, including food.

The Right to Health
Under the International Bill of Human Rights, everyone has a right to medical care as well as a right to share in the benefits of scientific advancement.

Introduction

Korean farmer Lee Kyung-hae had a history of using violence to make a political point. In 1990, he attempted to disembowel himself as he protested the direction of the Uruguay Round of trade talks. In 1993, he starved himself outside the Korean Parliament to protest a rise in the price of rice. But, in 2003, during the WTO Ministerial Conference in Cancun, he made the ultimate sacrifice. He climbed to the top of a security fence and told his fellow protestors, "Don't worry about me, just struggle your hardest." He then stabbed himself in the chest.[1]

Mr. Lee wanted to inspire other small farmers to fight against trade liberalization under the WTO.[2] He feared the WTO represented the end of small farming and the small-town way of life in Korea. He hoped his death would prod others to think broadly about how trade affected the rights of these small farmers to a sustainable livelihood.[3] However, his death did not seem to encourage the delegates to think along these lines. Although many delegations found his act deeply disturbing, the meeting proceeded as planned.

Nonetheless, Mr. Lee's dramatic suicide did bring greater attention to scholars and activists who claim the WTO system undermines human rights.[4] Some critics allege that the WTO promotes trade at the expense of human rights such as labor rights or the right to health.[5] Other WTO critics claim that it obliges member states to "take decisions that endanger the fundamental rights that they had freely agreed to protect and implement."[6] In this chapter, we do not purport to answer whether the WTO system conflicts with the international human rights system, whether increased trade promotes violations of human rights, or whether WTO rules make it harder to use trade sanctions or incentives to promote human rights compliance overseas.[7] These are controversial questions that must be answered in a separate book. As this is a book about policymaker behavior at the intersection of trade and human rights, we discuss how governments have introduced human rights concerns into the workings of the GATT/WTO. Although human rights concerns are not a central focus of the day-to-day workings of the WTO, we found that human rights concerns are seeping into WTO discussions. For example, when member states have discovered that WTO rules made it harder to achieve certain human rights

Examples of human rights issues seeping into the WTO

Issue	Response by members of the WTO
How to handle accessions of nations with significant human rights problems	Rule of law language in China accession. Discussion of human rights in trade policy reviews
Discussion of how trade liberalization may affect right to food and food security	WTO members agree to discuss food security as part of now-suspended agricultural trade negotiations
Concern that trade in diamonds is fueling/funding conflict	First trade waiver justified on human rights concerns
Liberalization of services (including those that are considered public goods and essential human rights such as education, water, health, housing, and food)	Many countries decline to participate in services negotiations for specific sectors such as water.
Ensuring access to affordable medicines in developing countries with public health emergencies	First-ever amendment of WTO delineating rights of WTO members in times of public health emergencies re: intellectual property obligations

objectives, they have at times found ways to clarify or rewrite WTO rules to ensure that national policymakers had space to achieve these goals. Moreover, members have introduced human rights concerns in trade policy reviews, negotiated waivers of WTO obligations and discussed human rights issues during both the Doha and Uruguay Rounds of trade talks.

The chapter begins with a short review of current scholarship on the WTO and human rights. We next discuss how the WTO works and the channels through which members can voice human rights concerns within the organization. Then, we examine how members of the WTO and members of the public have addressed labor rights and the right to food/food security during trade negotiations. When some members tried to include labor rights in the WTO's purview, they were stymied. Thus, these members had to find different ways to show that labor rights could affect trade. In the case of agricultural trade talks, policymakers early on recognized they must address human rights concerns related to agricultural trade liberalization and they agreed to include nontrade issues in the talks.

Finally, we discuss an interesting possible side effect of membership in the WTO: WTO rules require that member states put in place policies to grant citizens certain political and procedural rights related to trade. As citizens learn to take advantage of these rights, they may demand similar rights in other aspects of governance not related to trade. We argue that the habits of good governance, particularly political participation, fostered under WTO rules *may*, over time, spill over into other aspects of the polity.[8] We hope this preliminary assessment will stimulate other scholars to examine how WTO rules may affect how governments behave at the intersection of trade and human rights.

The WTO includes many agreements that govern trade in goods and services, special arrangements for special sectors, and related agreements such as the Agreement on Sanitary and Phytosanitary Measures. For the purposes of simplicity, we limit our discussion in this chapter to GATT 1994, Annex 2 (the Dispute Settlement Understanding), Annex 3 (the Trade Policy Review Mechanism), and the Agreement on Agriculture. We focus on GATT 1994, which delineates the basic norms and obligations of the world trading system. We do not discuss services and trade-related aspects of intellectual property agreements in this chapter.[9]

Recent Scholarship on Trade, the WTO, and Human Rights – and a Caveat

There are few studies that examine how WTO membership affects the *behavior* of governments regarding human rights. However, in recent years, scholars from many disciplines have examined the relationship between the WTO system and human rights.[10] Some scholars have argued that human rights issues are not trade issues and, therefore, the WTO has no authority to address them.[11] Yet others have proposed ways to find common ground between WTO trade law and international human rights law. Some scholars have suggested systematic reforms, such as making the human rights system more like the WTO (for example, with stronger dispute settlement and enforcement mechanisms) or, alternatively, making the WTO system more sensitive to human rights concerns.[12] Other academics have suggested bridging mechanisms to ensure better dialogue and coordination between trade and human rights officials.[13] For example, the legal scholar Ernst-Ulrich Petersmann argues that the world needs a new paradigm for global integration, one based on human rights and the sharing of the social adjustment costs of global integration. He argues that "citizens" must become recognized as legal subjects of the WTO.[14] Finally, some scholars have examined how the WTO's dispute settlement system might address a trade dispute involving human rights.[15]

Meanwhile, other academics have sought to empirically examine the relationship between trade flows or trade openness and human rights. As discussed in Chapter 1, some scholars have sought to statistically test the relationship between trade openness and different measures of human rights such as labor rights, personal integrity rights, or subsistence rights (such as the rights to water, food, and sanitation). Others have simply examined the relationship between trade (or foreign investment) and a particular human right. These studies have revealed that some rights (such as personal integrity rights) tend to improve, whereas others such as labor rights decline until a certain level of democracy is reached.[16]

These studies have not yet provided scholars with a broad understanding about how trade affects human rights or how protecting human rights may affect trade. Moreover, only one of these studies examined the effect of *WTO membership* and human rights. Scholar Mary Comerford Cooper tried to test the relationship between WTO membership and democratization (as opposed to protecting a particular human right) for the period 1947–1999. She could not determine whether democratic states were more likely to join the WTO or whether WTO membership makes countries more likely to become or remain democratic.[17]

We also performed a cursory examination of GATT/WTO membership, income level, and political rights (noting that the GATT governed trade from 1948 to 1994; the WTO thereafter.) Table 2.1 shows how the membership of the GATT/WTO has changed over time, particularly in regards to the percentage of free and democratic member states. We divided the countries by income

TABLE 2.1. *Democratic and free nations in the GATT/WTO**

	1948 GATT	1986† GATT	1994 GATT	2005 WTO
High income	12 (52%)	25 (27%)	32 (25%)	39 (26%)
Middle income	3 (13%)	38 (42%)	56 (44%)	67 (45%)
Low income	8 (35%)	28 (31%)	40 (31%)	43 (29%)
Total member countries	23	91	128	149
Free member countries		37	57	77
Percentage free (countries with higher civil and political freedoms)		40.66% (37/91)	44.53% (57/128)	51.68% (77/149)
Percentage free, excluding the high-income 24‡		19.40% (13/67)	31.73% (33/104)	42.40% (53/125)

Note: Table prepared by Jillian Bohinc.

* Information received from the World Bank Web site (http://www.worldbank.org), the Freedom House Web site (http://www.freedomhouse.org), and the WTO Web site (http://www.wto.org).

† The income information given for the 1986 column is actually for 1987. Data for 1986 were not available from the World Bank Web site; however, the income status for a country generally does not change very drastically between years.

‡ Yearly totals vary because, for instance, some countries dropped out; some countries split (the Czech Republic and Slovakia); and the nations of the European Union agreed to negotiate trade policies at the European Community level. According to Freedom House, democratic and free countries have a climate of respect for civil liberties, significant independent civic life, and independent media. In partly free countries, political rights and civil liberties are more limited, and these countries may also experience corruption, have weak rule of law, and one dominant political party enjoys dominance. In countries that are not free, people are widely and systematically denied basic civil liberties and political rights.

levels and found that the percentages of income levels stayed mostly constant, although more developing countries joined the WTO and more countries moved to a higher income level. We note that, if we exclude the high-income Organization for Economic Cooperation and Development (OECD) countries, a growing percentage of WTO members are considered to be "free" and democratic, using Freedom House's criteria. Here, too, however, the direction of causality is unclear. We don't know whether WTO membership is a factor moving states to become more democratic or whether more democratic states want to join the WTO.

We must make one important caveat before we use insights from these studies to examine what member states have done to promote human rights at the WTO. When scholars, activists, and policymakers discuss the WTO's impact on human rights, they often conflate the actions and decisions of WTO member governments' policymakers with WTO "diktat." However, there is no such thing as WTO "diktat."[18] The WTO *bureaucracy* cannot tell WTO member states what to do. The WTO system represents the *consensus of the member states.* [19] When those members agree on a course of action, they are collaborating to develop WTO policy. Nonetheless, many critics of multilateral trade liberalization argue that because the WTO has a binding system of dispute settlement, it forces members to make compliance with WTO rules a top policy priority.[20] Yet even here members have flexibility. If the Dispute Settlement Body finds that a member state's policies distort trade, that member can change its policies or not – and accept the consequences – whether retaliation or worsened trade relations.

Like the GATT that preceded it, the WTO agreements say very little about what governments should do when their trade obligations and human rights obligations intersect.[21] We next delineate what those obligations are.

The Human Rights Obligations of WTO Member States

Each government that is a member of the United Nations has committed itself to promote and protect human rights. Most of the 149 WTO member states have ratified or signed the two UN Covenants on Human Rights.[22]

In the 1990s, the members of the United Nations recognized that they needed to do more to ensure that international organizations, as well as nation states, collaborated to protect human rights; they worked to ensure that their activities did not make it harder for governments to promote human rights at home or abroad. At a historic meeting in Austria in 1993, UN members agreed – on paper – to coordinate their efforts by signing the Vienna Declaration on Human Rights.[23]

However, although the WTO and the UN Commission on Human Rights are both in Geneva, they have never met to coordinate policies. In fact, WTO staff cannot simply "coordinate" without a direct mandate from WTO member states. Nevertheless, officials from UN human rights bodies and WTO staff are beginning to communicate. In recent years, for example, the UN High Commissioner has issued several reports that provide "context" for the interpretation of WTO rules.[24]

The Trade Obligations of WTO Member States

The WTO is a cooperative legal system with two main functions: to govern trade through its set of international agreements and to stimulate trade through negotiations aimed at expanding market access for its member states.[25] The WTO system does not directly govern the behavior of people or firms engaged in trade – it governs the behavior of governments. The WTO agreements speak to relationships *between* states, rather than relationships *within* states, because that is generally the purview of domestic policymakers. According to law professor Steve Charnovitz, international trade law "takes as a given that the responsibilities of a government towards its citizens is a matter to be determined by each government, not by the international community."[26] As a result, the WTO agreements do not discuss human rights per se.

If they seek to use trade to protect human rights at home or to advance human rights abroad, WTO member states must adhere to certain principles. First, member states must automatically extend the best trade conditions granted to goods and services of one member to goods and services of every other nation that belongs to the WTO (the most favored nation [MFN] principle). Second, these countries must under GATT treat products of foreign firms in the same way they do those of local firms (the national treatment principle). Policymakers cannot discriminate between products originating in different countries nor between imported goods and *like* domestically produced goods.[27]

Avenues to Discuss and Act on Human Rights Concerns within the WTO System

WTO principles effectively limit how and when governments may apply policies that can distort trade, including policies put in place to promote human rights abroad or at home. Because of these limitations, some people perceive that the WTO system reduces the amount of policy options available to member states to promote and protect human rights. Yet we found that WTO members can use several avenues to discuss human rights or to act to protect human rights at home or abroad; they are summarized in Table 2.2.

TABLE 2.2. *The WTO system and where human rights may enter the discussion*

Accessions	Nations have not introduced human rights concerns, per se, in accessions, but some members have become increasingly concerned about human rights and, in particular, the rule of law in acceding countries. In the China accession, China was asked to enforce all of its laws in all of its territories, including export processing zones.
Nonapplication	When nations accede, WTO members may choose not to extend trading rights and privileges. The United States used nonapplication to deny trading rights to Romania when it was communist and undemocratic.
General exceptions	Article XX includes language allowing nations to restrict trade when necessary to protect life, protect public morals, secure compliance or conserve natural resources. Article XXI allows member states to restrict trade for reasons of national security.
Waivers	The Kimberley waiver for conflict diamonds was the first waiver approved for a human rights purpose. Stimulated by a UN Security Council Resolution and broad member interest and support. Preference programs were originally put in place under a waiver. Some preference programs have human rights conditionality.
Dispute settlement	There have been no disputes that centered directly on human rights questions. First dispute on public morals (Internet gambling) was in 2005. Food safety disputes to some degree center on the right to health (but not explicitly defended as human rights concerns, e.g., the beef hormones case).
Trade policy reviews (TPR)	The WTO Secretariat and member states jointly review trade policies and practices of member states. Larger trading nations are reviewed more frequently. Officials increasingly bring up human rights concerns, particularly labor rights, in these discussions.
Amendments to existing agreements or clarification	WTO members recognize there are times when they need to provide greater guidance to member states. In amendments, members agree to alter existing agreements to stipulate what member states can or cannot do, as in intellectual property rights (IPR) and the right to health (access to affordable medicines). In addition, members have agreed to further discussions to clarify the relationship between IPR and traditional knowledge.[28] Such actions are rare.
Negotiations	Some members sought to include labor rights in negotiations, but they failed. Members have discussed nontrade issues such as access to affordable food and food security in agricultural negotiations.

On Accession and Nonapplication

Like the GATT, the WTO does not have any human rights or democracy criteria for membership. Any state or customs territory with full autonomy in the conduct of its trade policies may accede to the WTO. However, WTO members must agree on the terms of membership, which differ for each country.[29] Members have successfully pressed for policy changes within states that want to accede to the WTO, and some of these changes are not strictly trade-related.[30] We examined all of the accessions (Cambodia, Saudi Arabia, Macedonia, Armenia, Nepal, and Vietnam) from 2003 to 2007 to ascertain if existing WTO members expressed concerns about the potential acceding country's human rights practices. Interestingly, each of these states has difficulty protecting human rights.[31]

When these countries applied for WTO membership, their applications (like those of all other countries seeking to accede) were reviewed by a working party composed of existing WTO members. The deliberations always began with a discussion of how these countries made and promulgated public policy, in general, and trade policies, in particular. Members then focused on how the applicant nation protected the rights of citizens, as well as noncitizens, to participate in trade.

For example, as Cambodia sought to accede to the WTO in 2003, members of the working party on its accession noted that its legal system did not afford adequate protection for individuals or businesses. The representative of Cambodia promised that the country would establish a commercial court system with trained judges and staff. Working party member governments then reminded Cambodia that when it established standards or technical regulations, it was obliged to develop "mechanisms for publication and dissemination of draft legislation and standards for public comment; [and] the establishment of a TBT (technical barriers to trade) Inquiry Point" where foreign and domestic producers could learn how to meet Cambodian standards.[32] After Cambodia agreed to these and many other changes, the WTO Ministerial Conference agreed to Cambodia's accession at the Cancun conference in September 2003.[33]

Members also examined Saudi Arabia's adherence to the rule of law as the working party deliberated the accession of that Gulf state. Members spent hours asking questions about the rights of Saudis and non-Saudis to participate in various elements of the economy. They also urged the country to publish notices of proposed measures related to trade and to provide an opportunity for "interested persons" to provide comments and views on such measures prior to their adoption and implementation.[34] In short, these officials were asking the Saudis for information about political participation in trade issues.

Saudi Arabia agreed to establish an official Web site for trade policymaking and to "provide a reasonable period . . . for members, individuals, associations and enterprises to provide comments to the appropriate authorities before such measures were adopted."[35] Nepal and Macedonia were required to address the same questions, and members of the working group seemed satisfied with the answers of the two governments.[36]

In October 2006, the United States sought to include language in the working party report related to Vietnam's accession. The United States noted that Vietnam had not ratified eight of the International Labor Organization's conventions relating to core labor standards and asked Vietnam to provide information on how it was applying these standards nationally. Several developing countries, however, objected to including language on labor rights in the working party report and it was ultimately not included.[37] Members attached stringent conditions for China's accession which required China to enforce the rule of law throughout China. These conditions will be discussed later in this chapter in the section on labor rights.

Thus, in general members did not use the accession deliberations to push potential members to change their human rights practices. But they did press for broad changes (such as improvements in the rule of law and greater transparency) that could facilitate human rights improvements over time.

WTO members decide not only conditions for membership but also whether to deny WTO benefits (known as *nonapplication*) to a potential member. Article XII allows members to deny application of WTO benefits to a new member, so long as they do so before the WTO Ministerial Council approves the member's accession agreement.[38] If countries use nonapplication under the WTO, they must use it for all of the WTO agreements.[39]

In principle, members are free to use this process to punish WTO applicants for their human rights practices. In practice, only the United States, Peru, and El Salvador have used the provision. The United States relied on nonapplication to deny trading privileges to terrorist nations or former members of the Soviet bloc, such as Romania.[40] In the United States, extension of MFN to Russia, Vietnam, and several other economies in transition from communism is contingent on these countries' adherence to the provisions of the Jackson–Vanik amendment to the 1974 Trade Act regarding freedom of emigration (see Chapter 6).[41]

On Trade Waivers, General Exceptions, and the Security Exception

Waivers
WTO members cannot expel another member for any reason, including the failure to protect and promote human rights.[42] Thus, countries that have

abused the human rights of their own citizens can remain members in good standing of the WTO. But under WTO rules, members can still use trade to address international human rights concerns in other countries. First, members can waive WTO obligations in cases where trade may exacerbate human rights abuses. Under GATT 1994, the members in attendance at a ministerial conference may waive an obligation imposed on a member, provided that any such decision is approved by three-quarters of the other members. (These waivers were supposed to be limited to exceptional circumstances and in fact such waivers are rare.)

For example, after the members of the United Nations called for a ban on trade in conflict diamonds, WTO member states called for and eventually agreed on a waiver under the WTO for such a ban.[43] Under the waiver, nations are allowed to trade only those diamonds certified under the Kimberley Process Certification Scheme. Members applying for the waiver had to commit to ensuring that the measures taken were consistent with international trade rules. The Kimberley Process Certification Scheme is a way for consumers and producers to ensure that they do not trade diamonds that indirectly fund wars in Sierra Leone or the Democratic Republic of the Congo.[44] As of April 2007, there were forty-seven official members of the Kimberley Process, although as of January 2005, fifty member states have applied for a waiver regarding their trade in conflict diamonds.[45] This was the first time that the members of the WTO approved a waiver of trade obligations based on a human rights rationale. Members agreed to this action in response to the United Nations General Assembly resolution to ensure that legitimate trade in diamonds could continue, that the diamond trade would not fuel conflicts or fund terrorism, and that human rights violations did not occur in the mining or processing of diamonds.[46] Thus, the Kimberley waiver sets an important precedent. Canadian Trade Minister Pierre Pettigrew stated, "This decision clearly shows that the WTO can be flexible when it comes to human security and development."[47]

The GATT/WTO has approved other waivers that could have an impact on human rights conditions, but these waivers were not designed specifically to protect human rights per se.[48] From 1971 to 1981, the WTO granted waivers to industrialized countries that wanted to provide preferential access to the trade of developing countries.[49] After that waiver expired in 1981, the contracting parties of the GATT developed and adopted a declaration entitled "Differential and More Favorable Treatment, Reciprocity and Fuller Participation of Developing Countries." The declaration, "the Enabling Clause," was adopted by a decision of the contracting parties and was not explicitly labeled as a waiver.[50] Under the Enabling Clause, tariff preferences granted by developed countries must not discriminate among developing countries, except for the possibility of providing more generous preferences to all least-developed countries.[51] The Enabling Clause does not, however, cover specific preferences for limited groups of developing countries granted by individual developed countries, such as those granted by the EU to certain developing countries under the Lomé Convention. In 2000, the EU applied for a waiver that would allow it to continue to provide the special trade preferences to these countries.[52]

Some of these preference programs have human rights conditionality clauses. The EU's Generalized System of Preferences-Plus (GSP-Plus), authorized under the Enabling Clause, provides additional market access to developing countries that support sustainable development and good governance policies. Specifically, these countries must have ratified key human rights conventions (as well as labor rights and environmental laws) and effectively implemented them through national law.[53] The Cotonou Agreement requires that recipients of preferential market access meet certain human rights obligations.[54] In addition, the United States GSP program requires GSP recipients to adhere to certain requirements related to workers' rights.

Finally, the WTO has also granted a waiver of obligations under Article 66 of the Agreement on TRIPS to ensure that nations can provide affordable medicines for their citizens. Members waived the obligations of least-developing country members with regard to pharmaceutical products until January 1, 2016.[55]

Taken in sum, these waivers (and the Enabling Clause) demonstrate that WTO members acknowledge that there are rare cases in which trade rules must be waived to ensure that human rights are not undermined (conflict diamonds). The WTO has also granted waivers that allow industrialized countries to provide trade preferences. Some of these trade preference programs use trade as an incentive to prod developing countries to promote human rights and development. But trade waivers may not be the most effective tools to use at the intersection of trade and human rights. Waivers are temporary measures, and human rights problems generally cannot be solved on a temporary basis.[56] Moreover, these waivers provide little guidance to trade policymakers on how to react to future conflicts between WTO rules and human rights objectives.

Exceptions

WTO members might find the foundation for a more effective approach to protecting human rights at home or responding to human rights abuses abroad in the GATT WTO's exceptions – Article XX and Article XXI. Article XX permits members to restrict trade when necessary to "protect human, animal or plant life or health; protect public morals; secure compliance with laws or regulations which are not inconsistent with the provisions of this Agreement" or to conserve natural resources.[57] However, members should not apply these measures "in a manner which would constitute a means of arbitrary or unjustifiable discrimination between countries where the same conditions prevail, or a disguised restriction on international trade."[58]

More specifically, Article XX paragraph (a) allows nations to ban trade under a public morals exception. Citizens in a WTO member state may be offended by human rights violations in another member state, but no nation has sought to justify a human rights ban on trade as an offense to public morals.[59] Article XX paragraph (e) covers measures directed at goods produced by prison labor. The paragraph explicitly refers to the products of prison labor rather than the labor conditions under which they are produced. Therefore it seems designed to protect domestic industries rather than workers from other countries that toil in unfair conditions. However, some scholars argue that governments might use paragraph (e) to ban trade from countries where workers toil in conditions of slave labor, forced labor, or child labor.[60]

In 2005, the UN High Commissioner for human rights noted that "member states' obligations towards their own populations could fall within the compass of the 'public morals,' 'public order' and human life and health exceptions of the WTO."[61] However, as noted earlier, in the fifty-nine years of the global trading system, no GATT or WTO member has successfully used this article to ban trade explicitly in the interest of human rights.[62] As a result, policymakers have little guidance from the Dispute Settlement Body or the Appellate Body regarding when and how these exceptions might be used to promote human rights.[63]

The Article XXI exception is quite different; its history reflects global political conditions at the time of the GATT's development. This exception allows nations to take any action that a member deems necessary for the protection of its essential security interests or to pursue its "obligations under the United Nations Charter for the maintenance of international peace and security." The language allows members to take action for their own security, but not to take trade action to protect another member's security or to protect the citizens of another member. However, members can take such steps if and only if the UN Security Council authorizes trade restrictions.[64] Member states have used this provision to put in place trade sanctions against nations such as South Africa and Somalia, which violated the human rights of their own people. The United States has also used this provision against countries such as Libya and Iraq, which it defined as terrorist nations.[65]

On Dispute Settlement

As noted above, the members of the WTO have never had a trade dispute that centered directly on human rights considerations. To some extent this is because a WTO member that violates human rights is unlikely to challenge trade restrictions put in place to pressure that government to alter its behavior. Such a country, with a long record of human rights abuse, say, Burma, would probably not want these issues discussed at the WTO and thus is unlikely to challenge the United States, which has put in place trade sanctions to influence Burma's human rights practices.[66]

For a brief moment, India appeared to initiate the first trade dispute centered on the use of a trade waiver designed to promote human rights. It initially challenged EU labor rights GSP conditions but ultimately limited its challenge. Nonetheless, the case has wide implications for how countries can use GSP programs to advance human rights with trade policy.

Under its GSP program, the EU grants developing countries either duty-free access or a tariff reduction on certain imported products.[67] But a beneficiary country is not automatically or unconditionally entitled to these benefits. The EU can withdraw trade preferences granted to developing countries under these arrangements if the beneficiary country systematically violates core UN and ILO conventions on human and labor rights or exports goods made by prison labor.[68] In recent years, the EU included additional preferences for countries engaged in efforts to combat drug production and trafficking. The European Union admitted it wanted to reward Pakistan for its new position on the Taliban regime in Afghanistan.[69] However, as readers might imagine, it is exceedingly difficult to get the members of the UN Security Council to agree that trade sanctions are an appropriate strategy to improve human rights conditions in other countries. However, according to trade scholar Lorand Bartels, "there was no mechanism for a beneficiary country to apply for these special preferences. The EC decided on the beneficiaries based on its own criteria."[70] Therefore, it appeared discriminatory to Indian policymakers.

On December 9, 2002, India requested the establishment of a WTO panel to determine whether provisions under the EU's GSP program relating to labor rights, the protection of the environment, and to combat drug production and trafficking were compatible with WTO rules.[71] The request received wide attention, largely because it was the first to contest a trade measure used to promote respect for a particular category of human rights. However, in March 2003, India informed the EC that it was withdrawing its challenge on tariff preferences granted under the GSP's environmental and labor clauses (but maintaining the rest of its challenge on drug production and trafficking).[72] Although India did not publicly explain its reasons for limiting its challenge, India had long been among the most vocal opponents of including labor rights in the purview of the WTO. To initiate a WTO dispute centered on labor rights would not only seem to directly contradict this position, but it might also spur other members to bring labor issues into the WTO's purview (something India and many other nations would like to avoid).

Despite narrowing its case, India still maintained that the conditions under which the European Union granted tariff preferences under this special incentive arrangement were discriminatory and violated the requirements set out in the Enabling Clause.[73] India argued that it violated the European Union's binding obligation to grant GSP preferences in a "generalized, non-reciprocal and non-discriminatory" way.[74] The panel found in favor of India.[75]

In January 2004, the European Union appealed the panel report's conclusions in the Appellate Body, and, in April, the Appellate Body issued its decision.[76] The Appellate Body found that in granting differential tariff treatment, preference-granting countries are required, by virtue of the term *nondiscriminatory*, to ensure that identical treatment is available to all GSP beneficiaries that have the same "development, financial and trade needs."[77] The European Commission altered its approach to bring it into compliance with WTO rules.[78]

This decision, however, has raised questions about how nations can use their GSP programs to promote human rights. For example, law professor Robert Howse fears that, in the future, policymakers will only be able to grant or withdraw GSP treatment by justifying such actions under the exception provisions in the WTO agreements (such as Articles XX and XXI).[79] Law professor Lorand Bartels, in contrast, is more hopeful. He has interpreted the panel's decision to mean that WTO members' GSP arrangements can differentiate among developing countries as long as the arrangements grant the same preferences to *all* developing countries that face the development, financial, and trade needs the arrangements try to address.[80] He believes that the report allows for differentiation between developing countries on three conditions: when there are legitimate development needs, when the preferences represent an appropriate and positive response to these needs, and when the preferences are available to all those countries with those needs.[81] Nonetheless, he worries that countries will find it difficult to withdraw trade preferences: "It is very difficult to argue that a withdrawal of trade preferences is a positive response to such [development] needs."[82] Thus, like Howse, he thinks it will be harder for industrialized countries to use trade policy to promote important nontrade policy objectives.

In the absence of a trade dispute directly related to human rights, prominent legal scholars have debated how the dispute settlement system could handle a trade dispute where one party used trade measures to promote human rights at home or abroad. According to WTO official and legal scholar Gabrielle Marceau, "WTO adjudicating bodies do not appear to have the competence ... to reach any formal conclusion that a non-WTO norm has been violated, or to require any ... action that would enforce a non-WTO norm over WTO provisions." By so doing, the WTO adjudicating body would effectively be adding to the members' WTO obligations without their assent. Law professor Joel Trachtman also notes that the WTO Appellate Body recently confirmed the principle that WTO adjudicating bodies do not have the competence to reach a formal conclusion that a non-WTO norm has been violated.[83] However, many scholars also believe that the WTO should give deference to human rights laws, which are perceived as *jus cogens* and thus have direct effect in WTO law.[84]

However, some scholars and human rights activists would welcome a trade dispute centered on human rights questions. They hope it would clarify whether the WTO agreements are superior to or of equal value to other international laws.[85] Moreover, depending on the nature of the dispute, it could provide insights into whether conditioning of trade (as in the EU preferences noted earlier or in the Kimberley waiver) based on nontrade policies such as human rights violates MFN privileges.[86]

On Trade Policy Reviews

Every member of the WTO is required to present its trade policy at a formal session, where members openly debate that nation's trade conduct.[87] According to the Secretariat, "the reviews have two broad results: they enable outsiders to understand a country's policies and circumstances, and they provide feedback to the reviewed country on its performance in the system."[88] Thus, we sought to ascertain if members of the WTO considered human rights an important element of a member state's policies and circumstances. We examined a sample of recent trade policy reviews reflecting developing and middle-income countries: Egypt (2005), Morocco (2003), Bolivia (2006), Romania (2005), El Salvador (2003), Gambia (2004), Brazil (2004), Slovenia (2002), Thailand (2003), and Malaysia (2005). We also examined reviews of the European Union (the EU) (2005) and the United States (2004). We found that WTO members occasionally discussed human rights as they provided feedback on member's trade performance.

In these reviews, some members acknowledged a relationship among economic growth, the rule of law, and human rights. The representative of Egypt stressed that it had put in place new laws to protect intellectual property rights and the rights of consumers. He added that "new laws had been enacted to foster political participation" and to strengthen civil society. He argued, "these landmark political reforms would enhance the trust in Egypt's commitment to the current economic and social reforms."[89]

The trade policy reviews also revealed that, although many countries were willing to change the various aspects of their legal systems to promote trade and investment, policymakers were also determined to preserve their social compact and their human rights priorities. For example, in its trade policy review, Romania stressed that it required investors to ensure that they would not violate environmental protection regulations, affect Romanian national security, or "affect the public order, health, or morality."[90] In Bolivia's review, the representative from Bolivia stressed that Bolivia had made "considerable efforts to adapt to world trade rules [and] trusted that its trading partners would appreciate what had been done, and urged the developed countries to make commitments that would lead to a substantial improvement in market access in order to enhance the economic and social welfare of their economies."[91]

But some members used their trade policy review as a platform to tout their activism on human rights issues. Ecuador's review noted that "Ecuador had established specialized tribunals to defend children's and women's rights, for example to deal with child pornography. These were priority areas."[92] With these assertions, Ecuador was trying to send a message about its human rights priorities and the role of the courts. Although many people may not see these issues as trade-related, Ecuador thought it important enough to discuss at its trade policy review.

China's trade policy review provided a particularly insightful window into how members view and act on the relationship between WTO obligations and human rights. Members did not specifically condemn or applaud Chinese human rights conditions or practices; yet some human rights concerns were clearly key elements of the discussion. The Chairperson (Claudia Uribe from Colombia) noted that China had dramatically reduced poverty from 73% of the population to 32% in 2003 and improved the rule of law to the benefit of its citizens and the global community. China, in response, stressed it would do more at home and abroad to "lift others out of poverty" and provide new opportunities. It pledged to expand its aid and technical assistance programs and invest in rural education and infrastructural development at home and abroad. The discussant noted for the first time that China was publicly debating "how to reform," especially how to put in place property rights and create jobs and how to address income inequality, especially between rural and agrarian areas.[93] He seemed to be applauding China for inviting public comment on some of these issues. But developing and industrialized country members also expressed concern about China's commitment to the rule of law, the right to information (not a human right under the UDHR although instrumental to democracy and effective governance), and inadequate protections for public comment (right to political participation and due process rights) on issues such as food safety. Members from around the world complimented China on its efforts to comply with its WTO commitments but expressed concern regarding its enforcement of intellectual property rights.[94] Moreover, the representative of the EC noted that China's trade policy "should contribute to more sustainable production patterns, rather than to lower standards" to meet new social and environmental challenges. In response, the representative of Cuba expressed concern "over questions . . . which involved value judgments about China's political, legal or social structure, and were not subject to WTO obligations."[95] WTO members commended China for openly discussing its challenges, and the representative of China in turn stated, "It was also a very useful exercise for China."[96]

Human rights concerns also seeped into the trade policy reviews of countries in the industrialized world. Both the European Union and the United States frequently talked about their commitments to promoting labor rights internationally (see below). But not everyone agreed with these strategies. For example, at the review of the European Community (EC) in 2004, Australia noted that "the EC's endeavor to pursue social and environmental objectives in its regional, bi-regional and bilateral trade arrangements raises some concerns."[97] It didn't delineate what these concerns were, but the Australian representative went on to ask if the EC had quantified the implications or the results of trade flows resulting from the inclusion of social and environmental provisions in its regional or bilateral agreements. The European Community responded, "Trade policy is . . . an important vehicle for social and environmental objectives, alongside a range of other policy areas." The European Community also claimed it was making an effort to understand the social and environmental impact of its trade policies with Sustainability Impact Assessments (SIAs) of its potential trade agreements. EC representatives stressed, "Initial results from these SIAs are now emerging, and show a broadly positive relationship between economic growth in developing countries and social development."[98]

With trade policy reviews, member states discuss the broad context in which trade occurs. Human rights concerns are a small but emerging component of these discussions.

On Amendments and Clarifications

From time to time, WTO members discover that they must either clarify or amend the language in particular WTO agreements. Such clarifications are rare, but when necessary, members can supplement existing language or issue a clarification. Although amendments and clarifications have generally not involved human rights questions, in recent years, WTO members found that they must clarify WTO rules in response to real-world conditions, such as the public health exceptions to the TRIPS agreement. We have already discussed this process in detail in Chapter 1.

Thus, members have several avenues to discuss how WTO rules can affect their human rights concerns. However, trade negotiations offer the most direct route to resolving perceived conflict between WTO rules and human rights. During such negotiations, WTO members can debate and develop rules to guide their own behavior. Although human rights are traditionally considered outside the WTO's purview, we found several instances during negotiations when members introduced human rights concerns.

How Member States Have Used Negotiations to Introduce Human Rights Concerns into the Purview of the WTO

The Intersection of WTO Rules and Labor Rights

Some scholars and policymakers have long argued that when governments undermine core labor rights (freedom of association and the right to organize and bargain collectively; nondiscrimination in the workplace; effective abolition of child labor; and freedom from forced labor), these governments are essentially allowing competition on the basis of unfair advantage. Thus, they conclude that the failure to protect core workers' rights may distort trade.[99] Reflecting that perspective, several European countries, as well as the United States and Canada, tried to introduce labor standards into GATT trade talks. But policymakers from numerous developing countries feared that these labor standards were the equivalent of de facto trade barriers (i.e., covert protectionism). In the end, GATT contracting parties did not succeed in including them in their purview.

With the creation of the WTO, labor activists, human rights activists, and many government officials wanted to make the negotiation of labor rights the first human rights issue discussed by WTO member states.[100] They also hoped to build on the findings of the Leutwiler Group report to the GATT. In 1985, this advisory group found that "there is no disagreement that countries do not have to accept the products of slave or prison labor."[101]

During the Marrakech ministerial conference of the GATT in 1994, policymakers from the United States, Norway, and several other countries hoped to include labor standards (and environmental issues) in the final Declaration, but representatives from many developing countries balked. The chair of the Trade Negotiating Committee referred to, but did not endorse, proposals for an examination of the relationship between international labor standards and the trading system.[102] In 1996, at the Singapore ministerial, some members demanded negotiations on core labor standards, but several developing countries again objected.[103] In the Singapore Declaration, members restated their commitment to observe internationally recognized core labor standards.

They affirmed that the ILO, rather than the WTO, was the competent body to discuss and address these standards and declared that governments must not use labor standards for protectionist purposes.[104]

In the preparations for the Seattle ministerial, the United States, the European Union, and Canada submitted proposals for the consideration of trade and core labor rights issues. These nations argued that public confidence in the WTO would rise if the members agreed to include core labor rights in the WTO's purview. They suggested various proposals to set up working groups on the relationship between trade and labor standards, but these proposals went nowhere.[105]

U.S. President Bill Clinton, the host of the ministerial, thought he could resolve this stalemate. In an interview with the *Seattle Post Intelligencer*, he argued, "I think that what we ought to do first of all [is] to adopt the United States' position on having a working group on labor within the WTO, and then that working group should develop these core labor standards, and then they ought to be a part of every trade agreement, and ultimately I would favor a system in which sanctions would come for violating any provision of a trade agreement." Representatives of several developing countries, including India and Mexico, responded angrily to President Clinton's proposal. They thought he was pandering to U.S. labor unions, and they refused to create such a working group. Moreover, they were particularly annoyed that he called for sanctions rather than incentives to advance labor rights abroad.[106] Clinton's efforts cast a pall over the ministerial. The delegates at Seattle could not find common ground on labor rights, development, or any of the other issues that brought them to that port city. The delegates left as disappointed and frustrated as many of the activists in the streets who were protesting the ministerial.[107]

Therefore, advocates of labor rights have had to find other ways to encourage a discussion about the relationship between trade rules and labor rights. They have achieved some success by delineating rules for export processing zones (EPZs). The WTO allows nations to use EPZs as instruments to attract investment and encourage economic development.[108] Although every country's approach to EPZs is different, many countries allow firms to breach national fiscal and sometimes labor laws in these zones.[109] According to the United Nations in 2003, at least sixteen countries had lower labor rights standards in their EPZs.[110]

In the 1980s, as more countries began to rely on EPZs to attract investment, some members of the GATT alleged that some EPZ incentives are the effective equivalent of an export subsidy. In the Uruguay Round, members agreed to discipline these "export subsidies" by gradually phasing them out. Governments can still maintain EPZs, but they can no longer provide them with financial incentives. Developing countries with less than $1,000 per capita GNP were exempted from these disciplines and were given until the end of 2003 to phase out these prohibited export subsidies.[111] However, many developing countries have asked for an extension of the phase-out date for these prohibited subsidies for their EPZs.

Some countries have also used the trade policy review process to press developing countries to improve their compliance with internationally accepted labor standards within EPZs. For example, the representative of the United States noted during El Salvador's trade policy review that there were reports of violations of workers' rights in the EPZs. The representatives of the United States and the European Union urged El Salvador to reconsider the use of these zones to stimulate growth.[112] The United States even used its own 2004 trade policy review to make a connection between labor rights and trade. The U.S. government report noted, in the context of the Doha Ministerial Declaration, that the subject of implementation of core labor standards was relevant for trade policy reviews.[113] However, some other nations were offended by this tactic. In the discussion of U.S. trade policies that followed, India noted that the ILO, not the WTO, was competent to deal with labor issues. Moreover, the Indian representative stressed that these reviews should not deal with "nontrade" issues. The government of Venezuela seconded these remarks.[114]

Some members were particularly concerned about labor rights and conditions in China's EPZs. China has used these zones (special economic zones) to experiment with market-based, outward-oriented policies.[115] In many of these zones, Chinese labor law is flouted or unenforced. As China sought to join the WTO, members of the WTO recognized that China might thus attract investment from countries that have more stringent workers' rights standards. They also noted that China lacked an impartial judiciary, an effective and transparent social and environmental regulatory system, and a strong central government capable of enforcing the law.[116] As a result, WTO members attached stringent conditions for China's accession, which were quite different from other countries' accession agreements.[117]

The 2001 Protocol on the Accession of the People's Republic of China is an unusual document. Unlike the Accession Protocols of previously admitted members, it specifically comments on the effectiveness of the rule of law in China. It states as a condition of accession that China must enforce "uniform administration of Chinese law" throughout China. "The provisions of the WTO Agreement and this protocol shall apply to the entire customs territory of China, including . . . special economic zones . . . and other areas where special regimes for tariffs, taxes and regulations are established." The agreement also calls on China to "apply and administer in a uniform, impartial and reasonable manner all its laws, regulations and other measures of the central government as well as local regulations, rules and other measures . . . pertaining to or affecting trade. . . . China shall establish a mechanism under which individuals and enterprises can bring to the attention of the national authorities cases of non-uniform application."[118] The agreement requires China to notify the WTO about "all the relevant laws, regulations and other measures relating to its special economic areas." Finally, it calls on China to ensure that "those laws, regulations and other measures pertaining to and affecting trade shall be enforced."[119] The China accession document did not address labor laws explicitly, but it reveals that members recognized that the failure to enforce human rights laws, whether labor law or intellectual property law, could distort trade.

The question of how labor rights relate to WTO rules remains an open sore within the organization. In December 2005, one day before the opening of the Hong Kong ministerial, WTO Director-General Pascal Lamy met with trade unionists. He told them "the WTO and its secretariat do not have a mandate to work on coherence between what is done in the WTO and what is done in the ILO." Lamy urged labor leaders to ensure they had enough leverage on their governments before they made a push for labor standards in future trade negotiations.[120] Lamy seemed to signal that advocates of labor rights must reassure developing country officials that uniform labor standards will not impede the competitiveness of their exports. Until they do, many WTO members will continue to oppose including labor standards in the WTO.

Human Rights, Nontrade Concerns, and Agricultural Liberalization

For many years now, the world's farmers and fishers have produced enough food to adequately feed the world's people. Yet millions of people are starving and more than two billion people worldwide suffer from malnutrition. Trade can be part of the solution to ending world hunger and malnutrition, but for many years trade policies and agreements have also been part of the problem. Trade in agriculture can both enhance and undermine human rights.[121] Although the UDHR does not explicitly delineate a right to food, it does delineate that everyone has the right to life and also states that "everyone has a right to a standard of living adequate for the health and well-being of himself and his family, including food." The Food and Agriculture Organization of the United Nations (FAO) has defined food security as the access for all people at all times to enough food for an active, healthy life.[122] According to the Commission on Human Rights, states are not to take actions that deprive people of access to adequate affordable food.[123] Moreover, under international law, governments are obligated "to take into account . . . international legal obligations regarding the right to food when entering into agreements with other States or with international organizations."[124] Trade negotiators have begun to take human rights concerns into account as they discussed how to liberalize trade in agriculture. However, in five years of discussion, they have found little common ground.

For most of the history of the GATT, many trade policymakers were unwilling to discuss agricultural trade liberalization. They recognized such talks would bring up complex questions about the trade compatibility of domestic policies established to achieve objectives such as food security, food safety, rural development, and environmental protection. During the Uruguay Round of trade talks from 1986 to 1993, however, policymakers finally agreed to begin to address these issues as part of comprehensive talks to liberalize trade in agriculture. Participants termed these issues *nontrade concerns.*

In Article 20 of the Agreement on Agriculture, they agreed that nontrade concerns (a term which was left undefined but that clearly included food security) must be discussed when the parties again met to negotiate further agricultural liberalization.[125] The participants also agreed to try to cushion the effect of trade liberalization upon the poor and upon developing countries. [126] Finally, the participants acknowledged that trade liberalization in agriculture could make food more expensive for citizens in developing and food-importing countries and therefore undermine access to food. Thus, they agreed to ensure that food-importing nations and developing countries could get both food aid and financial assistance to buy food if they needed.[127]

In the years that followed, many countries sought to define these nontrade concerns and ensure that they remained central to the negotiations. Policymakers occasionally brought up human rights issues during such discussions. For example, in 2000, the EC, Norway, Korea, Mauritius, and Switzerland organized a conference on nontrade concerns. These countries were part of a group of some thirty-eight countries that submitted a note on nontrade concerns to the WTO. In that note, they stressed that "every country has the right, in accordance with mutually agreed rules, to address non-trade concerns, such as ... food security." The attendees at the conference concluded "the question to be addressed is whether the actual provisions under the URAA (Uruguay Agreement on Agriculture) are sufficient to fulfill the multiple objectives assigned it by societies, because food is a most essential good." [128] In a jointly prepared paper, the Japanese and Koreans stressed, "everyone must have access to food and every government is responsible for ensuring a food supply sufficient for its people." The two governments concluded that market forces were not the answer and food security must be taken into account.[129]

When members agreed to agricultural trade negotiations at Doha in 2001, they proclaimed that they would work to establish a fair and market-oriented trading system with strengthened rules and specific commitments on government support and protection for agriculture. They also agreed to take nontrade concerns and the specific needs of developing countries into account as they proceeded with negotiations.[130]

However, the members struggled to find common ground on how to treat nontrade concerns as part of the negotiating process. As the International Institute for Sustainable Development (IISD) observed, "most countries accept that agriculture is not only about producing food and raw materials . . . it can serve a number of different social objectives." Countries disagreed as to whether and if so how other countries should be allowed to pursue such objectives if by so doing they distort trade. The Agreement on Agriculture allows all WTO members, and not just developing countries, to maintain some support measures designed to meet these objectives. These acceptable support measures are called the "Green Box." But WTO members disagree as to what measures belong in the Green Box, as well as what measures are appropriate strategies to address food security and access to food.[131]

The IISD concluded that by 2003, countries had divided into three groups on how to address nontrade issues such as food security and access to food in agricultural trade negotiations. The first group, which includes countries such as Norway, Japan, Switzerland, and South Korea, as well as the EC, want trade negotiations to authorize additional measures to address nontrade concerns. These countries argued that agriculture is unlike other traded goods and deserves special treatment and special rules. They occasionally made human rights arguments in defense of their position (see Chapter 5). The second group, composed of developed and developing countries (Canada, Australia, South Africa, and the United States, among other countries), opposes including other support measures in the Green Box. In general, this group argues that the best way to promote human rights and human welfare is to let trade flow without trade supports such as subsidies, export credits, or payments.[132] (However, because of its own trade subsidies [for example, cotton], the United States was often accused of undermining the rights of small farmers to participate in trade.[133] U.S. policymakers found themselves in the odd position of calling for an end to trade-distorting practices and defending its own subsidies.)[134] Finally, the third group, made up of developing countries, including India, Pakistan, and many African countries, favors the use of measures to address nontrade concerns for *developing* countries but argues against the use of any trade-distorting measures in *developed* countries. According to the IISD, these countries argue that their nontrade issues of food security, sustainable rural development, and poverty alleviation are more urgent than those of the industrialized world.[135] Policymakers from this third group of countries argue that the agriculture sector is the linchpin for economic growth and employment in many developing countries. These countries fear that if their agricultural sectors were weakened by new exceptions for industrialized countries, they would not be able to feed their people, ensure food security, create enough new jobs, and reduce poverty. This position has been seconded by many scholars of development.[136] Trade policymakers from these developing countries argue that only developing country food importers and exporters deserve increased special and differential treatment.[137]

These different perspectives on the role of nontrade issues and what support measures should and shouldn't be allowed began to undermine progress in the Doha Round. By 2003, it became clear that the members of the WTO could not find a consensus on nontrade issues in particular and agriculture in general. Developing countries walked out of the Cancun ministerial conference in 2003 over several topics, including agriculture.[138] However, in 2004 members agreed to continue talking. Although these talks made some progress, on July 24, 2006, the Director-General of the WTO, Pascal Lamy, suspended negotiations. He reiterated that he did not think members could find common ground on agricultural trade issues.[139] He warned the WTO members of the human rights consequences of their failure to find agreement. "Failure of this Round would be a blow to the development prospects of the more vulnerable Members, for whom integration in international trade represents the best hope for growth and poverty alleviation. This is why it is called the development round." Lamy concluded by saying, "Today there are only losers."[140] (It is important to note that the negotiations were resuscitated on February 7, 2007, but as of August 5, had made little progress).[141]

Whatever the ultimate outcome of these talks, the agricultural trade negotiations raised public awareness of how the right to food and food security affect the trade positions of all WTO members. Industrialized and developing countries alike were equally adamant about the need to protect the food security of their own people but were unwilling to examine the consequences of their positions upon food security for humankind. This disconnect between WTO members' domestic trade obligations and their global human rights obligations ultimately led to gridlock at the WTO. Despite their obligations to take into account the right to food and food security, participants developed their positions on these issues based on the needs of their constituents.

Taken together, these case studies reveal that countries are now willing to accept human rights issues as part of the purview of the WTO. But they have, thus far, failed to find common ground on *how* and *when* to include these issues.

A Potential Positive Externality of WTO Membership

Although many individuals argue about how the WTO may constrain the ability of national policymakers to advance human rights, they may be overlooking an interesting positive side effect of WTO membership. To comply with WTO rules, all members must regulate in a transparent, accountable manner and provide citizens and traders (both foreign and domestic) the opportunity to influence and participate in certain aspects of trade policymaking. WTO members have gradually modernized or put new laws and regulations into place to meet these obligations. As a result, membership in the WTO *may* indirectly promote individuals' rights to information, due process, and political participation.

Under GATT and now WTO rules, member states must guarantee individuals participating in trade certain civil and political rights. These rights include legal guarantees such as the right to submit comments about specific trade policies to a national agency and the right to appeal administrative rulings on trade. In addition, member states are required to provide information about their trade laws and regulations and to allow citizens to comment on these regulations. They must also apply the same rules to domestic and foreign market actors.[142] If WTO member states fail to put in place and uphold these rights to information, political participation, and due process, other WTO member states may challenge their trade policies under the WTO's binding system of dispute settlement.

Some, but not all, WTO agreements require governments to accord due process rights (such as the right to recognition before the law) to importers as well as exporters. For example, under the WTO's Safeguards Agreement, when workers or industries petition their government for import relief, the responding government must give public notice and hold hearings in which interested parties can respond to a safeguard investigation.[143] The Agreement on Technical Barriers to Trade requires governments to publish standards and technical regulations and allow interested parties (whether foreign or domestic) to become acquainted and respond to the regulation.[144] The Customs Valuation Agreement requires governments to establish in law the right of the importer to appeal a determination of customs value.[145] Finally, the Dispute Settlement Agreement has due process rules for member states and their citizens during dispute settlement.[146] In this way, individuals, firms, and associations (both foreign and domestic) can influence some of the administrative and regulatory processes of government.

Although not all WTO rules encourage political participation and due process rights, they do obligate members to regulate trade in a transparent manner.[147] Article X of the GATT 1994 requires that trade measures must be published "promptly in such a manner as to enable governments and traders to become acquainted with them."[148] (It does not mandate, however, that citizens receive the right to comment on all trade measures.) Moreover, it requires that governments publish all agreements "affecting international trade policy which are in force between the government or a governmental agency of any contracting party and the government or governmental agency of any other contracting party."[149]

The architects of the WTO aimed to ensure that "members and other persons affected, or likely to be affected, by governmental measures imposing restraints, requirements and other burdens, should have a reasonable opportunity to acquire authentic information about such measures and accordingly to protect and adjust their activities or alternatively to seek modification of such measures."[150] They established systems and procedures to check on whether new members were actually doing what they said. At accessions, new members were required to establish plans for putting WTO rules into effect.

In addition, all countries are required to notify other members about changes to their trade laws. If members need to postpone effective dates of WTO rules, they must ask for and receive permission for waivers. WTO members also established a system of trade policy reviews, wherein WTO member states and the Secretariat would review each member's compliance with the WTO system. The WTO Secretariat will then post the reviews on the WTO Web site.[151]

Taken in sum, these requirements are prodding many member states to change how they make trade policy. For example, when it develops trade policy, Malaysia claims it now consults extensively with stakeholders from business, government, and civil society.[152] El Salvador and Guatemala have held their first public hearings on the development of trade policies.[153] But policymakers have acknowledged that improving the process of governance does not guarantee public participation and support. In its trade policy review, El Salvador noted "the importance of convincing the population of El Salvador that free trade was synonymous with a better quality of life." They then twice asked for help and cooperation in this task. The representative of the European Union urged El Salvador to do more to include civil society in the formulation of trade policy.[154] Another example is Romania's development of an action plan to achieve a stable and predictable business environment based on the recommendations of the World Bank and civil society. It stressed that it would create a dialogue with business, government, and civil society on how business should be regulated.[155]

Members often find it painful to align their domestic policies and procedures with their WTO obligations. They also recognize that members need money, time, and assistance to make their trade policies more transparent and accountable. However, some governments are unhappy or ambivalent about these demands. The representative of Romania stressed that "Romania's recent progress in trade policy should be judged in light of the economic and social costs of the reform process."[156] Bolivia and Columbia noted they had "political, economic, and social costs" associated with implementing WTO commitments, which other members needed to acknowledge.[157] At Bolivia's trade policy review, the representative of Uruguay noted that "rather than demanding answers concerning Bolivia's trade policy, members should have been asking in what way they could help." Almost every government present noted that Bolivia had done all the right things, but these steps had not spurred growth and had stimulated public discontent.[158]

Yet WTO members continue to alter their public policies in spite of these costs. Although the threat of dispute settlement may be an obvious (negative) incentive, WTO members may be equally motivated by the potential of good governance to attract trade and investment. Moreover, policymakers may recognize that good governance in the trade arena may have additional benefits. When they meet their trade obligations, policymakers learn how to regulate in a transparent manner, which is generally less conducive to corruption. With such policies in place, foreign investors may begin to perceive well-governed countries as attractive locales for investment.

Citizens in member states may also become more active participants in governance. Citizens that learn how to influence their government on trade policies will probably want their voices heard on other aspects of public rule-making. Over time, it seems logical that habits of due process and political participation (influenced by WTO membership) may gradually spill over to other aspects of the polity.[159]

Scholars have not yet tested the relationship between WTO rules and political participation, and it is beyond the scope of our research to do so. However, using data on political rights, we performed a preliminary and rudimentary comparison. It revealed a potential association between GATT/WTO membership and improved political participation. Using the CIRI Human Rights Data Set developed by David Cingranelli and David Richards, we compared political participation scores, over time, with different lengths of GATT/WTO membership.[160] We excluded the twenty-four Organization for Economic Cooperation and Development (OECD) high-income countries, where we presumed political participation was already strong, and we divided the remaining 120 countries into three groups based on duration of WTO membership (short [less than ten years], medium [less than twenty years], and long [over twenty years]). The data set codes each variable as a 0, 1, or 2, with 0 representing little protection for political participation rights, 1 representing moderate protection, and 2 representing strong protection.

The data reveal that countries that were members of the GATT as well as the WTO (that is, were members for more than over eleven years) have higher scores for the protection of political participation (some 86% of the medium group and 92% of the long group) than those that joined the WTO after 1995. This seems to indicate that membership in the GATT/WTO over time may lead to more legal protections for political participation in member countries. And over time, these protections may motivate more people to participate in the governance process.

We did not control for a myriad of other variables that could affect this right to political participation, and we realize that small sample sizes and questions of the direction of causality impede our ability to make rigorous conclusions. Moreover, it is equally plausible that causality may run in the other direction – that citizens from countries with increased political participation demanded membership in the GATT/WTO. However, we hope the chart below provides a crude beginning to this discussion and an impetus for future empirical research on this issue. And we hope it gets people thinking about the potential human rights spillovers of WTO membership.

TABLE 2.3. *The WTO and political participation*

Duration of WTO membership	2004 political participation score				As a percentage of total for duration classification		
	# of 0s	*# of 1s*	*# of 2s*	*Total*	*% of 0s*	*% of 1s*	*% of 2s*
Short (*joined after 1996*)	6	6	9	21	28.57	28.57	42.86
Medium (*joined before 1995*)	5	12	21	38	13.16	31.58	55.26
Long (*joined before 1985*)	7	28	26	61	11.48	45.90	42.62

Conclusion

In April 2005, a representative from Rwanda wondered out loud about the WTO's role in promoting human rights as well as trade. She spoke in the context of the Terry Schiavo case, in which the U.S. Congress had gone to extraordinary lengths to protect the life of a brain-dead woman kept alive by life support. She quoted U.S. President George W. Bush: "Where there are serious questions and substantial doubts, our society, our laws, and our courts should have a presumption in favor of life." She then added that the members of the WTO should also attempt to "build a culture of life" that values the rights of the poor and sick over WTO rules designed to expand trade and (in her mind) thereby benefit rich countries and multinational corporations.[161]

The Rwandan diplomat wanted to make the point that the lives of poor and sick people in Africa are no less valuable than that of one woman in Florida. Thus, in her view, the members of the WTO must strive to ensure that WTO's rules do not make it harder for policymakers to advance a wide range of human rights, including the right to health and the right to life.

Some people may perceive the WTO system of rules as inherently antagonistic to human rights objectives, but they confuse WTO rules and agreements with the decisions of sovereign states. The WTO does not prohibit countries from protecting human rights, but its rules do constrain the behavior of governments at the intersection of trade and human rights. They require that member governments do not unnecessarily or unduly distort trade when they seek to promote human rights.

As members have become more aware of the potential for conflict between their trade and human rights objectives, history reveals they have worked to find solutions. Moreover, WTO member states as well as members of the organized public have found ways to introduce some human rights concerns into the WTO's purview. For example, member states have clarified that governments may waive their TRIPS obligations in the interest of ensuring affordable medicines for their citizens. Although some members have objected, other members have discussed human rights questions during trade policy reviews. They have used waivers to promote human rights indirectly or directly. And members have also taken steps to put in place procedures and protections for ensuring public participation and due process in trade rulemaking. These steps may, over time, prod citizens to demand similar procedures and protections in other aspects of policymaking.

But members still have little guidance regarding how they can address dissonance between their trade and human rights obligations. Perhaps such dissonance can be addressed only through a trade dispute that addresses whether the WTO should defer to human rights obligations.

Nonetheless, WTO member states must do more to ensure that the international system of trade rules does not undermine human rights. These countries must find ways to ensure that the deals they conclude do not make it harder for governments to ensure that their people have access to the resources they need to participate in local, national, and global markets. Moreover, they should find ways to examine how national policymakers, tasked to meet national trade needs, can reconcile that mandate with their international obligations to promote food security and the right to food.

Members should also examine how the WTO system might use approaches short of new negotiations to ensure that WTO members do not undermine human rights as they seek to expand trade. The members of the WTO should make it clear to governments that they must uphold the rule of law within their borders. One solution is for the WTO's member states to adopt and enforce a "no standards-lowering" clause.

Finally, we cannot ignore the fact that the responsibility for promoting and protecting human rights lies with member states. States are supposed to refrain from action that could interfere directly or indirectly with the enjoyment of human rights within their borders or in other countries.[162] Although Costa Rica's Supreme Court is examining the human rights impact of CAFTA, we know of no country that has effectively attempted to ensure that its trade objectives are consistent with its human rights obligations and with the human rights obligations of its trading partners.

We believe that multilateral trade liberalization and the progressive realization of human rights are compatible. But first the members of the WTO must set up mechanisms within their own governments to ensure greater policy coherence between their human rights objectives and their trade objectives. The WTO system is not the grim reaper for human rights.

3

South Africa

In the "Rainbow Nation" Trade and Human Rights Are Anything but Black-and-White

HUMAN RIGHTS DISCUSSED IN THIS CHAPTER

This chapter focuses on (1) the right to work, (2) the right to equality and nondiscrimination, (3) the right to health, and (4) labor rights.

Right to Work/Sustainable Livelihood
Under the International Bill of Human Rights, everyone has the right to work, to free choice of employment, to just and favorable conditions of work, and to protection against unemployment.

Right to Equality and Nondiscrimination
Under the International Bill of Human Rights, everyone has the right to equality before the law and equal protection of the law. Everyone also has a right to equality and nondiscrimination as regards the enjoyment of human rights and fundamental freedoms.

Right to Health
Under the International Bill of Rights, everyone has a right to medical care as well as a right to share in the benefits of scientific advancement. Governments are required to recognize the right of everyone to the enjoyment of the highest attainable standard of physical and mental health, including improving environmental and industrial hygiene; prevention, treatment, and control of epidemic, endemic, occupational, and other diseases; and creating conditions that would assure to all medical service and medical attention in the event of sickness.

Right to Basic Services
Under the International Bill of Rights, everyone has a right to a standard of living adequate for the health and well-being of himself and of his family, including food, clothing, housing, and medical care.

Labor Rights
Under the ILO Declaration on Fundamental Principles and Rights at Work (1998) all members of the ILO, even if they have not ratified the Conventions in question, are obliged to respect, to promote, and to realize the principles concerning the fundamental rights which are the subject of those Conventions, namely (a) freedom of association and the effective recognition of the right to collective bargaining, (b) the elimination of all forms of forced or compulsory labor, (c) the effective abolition of child labor, and (d) the elimination of discrimination in employment and occupation.

Introduction[1]

When Nelson Mandela speaks, the world listens. On January 6, 2005, Mandela made global headlines when he revealed that his fifty-four-year-old son, Makgatho Mandela, had died of AIDS, a cause of death rarely disclosed in South Africa. Mandela hoped some good could come from Makgatho's life and death. He wanted others to understand that "*AIDS is no longer a disease; it is a human rights issue.*"[2] Thus, he stressed, "Let us give publicity to HIV/AIDS and not hide it."[3]

Mandela's announcement was difficult for professional as well as personal reasons. The Nobel Peace Prize-winning leader has devoted his life to the fight for universal human rights. He led South Africa during its peaceful transition from a racist, apartheid state to a multiracial democracy in 1994. However, in recent years, he also acknowledged that he did not do enough to combat HIV/AIDS during his presidency (1994–1999) and that failure had major implications for the advancement of human rights in the new South Africa. Mandela understood that HIV/AIDS jeopardizes the South African government's ability to build what he described as "a nation in which all people – irrespective of race, color, creed, religion or sex – can assert fully their human worth."[4]

South Africa has the fifth highest prevalence of HIV/AIDS in the world.[5] Every year some 300,000 South Africans die from, and thousands more are orphaned by, HIV/AIDS. The stigma and misunderstanding of HIV/AIDS runs so deep throughout the country that many South Africans are reluctant to get tested or treated.[6] As a result, the disease has become so ubiquitous that it has taken a huge toll on the country's productivity.[7]

To be fair, most governments, including the richest and most competent, stumbled in their initial responses to HIV/AIDS. However, the new South African constitution obligates the government to ensure the right to health of all South Africans. Because some 80% of all South Africans lack access to private health care, the government must provide for the rest. But the government responded slowly to its public health responsibilities.[8] As an example, the government did not provide public treatment programs until 2003, after poorer African countries such as Uganda and Zambia had set up programs to provide medicines to their needy citizens.[9]

South Africa did not have the public health infrastructure or the money to prevent the rapid spread of the disease. But many observers argue that the South African government also lacked the will to thwart the disease.[10] For example, President Thabo Mbeki has at times inferred that HIV is not wholly responsible for the AIDS virus. Other key government officials have questioned the effectiveness of antiviral medications.[11] The South African doctor David Barnard described South Africa's approach as "inconsistent, tentative, and controversial."[12] *The Economist* called the government's response to the disease "disastrous and utterly ineffective."[13] In August 2006, Stephen Lewis, the Ambassador to Africa for AIDS for the United Nations, stressed that South Africa "is the only country in Africa whose government continues to propound theories more worthy of a lunatic fringe than of a concerned and compassionate state."[14]

Although the South African government in general has responded inadequately to the public health and human rights challenges of HIV/AIDS, its policies catalyzed a global debate over the relationship between the right to health and WTO rules. In 1997, the South African Parliament passed a law requiring the government to provide affordable medicines for its needy citizens. The law allowed policymakers to take steps to purchase drugs abroad where they might be cheaper or to breach patents and produce generic equivalents at home. In 1998, thirty-eight pharmaceutical firms challenged the constitutionality of this law. Although the firms ultimately dropped their case, South Africa recognized that it and other governments would need clarity regarding whether the country could use the public health exceptions under WTO intellectual property rules to provide its citizens with more affordable medicines. As the members of the WTO met to launch a new round of global trade talks at Doha, Qatar, in 2001, South Africa worked with other nations to ensure that the Doha Declaration clarified how governments could safeguard their rights to affordable medicines and their trade obligations in times of public health emergencies.[15]

* * *

South African officials learned from this experience that trade rules could affect the type and/or effectiveness of policies they adopted to advance human rights. But South African officials, like many of their counterparts abroad, have yet to develop a strategy and institutional structure to assess how trade may affect human rights at home or abroad. They struggle to ensure that the economic growth stimulated by trade accrues to the bulk of the South African people and not just to the country's more educated and affluent citizens. In its most recent review of South Africa's trade policy, the WTO noted that although trade liberalization has stimulated economic and factor productivity growth overall, the country has not been able to increase trade and investment sufficiently to produce more jobs and higher living standards for the great majority of its people.[16]

South Africa does not use trade incentives as a tool to improve human rights, nor does it use trade sanctions as a vehicle to inspire foreign policymakers to stop violating human rights. It continues to trade with its neighbor Zimbabwe, even as the government of Robert Mugabe undermines the rights to food, property, and shelter for many of the Zimbabwean people.[17] Moreover, the country trades with and accepts investment from major human rights violators such as Libya, China, and Sudan. In this regard South Africa acts no differently than many other countries that have a much weaker rhetorical commitment to human rights.

Yet South Africa is unique among our case study countries. First, it is the one country in our study that has experienced UN-approved trade sanctions, imposed to change its human rights practices.[18] The United Nations authorized these sanctions to bring down the apartheid regime, which systematically violated the rights of South Africa's black majority and other ethnic minorities.[19] Second, South Africa has an exceptionally strong commitment to improving and upholding human rights at home. The Constitution requires the government *as well as* private actors to progressively help citizens realize their rights.

In this chapter, we examine how South Africa has tried to reconcile its commitment to human rights with its trade agenda. We begin with a brief overview of the country's human rights ethos and discuss how South Africa tries to influence human rights in other countries. We then examine South Africa's trade objectives, policies, and approach to making trade policy. Next, we discuss several examples of how South African policymakers balance trade and human rights objectives at home and abroad. Finally, we develop some conclusions about how South Africa has responded to these complex issues.

Human Rights Ethos and Conditions

If, as some people allege, countries have a brand, the "Rainbow Nation" is characterized by its nonracial ethos and deep commitment to human rights. The black majority, remembering their bitter collective experience under apartheid, made sure that the Constitution delineated their rights. The white minority (as well as other minority ethnic groups such as Asians) also wanted to ensure that their basic rights were not undermined as the government attempted to redress years of oppression under apartheid.[20]

South Africa's constitution reflects this broad-based commitment to human rights; it is both modern and comprehensive. It includes not only traditional human rights (such as civil and political rights delineated in the International Bill of Human Rights) but also new rights such as environmental rights.[21] When interpreting the Bill of Human Rights, the Constitution requires that the courts *must* consider international law and *may* consider foreign law.[22] A series of court decisions established that the government should work to help its citizens progressively realize these rights.[23]

Policymakers also created a governmental infrastructure to monitor the government's performance in advancing human rights. The South African Human Rights Commission is tasked to monitor the government's performance on issues of human rights. This agency is independent, and it has the power to conduct investigations, issue subpoenas, and hear testimony under oath.[24] The agency is receptive (as are other government agencies) to the views of domestic and international human rights organizations. Human rights organizations (and research institutions) are visible, influential, and often highly critical of the government's human rights performance.

Advancing Human Rights at Home

Despite this mandate and strong institutions, South Africa has significant human rights problems. Rape, sexual harassment, and violence against women are pervasive and often unreported. The government and civil society have tried to prevent such violence and abuse, but they are hampered by societal attitudes and a lack of infrastructure, funds, and training for law enforcement officials. Human rights observers also report problems of forced child labor, vigilante violence, and mob justice. Inequalities are entrenched along racial lines – the black majority is the most likely to be poor, uneducated, and lacking access to basic resources and economic opportunities.[25]

In contrast with most nations, the South African Constitution delineates that nonstate actors have some human rights responsibilities. Section 8(2) of the Constitution "extends the duty to implement the Bill of Rights to private actors 'if it is applicable.'" The Constitution did not precisely establish the obligations of nonstate actors, but it did make clear that many different actors might have to cooperate and act in a concerted manner to enable the full realization of rights.[26] As a result, in recent years, South Africans have debated how the private sector can play a role in advancing human rights at home.[27] This debate has played out as the country has tried to privatize (and open to foreign investors) basic services such as water, education, and electricity and as it has tried to promote black economic empowerment. Under the South African Constitution, the government is required to ensure that all citizens have access to public services such as water, telephony, and electricity. Many human rights activists do not oppose privatization per se, but they want the government to regulate these providers to ensure affordable access to such basic services.[28] They note that many of South Africa's poorest citizens do not have access to many of the most basic services, including water, education, or electricity.[29] In recognition that privatization could make public services less attainable, policymakers recognized that the government should move cautiously on privatization and on opening these sectors to foreign trade and investment.[30] Yet the African National Congress (ANC) government recognizes that private capital can help to modernize, improve, and provide these services. In recent years, the government has begun to privatize some public enterprises.[31] But it has not opened up all key service sectors to *foreign* investment. For example, it has not included basic public services such as education or water in its schedule of specific services liberalization commitments.[32]

South Africans have also struggled to find a way to ensure that the black majority (often landless) gains access to land (land restitution) without unduly penalizing the bulk of landowners, most of whom are white. Policymakers recognized that land reform is an emotive issue that must be handled with sensitivity. Until recently the country rarely expropriated land from private owners to provide redress to original settlers. When it did, the Constitution required that "the amount of compensation and the time and manner of payment must be just and equitable, reflecting an equitable balance between the public interest and the interests of those affected."[33] The government moved cautiously, because it saw that land seizures in Zimbabwe had not only under-mined the rights of white farmers but also ruined the economy and left many Zimbabweans hungry.[34] But as more and more foreigners have purchased land in South Africa, land values and prices have skyrocketed, making it harder for the government to control the land reform progress. Thus, in February 2006, President Thabo Mbeki announced that the government would review its approach to land reform, reassess land acquisition models, and study the alleged manipulation of land prices. The government also announced it would regulate conditions on which foreigners can buy land.[35] However, many South Africans criticize the government for not moving fast enough on land reform. As of July 2006, only 3% of agricultural land previously owned by whites had been transferred so far. According to the South African newspaper *Business Day*, South Africa will have to increase delivery fivefold to meet the target of transferring 30% of land to black people by 2015. The International Crisis Group, a conflict resolution organization, has warned of increased rural vio-lence if the government fails to accelerate land reform. Thus, the government is struggling to attract foreign investment in land, protect the property rights of existing landowners, and ensure that land redistribution provides the disadvan-taged and the poor with land for residential and productive purposes.[36] These examples illuminate how difficult it is for governments to ensure equitable economic growth and promote human rights at home, let alone abroad.

Advancing Human Rights Abroad

In 1993, Nelson Mandela wrote that "South Africa's future foreign relations will be based on our belief that human rights should be the core concern of international relations.[37] In May 1994, Alfred Nzo, then minister of foreign affairs, noted, "Since South Africa has been on the scene of grave abuses of human rights…we have vowed to play a leading role in the promotion of human rights and democracy internationally."[38]

But South Africa does not try to prod other countries to be more sensitive to human rights. In general, it aims to lead by example. South Africa made the transition from oppression to democratic rule without outside interven-tion or the use of peacekeeping forces. In 1995, South Africa established the Truth and Reconciliation Commission to avoid bloodshed between the vic-tims and perpetrators of apartheid.[39] The Truth and Reconciliation process was designed to develop a culture that places a high value on human rights and, by so doing, prevent recurrences of injustice. In the interest of amnesty, the Commission offered something to everyone. It offered victims reparations if they did not sue; it offered individuals who publicly confessed their crimes amnesty from prosecution; and it promised to prosecute those individuals who did not receive amnesty. Many observers perceive the Commission as a great success, particularly because it facilitated the peaceful transfer of power from the white minority to the black majority. The South African approach has influenced settlements in the Balkans, Chile, Guatemala, Rwanda, and other countries.[40]

However, South Africa has not been very successful at "exporting" its model of racial harmony. For example, in 2001 South Africa hosted the World Conference against Racism, Racial Discrimination, Xenophobia, and Related Intolerance in Durban. But by most measures the conference failed; some participants walked out in the belief that the conference had been hijacked by individuals critical of Israel (and other states).[41] Recently, human rights activists in South Africa and abroad have criticized the government's failure to promote human rights in its neighborhood. They cite the situation in Zimbabwe, where the government has used violence against human rights activists and its opponents. According to the nation's second largest political party, the Democratic Alliance, "instead of furthering an agenda based on the protection and promotion of human rights, we are more concerned with using bureaucratic excuses to shield tyrants and despots from international scrutiny."[42]

More recently, South African officials have tried to promote democracy in southern African countries such as Angola, Lesotho, Swaziland, Nigeria, Sudan, the Comoros, and the Democratic Republic of Congo.[43] But here, too, policymakers have struggled. While some African officials view the country as a friend and a positive influence, other African countries view it with ambivalence. They distrust South Africa's economic and political intentions because the country is a major investor throughout Africa. According to analyst Chris Landsberg, some observers describe the country as an "economic bully" masquerading as a political democrat.[44] They fear that major South African investors (such as De Beers) will take advantage of their political and economic shortcomings. Moreover, as we will show, South Africa is a magnet for immigrants (especially skilled immigrants) from other poorer African nations. Other African countries do not want to lose their best and brightest to South Africa.[45] Thus, the country must tread carefully as it tries to influence the behavior of its neighbors.

In 2005, the South African Ministry of Foreign Affairs issued its Strategic Plan for 2005–2007, and the Minister of Foreign Affairs, Dr. N. C. Dlamini Zuma, made clear that promoting human rights is a key part of its mission: "Our vision is an African Continent, which is prosperous, peaceful, democratic, nonracial, nonsexist and united, and which contributes to a world that is just and equitable." But Minister Zuma also noted, "Our role is to push back the frontiers of poverty and underdevelopment in the world and to ensure the constant expansion of the possibilities for freedom and human advancement."[46] As we will show throughout this chapter, the government views trade liberalization as a vehicle to achieve these goals. But policymakers and the public are uncertain about how to drive the trade liberalization process so that they can encourage equitable growth at home and abroad.

Trade and Investment Overview

South Africa is the largest and most influential trade player in Africa. The country leads the continent in industrial output (40% of total output) and mineral production (45% of total production). It also generates the majority of the continent's electricity (over 50%). South Africa has an abundant supply of natural resources; well-developed financial, legal, communications, energy, and transport sectors; a stock exchange that ranks among the ten largest in the world; and a modern infrastructure supporting an efficient distribution of goods to major urban centers throughout the region.[47] South Africa is also a net food exporter.[48] The World Economic Forum's 2004 annual Global Competitiveness Index rated South Africa the most competitive economy in the sub-Saharan region and the most attractive country in Africa for investment. To a great extent, that attractiveness stems from the government's sound financial management and the expertise of the South African people.

The economy has grown on average a steady 3% since 2001. Mining comprises about one-third of the country's GDP, but in recent years its services sector has dominated in contribution to GDP.[49] Despite its large semi- and unskilled labor force, trade of manufactured products in South Africa remains weak, its manufacturing sector accounting for only one-fifth of GDP in 2004.[50]

However, most South Africans have not benefited from this economic growth. Although South Africa is a global economic player with a growing black middle class, it is also a country where most people are unskilled and barely eke out a living.[51] The country also has huge economic challenges, including persistent high unemployment, poverty, large wealth disparities, and, as noted above, a high incidence of HIV/AIDS.[52]

Just as South Africa has two economies, South Africa has two approaches to trade. On one hand, it is a leader of efforts to make trade policy reflect the needs of developing countries. But within Africa, South Africa is a huge exporter and foreign investor and the government wants to protect and expand its market share. Thus, the government's approach to trade must balance these dual perspectives.

**HOW TRADE POLICY IS DEVELOPED IN SOUTH AFRICA AND WHERE
HUMAN RIGHTS ENTERS THE DISCUSSION**

The Department of Trade and Industry (DTI) develops trade policies and moves
trade agreements forward. Although its staff does not have expertise on human
rights, per se, it does occasionally coordinate with staff from the Ministries of
Foreign Affairs, Communication, Labor, Education, and other ministries.

The trade policymaking process typically begins when DTI teams come up
with a proposal for trade policy. In some rare cases, the DTI may publish it as an
informal discussion paper or "green paper" either online or in the government
Gazette[53] and invites a period of public comment before proceeding.[54] *This provides the first opportunity for nongovernmental input on human rights concerns.*
In most cases, however, the DTI skips this step and presents the proposal directly
to subject area clusters. The clusters are composed of officials working on broad
issue areas such as the Economics or the International Affairs, Peace, and Security
clusters. These clusters of officials debate and refine the proposal. The clusters
often publish the refined proposal as a "white paper" in the *Gazette* and invite
public comment. *This is a second opportunity for civil society groups to introduce
human rights concerns.* The clusters next forward the proposed trade policy on
to the joint national/provincial coordinating body called the Minimec, made up
of ministers of the departments (national executive branch level) and the ministers of the economic cabinet (provincial executive branch level). The Minimec
negotiates the details of the proposal and incorporates feedback from the public
comment period if a white paper was issued. The Minimec then sends a revised
version to the DTI minister at the cabinet level.[55] The DTI minister makes the
final policy decision, with the president's approval, and begins the implementation process. If the proposal requires new legislation, then the DTI forwards the
policy to the parliamentary minister's office. This office distributes copies of the
policy to members of Parliament and conducts briefings to the relevant parliamentary working committees, such as committees on economics, social development,
labor, the environment, and others. After the working committees refine the proposal, members of Parliament take committee decisions to their constituencies,
allowing for a period of public comment, and soliciting feedback from community
groups, and then take the input back to the parliamentary working committees for
incorporation into the new legislation. Once this interaction period concludes,
Parliament revises and adopts the policy as a bill, after which it goes back to the
minister of the DTI for his or her approval, then on to the cabinet for approval by
the entire cabinet and the president.

Thus, South Africa develops trade policies in an open, accountable manner.
However, as in most democracies, trade policy is primarily formulated with input
from a small circle of influential elites (from business, labor, and academia).
This circle in South Africa often meets at an organization called the National

Economic Development and Labor Council (NEDLAC). The government created and funds NEDLAC to get business, labor, government, and civil society to cooperate in developing a consensus on socioeconomic issues.[56] Furthermore, although NEDLAC is involved in most trade negotiations, the government can choose to bypass consultations to push a policy or agreement forward. Although NGOs are members of NEDLAC, it does not yet include many human rights scholars or human rights NGOs. However, these groups are beginning to make their voices heard through independent research and outreach.[57]

Taken in sum, there are several avenues through which individuals can introduce human rights concerns in the trade policymaking process. However, human rights activists have rarely used these avenues (although their use is increasing). Moreover, the government has not developed staff expertise or interest in the relationship of trade and human rights objectives (policy coherence). International trade and human rights officials exist in separate spheres and rarely meet to ensure that human rights objectives complement trade goals or that trade goals do not undermine human rights objectives.[58]

South Africa has a transparent democratic process for making trade policy, which is directed by an executive branch agency, the Department of Trade and Industry (Figure 3.1). That department works closely with representatives of labor and business and is learning to work with NGOs.[59]

South African policymakers believe they can use trade liberalization to achieve multiple ends: development of the economy, promotion of small- and medium-sized enterprises, economic empowerment of previously disadvantaged persons, and reduction in inequality and poverty. They also want to use trade liberalization to spur regional growth and stimulate an Africa-wide market for goods and services.[60] To achieve these diverse goals, South Africa eagerly participates in a wide range of regional, bilateral, and international trade agreements (see Table 3.1).[61]

When South Africa speaks on trade policy, it does not just speak for its citizens. It also speaks for its fellow members of the South African Customs Union (SACU). SACU, the oldest customs union in the world, was established in 1910.[62] In 1969, South Africa and the other SACU members (Botswana, Namibia, Lesotho, and Swaziland) agreed to harmonize their tariffs, excise duties, customs valuation, rules of origin, and contingency trade remedies.[63] In 2002, the five member states agreed to jointly negotiate all new free trade agreements as a region.[64] However, these countries are at very different levels of development and often have dissimilar trade policy priorities.[65] As a result, South Africa has struggled to ensure that trade-derived growth promotes

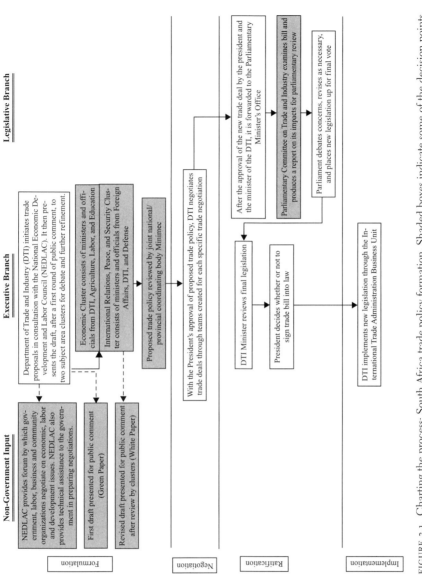

FIGURE 3.1. Charting the process: South Africa trade policy formation. Shaded boxes indicate some of the decision points where human rights can enter the process.

75

TABLE 3.1. *Overview of the agreements governing South African trade*

Trade agreement	Year	Other member enacted nations	Special attributes
Regional agreements			
South African Customs Union (SACU)	1910	Botswana Namibia Lesotho Swaziland	Agreement to harmonize tariffs, excise duties, customs valuation, rules of origin, and contingency trade remedies with permission to implement exceptional trade restrictions. South Africa leadership role. Jointly negotiate all free trade agreements. Finalized agreements w/ Mercosur and EFTA. Negotiating with the U.S.
Africa Growth and Opportunity Act (AGOA)	2000	United States and 37 other African nations	Regional preferential agreement with the United States designed to facilitate greater U.S. trade with Africa that grants preferential market access to certain categories of goods.
South African Development Community (SADC)	1992	SACU countries Angola Dem. Rep. of Congo Malawi Mauritius Mozambique Tanzania Zambia Zimbabwe	Designed with mission of "creating a development community that would achieve economic integration, including trade." Hope to establish a free trade area.
Bilateral agreements			
Trade, Development, and Cooperation Agreement (TDCA)	1999	European Union	Reinforced South Africa's ties to its largest historical trading partner. Excludes certain "sensitive sectors."
Zimbabwe	1964	Zimbabwe	Provides for duty-free trade and preferential quotas on selected items and concessional tariff rates on others.

Note: Table created by Eric Lundgren.

increased opportunities not only for its own citizens but also for those of the other SACU members.

Like other developing countries, South Africa wants the WTO to do more to address the unique trade needs of developing nations. Thus, it has argued that the Doha Round must lead to real improvements in market access and reduce industrialized country protectionism.[66] South African policymakers have called for the elimination of all tariff and nontariff barriers on products of export interest to developing countries (especially agricultural products), the provision of meaningful technical assistance and capacity building, and the adoption of special arrangements for the least-developed countries through duty-free and quota-free market access for all their products. Before the Hong Kong Ministerial of the WTO in December 2005, Mandisi Mpahlwa, the Minister of Trade and Industry, proposed a ten-point program to ensure that the new round was truly a development round.[67]

South Africa has close trade relationships with both the European Union and the United States – the giants of the trading world. Nonetheless, it has not been hesitant to criticize either government for their lack of concern for the needs of the developing world. For example, in the Doha Round of multilateral trade talks, Trade and Industry Minister Mandisi Mpahlwa said the United States and other major agriculture subsidizers need to give up domestic trade-distorting subsidies before expecting significant market access concessions from developing countries.[68] He singled out the European Union, saying, "The main challenge to moving agricultural negotiations forward lies squarely with the EU."[69] After the Round's suspension, senior trade officials frequently bemoaned the demise of trade talks, stressing this would undermine the ability of small farmers to compete against big global agribusiness firms.[70]

South Africa was equally assertive in regional trade talks between the United States and SACU. During negotiations for a potential free trade agreement, policymakers urged the United States to be patient in trade negotiations with SACU regarding issues such as intellectual property rights, services, labor, environment, government procurement, and investment.[71] But because SACU and the United States could not find common ground on many of these issues, negotiations ended in April 2006. However, SACU and the United States may move forward on a more limited investment agreement.[72]

South Africa is not counting on trade with the United States or the European Union alone. It is working to diversify its trade relationships to prevent overdependence on any single trading partner for important goods and services.[73] Thus, it is pursuing close trade ties with major global players India, Brazil, and China. These increasingly close relationships allow South African exporters to benefit from new markets as well as alternative sources of goods and investment.[74]

Linking Human Rights and Trade Agreements

South African policymakers argue that trade liberalization can enhance human rights by enabling more people to participate in global markets. But South Africa has had a hard time ensuring that trade liberalization enhances the human rights of the South African people. In the next section, we examine how South Africa links trade policy with its objectives of creating jobs for the unskilled and maintaining its relatively high labor standards. Here South Africa has acted creatively, but its actions have not stimulated enough job-creating investment. And in some sectors, policymakers have discovered they have few alternatives to protectionism to protect higher wage manufacturing jobs. We then examine how South Africa has balanced its need for foreign investment with its insistence that investors encourage black economic empowerment. Next we assess how the country worked to lead global efforts to clarify the public health exceptions under the WTO's TRIPS agreements. We then move to two examples of how South Africa seeks to promote human rights and trade internationally. We focus on trade with Zimbabwe and trade in one sector: diamonds, one of the country's main exports.

Current Areas of Tension between South Africa's Trade and Human Rights Objectives

Juggling Multiple Domestic Goals: Creating Jobs and Maintaining Labor Standards while Struggling to Attract Investment

South Africa has a jobs problem. Some 36% of the population is unemployed, and, despite the toll of HIV/AIDS, malaria, and other epidemics, the labor population is growing at 2% a year.[75] Many of the unemployed would welcome any job that provided a secure and regular income, but the economy has not created jobs for most of these workers, who are generally unskilled. At the same time, the country has maintained a strong and comprehensive system of labor rights. For example, according to the U.S. Department of State, some 42% of South Africans employed in the formal sector are unionized (some 4.5% of agricultural workers). Workers frequently exercise their rights to strike, to organize, and to bargain collectively. The government is widely seen as effective at setting and monitoring work conditions and ensuring that workers are treated fairly.[76]

In 2002, the government enhanced worker protections through an amendment to the Labor Relations Act.[77] Although the new laws strengthened labor rights, they also discouraged new investment in labor because labor costs were so high relative to capital. Increasingly, firms in the new South Africa have invested in plants and machinery (labor saving devices) rather than in labor.[78] The government's approach to labor rights, therefore, may have undermined its objective of job creation for the neediest South Africans.

To some extent, South African unemployment is a legacy of apartheid. For many years, the majority black population did not have access to capital, land, or adequate education. But the government has also admitted that the nation's jobs problem also stems from rigidities in the labor market, high labor standards, and an increase in the urban population, as many blacks were drawn to the cities after the end of apartheid.[79]

South Africans are losing jobs in some traditionally well-paying and labor-intensive industries, such as mining and manufacturing.[80] The textile sector provides a good example of this dilemma.[81] South African government statistics reveal that approximately one-third of those employed in textiles have lost their jobs since 1996.[82] South African workers and companies cannot compete with their counterparts from countries such as China, India, and Pakistan, where both wages and labor standards are significantly lower. Some labor leaders think the appropriate response to this dilemma is protection.[83] The government responded in June 2006, when it announced that the Chinese government had agreed to voluntarily reduce textile exports to South Africa.[84]

Agricultural workers are also losing jobs because of high costs associated with strong labor protections. In 2005, the international development NGO Oxfam reported that to maintain their competitiveness, South African farmers have cut back permanent jobs and reduced workplace protections for some workers. According to Oxfam, "All deciduous fruit farmers and more than half of wine grape farmers interviewed in a 2001 study were using contractors." Oxfam added that "the shift from on-farm to off-farm labour brings health risks" such as HIV/AIDS, as farm workers move to cities for jobs. These workers also receive fewer benefits and protections.[85]

The South African government, labor, and civil society sectors disagree over trade policy's role in causing such job losses. Whereas labor and civil society in South Africa often blame trade for job losses, policymakers attribute those losses mainly to technological change.[86] Policymakers believe that the best solution to job loss is retraining, which is expensive and difficult for the public sector to provide.

South Africa lacks a strong safety net to catch those workers who lose their jobs either from technological change or trade.[87] In 2003, the government instituted a "skills-development levy" on employment payrolls. This strategy was specifically designed to protect those workers adversely affected by trade liberalization by creating an incentive for companies to train their workers.[88]

They hoped such efforts would make it less likely for business leaders to replace these more skilled workers with new technologies.

In 2006, the government acknowledged that it must do more to upgrade the skills of its workers. Senior officials devised a two-pronged solution. They would eliminate fees at the poorest schools in the country and provide incentives for skilled workers (such as engineers and scientists) to immigrate to South Africa. The government also unveiled a new working group composed of representatives from government, civil society, business, and labor (the Joint Initiative for Priority Skills Acquisition) to respond to the country's skills challenges.[89]

In recent years, the South African government has started thinking creatively about ways to stimulate job growth. The South African government created a voluntary social label – "Proudly South African" – to encourage local production and jobs. To use the label, a company's products or services must incur at least 50% of their production costs, including labor, in South Africa and be "substantially transformed" in South Africa (in other words, a product that is merely imported and repackaged would not be eligible); all labeled products must also meet high quality standards. A company must demonstrate a commitment to fair labor, employment, and sound environmental standards. By meeting these criteria, consumers can be assured that companies and their products carrying the "Proudly South African" label are of a high quality, are created in a socially responsible manner, and support local jobs and the economy.[90] Policymakers claim that the label does not impede market access for foreign producers or act as a disguised trade restriction, in adherence with WTO rules.[91]

Although policymakers have been receptive to social labeling they have made it clear they will not lower labor standards. In 2004, the minority political party, the Democratic Alliance, proposed a two-tiered labor system with (1) a high-cost tier that maintains all current labor regulations for older, more skilled workers and (2) a low-cost tier with less stringent labor regulations for younger, presumably less-skilled workers.[92] The Democratic Alliance aimed to induce employers to hire larger numbers of unskilled workers. They hoped employers would then invest in these workers and train them. Some academics found the idea intriguing, but they acknowledged that it would be politically impossible to implement a proposal that calls for reducing the country's labor standards, even in just part of the economy. The proposal went nowhere.[93]

South Africa's strategies to simultaneously create jobs, upgrade skills, and maintain high labor standards are falling short. In the past five years, although foreign investment has increased, such investment has not created many new jobs for unskilled workers. Foreign investors have focused on the country's banking, insurance, or telecommunications sectors.[94] Some 27% of workers in

September 2005 were unemployed – the bulk of them unskilled black South Africans.[95] In spite of these problems, the government does not see reducing labor standards as an effective strategy to attract job-creating investment. The country believes that worker rights are a key component of human rights and, thus, these rights must be buttressed rather than reduced.

Cracking the Codes: Balancing the Need for Investment with the Priority of Black Economic Empowerment

When the ANC government first came to power, it recognized that South Africa could not achieve sustainable growth without attracting significant amounts of foreign investment. Policymakers reduced taxes, relaxed exchange controls, and offered liberal repatriation of profits. Policymakers even stressed the country's unique attributes: "South Africa offers investors a business destination combining . . . the stability of a developed country . . . the opportunities of a vibrant emerging market . . . and a climate that fosters growth." They also noted, "South Africa has a real competitive advantage in that its exchange rate makes it one of the least expensive countries in which to do business."[96]

Policymakers also decided that all investors, domestic and foreign, must help address the inequities caused by apartheid.[97] They knew the country could never develop unless the bulk of South Africans had access to credit, training, education, and job opportunities. When apartheid finally ended, the bulk of the country's wealth was concentrated in the white elite, with little capital available to the majority of the population. The wealthiest 10% of the population owned 45 percent of the national wealth, compared with just over 1% owned by the bottom 10 percent.[98] Some 62% of South Africa's blacks and 38% of its "coloured"[99] people lived below the poverty line, compared with 1.5% of its white population. Moreover, the black majority did not enjoy the same access to public education as whites and often did not have access to the resources needed to obtain better jobs. The apartheid government often denied blacks access to health care and to basic services such as electricity, water, and sanitation, as well as land ownership.

Policymakers were determined that the black majority (and other disadvantaged members of society, such as women, people with disabilities, and people in rural communities) receive the skills, land, and other resources they needed to improve their standard of living. One policymaker told us, "We cannot simply rely on the market to achieve equity redistribution on its own. Because of the history of this country, the government must force the market to address this issue."[100] These officials recognized that the government could use its market power to prod firms to provide more opportunities for those South Africans who had been denied access to such opportunities. But they also acknowledged that they must do so in a way that would not undermine economic growth.

In 2003, the South African Parliament passed the Broad-Based Black Economic Empowerment (hereafter the BEE) Act. This law required the government to take an entity's BEE status into account when determining qualification criteria for the granting of licenses and concessions, developing and implementing a preferential procurement policy, determining qualification criteria for the sale of state-owned enterprises, and developing criteria for entering into partnerships with the private sector.[101]

To measure a firm's compliance with the BEE Act, the government also established codes of good practice to measure the BEE across all sectors of the economy. These codes were intended "to level the playing field for all entities operating within the South African economy by providing clear and comprehensive criteria for the measurement of broad-based black economic empowerment." Citizens and corporate officials had the opportunity to comment on the codes in December 2004, and the government had a discussion "with selected private sector stakeholders who had provided substantial input." The government then prepared a second draft, which was approved by the cabinet in October 2005.[102]

The law stipulated that *only those firms wishing to sell or contract with the state* "must apply the codes." Thus, the government *did not require* any company to adhere to the BEE. However, almost every firm operating in South Africa would have to accommodate the BEE, because a firm's BEE rating reflects the rating of its vendors and suppliers, as well as factors directly within its control, such as ownership, management control, skill development, and employment equity.[103] If a company doing business – or wishing to do business – failed to comply with the BEE, they and their suppliers and subcontractors would receive a lower overall BEE rating and could find it harder to win government contracts, enter into partnerships, and receive licenses and concessions.[104]

Not surprisingly, the BEE strategy encountered significant opposition within South Africa's private sector. Although some business leaders and academics supported the objective, they worried about the strategy, particularly the BEE's equity ownership provisions.[105] The BEE originally set a target of 25% black ownership for all firms wishing to do business with the South African government. Because capital ownership resided almost entirely in white hands at the end of apartheid, many white-owned firms met the BEE target by selling at least 20% of their equity to one or more black business partners. However, many South Africans questioned whether this approach will benefit the bulk of South Africans, arguing instead that only a cadre of well-connected black elites profited.[106] These critics noted that to truly facilitate black participation in the economy, the government must ensure that workers and managers have the necessary skills.

Businesspeople and academics were not the only South Africans with concerns about the government's BEE strategy; skilled workers were also concerned. In July 2006, Neva Makgetla, an economist with COSATU (The Congress of South African Trade Unions), said that the negotiations on sector charters and the empowerment regulations often end up as class wars, as different groups try to grab more benefits or avoid costs. She maintained that increasingly affluent black businesspeople want more ownership, more financing, and less risk; workers demand higher targets for skills development, employment equity, and local procurement to safeguard jobs; and communities want more appropriate, lower-cost services. "Union members fear big companies will boost their empowerment scores by outsourcing activities to black entrepreneurs at the cost of workers' conditions and security."[107] Thus, some South Africans with skills fear that BEE strategies that empower some black South Africans may, in time, cause economic insecurity for others.

In addition, many foreign investors are also deeply concerned about the BEE's requirements.[108] A 2005 survey conducted by the American Chamber of Commerce in South Africa found that foreign investors supported the need for affirmative action, but these same investors acknowledged that the lack of clarity surrounding the application of Black Economic Empowerment dampened their willingness to further invest in South Africa.[109] A South African newspaper, *The Mail and Guardian*, surveyed multinationals in August 2006. They found that "foreign firms are wary of being forced to hook up with unknown empowerment partners." Those surveyed also cited vague criteria for equity equivalents, problematic procurement rules, and breaches of confidentiality as problems.[110] Another South African business paper, *The Financial Mail*, reported similar concerns.[111] However, the executive director of the Japanese External Trade Organization said that he accepted the BEE as an "African cost" to doing business in South Africa.[112]

In our interviews (conducted in 2005) we found some U.S. investors were deeply concerned about the BEE. For example, staff from the U.S.-South Africa Business Council claimed that the strategy was essentially an illegal expropriation of capital.[113] American Chamber of Commerce President Luanne Grant described the BEE as a form of "equity divestiture."[114] Interviewees cited several problems with the BEE strategy. First, most multinationals do not have large operations in the country and therefore generate few of their revenues and profits there. As a result, they do not think it is fair to require all companies to divest 25% of their equity to black South Africans. Second, many multinational corporations pulled out of South Africa amid human rights protests during the apartheid era, whereas others entered the South African market only after apartheid's end. Many executives feel it is unfair to ask them to help redress the harm done during that time when they did not participate in human rights abuses.[115] Third, the BEE Act may compel U.S. firms to take positions contrary to U.S. law. U.S. companies are forbidden under U.S. antidiscrimination law to categorize employees by race. The Foreign Corrupt Practices Act extends these prohibitions to U.S. companies operating abroad. However, South Africa's BEE provisions require U.S. firms to categorize and report on the racial composition of their workforces to receive points on the BEE scorecards. Finally, many multinationals also have strict policies on equity ownership, further complicating their ability or their willingness to comply with the equity divestiture provision.[116]

In response to these concerns, the South African government acknowledged that it may need to develop a different approach for foreign investors.[117] In 2006 *The Times* of London reported that the South African government was considering revising BEE requirements for foreign investors, in recognition that it needed to increase such investment if it was to grow sufficiently.[118] However, if the government were to put in place different standards for foreign investors than domestic investors, it must ensure that it does not violate national treatment obligations under WTO agreements such as the General Agreement on Trade in Services (GATS).[119]

The government is revising the BEE strategy to meet the concerns of its own citizens as well as foreign investors. In July 2006, the government acknowledged the BEE codes were still too complex and perhaps did not consistently meet their stated objectives. Policymakers agreed to revise the codes to ensure that truly needy black and "coloured" people achieved greater participation in ownership.[120] South Africa's Minister of Trade and Industry stressed that the government would further simplify the process and examine the impact of the BEE on investment and on actual empowerment of disadvantaged groups in South African society.[121] In October 2006, the government passed new legislation clarifying the responsibilities of multinationals and allowing these firms to substitute equity equivalents (which were left relatively vague).[122]

South Africa wants domestic and foreign investors to provide more opportunities for those South Africans who were historically denied access to resources, skills, and credit. It developed a strategy that leveraged the government's purchasing power to prod behaviorial changes among market actors. But that strategy has not created enough opportunities for the disadvantaged and it has aroused criticism at home and abroad. South Africa must tread carefully if it wants foreign as well as domestic investors to be part of an effective and equitable solution.[123]

Clarifying TRIPS Obligations and Domestic Obligations to Ensure South Africans' Right to Health

As noted in the introduction, HIV/AIDS has the potential to undermine the social and economic progress South Africa has achieved since the end of apartheid. The 2003 South Africa Human Development Report stated that, in 2001, almost 12% of black Africans were infected, compared with less than 2% of the white population. Many of these citizens are stricken at their most productive ages (20 to 40 years old).[124] More than 28% of black Africans aged 30 to 39 were estimated to be suffering from HIV/AIDS.[125] In 2001, *The Economist* reported that average life expectancy was set to fall from 60 years to 40 years by 2008. The International Labor Organization estimated that South Africa will lose almost 11% of its workforce by 2005. *Without productive people, the United Nations expects the epidemic to reduce South Africa's economic growth rate by 0.3% to 0.4%.*[126]

Most of the South Africans affected by HIV/AIDS are poor, young, and unemployed people without health coverage. These men and women are South Africa's future workers. Less than 20% of South Africans (and less than 10% of blacks) have some form of private medical coverage that would enable them to get the medicines and care they need.[127] The government has to fend for the rest. However, policymakers have not been very effective at either helping the sick or preventing new infections.[128] In South Africa's rural communities, citizens have tended to rely on traditional healers rather than modern medicine. In fact, the *Washington Post* noted that some South African communities shun HIV/AIDS victims, many believing the disease is the result of a curse or witchcraft.[129]

Traditional attitudes about the role of women and about how to treat infectious diseases have made it hard for public health officials to prevent the spread of the disease, but South African leaders have often been part of the problem.[130] According to Stephen Lewis, the United Nations Special Envoy for HIV/AIDS in Africa, leading government officials have questioned antiretroviral treatment and delayed providing it to pregnant women and AIDS patients. He stressed that gender inequality (endemic in South Africa) is driving the pandemic.[131]

However, although the government has often acted inconsistently and ineffectively, it used trade policy in a path-breaking way to promote access to affordable medicines (and the right to health). In 1997, the Parliament passed a new law, the Medicines and Related Substances Control Amendment Act.[132] The law allowed the government to take steps to ensure access to affordable medicines, including licensing firms to produce generic versions of patented drugs and importing drugs from other countries where prices may be lower.[133] These provisions were designed to enable the government to provide more drugs to more of its citizens in desperate need.

Policymakers took these steps with some ambivalence. On one hand, they recognized that the WTO's TRIPS allows nations to breach these rules in times of public health emergencies. South Africa's HIV/AIDS problem was clearly fast becoming such an emergency. On the other hand, policymakers feared that the country could be seen by foreign investors as taking steps that undermined its commitment to WTO rules and that such actions could jeopardize foreign investment.

Not surprisingly, executives at many foreign pharmaceutical firms were outraged. They feared that if they let South Africa take these steps, other countries would follow. In 1998, the Pharmaceutical Manufacturers Association launched legal action in the South African court system.[134] The Association claimed that the Act violated a range of its members' rights, citing, in particular, rights to property contained in the South African Constitution.[135] The manufacturers also alleged that the actions of the South African government threatened the international patent regime, as delineated in TRIPS. Finally, the drug companies claimed that the government's actions would undermine South Africa's obligations as a member of the WTO.[136] Meanwhile, pharmaceutical firms began to lobby their national governments for relief. In the United States, the U.S. Trade Representative (USTR) responded by placing South Africa on its intellectual property Special 301 Watch List. The two governments began to discuss the relationship between South Africa's public health problems and the WTO's intellectual property rules.[137]

In the same period, activist groups in the United States and Europe (such as Doctors without Borders, ACT UP, Oxfam U.K., and the Health Gap Coalition) publicly criticized the USTR's strategy. They forged a coalition to influence the outcome of the case and, ultimately, to clarify WTO rules. In 2001, the Treatment Action Campaign sought and received permission from the Pretoria high court to join the case with *amicus curiae* briefs, but the case went no further. On April 19, 2001, in the face of NGO activism, public attention, and perhaps concern about what this meant for their future, the pharmaceutical companies abandoned their suit. One year later, in April 2002, the government announced that it would make antiretroviral drugs readily available.[138]

In 2001, as well, public health activists and the COSATU urged President Mbeki and Parliament to declare HIV/AIDS a public health emergency. The Treatment Action Campaign called on the government to draft a treatment plan. The Campaign recognized that the government should not act hastily, noting that pharmaceutical companies were responding to the emergency by lowering their prices. The government should, thus, request "in writing from every drug company voluntary licenses for opportunistic infection and anti-retroviral medicines. . . . If they agree to voluntary licenses such an emergency may not be necessary." These activists, in short, were trying to find a way to enable South Africa to obtain needed medicines without alienating foreign investors.[139]

In the months that followed, South Africa joined with activists and other concerned governments to demand clarification of the WTO's intellectual property rules at a time of public health emergency (that story is detailed further in Chapter 4).[140] Today, South Africa reserves its right, under the Doha Declaration on the TRIPS agreement, to license and manufacture generic drugs to combat public health emergencies such as HIV/AIDS and malaria.[141] However, despite a government-run communication campaign, South Africans remain at great risk for HIV/AIDS, as well as other infectious diseases such as tuberculosis and malaria. Until the country can address factors such as illiteracy and gender inequality, South African policymakers and public health officials will have difficulty thwarting the spread of infectious diseases.[142]

In sum, South Africa struggled to find a way to ensure that it could provide access to medicines for all its people. Some observers blamed the WTO's TRIPS agreement for making it harder for the government to meet its human rights obligations. But in fact, South Africans used the country's public health emergency to pressure pharmaceutical firms and WTO members to more clearly delineate what governments can do in times of public health emergencies. South Africa's difficulties in ensuring the right to health of its citizens stemmed less from trade than from its own failure to develop effective public health strategies.

The Choice: The Decision Not to Use Trade and Investment Policies to Promote Human Rights Abroad

South Africa is different from many other advanced developing countries in that it claims that it wants to promote human rights *internationally*. The Strategic Plan published by the Department of Foreign Affairs in October 2005 asserts "our role is also to push back the frontiers of poverty and underdevelopment in the world and to ensure the constant expansion of the possibilities for freedom and human advancement." President Mbeki has added that "We shall fulfill this task, conscious of the responsibility that we have not only to our own citizens, but also to the rest of humanity in pursuing the goal of a better world."[143]

Despite this rhetorical commitment, the country is unwilling to use force or *unilateral* trade policies to alter the behavior of other countries. Zimbabwe provides a good example of how the country has tried to find a clear path between its human rights priorities and its desire to stay out of the affairs of other countries. As in South Africa, the black majority in Rhodesia (now Zimbabwe) struggled to achieve their rights. Ultimately, they democratically elected a leader from the black majority, Robert Mugabe. In recent years, Mugabe has become a despot, arresting and intimidating his democratic opposition. Yet he was reelected in March 2002 (in elections that the U.S. Department of State and others deemed neither free nor fair). Under his direction, the country has seized land and forced individuals to move from their homes. Many Zimbabweans today are starving and have no jobs or income.[144]

Although South Africans, including government officials, are increasingly alarmed about the situation, the South African government continues to encourage trade and investment between the two countries. Some observers in the human rights and business communities fear that President Mbeki's failure to condemn President Mugabe sends a message that South Africa might follow Zimbabwe's pattern of corruption, incompetence, and inhumanity.[145]

There may be several reasons why the South African government has not taken stronger steps to use trade policies to change its neighbor's policies. First, Mugabe sheltered and supported the ANC during the years it fought apartheid. Second, South African policymakers may not feel comfortable publicly criticizing another government in southern Africa – it is not in the African tradition.[146] Finally, there may be a direct economic reason why the government will not take more forceful steps with Zimbabwe. Policymakers and many South Africans fear that if South Africa and other nations were to use the country's economic power to challenge or to bring down Mugabe's government, South Africa would be swamped by a tidal wave of refugees. According to reporter Charlayne Hunter-Gault of National Public Radio (USA), South Africa has absorbed some 2 million Zimbabweans since the crisis began (and in 2007, some 50,000 a month.)[147]

The South African populace is not supportive of easing immigration restrictions. In December 2004, Somali refugees were attacked in the Western Cape, and seven immigrants were murdered. The U.S. Department of State reported rising xenophobia and attacks on foreigners in South Africa. Given the country's high unemployment rates, anti-immigrant groups such as the Unemployed Masses of South Africa blamed immigrants for rising unemployment.[148] Thus, South Africa must juggle its desire to promote human rights abroad with its need to ensure that Zimbabwe's destabilization does not spill over into South Africa.[149] Policymakers have concluded that trade sanctions would exacerbate this dilemma. But some human rights observers are frustrated by the country's failure to resolve the issue. The head of South Africa's Human Rights Commission, Jody Kallapen noted, "Our ability as a country, as a region, as a continent is undermined when our own track record is as poor as that."[150] Mugabe's ability to stay in power and his continued violence against opponents have led some critics of South African policy to argue that the South African government has a "fundamental misunderstanding" of the role of human rights in the nation's development.[151]

Zimbabwe is not the only country where the South African government has difficulty squaring its trade policy with its progressive human rights rhetoric. The country also has trade and investment relationships with other countries that systematically violate human rights, such as Libya, Iran, Burundi, and Sudan. In some cases, the South African government has exported arms to these governments that were then used to oppress their citizenry.[152] These trade actions seem to contradict the country's commitment to human rights as the cornerstone of its foreign policy.

South African policymakers argue that they prefer to rely on "quiet diplomacy" rather than economic statecraft to press for human rights changes in other nations.[153] They believe that unilateral attempts to invoke policy changes abroad should come only as a last resort and even then preferably through incentives rather than disincentives such as direct trade sanctions.[154] However, South Africa intervened in Lesotho during a constitutional crisis that posed a threat to the country's democracy, and it also made efforts to ease tensions in Angola. South Africa keeps peacekeepers in Burundi and the Democratic Republic of the Congo.[155] Thus, the country is willing to use its own financial and human resources to pursue peace and human rights, but it has not yet used unilateral trade or investment policies to achieve these ends.

Diamonds Are Forever: Prodding the WTO to Allow Only Trade in Certified Diamonds

The South African government has, however, led *global* efforts to stop trade in conflict diamonds. In the 1990s, members of the United Nations became increasingly concerned about the role of conflict diamonds in fueling civil conflicts and financing terrorism. The international community struggled to find ways to address this issue. South Africa was deeply involved in these efforts. The country is home to the world's largest diamond producer, De Beers. Both the company and South African officials were concerned that consumers in the largest market, the United States, might turn off to diamonds.[156]

In May 2000, at the invitation of the South African government, southern African diamond-producing states met in Kimberley, South Africa, to devise a plan to stop the trade in conflict diamonds and to reassure consumers that their purchases have not contributed to violent conflict and human rights abuses in the countries of origin.[157] Participants recognized they could build onto the existing certification process (diamonds are already certified for their quality). In November 2002 – after nearly two years of negotiation – governments, business, and civil society groups found common ground on the Kimberley Process Certification Scheme. The scheme informally regulated the diamond trade by certifying that diamonds are not produced in conditions where human rights are abused. All parties – government officials, rough-diamond trading entities, and civil society groups – agreed to abide by the certification process.[158]

In 2003, members of the WTO agreed to link the Kimberley Process to the WTO through a trade waiver. They decided that only diamonds certified through the Kimberley Process could be traded. This action set two important precedents. It was the first time that the WTO approved a waiver of trade obligations based on a human rights rationale. In addition, it was the first time that the WTO accepted a waiver based on a link to a private, voluntary certification process.

The Kimberley Process remains a work in progress. Not surprisingly, many civil society groups have criticized the results of this agreement, which, they allege, increased the market power of De Beers and did not address the underlying problems that can lead to conflict or human rights violations in Africa.[159] Interestingly, the participants seem determined to make the process address these underlying problems. In 2005, De Beers, Global Witness, and Partnership Africa Canada has set up the Diamond Development Initiative to "gather all interested parties into a process that will address, in a comprehensive way, the political, social, and economic challenges facing the artisanal diamond mining sector in order to optimize the beneficial development impact of artisanal diamond mining to miners, their communities and their governments."[160] However, many civil society groups remain dissatisfied. For example, in June 2006, Amnesty International reported that the Kimberley Process still lacks the monitoring and transparency needed to ensure enforcement.[161] Moreover, NGOs such as Global Witness and others are now calling for legally binding regulations imposed by governments on the international diamond industry to ensure that diamonds no longer fund conflict or human rights violations in Africa.[162]

Conclusion

In ten short years since the fall of apartheid, South Africa has transformed itself from a human rights pariah to a human rights role model. Although South Africa must overcome its massive unemployment problem, resist the spread of

HIV/AIDS, and eliminate inequalities of access and opportunity, it has made great progress. It has created more opportunities for more of its people.

Trade played an important role in that expansion. South Africa aggressively liberalized its tariff structure and improved its trade policymaking and evaluation capacities. Moreover, it has led its southern African neighbors in regional negotiations and has worked to take their interests into account, sometimes at the expense of its own development needs.[163]

However, South Africans have learned that although trade policies can bring growth, they can also exacerbate or bring to the fore existing human rights problems. For example, trade agreements did not cause South Africa's public health problems, but for a time trade rules appeared to make it harder for the country to provide access to medicines for all of its needy citizens. However, when South Africa declared a public health emergency, it was able to negotiate with pharmaceutical companies and devise strategies to provide more people with more affordable medicines. The problem exposed a larger dilemma – the country had not and still has not devised an effective strategy to ensure that all of its people have access to effective public health programs. Nor has the country developed effective comprehensive strategies to halt the spread of the disease. In another example, some South Africans have blamed trade for unemployment and underemployment, but trade and foreign investment are in fact creating jobs for South Africans. Unfortunately, many South Africans don't have the skills or education for these jobs and, thus, policymakers acknowledge they must invest more in education and retraining. Thus, trade has helped expose South Africa's existing problems in ensuring access to education and opportunities.

South Africa has also had to reevaluate some of its strategies for advancing human rights, which may distort trade and investment. South African officials have made it clear that although the country desperately needs sustained increased investment (especially investment that will create more jobs for the black majority), the country will neither reduce its labor standards nor abandon policies adopted to ensure black economic empowerment. South Africa is adamant that these human rights will remain top priorities. However, at this writing, South Africa has announced it will *alter* BEE standards for foreign investors. Government officials concluded that South Africa's investment needs outweigh rigid standards applied to all companies that seek to do business with the state of South Africa. They have also acknowledged that foreign investment in land has led to skyrocketing land prices, making it harder for the government to balance land reform, food security, and restitution – important human rights objectives.

Thus, South Africa is struggling to find ways to ensure that trade advances rather than undermines human rights at home. But it has consistently made protecting human rights a priority. These examples reveal it is willing to tinker with its domestic strategies or work at the WTO rather than resort to protectionism.

The country is less sure-footed, however, in its attempts to link trade and human rights abroad. The South African government stresses that "the content of our engagement with South Africa determines our engagement with the world: thus our foreign policy is guided by the same goals we pursue at home."[164] But South Africa has found it hard to achieve human rights goals internationally, refusing to use force or unilateral trade sanctions. It prefers to lead by example or with incentives (such as its common market). Alas, these approaches do not seem to be working in Zimbabwe.

At the same time, South Africa has acted effectively to link human rights and trade at the WTO. It led efforts to adopt a trade waiver to support the Kimberley Process certification (although some argue that the certification preserved the market power of De Beers). Working with Brazil and India, South Africa also pushed for clarification of the TRIPS public health exceptions.

South Africa does not officially examine how trade policies may affect its human rights objectives. To some extent, this is because South Africa, like most nations, lacks a mandate to do so. Moreover, in South Africa as in many other nations, there are few opportunities for human rights activists as well as trade officials and NGOs to collaborate with government officials to achieve both goals.

South Africa has considerable experience navigating traffic at the intersection of trade and human rights. But citizens of the "rainbow nation" are not finding it easy to read the signs. South African policymakers will need to find ways to better anticipate how trade policies and agreements might affect the country's human rights objectives at home and abroad.

4

Brazil

Creating New Rules of the Road

HUMAN RIGHTS DISCUSSED IN THIS CHAPTER

This chapter focuses on (1) rights to health, (2) traditional knowledge/ indigenous rights, (3) the right to the abolition of slavery/forced labor, and (4) labor rights.

Right to Health
Under the International Bill of Human Rights, everyone has a right to medical care as well as a right to share in the benefits of scientific advancement. Governments are required to recognize the right of everyone to the enjoyment of the highest attainable standard of physical and mental health, including improving environmental and industrial hygiene; prevention, treatment, and control of diseases; and creating conditions that would assure to all medical service and medical attention in the event of sickness.

Indigenous Rights and Traditional Knowledge
Under the International Bill of Human Rights, in all states in which ethnic, religious, or linguistic minorities exist, persons belonging to such minorities shall not be denied the right, in community with the other members of their group, to enjoy their own culture, to profess and practice their own religion, or to use their own language. The Convention on Biodiversity (CBD) includes measures to protect and use traditional knowledge related to the conservation and sustainable use of biodiversity.

Freedom from Slave Labor
Under the International Bill of Human Rights, no one shall be held in slavery or servitude; slavery and the slave trade shall be prohibited in all their forms. The ILO's Forced Labor Convention 29 (1930) and Abolition of Forced Labor Convention 105 (1957) concerning Forced and Compulsory

Labor also defines this right and provides the primary point of reference for national and international efforts aimed at its eradication.

Child Labor
Under the International Bill of Human Rights, children and young persons should be protected from economic and social exploitation. Their employment in work harmful to their morals or health or dangerous to life or likely to hamper their normal development should be punishable by law. States should also set age limits below which the paid employment of child labor should be prohibited and punishable by law. The ILO's Minimum Age Convention 138 (1973) and Worst Forms of Child Labor Convention 182 (1999) also reiterate this right.

Introduction[1]

In many countries, the military serves one objective – to defend the nation's security. But 21st-century Brazilians early on understood that the armed forces could also help defend the nation's health.[2] Thus, on March 9, 2002, Brazil's military joined firefighters and health workers on the crowded streets of Rio de Janeiro, Brazil's second-largest city. The soldiers, firefighters, and health workers sought to defeat a tiny, numerous, and occasionally deadly adversary: the mosquitoes that spread tropical diseases such as dengue fever.[3]

Policymakers called on these public health troops to persuade the citizens of Rio to join them in this fight. In Rio's *favelas* (slums), as well as in middle-class neighborhoods, the volunteers made a connection that probably seemed strange. These public health volunteers linked the dreaded disease to the many abandoned tires that dotted the city.[4] Although discarded tires did not cause Brazil's dengue fever outbreak, the many used tires left to rot in landfills throughout the country have exacerbated the problem. Because there is no environmentally safe way to dispose of these tires, they are abandoned and left to collect water, providing perfect breeding grounds for disease-carrying mosquitoes.[5]

The retreaded tire market in Brazil is the largest in the world and continues to grow. Several Brazilian companies import used tires, retread them, and sell them at home and abroad at a fraction of the price of new tires.[6] However, these companies do not require their suppliers to ensure that all the tires they import can be retreaded. Thus, many of the tires these companies receive are unusable and must be discarded as trash.[7] The combination of tires abandoned by individuals and by companies is a real threat to public health.

Brazilian government officials have been trying since 1992 to reduce the supply of used tires in Brazil. But they did not devise an effective approach.

For example, in 1992, the Brazilian Institute for the Environment (IBAMA), a part of the Ministry of the Environment, tried to limit the importation of used and dangerous goods, including used tires.[8] But the decree was revoked because import prohibition is outside the competency of that ministry.[9] In 1999, the National Council on the Environment issued resolution 258/99, which ordered the tire industry to recycle used tires in gradually increasing quantities on par with production of new tires in 2004.[10] And on September 25, 2000, the Brazilian Ministry of Development, Industry, and Foreign Trade issued a decree that explicitly banned imports of all used *and* retreaded tires into Brazil.[11] However, these strategies did little to change the behavior of Brazilian citizens and companies, who continued to abandon tires.

Yet with the import ban, Brazil's tire problem had become a regional trade issue. Uruguay, a close trading partner, a member of the Common Market of the South (MERCOSUR), and an exporter of tires, challenged the ban. In 2001, a MERCOSUR ad hoc tribunal found the bill in violation of Brazil's trade obligations.[12] As a result, each year Brazil must import 130,000 used tires from Uruguay, providing more fodder for Brazil's tire dumps.[13]

Brazilian policymakers did not use a public health or environmental rationale to justify their trade ban at the MERCOSUR tribunal. However, in 2001, Brazilian policymakers concluded that the tire problem had become a public health problem. They officially linked the glut of used tires to the rise in dengue fever (as well as a host of other health and environmental problems).[14]

In July 2001, the president of Brazil decreed that retreaded tire manufacturers must "destroy" as many tires each year as they sell into the Brazilian market. In September he issued Presidential Decree No. 3919, which provided for fines on the importation, marketing, transportation, and storage of imported used and retreaded tires (but not on domestic retreaded tires).[15] Finally, in December 2003, the Ministry of Development, Industry, and International Trade announced that MERCOSUR countries would be excluded from the import ban of used tires.[16]

Consequently, because of these strategies, Brazil's tire ban became an international trade issue. The European Commission (a major exporter of used tires to Brazil) challenged the presidential decree.[17] After bilateral talks failed, the WTO established a panel to examine the dispute on January 20, 2006.[18] Brazilian officials argued that there is no safe way to dispose of these tires and that their disposal causes serious risks to human, life, and environmental health. They justified the import ban under Article XX (b) of the WTO.[19] With this action, Brazil became one of the first countries to argue that a trade ban is "necessary" to protect the life and health of its people. It also argued that it had no reasonable alternative measure to such a ban to protect the right to health.[20]

However, on June 12, 2007, a panel established under the WTO's dispute settlement body found that Brazil's import restrictions on retreaded tires were inconsistent with WTO rules. The panel also went on to say that Brazil's ban on imports of retreaded tires could be justified as an exception to WTO rules based on public health concerns if the Brazilian government had applied the ban without distorting trade. The Brazilian government expressed "great satisfaction" with the decision and said it would not appeal.[21]

✻   ✻   ✻

The tire trade dispute signaled a major change in Brazilian trade policy. For much of Brazil's recent history, Brazilian officials developed trade policies as if these policies had little or no effect on other foreign or domestic policy priorities.[22] They asserted that trade policies were commercial and economic policies that had little to do with human rights. Although many senior Brazilian policymakers still hold this view, their actions reveal they are rethinking the relationship between trade policies and other important policy objectives.

Brazil's approach to these issues is important because Brazil is the world's eighth-largest economy, a major influence on global trade policies, and Latin America's largest and most influential democracy. Brazil is both a powerful industrialized country and a developing nation. In this chapter, we examine how Brazil has tried to reconcile its diverse human rights objectives with its trade agenda. We begin with a brief overview of human rights conditions in Brazil and discuss Brazil's human rights ethos. We then examine Brazil's policies toward trade and investment. We focus on Brazil's trade policymaking process, and we discuss how Brazilian officials reconcile their dependence on trade for economic growth with their desire to promote human rights at home. From there, we discuss how Brazilian policymakers (and members of the concerned public) have responded when they perceived conflict between the country's trade and human rights objectives. Finally, we develop some conclusions about how Brazil behaves at the intersection of trade and human rights.

Human Rights Ethos and Conditions

Brazil has a strong commitment to human rights at home and abroad, but when it acts to advance human rights, it proceeds differently than other activist nations. Brazil does not publish human rights reports, use trade sanctions, or try to mediate international disputes like the United States or the European Union. Instead, Brazilian policymakers and citizens have put forth new strategies to advance human rights (such as the right to health) at home and abroad. Brazil's less traditional approach may stem from the experience of its people under military rule, when the government relied on policies that favored certain sectors of the economy and populace.

From 1964 to 1984, Brazil was a military dictatorship; the generals did not make human rights at home or abroad a top priority.[23] Brazil's military rulers frequently jailed those individuals who spoke out against their rule. Moreover, Brazilian economic policies made it harder for poor and middle-class citizens to obtain access to resources such as education, credit, and public health. From the 1930s through the 1980s, Brazilian policymakers maintained import substitution policies designed to substitute domestically produced manufactures for imports. However, to finance investment in key sectors, Brazilian manufacturers and the government both took on high levels of debt.[24] In the aftermath of the 1973–1974 oil crisis and related adjustments, Brazil's growth began to falter and inflation grew. By the late 1970s, Brazilian policymakers struggled to cope with stabilization problems caused by rising interest rates, the second oil shock, and spiraling inflation. In the 1980s, they put in place a painful International Monetary Fund (IMF) austerity program, which required policymakers to cut government services and subsidies as well as to hold down wages to fight inflation. Brazil's poor and middle class suffered under these inflation-fighting tactics.[25]

However, these economic policies had unintended political consequences. In 1983, millions of Brazilians took to the streets to demand both democracy and public policies more responsive to the economic situation of the poor and the middle class. In 1985, after months of protest, the military government agreed to hold free elections. Human rights and democracy activists, academics, politicians, and others were determined to develop policies that made human rights the centerpiece of the new democracy. The new government that took over in 1985 was a broad coalition between business leaders and middle- and working-class pro-democracy groups.[26] With input from these many different groups, Brazil's legislators drafted a new constitution that included provisions to promote and protect civil, political, economic, social, cultural, and collective rights.[27]

Brazil's new democratic leaders recognized that they must first get the economy on track before they could focus on the needs of Brazil's poorest citizens. Both the Sarney (1985–1989) and Collor de Mello (1989–1993) presidential administrations devised new economic policy "shock plans" intended to stabilize prices and wipe out inflation. Both plans had limited success.

In 1994, President Fernando Henrique Cardoso and his staff implemented a new economic stabilization plan, the Real Plan, designed during Cardoso's tenure as finance minister under Itamar Franco's regime. The Real Plan gradually increased interest rates, introduced fiscal and labor market reforms, stabilized monetary policy, and reduced reliance on foreign debt. As the economy rebounded, Brazil again began to attract foreign investment. President Cardoso was then able to focus on the country's human rights agenda. He made primary education a priority, and dropout and illiteracy rates declined. His administration also developed programs to address issues such as poverty, discrimination, and the rights of minorities, children, and women. But the president, constrained by budget realities, was unable to invest sufficient funds in improved access to education, public health, and sanitation.[28]

In 2002, Brazilians elected a new president, Luiz Inácio Lula da Silva, who promised to promote greater access to opportunities and resources for all of the Brazilian people. Like the leaders he followed, President Lula was constrained by economic realities. And like previous presidents, he pledged to reform the Brazilian economy. His administration met stringent fiscal targets, reduced Brazil's debt burden, and attempted to reform fiscal and social security policies.[29] However, he also put money, time, and expertise toward solving some of Brazil's long-standing human rights problems. For example, President Lula prodded Congress to approve a stringent gun control law that restricted access to firearms. However, the Brazilian electorate repudiated the law in a nationwide referendum in October 2005.[30] The government has also tried to address poverty, hunger, and income distribution through generous assistance programs. For example, the administration improved on earlier efforts to reduce child labor by addressing family behavior patterns. The "Bolsa Familia" program, which is supported by the World Bank as well as federal funds, provides families with a general stipend based on the level of income and number of children.[31] Policymakers are now trying to coordinate this approach with child labor eradication efforts initiated in the early 1990s by the ILO, UNICEF, and other international agencies. Moreover, policymakers have engaged broad sectors of society in the fight to improve public health. As noted in the introduction to this chapter, public health officials mobilized an army of volunteers to educate the citizens of Rio on dengue fever. Finally, in their quest to fight the spread of HIV/AIDS, government officials have worked with prostitutes to encourage their partners to use condoms.[32]

Despite these actions, independent observers still find pervasive human rights abuses in Brazil. They report that the judiciary is often inefficient and corrupt. Justice is slow and unreliable, and states have poor records regarding personal integrity and judicial rights. Child labor, violence against women, and child abuse persist in Brazil. Although the country has strong unions and a constitutional commitment to labor rights, in reality freedom of association and other worker rights are limited. Because many people work in the informal sector, many of Brazil's workers have few legal rights and protections.[33] According to the NGO Human Rights Watch, "Human rights defenders suffer threats and attacks; police are often abusive and corrupt; prison conditions are abysmal; and rural violence and land conflicts are ongoing. And while the Brazilian government has made efforts to redress human rights abuses, it has rarely held to account those responsible for the violations."[34] Widespread corruption undermines the ability of the government and the Brazilian people to advance human rights in Brazil.

Meanwhile, many Brazilian NGOs believe that Brazil's foremost human rights problem is its failure to provide opportunities and resources for the poor. NGOs such as Conectas and Justicia Global criticize the government for inadequate public investment in education, health care, and sanitation.[35] But Brazilian policymakers are in a bind. Without sufficient economic growth, they lack the resources to address these problems, but those same economic policies that favor growth have, at times, hit hardest on the poor.[36]

Brazilian policymakers are trying to monitor the effectiveness of using domestic policies to promote human rights. In 1996, Brazil became the first country in the Western Hemisphere (and the third in the world) to establish a National Program for Human Rights.[37] The Program was designed to identify the main obstacles – be they administrative, legislative, political, or cultural – to the promotion, protection, and full realization of human rights in the country.[38] The Ministry of Justice, collaborating with other government officials and civil society groups, issued a National Action Plan for Human Rights in 1996, which was updated in 2002.[39] In 2003, the government established a Special Secretariat of Human Rights within the Office of the Presidency. The Special Secretariat helps other departments monitor and enforce human rights laws and works with the Ministry of Justice on the National Program for Human Rights.[40] However, although the Special Secretariat and the Ministry of Justice are responsible for monitoring the implementation and effectiveness of the action plan, these officials do not have a mandate to evaluate the effects of trade policies on human rights at home or abroad.

Brazilian policymakers also try to influence international human rights developments. Article 4 of the Constitution enshrined the "prevalence of human rights" as a defining principle to guide the country's foreign policy.[41] Brazil became a party to most international human rights covenants and treaties and became increasingly active in the UN system.[42] However, Brazil rarely unilaterally criticizes other countries for their human rights practices.[43] In fact, Brazilian policymakers have publicly chastised the United States for "politicizing" its international human rights agenda.[44] Yet independent human rights observers such as Human Rights Watch and the Brazilian human rights NGO Conectas have criticized Brazil's strategy for promoting human rights abroad as inconsistent and incoherent. They note that Brazil occasionally votes against or abstains on international human rights questions, as it has done with countries such as Cuba and Turkmenistan or Russia's treatment of Chechen citizens in Chechnya, a rebellious Russian province.[45] Human Rights Watch argued that these votes "seemed to reflect political selectivity or diplomatic expediency.... Brazil has rightly criticized the selectivity of the Bush administration; it should not...yield to the same considerations."[46] Conectas also released a report detailing the inconsistencies between Brazil's human rights and foreign policy agenda – particularly relating to Brazil's voting patterns at the UN – which it presented to the Brazilian Congress in 2005.[47]

Although Brazil has not always consistently pushed to promote human rights, it has suggested that UN members adopt a different approach to monitoring human rights. Brazilian policymakers expressed concern that only industrialized countries and independent observers (mainly from the developed world) prepare evaluations of national human rights performance. These reports, they argued, reflected their countries' norms and values rather than norms and values of citizens of the developing world. Thus, in 1998 and 2005, Brazil suggested that the United Nations create a global monitoring and reporting system for human rights to serve as a "thermometer of the global human rights situation."[48] However, this proposal has not made much headway among the members of the United Nations.[49]

In sum, Brazil continues to have pressing human rights problems at home. Yet, commensurate with its global political and economic clout, Brazil is beginning to assert its influence on international human rights issues.

Trade and Investment Overview

Brazil is a major force in global trade and finance. It has advanced agribusiness, banking, and manufacturing sectors. Brazilian companies export first-class planes, steel, shoes, and textiles. The country is also a world leader in soybean, orange juice, and cotton production.[50] Brazil attracts substantial trade and investment because of its size, population, resource base, and competitive industrial and banking sectors.

At the same time, Brazil has many of the problems of developing countries. Governance, particularly at the state level, is often inadequate and corrupt. Brazil is often not an easy country in which to do business.[51] Foreign investors and local businesses have great difficulty steering through Brazil's bureaucratic maze. Moreover, business and employment taxes are high.[52] These reasons, combined with limited law enforcement, help explain why some 40% of Brazilian economic activity occurs outside of the formal sector.[53]

Brazil is simultaneously a partner of the industrialized world and a leader of the developing world.[54] Not surprisingly, Brazil takes on both personas at the WTO. For example, it has pushed for banking services liberalization in the Doha Round, because it is a leader in that sector. Like other industrialized countries, it is quite willing to challenge the trade practices of other countries in the WTO's Dispute Settlement Body.[55]

But Brazil is also the voice of middle income/developing country frustration with the WTO status quo. In fact, during the Uruguay Round of the GATT, Brazil's sophisticated trade officials led (with India) the so-called G-10 effort to block the inclusion of the "new issues" such as labor, investment, and competition policies into the purview of the WTO.[56] During the four years of Doha Round trade talks, Brazil's trade minister was frequently quoted criticizing both the orientation and progress of the round.[57] Brazil was frequently willing to confront the United States and the EU on their trade policies – in particular, their export subsidies. In August 2003, Brazil organized and continues to lead a bloc of countries that challenge agricultural protectionism. These countries argue that developed countries often justify their agricultural support on the grounds that such support promotes food security, but Brazil and its allies argue that richer countries should not be allowed to maintain such agricultural supports. This group of countries (the G-21 includes India, South Africa, China, and other countries) has consistently taken the position that without significant agricultural trade liberalization the Doha Round won't really be a development round. Because of Brazilian activism, U.S. and EU policymakers have frequently blamed Brazilian trade officials and Brazilian trade policies for the collapse of the talks.[58] Meanwhile, some developing country officials and academic observers criticized Brazil (and India) for leading the developing world on agricultural interests and playing along with the industrialized world on services.[59]

And at the same time that it criticizes industrialized country policies, Brazil (like many other middle-income countries) continues to receive substantial trade preferential benefits from the United States and the European Union, as part of their Generalized System of Preferences (GSP) program. (However, in August 2006, the United States hinted it might graduate Brazil and other countries from that program.) Brazil also benefits from an extended transition period afforded to developing nations to implement various WTO commitments.[60]

Brazil has developed a democratic process for trade policymaking, but it is relatively insular. It is dominated by executive branch officials (Figure 4.1).

Trade Relationships

Brazil participates in many trade agreements at the multilateral, regional, and bilateral levels. Brazil was a founding member of both the GATT and the

HOW TRADE POLICY IS DEVELOPED IN BRAZIL AND WHERE HUMAN RIGHTS CAN ENTER THE DISCUSSION

In Brazil, the trade policymaking process begins, and remains primarily, within the executive branch. In fact, the executive's authority is more absolute than in many other countries. The president appoints the members of the Government Council of the Presidency of the Republic, which houses the chamber in control of trade policy formulation, the Chamber of Foreign Trade (CAMEX). The president can often amend, update, and even bypass the legislature through presidential decrees and provisional measures. In fact, the Brazilian Parliament plays a relatively minor or passive role in the trade policymaking process, beyond voting on and approving trade-related legislation.[61] For much of its modern history, Brazilian trade policymaking has been the turf of technocrats who reported to the president. However, as Brazilian trade policy has evolved (from import substitution to more international policies focused on market access), so has the trade policymaking process.[62]

In 1995, the president created a new multiministry council, the CAMEX, to discuss and develop trade policy.[63] The CAMEX is governed by a Council of Ministers, composed of the Ministers of Finance, Development, Industry, and Foreign Trade (MDIC), which presides over the CAMEX; External Relations (MRE); Agriculture; and Planning and Budget; as well as the Civil Cabinet Minister. The CAMEX is responsible for formulating, adopting, coordinating, and implementing trade policy; establishing guidelines for trade negotiations; and coordinating implementation of trade policy decisions. The CAMEX does not formally facilitate the introduction of human rights concerns into the policymaking process, nor do any of its members have human rights expertise per se. However, other public bodies, such as the Ministries of Health or the Environment, must consult with the CAMEX on any of their potentially trade-related decisions. *This is one avenue through which public officials could bring human rights concerns into the policymaking process.*

The process is as follows: The CAMEX's Council of Ministers acts as the decision-making body on all proposed trade policies and negotiations. The Council is divided into four subcommittees: the Executive Management Committee, the Executive Secretariat, the Export Finance and Guarantee Committee, and a Private Sector Consultative Council. *This private sector council is the only formal avenue for nongovernmental input at the CAMEX (decision-making) level. Although this is an additional avenue for human rights to enter the discussion, we found no evidence that this council has ever used it to do so.* Once the Council of Ministers makes trade policy decisions, they send the decisions back to the respective ministries for implementation. The majority of trade policy implementation lies within the Secretariat of Foreign Trade (SECEX) of the Ministry of Development, Industry, and Foreign Trade (MDIC). However, the Ministry of Foreign Affairs is responsible for the negotiations of all trade agreements.[64] Finally, the Congress analyzes and ultimately votes on all proposed new or amended trade policies, though in general their participation in the overt trade poli-cymaking process is minimal and at times bypassed.[65] *However, Parliament does at times hold public hearings on proposed legislation, offering another avenue through which human rights can enter the process.*

The structure of trade policymaking in Brazil is designed to facilitate quick decision making, but it does not allow much opportunity for government officials or NGOs to raise human rights concerns within the policy debate. Moreover, policymakers rarely involve or consult members of the general public or the Parliament. Beyond the CONEX, the CAMEX offers no avenues for civil society or labor groups to participate in trade policy formulation. However, since 1995, the Ministry of External Relations has created several National Secretariats (composed of invited representatives from business, civil society, and labor) that offer a formal outlet for public participation in trade negotiations.[66] *Although this drastically increases the transparency of negotiations and the means by which they bring human rights issues into the trade discussions, the MRE more informs these secretariats of their (already decided) negotiations agenda than consults with them on strategy.*[67]

Thus, Brazil differs from our other case studies in that it offers few opportunities for policymakers or members of the general public to bring up human rights concerns as trade policy is developed. The process is particularly insular. However, public officials and members of the concerned public are finding greater receptivity to human rights concerns.

WTO and knows how to use the system of rules both to stimulate trade and to defend its interests.

As Table 4.1 illustrates, Brazil actively negotiates regional and bilateral trade agreements (Brazilian policymakers consider these agreements to be complementary to the multilateral trading system.) Like South Africa, Brazil participates in fewer of these agreements than the United States or the EU.

In November 1991, Brazil joined with Argentina, Paraguay, and Uruguay to create MERCOSUR, a common market and trade agreement.[68] The members of MERCOSUR have concluded free trade agreements with Bolivia, Chile, and Peru, as well as the three other countries of the Andean Community. They also have signed framework agreements with India, Mexico, and South Africa.[69] Such agreements serve as templates for future more comprehensive agreements. Brazilian officials attach great importance to MERCOSUR.

Linking Human Rights and Trade Agreements

Although Brazil is a leader on trade issues at the regional and multilateral levels, Brazil has not taken a leadership role in linking trade to human rights.

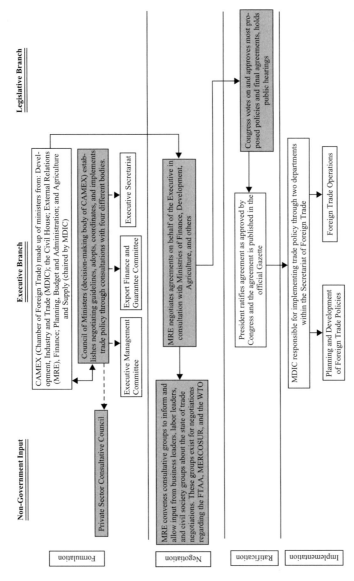

FIGURE 4.1. Brazilian trade policy formation. Shaded boxes indicate some of the decision points where human rights can enter the process.

TABLE 4.1. *Overview of Brazil's major regional and bilateral trade agreements*

		Framework and free trade agreements concluded by MERCOSUR, 2004	
Trade agreement	Year enacted	Other member nations	Special attributes

		Free trade agreements	
MERCOSUR – Chile	1996	Chile	Duty elimination for at least three-quarters of tariff lines by January 2004 and for all tariff lines by 2014
MERCOSUR – Bolivia	1997	Bolivia	Establishment of a free trade area by January 2006
MERCOSUR – Andean Community	Signed 2003 (not yet in force)	Ecuador, Peru	Gradual establishment of a free trade area within a transition period of 10 years; rounds of negotiations currently taking place
MERCOSUR – Peru	Signed 2003 (not yet in force)	Peru	Establishment of a free trade area within a maximum transition period of 15 years
		Framework Agreements	
MERCOSUR – South Africa Framework Agreement	2000	South Africa	
MERCOSUR – Mexico	2002	Mexico	Gradual establishment of a free trade area; negotiations ongoing
MERCOSUR – India Framework Agreement	2003	India	
MERCOSUR – India Preferential Trade Agreement	2004	India	Trade agreement; concessions yet to be finalized
MERCOSUR – Eygpt Framework Agreement	2004	Egypt	

Source: MERCOSUR Secretariat.

Brazil's position is quite similar to South Africa's. Like that country, Brazil trades with prominent human rights – abusing nations, such as China, Cuba, Sudan, Saudi Arabia, North Korea, Iran, and Syria.[70] Brazilian policymakers do not believe that it should use trade policies or agreements to promote human rights abroad. Moreover, Brazilian policymakers appear to believe that unilateral trade sanctions are ineffectual at changing the behavior of their overseas counterparts.[71] However, Brazil is willing to use trade sanctions when they are authorized by the UN Security Council and applied multilaterally.[72] Brazil has also been open to devising special multilateral agreements or treaties that connect trade with the promotion of human rights. For example, Brazil was an early supporter of the Kimberley Process trade-waiver on conflict diamonds, as well as an advocate of an international arms trade treaty.[73]

Brazilian policymakers often told us that they do not need to do more to coordinate trade and human rights objectives at home.[74] They argue that trade and human rights are "already compatible." They claim that trade spurs growth, which will reduce poverty and increase revenue to spend on social programs and on tackling human rights issues.[75] But trade-fueled growth has not always trickled down in ways that increase the opportunities for all of Brazil's people.

As MERCOSUR is a trade agreement as well as a common market, its members have frequently met in working groups to discuss other policy objectives that can be affected by trade policies. Officials from these countries occasionally discuss human rights concerns. Although the MERCOSUR agreement has some human rights language, there are no human rights obligations within the treaty that establishes their common commercial policy. For example, the MERCOSUR countries included labor commitments and institutions, such as commitment to the ILO core labor standards, in their common market architecture. Thus, if any party to MERCOSUR fails to protect labor rights, a supranational Commission on Social and Labor Matters can review allegations at the behest of another member state. However, the Commission cannot impose trade sanctions or other penalties in the event of such a violation.[76]

In 1998, MERCOSUR members adopted the Ushuaia Protocol on democratic commitment, which prohibits the entry of undemocratic states into the common market.[77] Although the Protocol text itself makes no explicit mention of human rights, the members of MERCOSUR invoked the Protocol as a joint response to a 1996 coup d'état in Paraguay. Furthermore, the Brazilian delegation cited numerous human rights motivations when it announced the protocol to the United Nations in 2000. For instance, when explaining the rationale for a democracy clause, Brazilian policymakers argued that "democracy, development and respect for human rights and fundamental freedoms are interdependent and mutually reinforcing."[78] Thus, although the

MERCOSUR trade agreement has no binding human rights commitments, Brazil and its MERCOSUR partners see the protection of human rights and democracy as a rationale for – and a side effect of – the agreement.

In sum, Brazil participates in a wide range of trade agreements in the belief that trade will stimulate economic growth and increase opportunities for the Brazilian people. However, Brazilian trade policymakers have come to recognize that some trade agreements may limit the range of policies they can take to address domestic human rights problems. Some Brazilian officials have begun to think about how to protect human rights at home as they negotiate new trade agreements or work to meet existing trade obligations. But the trade policymaking bureaucracy, as we noted above, does not include human rights officials and has no mandate to examine how a particular trade policy or agreement might affect human rights. As a result, Brazilian policymakers, like those of other countries, have a hard time reconciling their trade and human rights objectives.[79]

Current Areas of Tension between Brazil's Trade and Human Rights Priorities

Home Remedy: How Brazil Uses the Leverage of Its Market to Ensure Access to Medicines and Bolster the Local Generic Drug Industry

Brazil reported its first diagnosed case of HIV/AIDS in 1982.[80] As in South Africa, the disease spread rapidly among the poor, many of whom had no access to medicine or health care. However, Brazilian policymakers and public health officials worked closely with medical personnel, NGOs, drug manufacturers, sex workers, and public and private funders to develop innovative and cost-effective strategies to slow the spread of the disease. Today only 600,000 Brazilians – around 0.07% of the population – live with the HIV/AIDS virus.[81] Both the United Nations and the World Bank consider Brazil's National AIDS Program to be "among the best in the world."[82]

Brazilian policymakers were committed to ensuring that their constituents could get the medicines they needed, regardless of their economic or social status. In 1996, the government established law 9.313, which mandates the free provision of "all medication necessary for the treatment" of HIV/AIDS patients in the country.[83] Policymakers initially hoped to persuade foreign drug makers to voluntarily reduce the price of the needed medicines. In return, Brazil would purchase these drugs in bulk amounts. However, although many companies did reduce their prices, the drugs were still too expensive for the majority of Brazilians.[84] As a result, Brazilian policymakers recognized they would not be able to ensure that all Brazilians who needed AIDS drugs could obtain them. Brazilian policymakers had to find a way to balance their trade obligations with their domestic responsibility to ensure affordable access to medicines. They felt strongly that TRIPS allowed nations to breach their obligations in times of public health emergencies such as the AIDS crisis.[85]

In 1997, Brazil revised its industrial property (patent) law. Article 68 of that law obliged the holder of a patent in Brazil to ensure that the subject matter of a patent is made – or, as the law delineated, "worked" – in Brazil. If a patent was not worked in Brazil, the law authorized the Brazilian government to issue a compulsory license allowing others to utilize the patent against the patent holder's wishes.[86] Other governments expressed concerns about Brazil's revised patent laws. This new requirement also seemed to curtail foreign patent holders' rights.[87]

In 1999, the Brazilian president issued a decree that allowed him to grant compulsory licenses for patents for noncommercial public use in cases of national emergency or *public interest*, provided that the government ascertains that the patent holder or his licensee would not or did not fulfill these needs.[88] Empowered by this new decree, policymakers warned drug makers that if they did not lower the price of their drugs, Brazil would be compelled to issue compulsory licenses. Brazil's threats generally convinced many drug makers to lower their prices in Brazil.[89]

This bullying strategy received a mixed reception at home and abroad. Many NGOs and public health officials praised Brazilian policymakers for their comprehensive approach, but the strategy also alienated foreign drug makers.[90] Policymakers in the United States, the European Union, and Switzerland – home to some of the world's biggest names in drug making – made it clear that they did not take kindly to Brazil's strategy.

The United States became the most outspoken opponent of Brazil's approach. On October 6, 1999, Secretary of Commerce William Daley traveled to Brazil, accompanied by senior officials from some of America's most prominent drug makers. He asked the Brazilian government to derogate the decree on patents, but Brazil refused. The government argued that it needed to either demand these discounts or develop generics to provide the necessary bulk medicines for all of its needy citizens.[91] In January 2001, the U.S. government requested a dispute panel challenging the compatibility of Brazil's patent law with the WTO's TRIPS agreement.[92] The U.S. government argued that Brazil's patent law was not designed to protect public health and that "Article 68 is a protectionist measure intended to create jobs for Brazilian nationals."[93] On April 30, 2001, the U.S. Trade Representative placed Brazil on its Special 301 Priority Watch list for nations that did not adequately protect intellectual property rights (IPR). Brazil's health minister responded, "Our patents law adheres scrupulously to the guidelines of the World Trade Organization." Brazil also noted that, although it had not used compulsory licensing, the threat to do so "has led a number of foreign laboratories to lower their prices."[94] In other words, Brazil felt bullying had achieved the results policymakers needed.

Brazil saw its attempts to juggle its IPR trade obligations with its human rights obligations in a rather different light than did American policymakers. On April 1, 2001, Brazil presented a resolution to the UN Human Rights Commission advocating the universal right to access to medicines, particularly in the case of the HIV/AIDS pandemic. It also lobbied other nations at the WTO to press for a clarification of the WTO's IPR rules.[95]

Brazil was clearly winning public support around the world for its strategies. On June 25, 2001, the United States dropped its WTO case against Brazil.[96] U.S. Trade Representative Robert Zoellick noted that Brazil and the United States had developed a consultative mechanism to seek "creative solutions to bilateral trade and investment disputes." Zoellick said this solution represented evidence of the U.S. administration's "flexible approach" to intellectual property issues.[97] Flexibility also became the watchword at the WTO. On November 14, 2001, when members met at Doha, they issued the Doha Declaration on the TRIPS Agreement and Public Health. It states that "the TRIPS agreement does not and should not prevent members from taking measures to protect public health." It also expressly affirms the rights of developing nations to authorize the production of generic versions of patented drugs (compulsory licensing) and allows countries to import patented drugs at the lowest prices available.[98]

Meanwhile, Brazilian officials also recognized they needed a stronger institutional structure to facilitate trade policymaking related to the public health needs of the country's citizens. In August 2001, policymakers within the Chamber of Foreign Trade (CAMEX) set up an interministerial group to discuss trade-related intellectual property issues. The group works to ensure that Brazil meets both its domestic public health obligations and its international trade obligations.[99] But this coordinative body could not prevent continued sparring between Brazilian officials and foreign drug makers. Between 2002 and 2005, the government negotiated price reductions with pharmaceutical companies such as Merck, Bristol-Myers Squibb, and Roche, but these negotiations were often conducted under the threat of compulsory licensing.[100]

Although Brazil continued to bully drug makers, the United States continued to bully Brazil. In 2004, Brazil remained on the Special 301 Priority Watch list, and the United States threatened to suspend economically important

GSP benefits.[101] Brazil's National Council to Combat Piracy and Intellectual Property Crimes responded by adopting a National Action Plan on March 17, 2005. The government agreed to work with the International Intellectual Property Association to stiffen IPR enforcement, and it enacted tougher penalties against IPR infringement.[102] The United States extended its review of GSP benefits to Brazil from May 2005 until September 2005 to allow more time for new programs and legislation to take effect. On January 13, 2006, the U.S. government closed their review of Brazil, deciding that it had taken sufficient steps to continue receiving GSP benefits.[103]

Like South Africa, Brazil continued to work internationally to clarify the rights of nations to breach IPR rules in times of public health emergencies. In 2003, it played a leading role in clarifying TRIPS to ensure that members could use compulsory licenses to produce drugs in times of public health emergencies.[104] Brazil also led efforts to amend the TRIPS agreement and to allow countries without a generic drug industry to use parallel importation to import low-priced drugs from a country producing generics, such as Brazil.[105]

In conclusion, Brazil has used a variety of tactics to provide affordable medicines for its people (and citizens in other countries). Based on revisions in its patent law, it used the threat of breaking patents to induce foreign drug makers to lower their prices. Brazil also worked tirelessly at the WTO to develop rules that clarified how countries could juggle their public health obligations with their trade obligations. These strategies came at a price: drug company executives, foreign investors, and key allies became distrustful of Brazil's intentions. Brazil has developed the world's tenth-largest market for drugs and Brazilian drug makers (both name brand and generic) are gaining an ever-larger share of that market. By the end of 2005, Brazil's generic drug makers had captured some 12% of the Brazilian market. Thus, some observers have argued that, although Brazil justified its strategy as focused on the right to health, it was deliberately working to build a stronger generic drug industry to compete directly with industrialized country pharmaceutical firms.[106] Whether or not there is any merit to these claims, the global pharmaceutical industry seems less interested in Brazil. In the past several years, foreign drug makers have significantly reduced their investment and employment in Brazil.[107]

Brazilian policymakers maintain that their approach has allowed the country to protect intellectual property while meeting the public health needs of the Brazilian people.[108] Brazil has been able to reduce the price of many AIDS drugs through bulk purchases and through encouragement of local generic production. However, Brazil still must import many other expensive drugs, which in 2005 consumed 70% of Brazil's AIDS budget.[109]

And a Little Frog Shall Lead Them: Linking Global Rules That Protect IPR with Global Rules That Protect Biodiversity and the Right to Traditional Knowledge

Scientists at the University of Kentucky in Lexington (USA) were able to turn a frog into a pile of money. The phyllomedusa frog (or *kambo*, as it is referred to in the Amazon region) provides a vivid example of Brazil's difficulties protecting its native plants and knowledge.[110] This frog's venom has been used by the Katukina people of the Juruá Valley (considered to be the most biologically diverse region in the world) in the Amazon rain forest for generations to treat a number of different maladies.[111] In 1999, researchers from the University of Kentucky collected a sample of *kambos* from the Juruá Valley and proceeded to complete research on the frog and to develop patented medicines to treat conditions such as ischemia.[112] But that pile of money did not end up in Brazil. Neither the university nor the pharmaceutical companies that patented the frog's unique venom provided Brazil – or the indigenous groups who originally developed the traditional remedies – with the dues stipulated in the CBD for benefit sharing.[113] Nor was Kentucky the only industrialized country institution or company that profited from indigenous plants or knowledge. After numerous such experiences, Brazilian policymakers recognized that they must find ways to protect their native people and their tribal cultures, as well as Brazil's diverse ecosystem.[114]

Indigenous people are a prominent minority in Brazil. Some 400,000 native persons from some 215 "nations" have ancient ties to the land, water, and wildlife of their ancestral domain. Brazilian as well as foreign investors exploit indigenous land for mining, logging, and agriculture, destroying the environment and wildlife and provoking violent confrontations.[115] As a result, Brazil's indigenous people are increasingly threatened by the actions of Brazilian policymakers, miners, farmers, and investors.[116]

The 1988 Constitution required the federal government to protect indigenous rights and to demarcate indigenous areas, but the federal government has moved slowly. Consequently, Brazil's indigenous population remains in great danger: they are often harassed and are occasionally killed for their land.[117] Many of these indigenous people live near the Amazon rain forest, which comprises 40% of all the tropical rain forest left in the world.[118] Not surprisingly, environmentalists as well as Brazil's indigenous groups are keen to protect this land, which is home to many rare and endangered species. However, Brazilian policymakers are also under significant domestic pressure to allow exploitation and development of the land. Many Brazilians are landless, the country has limited areas of highly fertile land, and only a small proportion of Brazilian territory is under cultivation.[119]

Brazilian law provides indigenous people with the exclusive beneficial use of the soil, water, and minerals on indigenous lands – but only if the Brazilian Parliament approves each case. The law also grants the indigenous population broad rights, including the protection of their cultural patrimony and the exclusive use of their traditional lands.[120] However, indigenous leaders and activists complain that they have little influence over decisions taken by the government affecting their cultures, traditions, land, and natural resources. These leaders claim that the government does not adequately protect their rights.

Outsiders have come to the defense of these indigenous populations. For example, ecologists argue that the lifestyles of indigenous people "provide valuable lessons for the conservation and sustainable consumption of biological resources." They seek to learn from indigenous peoples by preserving their traditional ways of life.[121] Other scientists, however, see profit in traditional knowledge. Pharmaceutical companies and institutes from the United States, Japan, and Europe routinely collect samples from plants and animals in the Amazon region, assess their biological properties, and patent their uses for financial gain, with little or no regard to the indigenous and traditional knowledge rights of the groups who cultivated the therapy or own the land.[122]

Given its plant diversity and indigenous population, Brazil has led global efforts to link biodiversity, indigenous rights, and trade rules. In 1992, at the UN Conference on the Environment and Development in Rio de Janeiro (ECO-92), policymakers, activists, scholars, and others began discussing questions of biodiversity and "traditional knowledge" and its relationship to international trade. In 1992, representatives of one hundred fifty nations agreed to the CBD – measures to ensure the protection of biodiversity and traditional knowledge. They agreed to respect and preserve traditional knowledge, to promote the wider application of traditional knowledge with the approval and involvement of the holders of such knowledge, and to encourage the equitable sharing of the benefits arising from utilization of such knowledge. Although the CBD spelled out guidelines for such cooperation it did not delineate how signatories were obligated to address their rights under the Convention to their obligations under the WTO.[123] Moreover, although 168 countries have signed the Convention, several industrialized nations, such as the United States, the Netherlands, Finland, and Japan, have not ratified the Convention and are unlikely to do so. Because of the importance of these countries in the global economy, the contracting parties to the Convention will have a hard time enforcing it.[124]

Thus, the CBD is not preventing non-Brazilian companies, universities, and individuals from profiting from traditional knowledge or native plants indigenous to Brazil. The chief prosecutor for the Brazilian state of Amazonas, who opened an inquiry into biopiracy in 1997, estimated in 2002 that about 20,000 individual plant samples are illegally removed from the country every year.[125] According to the Brazilian Institute for the Environment, "The scientists congregate in small frontier towns. Then they ask the Indians what they would do if they had a headache, muscle pains, or a bad stomach. The local people then take them into the jungle and show them which plant they would use to cure those symptoms. The scientists pay the Indians a little money, then take the plant back to their labs. There, they discover the principle by which the plant works and sell their preliminary research on to the pharmaceutical companies for development." The Institute also noted that the Indians were never paid for their knowledge.[126]

Brazilian officials recognized that they could not rely on the CBD to protect traditional knowledge and indigenous rights. They sought clarity at the WTO on the relationship among the TRIPS agreement, the CBD, and the protection of traditional knowledge.[127] At Doha, members agreed to further discuss this issue as part of the TRIPS Council mandate.[128] Since 2001, Brazil has frequently worked with India to find common ground on these issues. In documents prepared for their fellow WTO members, they stressed that although the TRIPS agreement allows members to grant patents for inventions or processes that use genetic material or traditional knowledge, TRIPS does not refer to the CBD.[129] Brazil, China, Cuba, the Dominican Republic, Ecuador, India, Pakistan, Thailand, Venezuela, Zambia, and Zimbabwe have all requested that TRIPS be amended to include, for example, rules requiring the disclosure of the country of origin of biological resources and traditional knowledge used in inventions; disclosure of evidence of informed consent prior to the exploitation of another nation's resources; and establishment of and compliance with rules for benefit sharing under relevant national regimes.[130] Ultimately, Brazil would like to see TRIPS amended to make it fully compatible with the CBD.[131]

However, other nations have a different perspective on the relationship between traditional knowledge, biodiversity, and WTO rules. The Swiss have recommended reforms at the World Intellectual Property Organization (WIPO), and the European Commission has proposed reforms that place legal obligations outside the scope of patent law.[132] The United States maintains that there is no inherent conflict between TRIPS and the CBD and that mandatory disclosure mechanisms are inappropriate, as they are likely to lead to uncertainties in the international patent system. The United States favors a contract-based approach that is regulated through national laws outside the patent system.[133] Given this range of opinion, the members of the WTO have not found any common ground clarifying this relationship.[134] When WTO trade policymakers met in Hong Kong in December 2005, they were unable to delineate the relationship between TRIPS and the CBD. Thus, the members recommended that the director general "intensify his consultative process on all outstanding implementation issues under article 12(b)" of the Doha Ministerial Declaration, including "those related to the relationship between the TRIPS Agreement and the CBD."[135] But in October 2006, a WTO panel limited the ability of WTO member states to apply multilateral environmental agreements such as the CBD in WTO disputes. If the ruling is upheld, then WTO panels will only interpret the relationship between WTO rules and environmental agreements in circumstances where all disputing parties are signatories to both agreements.[136]

Brazil also turned to the World Intellectual Property Organization(WIPO) to clarify the relationship between biodiversity and intellectual property. As a UN agency, WIPO is designed to promote the protection of intellectual property throughout the world through cooperation among states and, where appropriate, in collaboration with any other international organization. Brazil submitted a proposal on behalf of the self-named "Group of Friends of Development," which proposed that WIPO look at the relationship among trade, IPR, biodiversity, and development more broadly.[137] In February 2006, WIPO held the first session of a Provisional Committee on Proposals Related to the WIPO Development Agenda.[138]

In recognition that they may have to wait years for international agreement on these issues, Brazilian policymakers have taken action at home to protect the country's biodiversity. In 2005, Brazil introduced a new law with tough penalties for those who use indigenous resources either without permission or without sharing the benefits with the state or local communities. Biopirates can face fines of up to $20 million, as well as other penalties.[139] This new approach has not appeased Brazil's native peoples, whose spokespersons contend that they still have little influence on government decisions about their destiny.[140] Meanwhile, the Brazilian government is increasing its investments in research on native plants and animals. In 2005, the Brazilian Ministry of Environment began Project Kambo, a project to investigate the potential pharmaceutical uses of the *kambo*'s poison. The government promises to share the benefits of their research and development with Katukina people. The government now argues that such research "could be the key to Brazil's transformation in the global political and socio-economic context."[141]

Thus, Brazil has developed international and domestic policies to protect biodiversity and indigenous rights. Ironically, although it has been an activist internationally on behalf of these issues, its own indigenous population perceives Brazilian efforts as half-hearted and ineffective.

Naming and Shaming on Labor Rights at Home, but All Quiet at the WTO

Like most countries, Brazil would like to ensure that none of its people work in conditions of forced labor. But in November 2006, Brazilian labor inspectors discovered forced labor in charcoal and pig iron mines deep in the heart of the Amazon. The charcoal is a key component of pig iron, which is used to produce steel. That steel is then incorporated into products such as cars and dishwashers produced by major multinational corporations such as General Motors and Toyota. The head of the Ministry of Labor's Mobile Inspection Group admitted, "Slavery is endemic to the charcoal camps that supply the pig iron industry. . . . And none of it would exist without multinational companies demanding the products they produce. They are a key part of the globalized, export-oriented economy Brazil thrives upon."[142]

Few people in Brazil were shocked by the news. Brazil has had a slave labor problem for many years.[143] That problem is not limited to the mining sector. Agricultural goods such as coffee, meat, soybeans, and orange juice are often produced by men, women, and occasionally children who toil in terrible conditions with few rights and little job security.

The world has not yet paid much attention to these conditions. Many agricultural products are not labeled by company, and it would be hard for consumers or activists to identify goods from those producers who contract with firms that abuse workers. But these foreign investors as well as Brazilian policymakers are increasingly concerned about them.

Forced Labor and Naming and Shaming

According to the ILO, Brazil has had a hard time combating this problem because of a wide range of factors, including accessibility challenges, poor communication, and inadequate law enforcement policies.[144] In 2003, policymakers admitted that some 25,000 workers – including women and children – were trapped in forced labor schemes, mostly on remote Brazilian ranches or estates. Black market contractors frequently lure young and illiterate workers into debt-related slavery with promises that they will be well compensated for their work. Once trapped in these arrangements, the workers have little ability to escape or alter their circumstances.[145]

In 2002, the ILO and the government of Brazil initiated a technical cooperation project entitled "Combating Forced Labor in Brazil."[146] As part of this effort, in 2003, President Lula signed into force a National Plan for the Eradication of Slave Labor.[147] The government committed to bolstering existing mobile inspection units which raid remote farm estates in search of abusive labor conditions, including slavery. These mobile task forces are directed by the Inspection Bureau of the Labor and Employment Ministry; they include federal police officers and labor inspectors as well as labor prosecutors with powers to initiate lawsuits through the federal courts. The president also created a National Commission to monitor the National Plan for the Eradication of Slavery. And he directed the Ministry of Labor and Employment to create and maintain a "dirty list" of companies that have been found by the Ministry to have workers in conditions "analogous" to slavery.[148] The Ministry updates the list biannually, informing other government ministries of the list as well as making it publicly available. Employers and companies remain on the "dirty list" until they pay all fines and penalties and prove that they have abolished slave labor practices on their premises. The general public can easily access the list on the Internet, and the list can be searched by company name or product.[149] The Lula administration also proposed a constitutional amendment that would allow the government to confiscate the land of any landowner found using forced or slave labor.[150] Although the Congress ultimately rejected that amendment, in 2006 the Senate unanimously approved instituting the "dirty list" into Brazilian law.[151]

The strategy of "naming and shaming" human rights violators could have positive results over time, but the plan has lacked the teeth to encourage real change in the behavior of these employers. The plan's penalties were weak and policymakers enforced the law sporadically.[152] Not surprisingly, some Brazilians seemed to ignore the law. In 2004, the Mobile Inspection Unit rescued thirty-eight forced laborers on a farm owned by Senator João Ribeiro and fifty-three workers on a ranch owned by Inocêncio Oliveira, a member of the Federal Chamber of Deputies (Brazil's House of Representatives).[153] Moreover, although the number of companies on the list has increased from 53 in 2003 to 180 in 2005, some companies have actually shown increases in the number of workers employed under forced or slave labor conditions over the two-year period to 2005.[154]

Several NGOs and business groups decided they must lead the way toward a more effective approach. The Confederation of Trade Unions, the ILO office in Brazil, several human rights NGOs, including the Ethos Institute of Enterprises and Social Responsibilty, and business organizations collaborated on a multistakeholder initiative: the National Pact for the Eradication of Slave Labor in Brazil.[155] The Pact builds on the objectives of the government's National Plan (which includes auditing companies, criminalization of employers, and reincorporating enslaved laborers back into the economy) by educating business and civil society and involving them in the struggle.

Until the National Pact initiative began, many companies seemed blissfully unaware that they or their affiliates and subsidiaries employed slave or forced labor. Representatives from the Ethos Institute in cooperation with the National Commission for the Eradication of Slavery and the ILO, worked to educate various sectors about the existence of slave labor in Brazil. They invited representatives from different sectors to discuss the problem and the Pact's proposed strategy. They informed businesses about the magnitude of the problem in Brazil. The Ethos Institute also tried to convince business leaders that the Pact would be good for business, because it would "place Brazil as a globally recognized case of effective combating of slave labor, increasing the value of the national product in the international market, and not the opposite." They also proposed that Brazilian manufacturers adopt a social label to reassure consumers that they were not purchasing products made with slave labor.[156]

Ethos' actions pressed the government to become more visible in its efforts to promote slave labor. The government officially launched this National Pact in May 2005.[157] Companies that sign the Pact promise not to use slave labor in any part of their supply chains.[158] They also commit to constantly review their efforts.[159] The companies also use the pact to discuss challenges and goals in the fight against slave labor.[160] On May 19, 2005, seventy-five companies, eleven labor federations, and thirteen civil society organizations signed an agreement with the Ministry of Labor and Employment. The signatories promised to ensure that their suppliers did not engage in slavery.[161] By the end of 2005, nearly 140 companies, from small and medium enterprises to large, exporting multinational corporations, signed onto the Pact.[162] In 2005, Bolivia and Ecuador announced that they would adopt similar initiatives.[163]

At the behest of civil society and labor groups, Brazil has begun to address its huge and continuing problem of slave and forced labor. It has achieved considerable buy-in from the private sector. Leaders clearly recognize that labor rights could affect Brazil's exports. Yet policymakers insist that labor rights should not be regulated by language in trade agreements. Brazil has consistently opposed the inclusion of labor rights in the WTO's purview (as well as the FTAA and MERCOSUR).[164]

Child Labor, Business, and a Social Label

Brazil not only has a slave labor problem, but many of its children work illegally in dangerous or unfair working conditions. Although the law restricts work that may be performed by children, some 6.7% of children age fourteen and under worked in 2003.[165] The majority of these working children and adolescents toil in the rural areas of northeast Brazil, producing charcoal or picking oranges, sisal, sugar cane, cotton, and tobacco.[166]

Over the years, the Brazilian government has developed several programs to combat child labor. In 1994, Brazil established the National Forum on the Prevention and Eradication of Child Labor, with support from the ILO and UNICEF. Policymakers hoped to engage all sectors of society, including the media, in efforts to prevent and eradicate child labor. In the next year, the Ministry of Labor launched mobile inspection units against child labor, targeting factories and other formal businesses. Policymakers also hoped to expand children's access to school and improve school attendance. In 1996, the Cardoso administration developed the Program for the Elimination of Child Labor (PETI) aimed at providing family income assistance conditioned to school enrollment. Taken in sum, these efforts helped reduce the number of working children between 5 and 17 by about 23%, from roughly 8.4 million in 1992 to 6.6 million in 1999. Over the same period, the 5- to 15-year bracket was reduced 30% from about 5.7 million to 4 million.[167] Although this initiative has been repeatedly tailored to meet changing conditions, Brazil still struggles to find effective policies to eliminate child labor.[168] And unfortunately, policymakers have made little headway in reducing child labor in the sector.

Several Brazilian business leaders recognized early on that government-led efforts could not solve the problem. They recognized that they could help change the incentives that led employers to hire children. In 1990, executives from Brazil's toy manufacturers' association started a new foundation, Abrinq.[169] Abrinq developed the Programa Empresa Amiga Da Criança (Child-Friendly Company Program) and began awarding a social label, the Child-Friendly Company Seal, to businesses that complied with ten commitments.[170] These commitments ranged from not using child labor anywhere in the supply chain to funding social projects that benefited children and adolescents.[171] In 2004, 1,041 companies (from small and medium enterprises to major exporting multinationals such as Wal-Mart, Unilever, and Volkswagen) earned the Abrinq seal.[172] In an increasingly socially conscious Brazil, consumers are beginning to pay attention to the way in which the goods they purchase are produced.[173] Polling data reveal that Brazilian consumers seek out goods made by companies that have been awarded the Abrinq seal.[174]

Abrinq has also worked with associations of business sectors that are most vulnerable to child labor, such as agriculture, to sign sectorwide pacts committing to the fight against child labor. NGOs report that this strategy has dramatically reduced child and adolescent labor in the sugar cane, oranges, footwear, and tobacco industries, which are all key export sectors.[175]

The Abrinq Foundation has also pushed the government to do more to promote the rights of children. During Brazil's 2002 presidential election, Abrinq and other organizations challenged the four main contenders to pledge to meet the United Nations' "World Fit for Children" goals. In 2003, President Lula developed a Child-Friendly President's Plan of Action (PPAC) for 2004 to 2007. The Plan of Action is designed to "combat all forms of child labor, as defined by ILO Convention 182 (1999), through supervisory actions aimed at the eradication of child labor." The program includes a public awareness plan and a direct income-transfer program for families with children age five to fifteen who have been "engaged in the worst forms of child labor."[176] However, only 2% of the 56 billion Real Dollar budget for the PPAC was allocated for programs to protect children and adolescents from child labor.[177]

The multistakeholder approach has led to some progress, but many industries (including export sectors) continue to rely on child labor. Unfortunately, the Brazilian government has done little to support the social labeling strategy initiated by the Abrinq Foundation or to promote its child labor eradication strategy (lauded by the ILO as among the best in the world) internationally.[178] Although the government seems to recognize that the public perception that Brazilian goods are made with child labor could alienate foreign consumers, it continues to act as though labor rights are purely a domestic policy issue.

Conclusion

Brazil led several efforts at the intersection of trade and human rights. Working with South Africa, it played an important role in pressing other WTO members to clarify the public health exception to TRIPS.[179] In partnership with India, it has tried to spearhead efforts to find common ground on traditional knowledge, protecting biodiversity, and protecting indigenous rights. Finally, Brazil has been among the most vociferous critics of the agricultural trade positions of the United States and the EU; it has consistently argued that the industrialized world must reduce agricultural support, even though many industrialized countries justify such support as necessary to ensure food security.

Brazil's activism on issues of trade and human rights reflects its increased activism on human rights issues. For example, Brazilian policymakers have proposed major reforms to the international system to monitor human rights. Brazilian officials don't just talk about protecting human rights: today Brazil commands the peacekeeping force on Haiti.[180]

Although Brazil is one of the few countries to establish a national monitoring system on its human rights performance, Brazil has major human rights problems. As trade has expanded, some of these human rights problems have become increasingly visible to Brazil's trade partners around the world. Brazil has adopted innovative approaches such as "naming and shaming" and social labeling to encourage producers to improve workplace conditions, but these strategies have not changed the behavior of many Brazilian (or Brazil-based) firms. Moreover, although Brazil has led global efforts to protect indigenous rights, the country has not been effective at protecting those rights at home.

Brazil appears determined to create new rules of the road at the intersection of trade and human rights. But its positions are confusing – sometimes it argues that human rights are trade issues; at other times it argues that human rights are nontrade issues that *should not* be discussed at the WTO; and in other instances it argues that human rights are nontrade issues that *should* be discussed at the WTO. For example, Brazilian policymakers have argued that the WTO's TRIPS rules have undermined human rights in Brazil and elsewhere (they are saying these *are* trade issues that should be clarified by the WTO system). Brazilian policymakers have also adamantly argued against including labor rights in the WTO's purview in the belief that *these are nontrade* issues that should not be part of the WTO. With the tires case, Brazil tried to clarify how and when WTO member nations can use trade restrictions to protect their citizens' right to health. In this example, Brazil argued that the right to health can be a trade issue.[181] Finally, Brazilian policymakers agreed that *nontrade* issues such as food security can be negotiated as part of agricultural negotiations under the Doha Round, yet these same policymakers say that WTO rules should allow only developing countries to rely on such supports.

Brazil's inconsistencies on these issues may stem from its determination to forge a different path from the United States and other nations. These discrepancies may also stem from its trade policymaking process: Brazil has not evolved an institutional structure to weigh human rights concerns as it makes trade policy. Trade policymaking in Brazil is not very transparent or very open to the views of NGOs and unions; although the private sector seems better positioned to influence trade negotiations.[182] Nonetheless, at the intersection of trade and human rights, Brazilian policymakers (and many Brazilian activists and business leaders) seem determined to find new paths to ensure that trade bolsters access to resources and opportunities.

5

The European Union

The Behemoth Is Not a Dinosaur

HUMAN RIGHTS DISCUSSED IN THIS CHAPTER

This chapter focuses on (1) the right to cultural participation, (2) right to political participation, (3) labor rights, and (4) the right to a sustainable livelihood – all human rights delineated in the International Bill of Human Rights or the ILO Declaration on Fundamental Principles and Rights at Work. The chapter also discusses the right to information.[1]

Right to Cultural Participation
Everyone has the right to freely participate in the cultural life of the community, to enjoy the arts, and to share in scientific advancements and its benefits. Governments can protect this right by not interfering in artistic expression or by intervening to protect national cultures and identity.

Right of Political Participation
Everyone has the right to take part in the government of his country, directly or through freely chosen representatives.

Labor Rights
Under the ILO Declaration on Fundamental Principles and Rights at Work (1998), all members of the ILO, even if they have not ratified the Conventions in question, are obliged to respect, to promote, and to realize the principles concerning the fundamental rights which are the subject of those Conventions, namely (a) freedom of association and the effective recognition of the right to collective bargaining, (b) the elimination of all forms of forced or compulsory labour, (c) the effective abolition of child labour, and (d) the elimination of discrimination in respect of employment and occupation.

Right to a Sustainable Livelihood
Everyone has the right to a standard of living adequate for the health and well-being of himself and of his family, including food, and the right to security in the event of unemployment. Governments protect this right by assisting those who are unable to provide for themselves or their families.

Right to Information
Everyone has a right to impart and receive information from policymakers at the local, national, and international levels. In recognition that there cannot be democratic participation in decision making if governments do not act in a transparent and open manner, governments are required to take steps to promote the right to information and act in a transparent and open manner.

Introduction

October 20, 2005, was a glorious day for French President Jacques Chirac.[2] He had convinced the majority of nations of the world to embrace a long-standing French objective: a treaty establishing principles governing trade in cultural goods and services.[3] Moreover, with this new treaty, France had embarrassed its occasional adversary, the United States, the world's leading advocate of "freer trade."[4]

Chirac's staff had worked closely with Canadian officials to develop the new treaty under the aegis of the United Nations Educational, Scientific and Cultural Organization (UNESCO).[5] France and Canada had turned to UNESCO to counter U.S. pressures to liberalize trade in cultural goods and services under the WTO.[6] After only three years of negotiations, the members of UNESCO approved the Convention on the Protection and Promotion of the Diversity of Cultural Expressions. The United States and Israel were the only two countries to reject the treaty.[7]

The UNESCO Convention is historic for several reasons. First, although the right to cultural participation is part of the UDHR, the new treaty enshrines in international law a much more detailed interpretation of the right to cultural, religious, and linguistic diversity.[8] Second, the treaty filled "a legal vacuum in world governance by establishing a series of rights and obligations, at both the national and international level, aimed at protecting and promoting cultural diversity."[9] Its signatories agreed that, because culture is an expression of national values and norms, they should not treat trade in films, books, and art in the same manner as trade in shoes, tires, or cups.

The French were long determined to protect their cultural heritage. To many people, France is a locus of high culture: home to the world's best food, museums, writing, wine, artwork, and couture. French officials and many members of the French public do not want that culture bastardized or jeopardized by foreign competition or contagion.[10] French officials argued that because the right to culture epitomizes the identity of nations, policymakers need leeway to protect their culture to maintain their sense of national identity.[11]

Although the European Union also participated in the negotiations, not all members of the EU agreed with France that trade in cultural goods and services should be governed outside of the WTO. Several of these governments saw no urgency to spell out the policy obligations of governments to promote cultural diversity. But policymakers from these countries did not want this issue to damage trade relations. Thus, when the Convention was approved, EU officials emphasized that they envisioned the treaty as a complement, rather than a threat, to the WTO.[12] But no one knows how the convention will be enforced or how WTO rules and the Convention's principles could truly be made complementary.

Not surprisingly, U.S. officials did not see the relationship between trade and the right to cultural diversity in quite the same way as their French counterparts. The United States is the world's largest exporter of cultural goods and services. Although U.S. policymakers acknowledged that many people around the world feared their culture could be undermined or changed by globalization (for example Egyptian rap, Russian jazz, or Swedish reggae), they also insisted that countries could use the Convention to erect new barriers to trade. The United States noted the European Union's insistence that many cultural goods (such as films or services related to libraries or museums) should not be subject to trade disciplines and had strongly argued to maintain "cultural exceptions" in the WTO.[13] Thus, the United States argued that the Convention should be redrafted so that "it can not be misinterpreted to authorize governments to impose protectionist trade measures in the guise of protecting culture."

The U.S. ambassador to UNESCO, Louise Oliver, justified her position based on human rights. She contended that the new treaty could be abused by repressive regimes to stifle domestic dissent or oppress cultural minorities. She stressed, "The main proponents of this convention seemed more interested in control over international trade flows and the lives of their citizens than in promoting freedom and cultural diversity."[14]

* * *

The European Union and its member states – more than any other case study – use trade agreements and trade policies to promote human rights. But EU member states are not always motivated by altruism. As this example of the

UNESCO Convention illustrates, one member state was able to move the EU and the members of UNESCO to agree to a brand new treaty addressing trade in cultural goods. France used human rights language to justify the treaty, although France also sought the treaty to "protect" cultural interests, which comprise key elements of its economy (e.g., fashion, wine, or tourism). This is not the only time that European Commission policymakers used human rights arguments to justify trade restrictions. For example, these officials have argued that EC trade restrictions on genetically modified organisms are necessary to protect the right to health of EU citizens, because the scientific community has not established whether genetic engineering is safe.[15] The European Commission has also argued that it must ban imports of beef grown with hormones to protect public health.[16]

Clearly, EU decision makers are weighing how some trade policy decisions may affect important human rights objectives within the European Union. However, like our other case studies, the European Union has not conducted a systematic study of how trade policies and agreements affect human rights at home or abroad.

The member states of the European Union have a hard time developing comprehensive policies at the intersection of trade and human rights for four reasons. First, the European Union is an economic union, but not every member adheres to the same economic rules. Although most EU countries use the euro, some member states, including Denmark, Sweden, and the United Kingdom, have retained their own national currencies. Members set their own fiscal and budgetary policies, but some member states have centralized their monetary policies. Second, EU policymakers from the EU executive (the European Commission) must coordinate trade and human rights policies for twenty-five very different countries with different social, political, and economic cultures.[17] Third, that same executive body does not have the authority to make all aspects of human rights or trade policies. For example, the states have competence to negotiate investment, and member states and the European Union share competence on human rights policies as well as authority to negotiate agreements relating to trade in social, cultural, educational, and health services.[18] Finally, policymakers must find common ground between officials from the trade and the human rights communities, two groups of individuals with very different policy goals.

But trade is not the only area of public policy where member states struggle to find common ground. To facilitate decision making and to clarify Europe-wide responsibilities versus member state responsibilities, in 2004, EU policymakers drafted a new Constitutional Treaty for Europe, which was approved by fourteen member states (Austria, Belgium, Cyprus, Germany, Greece, Hungary,

Italy, Latvia, Lithuania, Luxembourg, Malta, Slovakia, Slovenia, and Spain). However, in 2005, citizens of the Netherlands and France rejected the new constitution.[19] Although the EU is moving forward on admitting new members, EU member leaders and European Community officials have put plans for further integration on hold.[20]

As in earlier chapters, we discuss human rights issues in the European Community and then examine the EU's policies toward trade and investment. From there, we examine three additional issues where trade and human rights policies may intersect. We begin with an in-depth examination of the trade policymaking process in the EU, which may undermine the rights of political participation and freedom of information of the European people. Next, we discuss how the EU promotes human rights through trade policy. Finally, we discuss EU agricultural trade policies and how these policies may affect human rights at home and abroad. For the purpose of simplicity, we generally refer to the European Union or EU in this chapter – but at times we also refer to the European Community or EC (which is the economic union of the members of the EU).[21]

Human Rights Conditions and Ethos

The countries of the European Union are lively democracies; their leaders and citizens have learned from centuries of war and intolerance that they must protect human rights. And like many democracies, they still have human rights problems. In many European nations, citizens have attacked immigrants, Roma (gypsies), the handicapped, and homosexuals. Human rights observers have reported rising incidences of racism, anti-Islamism, anti-Semitism, and xenophobia.[22] In the aftermath of the September 11, 2001, attacks on the United States, several countries, including the United Kingdom and France, put in place emergency measures that threatened to undermine civil liberties and the rights of refugees and migrants. They have justified these derogations from their human rights commitments on the basis of national security.[23] Despite these problems, the individual nations of Europe and the European Union have a strong commitment to human rights at home and abroad.

Promoting Human Rights at Home

When European policymakers laid the groundwork for what would become the European Union, they did not focus on human rights.[24] Their initial goal was to establish a common market, not a unified political system with human rights at its core. But as the common market became ever more successful, European policymakers wanted to encourage greater political integration. They gradually established a common currency, a policy on justice and criminal affairs, and a Common Foreign and Security Policy.

As economic and political ties strengthened, however, EU member states gradually introduced human rights objectives into the operations and institutions of the European Union. The current (2002 Nice) Treaty on the European Union defines liberty, democracy, respect for human rights and fundamental freedoms, and the rule of law as the founding principles of the Union. It mandates that the European Union must respect fundamental rights as general principles of Community law.[25] The European Council can suspend certain rights (including voting rights) of EU member states that violate these principles in a "serious and persistent" way.[26] EU institutions and member states are forbidden to violate human rights when they develop or implement community policies.[27] Citizens are guaranteed certain rights as Europeans, such as the right to vote and stand for office in the local elections of the country in which they happen to reside.[28] But, in general, EU institutions can only advance certain human rights linked to the common market, such as gender rights and safety and health conditions in the workplace. Moreover, because members are responsible for human rights within their borders, current law only addresses their behavior (or EU institutional behavior) when these institutions develop or implement Community policies.[29]

As part of the new EU Constitutional treaty, EU officials wrote a new EU human rights charter, the EU Charter of Fundamental Rights. The proposed Charter includes a wide range of traditional human rights, such as workers rights and the right to health, as well as new (third-generation) rights, such as the right to protection against the abuse of genetic engineering and biotechnology (Article 3) and the protection of personal data (Article 8).[30] However, the Charter cannot come into force until the new Treaty is approved. Thus, promoting human rights remains the bailiwick of member states.

Advancing Human Rights Abroad

Although the European Union has limited powers to advance human rights throughout the twenty-five member states, it has a clear mandate, institutional structure, and funds to promote human rights abroad. The European Union has made human rights a priority in its Common Foreign and Security Policy (which remains a matter of the EU member states), its foreign aid policy (which supplements the development cooperation policies of individual states), and its trade policy.[31] The European Union does not set out to impose its human rights norms upon other countries but uses dialogue to convince policymakers in other countries that advancing human rights is in their interest. The EU Council of Ministers have made abolition of the death penalty (1998); the fight against torture and other cruel, inhuman, or degrading treatment or punishment (2001); the protection of children in armed conflict (2003); the rights of human rights defenders (2004); and the promotion of international humanitarian law (2005) their top international human rights priorities. Officials in the Human Rights and Democracy Unit of DG External Relations (the European Commission agency responsible for foreign policy) try to implement these goals.[32] Officials in DG Development supplement this work with human rights capacity-building projects, paying particular attention to gender rights, children's rights, and the rights of indigenous people.[33] The European Union also tries to increase the demand for human rights overseas by supporting the activities of civil society groups and international organizations (such as the International Criminal Court) working to promote democratization, good governance, and the rule of law, and the elimination of racism, xenophobia, and discrimination against minorities and indigenous people.[34]

EU officials learned how to build human rights capacity abroad when the European Union expanded to include countries from southern, eastern, and central Europe. For example, Spain and Portugal joined the EU after years of being ruled by dictators. Thus, to join the EU, policymakers required potential members to respect human rights, and it gave these countries considerable assistance to help put laws, policies, and monitoring institutions in place.[35] The European Union provides similar assistance today to the current candidate countries (Bulgaria, Romania, Turkey, Croatia, and the Former Yugoslav Republic of Macedonia) and possible future candidate countries (such as Albania and Bosnia and Herzegovina).[36] As we will show later in the chapter, EU officials apply a similar approach to developing countries outside of Europe.[37]

Trade and Investment Overview

The European Union is a trade behemoth: it is the world's largest trading block, with some 460 million generally middle-class consumers. Not surprisingly, it has an enormous influence on global trade. It is the world's largest trader of services and agricultural products, and it accounts for some 40% of outward foreign investment.[38] But the European Commission and the twenty-five member states sometimes have a hard time defining common trade priorities. For example, in negotiations that cover goods as well as services, EU officials must juggle issues requiring community-wide decisions with issues that are decided by national policymakers. To facilitate common ground and effective decision making, they have created a complicated bureaucratic procedure.

HOW TRADE POLICY IS MADE IN THE EUROPEAN UNION AND
WHERE HUMAN RIGHTS CAN ENTER THE DISCUSSION

The European Commission's Directorate General of Trade (DG Trade) negotiates and monitors trade agreements on behalf of the EU member states. DG Trade is headed by the EU trade commissioner, who is appointed by the governments of the EU member states in consultation with the president of the Commission.[39] To carry out their responsibilities, DG Trade officials regularly consult with officials from other departments such as Internal Market, Industrial Affairs, Competition, and Agriculture. *They also consult with constituents concerned about trade by setting up hearings, expert committees, or high-level working groups, where representatives from business, labor, and civil society can provide input for DG Trade officials.*[40] *In recent years, these officials have also begun to solicit public opinion on trade policy through the Internet.*

When the European Commission approves a proposal, DG Trade officials then move it for discussion to the Article 133 Committee. This committee, which is composed of national trade officials and experts appointed by the EU member states, reviews all aspects of EU trade policy on a weekly basis.[41] The members of the committee tend to be senior civil servants who are close to the trade ministers they serve.[42] These men and women consult with government officials in the different capitals to work out and defend national positions on mostly the technical and tactical aspects of the Commission's proposal. Many EU member states try to involve national business, labor, and civil society in this process.[43] The Article 133 Committee has no formal operating guidelines, but it rarely votes and always tries to reach consensus.[44]

Once DG Trade has worked out a recommendation with the Article 133 Committee, any remaining issues are passed on for deliberation to the Committee of Permanent Representatives (COREPER). It is comprised of the heads or deputy heads of mission from the EU member states in Brussels. Like the Article 133 Committee, it will try to avoid a formal vote and seek a consensus on the issues on the table.[45] Ultimately, the General Affairs and External Relations Council gives the final approval to the Commission's proposal for a negotiating mandate.[46] The Council is composed of the twenty-five foreign affairs ministers of the European Union, who, depending on the issue on the agenda, are joined by the EU ministers responsible for trade, European affairs, or development.[47] If a policy, strategy, or negotiating mandate is approved by the EU ministers, DG Trade is empowered to conduct, under the leadership of the EU trade commissioner, the actual negotiations in consultation with the Article 133 Committee. The committee closely monitors the negotiations to ensure that DG Trade's negotiators remain within their mandate. In the end, the General Affairs and External Relations Council must decide whether to ratify the agreement negotiated by DG Trade.[48]

Trade and foreign policy officials elected in member states meet under the aegis of the Council of Ministers and set the ultimate objectives for trade negotiations and policies.[49] In discussing trade, the foreign affairs and/or trade ministers represent their countries and make decisions by qualified majority vote (or by unanimity on services or intellectual property issues). In practice, however, the council tends to reach decisions by consensus.[50]

The members of the Council of Ministers are elected officials who vote on trade policy – thus, they seem to function like legislators. However, no legislative body at the national or European level acts as a counterweight to the European Commission during the process.[51] DG Trade maintains a "Civil Society Dialogue" to inform, discuss, and consult with European civil society on all aspects of EU trade policy, including negotiations. But it does not have to consult with them and they have no formal or official role in the development of policy. Consequently, the public has little direct influence over trade policy decisions. EU trade policy is made behind closed doors by a small circle of elites who must deliver results for their member states. *However, as the next chart illuminates, human rights can enter the discussion at multiple points. Policymakers as well as constituents can bring up human rights concerns during the policy formation, negotiation, and implementation process. But the government is not obliged to respond to these concerns.*

EC policymakers, like their counterparts around the world, hope that trade will stimulate growth and create jobs at home. They want trade policies to reduce poverty and advance sustainable development abroad. EU officials claim these two objectives are complementary.[52] But EU officials, like other industrialized country officials, find it difficult to achieve both objectives.

In March 2000, EU leaders decided that their policies should be directed toward helping Europe become "the most competitive and dynamic knowledge-based economy in the world, capable of sustainable economic growth with more and better jobs and greater social cohesion" by 2010.[53] But many individual European countries are growing slowly, if at all, and unemployment is high.[54] EU policymakers worry about how they can sustain their generous welfare systems and support their rapidly aging populations as they compete with nations such as China, which have an ample supply of young workers willing to work for relatively low (albeit rising) wages.[55] Under President José Manuel Barroso, the European Commission has made economic growth and jobs the number one priority for the European Union (2005–2009).[56] EU policymakers believe trade liberalization can help achieve these goals by creating new export opportunities as well as encouraging productivity growth and innovation. In the future, they argue, Europeans will work at better jobs in a knowledge-based economy.[57]

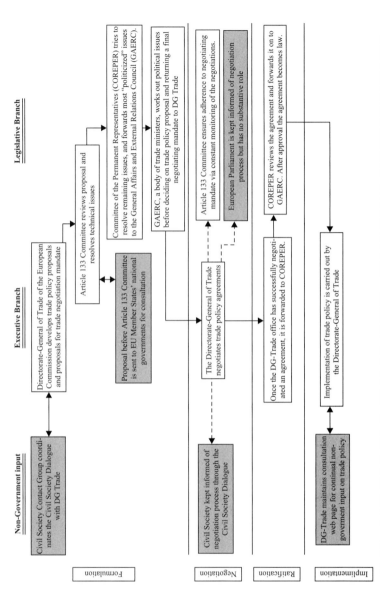

FIGURE 5.1. European Union trade policy formation. Shaded boxes indicate some of the decision points where human rights can enter the process.

Note: In the context of the EU, the "Legislative Branch" includes the Council of Ministers and the European Parliament. In most domains they work together to approve policy, but in trade policy, decisions are made by the trade ministers (and/or foreign ministers) in GAERC, acting for the Council of Ministers.

But growing numbers of European policymakers and citizens are not sure that the knowledge-based economy will provide enough "better" jobs for all Europeans, especially those without a college education. For example, policymakers in France, Italy, and Poland, among other countries, are increasingly using local policies to protect jobs and "national champions" – important local firms.[58] In addition, many European citizens do not believe that trade liberalization will yield a virtuous circle of new investment, high-wage jobs, and economies of scale.[59] A 2005 poll by the German Marshall Fund found that some Europeans fear that EU companies will move jobs and investment overseas under the rubric of trade liberalization.[60] Some 69% of those polled in Europe believe that free trade "mostly benefits multinational companies, not ordinary people or small companies." Moreover, in Italy and France, people think they are more likely to suffer from trade than to benefit from it.[61] These public concerns reveal that either the European Union needs to do a better job of explaining its policies or it needs to change them.

The European Union claims that its external trade policy "is conceived not only as an end in itself, but as a means to promote sustainable development."[62] Sustainable development has two broad components – core labor standards (the right to collective bargaining, freedom of association, elimination of discrimination in the workplace, elimination of all forms of forced labor, and the abolition of child labor) and respect for the environment.[63] The European Union's trade agreements often include social and environmental capacity-building programs that are designed to help their trade partners achieve good governance in these areas over the long term.[64]

EU policymakers argue that the best way to promote trade and sustainable development is under the aegis of the WTO.[65] EC policymakers try to support the WTO in several ways. First, they are actively involved in the Doha Round talks and rely on its good offices to mediate disputes. The European Union and its individual member states also provide a significant amount of funds to help developing countries effectively participate in the WTO (WTO capacity building).[66]

However, like the other countries we surveyed, the European Union actively negotiates regional and bilateral trade agreements. It believes that such agreements can complement and reinforce the WTO, provided that they are outward looking and lead to lower external trade barriers.[67] Since the 1990s, the European Union has negotiated an increasing number of bilateral trade agreements with countries such as Mexico, Chile, and South Africa.[68]

EC policymakers see trade agreements and policies as tools that can change the behavior of countries where human rights are not adequately protected. For

TABLE 5.1. *Overview of the European Union's Major Regional and Bilateral Trade Agreements*

Trade agreement	Other member nations	Special attributes
Regional Agreements		
Agreement on the European Economic Area (EEA) 1994	Norway, Liechtenstein, Iceland	The EEA extends the European Union single market and its legislation to these EFTA countries, with the exception of agriculture and fisheries.
Bilateral Agreements		
Europe Agreements 1993	Bulgaria, Romania	The EAs are a prelude to accession to the European Union.
EU-Turkey Association Agreement 1995	Turkey	Liberalizes all trade in industrial goods.
Euro-Mediterranean Association Agreements 1997–2006	Egypt, Israel, Jordan, Morocco, Tunisia, Algeria, Lebanon, Palestinian Authority	Gradual liberalization of trade in industrial goods and agricultural products through reciprocal preferential access.
Stabilization and Association Agreements 2004, 2005	Former Yugoslav Republic of Macedonia, Croatia	Gradually establish a free trade area.
EU-South Africa Trade, Development, and Cooperation Agreement (TDCA) begun 2000	South Africa	Gradually establish a free trade area over a period of twelve years.
EU-Chile Association Agreement begun 2003	Chile	Gradually establishes a free trade area.
EU-Mexico Global Agreement 2000	Mexico	Aims to gradually establish a free trade area.
Nonreciprocal Preferential Agreements		
ACP-EU Partnership Agreement (Cotonou Agreement) 2000	Seventy-nine African, Caribbean, and Pacific (ACP) countries	Unilateral preferences will be replaced by reciprocal Economic Partnership Agreements (EPAs) beginning in 2008.

Source: DG Trade, http://europa.eu.int/comm/trade/issues/bilateral/index`en.htm.

example, the European Union is negotiating a free trade agreement (FTA) with the Gulf Cooperation Council, which includes human rights violators such as Saudi Arabia, Oman, and the United Arab Emirates.[69] In addition, for several years, the European Union has been trying to prod Iran to abandon its nuclear program in exchange for security and trade guarantees.[70] European Union policymakers clearly believe that trade offers an opportunity for dialogue, and with such dialogue, EU policymakers will convince its trade partners that promoting human rights is in their interest.

Linking Human Rights and Trade Agreements

Since 1995, the European Union has also included a human rights clause in all its trade, cooperation, partnership, and association agreements, except the WTO agreements.[71] The clause defines respect for fundamental human rights as an "essential element" of the agreement.[72] EU policymakers want their counterparts to recognize that if they promote human rights and develop the habits of good governance, they will gradually attract long-term investment, stimulate trade, and achieve sustainable development.[73]

Europe's view that human rights and trade objectives can and should be linked is not a new development. Throughout the history of the GATT, countries such as Germany, the United Kingdom, and France tried to include labor rights in its purview. However, after WTO members made no progress on these issues at the WTO's Seattle ministerial (1999), the European Union developed other approaches.[74] The European Union now argues that the International Labor Organization (ILO) needs greater authority to work with its members and the WTO on the promotion and supervision of core labor standards.[75] The European Union also funds specific labor rights capacity-building projects such as the Joint Initiative on Corporate Accountability and Workers Rights to attempt to improve workplace conditions in global supply chains.[76]

But the EU states it rarely tries to promote particular groupings of human rights because policymakers believe that human rights are universal and indivisible. Thus, its GSP program aims to prod developing countries to promote a wide range of human rights delineated in international conventions.[77] The European Union has developed several different approaches to GSP which allow developing countries to export to the EU without duties or with slightly lower duties.[78] The forty-nine least-developed countries (LDCs) can take advantage of the Everything but Arms Initiative, which grants duty-free access to imports of all products except for arms and munitions.[79] The European Union hopes this will be a strong incentive to these countries to avoid producing or trading arms and munitions and will ultimately promote rights such as personal integrity rights, labor rights, and the right to life. Meanwhile, the GSP-Plus arrangement grants additional market access to "dependent and vulnerable" countries that have ratified and effectively implemented key international conventions on human and labor rights, environmental protection, and good governance.[80] In December 2005, the European Commission granted GSP-Plus benefits to Bolivia, Columbia, Ecuador, Peru, Venezuela, Costa Rica, El Salvador, Guatemala, Honduras, Nicaragua, Panama, Moldova, Georgia, Mongolia, and Sri Lanka for the period from 2006 to 2008.[81]

The European Union has not only adopted a country-specific approach to linking trade and human rights but it has also focused its efforts on specific sectors. The EU guidelines on torture commit the European Union to "prevent the use, production and trade of equipment which is designed to inflict torture."[82] Thus, on June 27, 2005, the European Union banned the export and import of goods that can exclusively be used for this purpose, such as gallows, guillotines, electric chairs, electric shock belts, air-tight vaults, and automatic drug injection systems.[83]

Specific member states have also developed some innovative approaches at the intersection of trade and human rights. For example, in January 2002, the Belgian Parliament approved a law aiming to promote socially accountable production by introducing a voluntary social label on workers rights. According to the Belgian government, the law "offers companies the possibility to acquire a label, which is granted to products whose chain of production respects the eight fundamental ILO conventions." The Ministry of Economic Affairs grants the label for a maximum of three years after a committee comprised of stakeholders (government officials, social partners, business federations, consumers, and NGO representatives) reviews a company's proposals. This committee establishes a program of control for the company and monitors its compliance. Certification is carried out by the inspection bodies accredited by the Minister of Economic Affairs. This social label was not linked to a specific trade agreement but was vetted by both the Belgian government and the European Commission to ensure that it was compatible with WTO rules. The label is not just for Belgian or EU firms. A U.S. NGO, Social Accountability International, has been accredited under the Belgian social labeling law. Thus, it does not seem to violate WTO national treatment rules – it treats foreign and domestic market actors similarly. Because this approach is voluntary, it probably does not violate WTO norms. Nonetheless, both the Belgian government and the European Commission sought to ensure that it was compatible with WTO rules.[84] The Dutch government requires companies that want taxpayer-funded export subsidies to declare in writing that they are familiar with the OECD Guidelines (a voluntary code of conduct that includes sections on human rights and labor rights). These companies must note they will make an effort to apply the Guidelines in their corporate practices. Austria is considering a similar link.[85]

In sum, EU policymakers at the national and supranational levels are committed to using trade policies and agreements to promote human rights internationally. But the European Union does not examine how trade policies may affect human rights at home, although it has used human rights arguments to justify some of its trade positions. We begin by examining how the trade policymaking process affects citizens' rights to political participation.

Current Areas of Tension between the European Union's Trade and Human Rights Objectives

For the People but Not Directly by the People: The EC Trade Policymaking Process

For a democracy to function effectively, citizens must participate in the government of their country, either directly or indirectly.[86] But citizens cannot effectively participate in public life unless policymakers share information. With such information, citizens can provide feedback to policymakers and make government more efficient and more responsive.[87] Thus, political participation and constant feedback ensure that public policies will reflect the needs and perspectives of the citizenry and citizens will perceive government decisions as both fair and legitimate.

Political participation and information sharing are alive and well in every individual member state of the European Union. But the public perceives – and the European Union admits – that EU policymaking has a "democratic deficit." The bureaucracy set up to manage relations between and among member states has grown increasingly removed from the people whom it serves. Every day, with little direct public oversight, EU technocrats make decisions that can affect the daily lives of Europeans. Although many understand the reason for such an approach, they are often frustrated by it.[88] And, away from Brussels, citizens do not feel they have the information, opportunities, or even the ability to influence such European Union–wide policies.[89] Trade policymaking provides a perfect example of this problem.

In the EU, trade policies are generally (but not always) made by EC officials with little direct public involvement or oversight.[90] The trade commissioner is appointed by the national governments of the member states in consultation with the president of the European Commission.[91] DG Trade staff are unelected civil servants who are not required to directly consult citizens in member states. The Article 133 Committee deliberations are not made public and no formal votes are recorded.[92]

Other EU trade policymaking bodies operate in an equally unaccountable manner. Trade policy is made behind closed doors by national government officials from EU member states.[93] Neither the press nor members of civil society, business, or labor can attend these meetings or directly influence the deliberations.

The European Union's legislative body, the European Parliament, plays no direct role in trade policymaking.[94] *Trade is the only common policy without a formal role for the European Parliament.*[95] Although the trade commissioner does try to inform and consult with European Parliament representatives, the democratically elected representatives in the Parliament generally can't alter European Union–wide trade policy.[96]

National parliaments also play a limited role in trade policymaking, except in the areas of services and investment.[97] Only three of the twenty-five parliaments – the Danish, British, and French – require their national government to consult with them on *all* EU policies, including EU trade policies and agreements.[98] Other countries simply brief their parliaments.[99] A former senior EU official told us that national parliaments in the European Union seem to have "given up" on scrutinizing their governments' representatives in Brussels when they decide on trade policy.[100]

Given the opacity of trade policymaking, the European Parliament has pushed to make the process more transparent and accountable.[101] The Parliament called on the member states "to revise the provisions of the European Community Treaty concerning the common commercial policy so as to guarantee full involvement of the European Parliament in this sphere, by providing for Parliament to be consulted on the negotiating mandates to be given to the Commission, opening up the 133 Committee to Parliament's representatives, and requiring Parliament's assent to all trade agreements."[102] However, none of these suggestions have been implemented.[103]

The European Parliament has also pushed for changes to European Commission policymaking, noting that its "unacceptable" secrecy hinders the scrutiny role of the European and national parliaments and undermines the legitimacy of Council decisions.[104] It has demanded that the Commission make more documents accessible and available to the public.[105] Yet the Commission has not implemented these recommendations either.

However, the European Commission has made some progress in involving citizen participation in the trade policymaking process. Since 1999, representatives from the EU Parliament, business, and civil society have joined the official delegations to WTO ministerials (but they do not negotiate). In 1999, as well, DG Trade officials established channels for civil society consultations. DG Trade staff, for example, sponsor public meetings with the EU trade minister.[106] These officials also set up a formal advisory committee, the Contact Group, which includes representatives from NGOs, businesses, consumer protection groups, agricultural groups, and labor organizations.[107] DG Trade staff regularly brief civil society on trade negotiations and answer questions.[108] According to DG Trade, this dialogue is open to employers' associations, trade union movements, agricultural producers' organizations, and NGOs such as Oxfam, Greenpeace, Friends of the Earth, and Action Aid. Members of the European Parliament and members of national parliaments are also welcome to participate in these meetings.[109] DG Trade has also convened several issue groups to discuss controversial topics such as the relationship between trade policies and access to medicines. NGOs have used these discussions to present their own proposals.[110] These meetings and mechanisms have made the EU trade policymaking process more responsive to the perspectives of civil society groups. However, NGOs and citizens are often involved late in the policy debate, after crucial decisions have been made.[111]

DG trade officials have also tried to do a better job of communicating with the broader public. Many trade documents and policies are posted and explained on the Internet.[112] The European Commission has developed a specific Web site, Public Consultations, to involve a broader cross section of the public in the discussion over specific trade issues. Trade staff have also developed dedicated Internet forums or Web sites for written public comments.[113] For example, on May 8, 2006, the European Commission launched a public consultation on how policymakers should manage trade and economic relations with China.[114]

Despite these attempts to expand the circle of those making trade policies, many NGOs, such as Oxfam, World Wildlife Fund, and Friends of the Earth Europe, remain critics of the process.[115] These groups complain that they do not have the time or money they need to influence EU officials the way business groups can.[116] They are tired of talking without being heard.[117]

Polling data reveal that although most Europeans support EU trade policy, a significant minority have very real concerns about the process. A 2003 Eurobarometer poll noted that 61% of EU citizens trust EU officials to ensure that globalization follows the right course, whereas 58% of EU citizens respond positively about the Commission negotiating trade issues on behalf of the member states.[118] At first glance, these numbers seem to reveal strong support for the EU trade policymaking process, but, in the United Kingdom, Finland, Greece, France, Spain, Germany, and Ireland, over 35% (and often as much as 54%) of respondents do not think it is a good thing that the European Union negotiates on behalf of member states. They believe that their home countries are more responsive to their needs, and, thus, they prefer that member states negotiate on behalf of their citizens.[119] Such a view is perhaps not surprising, because "all politics are local." However, the poll also found that 79% of citizens believe that critics of globalization raise important points that deserve to be debated but are not heard in the EU trade policymaking process.[120] A 2005 poll of 7,515 Europeans found that 63% are in favor of globalization and 61% trust the European Union to ensure that globalization will head in the right direction. But they think that multinationals (64%) and financial interests (62%) have too much influence on the trade policymaking process. The poll also found that "anti-or alter-globalization movements are widely deemed to ask relevant questions . . . but are seen as failing to influence political decision makers." The pollsters concluded that "mistrust of many key players is blatant."[121] The results of these polls show a level of discomfort with the management and direction of EU trade policies.

In sum, the European Union claims that human rights "values underpin the EU's internal ethos."[122] Yet, in the interest of meeting the political needs of twenty-five member states, the European Union's policymaking processes appear to have frustrated some of its citizens' democratic rights.

Promoting Human Rights Abroad: Trade Can Be a Mighty Lever When Pulled

In January 2006, the Russian government briefly shut off Ukraine's supply of natural gas. Supposedly, the two nations were disputing how much Ukraine should pay for gas. The action set off alarm bells in much of the world as many European leaders were pushing their panic buttons. Analysts saw the shutoff as an attempt to punish Ukraine for its Orange Revolution, when Ukrainian citizens took to the streets to demand (and achieve) democratic regime change. The shutoff led to deep reductions in gas delivery to Western Europe, which relies on the East for much of its energy.[123]

EU policymakers have become increasingly concerned about Russia's human rights practices at home and abroad. In its 2005 human rights report, the European Union expressed "concerns about human rights in Russia, and in particular about the human rights situation in Chechnya, the situation of human rights defenders, the rule of law, and freedom of the media."[124]

The European Union and Russia have much to gain by close economic and political ties. The European Union wants a stable Russia and friendly relations with Russian officials. But it is deeply concerned by Russia's unwillingness to consistently protect human rights and the rule of law. Nonetheless, the European Union is increasingly dependent on Russia for much of its energy. By 2020, three-quarters of Europe's natural gas will be imported, the bulk of which will come from Russia. Thus, Europe's reliance on Russian gas is problematic, particularly if Moscow makes a pattern of using energy as a tool for foreign policy.[125] Meanwhile, Russia wants to increase trade with the European Union, obtain more EU investment, and gain EU support to join the World Trade Organization. This provides the EU with some leverage over Russia's behavior.

The European Union has a Partnership and Cooperation Agreement with Russia, which entered into force December 1, 1997. This agreement acts as a framework for cooperation on a wide range of issues, including trade, culture, national security, crime, and immigration.[126] The agreement also includes a human rights clause. Thus, it gives the European Union the option to use "appropriate measures" to protect human rights in Russia. But the European Union has not invoked this clause despite its serious concerns.[127] Some critics allege that Europe has been hesitant to criticize Russia for human rights abuses because of its need for a stable supply of Russian energy. In November 2004, the European Union and Russia began a regular human rights dialogue, and the European Union has consistently expressed its concerns about the declining human rights situation in Russia.[128] EU policymakers seem to have concluded that dialogue is the right strategy to improve human rights conditions in Russia and to prod the Russians to ensure that they don't use trade in ways that undermine the human rights of citizens of other countries. But so far, this dialogue has prompted little change in Russian human rights practices.

EC policymakers have introduced human rights clauses into more than fifty trade agreements, which apply to more than 120 countries, including many former colonies of the great European powers (France, the Netherlands, Spain, Portugal, Germany, and the United Kingdom).[129] Many of these agreements (such as the Cotonou Agreement and the Association Agreements) include preferential trade arrangements.[130] Others (such as Partnership and Cooperation Agreements) provide a framework for cooperation and future trade agreements. Although these agreements reflect the different social, economic, and political status of the European Union's trade partners, they all have one thing in common. The parties to these agreements are supposed to use dialogue and review mechanisms and assessments to improve human rights.

But EU policymakers have not left sanctions out of their human rights equations. They can withdraw development funds or take "appropriate measures" such as suspending the agreement in full or in part if an offending partner country (mostly following a consultation procedure) fails to bring satisfactory change in its human rights record.[131] Such "appropriate measures" may include trade or arms embargoes.[132]

Since 1995, the European Union has invoked the human rights clause in twelve cases.[133] Except for Uzbekistan, all these cases concerned countries bound to the European Union by the Cotonou Agreement. These countries were former colonies, where the European Union had strong political and economic relationships and influence. In six out of the twelve cases, the European Union decided to impose "appropriate measures" (arms embargoes, as well as restrictions on admission – visa or travel bans – and the freezing of funds) when talks broke down.[134]

Although policymakers argue that "the principal role of the clause is to provide the EU with a basis for positive engagement . . . with third countries," they struggle to find a consistent and workable balance between persuasion and coercion. According to Princeton scholar Emilie Hafner Burton, the European Union has successfully used the threat of targeted measures against Togo (1998), Fiji (2000), Comoros Islands (1999), and Niger (1999).[135] These are all relatively small trading partners for the European Union, and they are countries with which EU member states had colonial relationships. In addition, the European Parliament notes that, in general, the European Union has invoked the human rights clause mainly in response to undemocratic changes of government such as coups, but the European Union has not used coercion in other instances where it might be equally useful. For instance, the European Union has never invoked the human rights clause in response to violations of economic, social, or cultural rights in countries such as Egypt and Tunisia.[136]

Human rights NGOs are critical of the EU's failure to consistently use the human rights tools embedded in trade agreements. In November 2005, the EU office of Amnesty International noted in 2005 that although human rights are violated "on a serious and systematic scale in most of the Mediterranean partner countries," policymakers have failed to intervene and to effectively apply the human rights clause.[137] They concluded that "while the EU develops frameworks and allocates significant resources to promote human rights, it tolerates or turns a blind eye to practices which have undermined human rights protection in partner countries."[138] Activists are not the only critics of how EU policymakers link human rights and trade policies. The EU Parliament has noted that the EC has not responded to human rights abuses in Vietnam, Laos, and Cambodia, with which the European Union has signed Partnership and Cooperation Agreements, despite dramatic calls from local human rights organizations.[139]

Clearly, EU policymakers are not eager to cut off trade in the interest of promoting human rights. The EU (in dramatic contrast with the United States) has never used a full or partial trade embargo to change the behavior of those countries with which it has signed bilateral or regional trade agreements. EU policymakers stress that they do not want to inflict high economic and humanitarian costs on the population.[140] EC officials rely instead on targeted (or "smart") sanctions such as arms embargoes or visa or travel bans.[141] EC policymakers recently used such smart sanctions in the hopes of improving human rights conditions in Zimbabwe.[142] Additionally, the European Union froze the assets of the president and senior officials of Belarus in response to that country's flawed election and its suppression of human rights.[143] EU policymakers believe a targeted approach allows trade to continue (benefiting citizens in both countries) but hurts policy elites.[144] However, by allowing trade to continue, the European Union may be propping up repressive regimes.

Scholar and current EU official Hadewych Hazelzet says that the European Union's failure to use negative sanctions in its cooperation, association, or preferential agreements stems not from a lack of will but rather from the collective decision-making process at the EU level.[145] The twenty-five EU member states in the General Affairs and External Relations Council have to decide *unanimously* on a common position in imposing such sanctions in accordance with the framework of the European Union's Common Foreign and Security Policy. Thus, one member state can derail the use of sanctions.[146] These decisions then have to be implemented by either a regulation proposed by the European Commission (in the case of trade sanctions) or national legislative measures (in the case of arms embargoes).[147] Thus, each EU member state has several opportunities to block or complicate EU decisions on sanctions that would harm that member state's bilateral relations with the targeted country.

Human rights activists and the EU Parliament have a different explanation for the European Union's reluctance to fully utilize the trade policy tools at its disposal to promote human rights. They believe that because decisions are made in secret, policymakers place commercial considerations over human rights concerns.[148] In a February 2005 report, the EU Parliament's Committee on Foreign Affairs noted, "the way the clause has been used, or not used, over the years . . . leaves room to ask if criteria for initiating a consultation procedure, or applying restrictive measures, are objective, or rather dependent on political and commercial interests." The Parliament also stressed that the wording of the clause "does not spell out detailed procedures for 'positive' and 'negative' interventions, leaving the EU member states' national imperatives to hold sway over the more general requirements of human rights."[149] The European Parliament called for a new human rights clause that would delineate when to use incentives and when to use disincentives.[150] In 2006 the Parliament called on the EC to "identify a list of "Countries of Particular Concern" with respect to human rights violations and prodded the EU to weigh imposing aid or trade sanctions if human rights breaches occur. "EU officials need this kind of specific policy directive if they are to promote human rights clearly and consistently."[151]

NGOs have also tried to influence decisions regarding how the European Union links trade and human rights. Some NGOs have asked EU policymakers not to conclude or to ratify international agreements with countries that have a questionable human rights record. These NGOs fear that such agreements will strengthen repressive regimes.[152] Nevertheless, the European Union has signed a Partnership and Cooperation Agreement and is about to ratify an Interim Agreement on Trade and Trade-Related Matters (which covers the trade-related aspects of the Partnership and Cooperation Agreement) with Turkmenistan, one of the most repressive and closed countries in the world.[153]

Thus, the EU relies on dialogues when it links trade and human rights. Yet EU officials admit that these dialogues are inconsistent, too general, and too informal. In assessing this dialogue, some government officials acknowledge, "If no progress has been made, the European Union should either adjust its aims or consider whether or not to continue."[154] EU policymakers, however, still believe that dialogue is the best means to change the behavior of other countries.[155] Because there are so many dialogues, EU officials have had to give their greatest attention to the most egregious human rights violations in their partner states. As a result, these officials rarely use the human rights clause to respond to violations of economic, cultural, and social rights. Thus, despite EU belief in the universality and indivisibility of international human rights, policymakers concentrate on the most egregious human rights violations among its trade partners.[156]

If dialogue doesn't yield changes among Europe's GSP partners, it can use sanctions. In fact, it is easier for the European Union to impose sanctions under the GSP scheme than sanctions under the human rights clause.[157] Nonetheless, the European Union has withdrawn GSP benefits from only one country, Burma, because of its use of forced labor. NGOs and parliamentarians have pressured DG Trade to withdraw GSP from Belarus – a country where labor rights and freedom of association are repeatedly denied.[158] In December 2003, the European Commission began to investigate these allegations as a first step toward a possible withdrawal of the trade preferences that the "last dictatorship in Europe" enjoys under its GSP scheme. After years of debate, on June 15, 2007, the EU announced it would withdraw preferential trade benefits from Belarus for its failure to protect labor rights.[159]

The EU, like our other case studies, does not examine the broad impact of its trade policies on human rights. But the EU does hire independent consultants to carry out sustainable impact assessments. These consultants weigh the impact of trade agreements on biodiversity, income, poverty, equity, and so on, in the EU and its trade partners, and sometimes even assess the trade impact on third countries. EU policymakers could add a human rights impact assessment to this existing mechanism.[160]

In conclusion, the European Union, more than any other case study, is willing to link trade and human rights as part of its larger objective of promoting human rights. But the European Union has been reluctant to use all of the tools (from human rights clauses to sanctions) in its toolbox when needed. Moreover, it uses these tools inconsistently. Because of this reluctance, the European Union sends conflicting signals to its trade partners about the importance of human rights.

Not All Quiet on the Home Front: Stimulating Sustainable Development Abroad while Maintaining a Sustainable Livelihood at Home

The European Union's agricultural commissioner, Mariann Fischer Boel, likes to tell a story about the European Union's Common Agricultural Policy (CAP), the EU system of agricultural subsidies. These subsidies are designed to guarantee a minimum price to farmers and to pay them a direct subsidy for the crops they plant. Boel reminds listeners that before Europe was the name of a continent, *Europa* was a woman in Greek legend. The god Zeus was so impressed by her beauty that he disguised himself as a bull and carried her off to the island of Crete as his prisoner. She notes that just as Zeus was Europa's jailer, many people believe that the CAP is the European Union's jailer. But, she argues, this "myth" is wrong. The CAP is being revamped to ensure that farmers "receive public money to produce the public goods we want – a pleasant, well-tended countryside with high environmental standards."[161]

Many people disagree with Commissioner Boel's interpretation of the myth. In their view, it is not Europeans that suffer, but poor farmers in other countries (particularly those from the developing world).[162] They argue that Europe's comprehensive system of agricultural subsidies undermines human rights in the developing world, such as the right to work and the right to a sustainable livelihood. They stress that these subsidies contradict Europe's commitment to sustainable development. Europe's problems with the CAP, they argue, reveal the difficulty of reconciling Europe's internal trade objectives (maintaining and creating jobs at home) with its external trade objective of reducing poverty and encouraging sustainable development.

The EU's agricultural support programs were designed to ensure that the people of the EU would have a sufficient supply of food. After World War II, Europe had many food shortages. Blizzards during the winter of 1947 brought Europe to a standstill. Farmers left their land fallow and flooded into the cities, reducing wages and opportunities for urban workers. Food supplies ran low. To ensure that this would never happen again, France, West Germany, Italy, the Netherlands, Luxembourg, and Belgium devised policies to keep farmers on their land, rather than seeking jobs in the city, to prevent food shortages and to preserve the land rather than exhaust it.[163] European officials hoped this program (the precursor of the CAP) would ensure that Europeans had food security and farmers could earn a sustainable livelihood from their hard work.

Today, the CAP includes three elements: price supports, a tariff arrangement, and subsidies. These domestic policies can distort market pricing and create incentives for overproduction by European farmers. For example, policymakers set external tariffs to raise the price faced by consumers of imported commodities to the European Union's target price.[164] But, in recent years, the European Union has taken a number of steps to make the CAP less trade distorting. It now provides direct income payments rather than price supports for many farm products, and these payments are linked to other objectives such as environmental protection, food quality, and animal welfare.[165] However, the European Union still subsidizes farmers for production and provides export refunds. Moreover, farmers are given subsidies based on the area of land growing a particular crop rather than on the total amount of crop produced.[166] Thus, these policies continue to distort market signals, encourage farmers to overproduce, and shield farmers from global price fluctuations.

Whatever its flaws, the CAP has achieved many of its goals. Today, the European Union is the world's second-largest exporter of food and agricultural products. EU farmers accounted for about 20% of the world's agricultural exports and imports in 2002–2003.[167] However, the CAP is expensive. Although agriculture represents only about 1.7% of EU GDP, taxpayers provided 58.8 billion euros or about 45% of the European Union's budget to support farmers in

2006.[168] Moreover, the CAP tends to benefit mainly large farmers. Approximately 80% of the CAP subsidies go to the richest 20% of European farmers.[169]

Not only is the CAP expensive and inequitable, but it has political liabilities as well. EU members are deeply divided on how to reform the CAP, with France being its most ardent defender.[170] France's trade minister, Christine Lagarde, has argued that agriculture is "fundamental to our identity" and that "the CAP is the cornerstone of [our] relationship with our land."[171] Thus, to the French, these subsidies protect their right to culture and maintain the European way of life. France's determination to keep these subsidies in place has been supported by some of the new entrants to the European Union, such as Poland, which has many small family farms.[172] However, other EU member states, such as the United Kingdom, the Netherlands, Denmark, and Sweden, are net contributors to the CAP, and they are demanding gradual reform of these policies.[173] But the European Union has been unable to achieve consensus on these issues because any three countries can collaborate to block a decision on reform.[174]

Today, some of the most vociferous opponents of the CAP include not just EU citizens but also development activists, policymakers, scholars, and trade officials concerned about the trade distortions created by this policy. During the Uruguay Round of trade talks (1986–1994), GATT contracting parties developed an Agreement on Agriculture, which was designed to gradually reduce tariffs and trade-distorting subsidies for agricultural products.[175] But in the eleven years since the agreement came into effect as part of the WTO, developing countries still confront significant trade barriers to their agricultural exports, particularly in the European Union. (The poorest countries, however, have free access to the EU market under the Everything but Arms initiative.)

Agricultural trade liberalization is also supposed to be a key component of the Doha Development Round. But agricultural exporters, food importers, and big subsidizers have many different perspectives on what trade-offs they will make and accept. The European Union has insisted that the United States must first revamp its agricultural support policies, while it insists that developing countries must make concessions in other sectors to compensate the European Union for agricultural reforms. In the four years of negotiation since the Doha Round agricultural trade talks commenced, the members of the WTO have achieved some success in developing modalities for agricultural trade liberalization.[176] However, in September 2003 at the Cancun ministerial meeting of the WTO, developing countries walked out when the industrialized countries could not find common ground on trade facilitation and market access issues. Developing countries – in particular, India and Brazil – made it clear that they would prefer no deal to a bad deal.[177] But some good came out of this failure when, in 2004, WTO members achieved a framework agreement for negotiations on agriculture.[178] As of this writing, policymakers from countries such as the United States, Canada, South Africa, India, and Australia continue to blame the European Union for the failure to achieve a final agreement on liberalizing agricultural trade.[179]

The international development NGO Oxfam has repeatedly chastised the European Union for its agricultural policies. It blames the European Union for overproducing, dumping its excess production, and protecting its home markets. Oxfam has called this situation "one of the principal injustices of world trade."[180] It has concluded that the CAP has a "disastrous" impact on the livelihoods of the many farmers in developing countries and obstructs these countries' economic development process.[181] Farmers, activists, and development officials also make human rights arguments against the CAP. They claim that if the CAP were truly reformed, farmers around the world – in particular, developing country farmers – could export more, gain greater access to resources, and compete more effectively on world markets. In addition, they argue that more people would have access to affordable food under more competitive markets.[182]

Some economists have provided supportive economic arguments to buttress these opinions. According to William Cline of the Center for Global Development, the liberalization of agricultural markets could reduce the number of people in poverty worldwide by 200 million or about 7%.[183] The World Bank concurs, noting "growth in agriculture has a disproportionately positive effect on poverty reduction because more than half the population in developing countries lives in rural areas, and poverty is highest in rural areas."[184] The World Bank has thus called for "coordinated, global trade reforms if we are to help the rural poor."[185]

Nonetheless, many of the rural (and urban) poor in the developing world live in countries that are net food importers. These people depend on cheap dumped or subsidized food from the European Union. Thus, agricultural trade reforms will not automatically increase access to food or the right to a sustainable livelihood around the world. The impact of agricultural liberalization depends on factors such as a country's level of development, its resource base, and its food needs. A 2005 *New York Times* article summarized the contradictions in arguments that subsidies hurt smaller, poorer farmers and help rich farmers in the industrialized world: the article stressed that most economists believe that, rather than focusing on EU/U.S. agricultural trade liberalization, developing countries could help themselves even more by focusing on internal reform. Poor countries often heavily protect their farms and support vast, uncompetitive agricultural sectors, drawing investment and labor into farming when it could be better used elsewhere.[186]

According to EU Trade Commissioner Peter Mandelson, the EU cannot work toward trade justice by simply abandoning agricultural subsidies: "Trade justice cannot be equated with big bang agricultural liberalization, and with it, a race to the bottom for EU agriculture and a free market mayhem that would gravely damage the interests of some of the poorest countries in the world."[187] Moreover, Mandelson has argued that only highly competitive agricultural exporters such as Brazil and Argentina, rather than poorer developing countries such as Guatemala or Cameroon, will benefit.[188]

Thus, while EU taxpayers and consumers may benefit from changes to the CAP, such changes would not necessarily have positive human rights or economic spillovers in Europe or abroad. Some farmers will have difficulty adjusting to market conditions, and some may lose their livelihood and land.[189] Nonetheless, change in the CAP is inevitable: it is expensive, it may no longer make political and economic sense, and many of the EU's trade partners will no longer abide it.

Conclusion

The European Union is the behemoth of global trade and investment. It is the world's leading merchandise exporter, the world's largest trader in services, and the source of over 40% of all outward investment. But like many behemoths, it moves slowly and carefully. It has trouble developing trade policies that can meet the diverse needs and perspectives of its 460 million citizens. Yet this same behemoth has taken a radical position – that human rights should be at the heart of many trade agreements.

Unfortunately, the European Union's view of human rights is often inconsistent. Although the European Union consists of twenty-five vibrant democratic nations, policymakers have not developed a process for trade policymaking that can both accommodate national trade policy needs and objectives and ensure that the public is involved, informed, and supportive of trade. EU policymakers can and should do more to ensure that public opinion can make its way up into that very insular and bureaucratic process. One key area should be human rights, yet the European Union has not focused any of its public consultations on human rights questions.[190]

EU policymakers have at times justified EU trade policy decisions as necessary for advancing or upholding human rights at home. Thus, it maintains trade barriers on beef and genetically altered corn in the interest of promoting its citizens' right to health. It created a new treaty to promote cultural diversity and to ensure that trade did not undermine national culture. But the European Union has not performed a comprehensive review of how trade policies and agreements may affect important human rights at home. Moreover, as the CAP example shows, policymakers have difficulty ensuring that domestic policies do not have a negative impact on human rights abroad. Although agricultural liberalization will not necessarily advance human rights for all of the poor, especially those in food-importing nations, the CAP story reveals how difficult it is for even the most advanced economies to ensure that external and internal trade policies are complementary and promote sustainable development at the same time.

We found that the European Union has been inconsistent in the way it has applied its two primary trade-related human rights instruments: the human rights clause and the human rights conditionality in its GSP scheme. The European Union almost always focuses on dialogue to deal with a wide range of human rights dilemmas. Moreover, when a country is economically or politically influential (as in the case of Russia), the European Union will rarely use all of the tools at its command to promote human rights. Finally, the European Union is reluctant to use trade policy tools to address economic, social, and cultural human rights violations. Some observers view this as a signal that the European Union is more committed to some human rights than others, and others argue that the European Union's commitment to the indivisibility of human rights rings hollow.

Although the European Union has worked to ban trade in certain sectors (conflict diamonds and tools for torture), it has been reluctant to use disincentives such as sanctions to address a broad range of human rights violations. Thus, without deliberate intent, it may be signaling that certain human rights are more important than others, that certain countries are easier to influence than others, and that it will not always use trade as leverage.

Given the importance of human rights to the European Union's foreign policy objectives, we were surprised that the European Union has yet to define criteria regarding when to use dialogue and when to use alternative tools to promote human rights. But EU policymakers and activists are at least thinking about these questions. For example, in May 2006, the EU Parliament "asked the Council and the Commission to ensure compatibility of trade agreements with existing UN treaties on human rights . . . and to monitor, review and reverse any negative impact of existing and proposed trade rules in respect of human rights."[191] Although the Parliament's resolution does not have the force of law, it is important. Perhaps it will prod the member states of the EU to use its sustainability impact assessments to examine the human rights impact of EU trade initiatives.

Thus, the European Union may be a behemoth, but it is not a dinosaur. The European Union's approach is evolving in the right direction: toward greater coherence between human rights and trade objectives.

6

The United States

At Cross Purposes – Americans at the Intersection of Trade and Human Rights

---

HUMAN RIGHTS DISCUSSED IN THIS CHAPTER

This chapter focuses on (1) labor rights, (2) the right to information and administrative due process, and (3) intellectual property rights, and (4) the right to health – all human rights delineated in the International Bill of Human Rights or the ILO Declaration on Fundamental Principles and Rights at Work.

Right to Political Participation
Under the International Bill of Human Rights, everyone has a right to take part in the government of his country, directly or through freely chosen representatives. The will of the people shall be the basis of the authority of government; this will shall be expressed in periodic and genuine elections which shall be universal and equal suffrage and shall be held by secret vote or by equivalent free voting procedures.

Administrative Due Process Rights
Under the International Bill of Human Rights, everyone has a right to recognition everywhere as a person before the law, protection against discrimination, the right to an effective remedy by competent national tribunals, and fair and public hearings by an independent and impartial tribunal, whether in civil, criminal, or administrative proceedings. In recognition that there cannot be democratic participation in decision making if governments do not act in a transparent and open manner, governments are required to take steps to promote the right to information, ensure due process in administrative procedures, and act in a transparent and open manner.

Labor Rights
Under the ILO Declaration on Fundamental Principles and Rights at Work, all members of the ILO, even if they have not ratified the Conventions in question, are obliged to respect, to promote, and to realize the principles concerning the fundamental rights which are the subject of those Conventions, namely (a) freedom of association and the effective recognition of the right to collective bargaining, (b) the elimination of all forms of forced or compulsory labor, (c) the effective abolition of child labor, and (d) the elimination of discrimination in employment and occupation.

Intellectual Property Rights
Under the International Bill of Human Rights, authors have a right to protection of the moral and material interests resulting from their scientific, literary, or artistic productions, tempered by the public's right to enjoy the arts and to share in scientific advancement and its benefits. This is not an easy balance to achieve. Governments have tried to protect the rights of authors through copyright, patent, and trademark regimes, but many critics argue that these regimes privilege mass manufacturers and distributors of creative works over both their authors and audiences.

The Right to Health
Under the International Bill of Human Rights, everyone has a right to medical care as well as a right to share in the benefits of scientific advancement.

Introduction

U.S. Representative Eliot Engel did not want to get between Americans and their chocolate. However, after reading a series of articles about forced child labor on cacao (the key ingredient in chocolate) plantations, he was left with a bitter taste in his mouth.[1] Recognizing that chocolate has long been America's guilty pleasure, Congressman Engel realized he would have to think creatively to address the problem. In 2001, he added a rider (an unrelated item) to an appropriations bill for the U.S. Food and Drug Administration. It required the agency to develop a label for chocolate products that would indicate that child labor was not used in the growing and harvesting of cocoa. The Republican-dominated House of Representatives passed the measure by an overwhelming margin.[2] Soon thereafter, Senator Tom Harkin, Eliot Engel's friend and a long-time activist against child labor, joined in this effort. The two men were determined to ensure that U.S. chocolate lovers were not complicit in a system of child labor.

Executives in the chocolate industry (a thirteen-billion-dollar industry in the United States alone) panicked. They feared that congressional attention – or worse, a congressionally legislated solution – could lead to public attention and ultimately lower chocolate industry sales.[3] Thus, chocolate industry leaders teamed up with Congressional staff, as well as civil society groups, labor unions, and others, to create a voluntary initiative, the Harkin–Engel Protocol, in September 2001. The Protocol's participants agreed to join forces to eliminate the worst forms of child labor in the growing and processing of cocoa beans and their derivative products. The signatories to the Protocol agreed to meet a number of date-specific actions, including developing a credible, mutually acceptable, industry-wide standard of public certification by July 1, 2005.[4]

The Harkin–Engel Protocol was historic for two reasons. First, companies throughout the chocolate supply chain (plantation owners, traders, and chocolate manufacturers) took responsibility for addressing, monitoring, and working with governments to alleviate child labor in the cocoa industry around the world. Second, it provided an example of how two U.S. officials could use their "bully pulpit" to ensure that children were not forced to work picking cacao beans.[5]

The Harkin–Engel Protocol has not yet been entirely successful.[6] Although the chocolate industry met many of the initial requirements and deadlines, they did not meet their promised July 2005 deadline of establishing an industry-wide monitoring system.[7] Nonetheless, the protocol prodded government officials (as well as corporate executives) to take steps to prevent child labor, to place children in school, and to beef up their enforcement efforts.[8] Forty-two countries in the chocolate supply chain endorsed the protocol and agreed to abide by its strictures.[9] Both Ghana and Ivory Coast developed plans and programs and asked for foreign assistance to address their child labor problems and to ensure effective enforcement.[10] As of this writing, however, children still toil in cacao plantations in West Africa.

*   *   *

The Harkin–Engel Protocol provides an example of U.S. activism at the intersection of trade and human rights. The United States often uses trade policies (both incentives and disincentives) to promote particular human rights in specific countries overseas. Yet U.S. policymakers have a hard time ensuring that its trade policies and positions (such as its agricultural subsidies for sugar or cotton) do not undermine human rights abroad and at home. With the exception of labor rights, U.S. officials do not officially try to ascertain the human rights impact of particular trade agreements on the American people or citizens abroad.[11]

In fact, the United States acts differently from other countries at the intersection of trade and human rights. First, the Congress rather than the executive branch sets the objectives for trade policymaking and maintains tight control over executive branch discretion. Second, Congress has its own human rights agenda, which includes acting on human rights issues without the involvement of the executive (as in the Chocolate Initiative example). Third, policymakers in the executive and legislative branches frequently do not act as if human rights are universal and indivisible, as outlined in the UDHR. And finally, U.S. policymakers use trade policies and agreements to advance particular human rights that the United States views as important, such as labor rights and the right to public participation.[12]

In the pages that follow, we describe how the United States government acts at the intersection of trade and human rights. The first case study examines how U.S. policymakers advance labor rights abroad through trade policies and agreements. Although Congress made labor rights an overall trade negotiating objective, policymakers are divided as to how to best advance these rights. In the second case, we show how U.S. trade policymakers use bilateral trade agreements to encourage due process rights and political participation. The environmental chapters of recent free trade agreements (FTAs) include provisions designed to encourage public submissions, public discussions, and public involvement in trade- and environment-related policymaking. But U.S. government officials have not devised an effective strategy to promote such public participation in countries where free speech rights are not protected. Finally, we examine how the United States seeks to reconcile its mandate to protect intellectual property rights with its human rights responsibility to ensure access to affordable medicines.[13] We discuss how the United States has responded to allegations that it was more devoted to protecting the IPR of its drug makers than to assisting countries overseas to provide access to affordable medicines. After the negotiation of the U.S./Australia FTA, policymakers discovered that U.S. efforts to promote transparency and accountability in drug purchasing programs overseas could make it harder for state and local governments to provide access to affordable medicines at home. This example reveals that the United States has a hard time anticipating the effect of its trade policies on human rights at home as well as abroad. U.S. policymakers often act at cross-purposes, in ways that may undermine the achievement of trade and/or human rights goals at home and abroad. For the purpose of simplicity, we often use the term "Americans" to describe citizens of the United States.

Human Rights Ethos and Conditions

U.S. citizens tend to have a different view of human rights than many of their counterparts overseas.[14] As historian Thomas McCraw notes, "Americans value competitive individualism and individual autonomy above the collective needs of the community."[15] Moreover, U.S. citizens and policymakers tend to equate human rights with human freedoms and to emphasize individual, responsibility, initiative, and competition.[16]

The United States not only has a different perspective on human rights but it also acts differently when promoting human rights.[17] As Harold Hongju Koh, the dean of Yale Law School notes, Americans have double standards on human rights. The United States does not always play by the rules, processes, and timetables of the international human rights institutions that it helped create at the end of the World War II. Yet it often uses those same standards to hold other nations accountable for their human rights practices. Moreover, the United States has lagged behind other industrialized countries in ratifying international human rights conventions (although some of the delay can be attributed to the U.S. system of checks and balances and the U.S. system of federalism. Under U.S. law, states as well as the federal government have human rights responsibilities.) Finally, the United States often prefers to use unilateral rather than multilateral tools to promote human rights.[18]

Perhaps because of these differences, America's credibility as a nation devoted to advancing human rights may be on the decline. As other countries and international bodies document and publicize U.S. human rights problems at home and abroad, fewer people see the United States as a model for their own countries.[19] Although the United States is traditionally viewed as a land of opportunity, a 2005 Pew Global Attitudes Poll found that people perceive Americans as not sufficiently interested in ensuring that governments provide individuals with the resources they need to achieve their potential.[20]

Protecting Human Rights at Home

The U.S. Constitution and its amendments outline the basic rights of U.S. citizens. Those rights have been gradually supplemented over time with new legislation such as the Americans with Disabilities Act. These rights are protected through federal and state institutions and a strong and transparent judicial system at the local, state, and federal level.

Although U.S. governance institutions are generally effective, respected international human rights observers report that the United States has many human rights problems. For example, in 2005, Amnesty International stated that the United States detained hundreds of individuals without charge and denied their basic rights, and U.S. officials sometimes used excessive force, unjustly detained aliens, imprisoned children for life without parole, relied on the death penalty, and ignored international laws.[21] Human Rights Watch concurred with these criticisms and also noted that U.S. minorities were increasingly unable to get access to resources such as health care and education.[22] For example, according to the Federal Centers for Disease Control, Hispanic Americans were most likely to be uninsured. Some 30% of Hispanics, 10% non-Hispanic white persons, and 16.5% of non-Hispanic African Americans had no health insurance in 2005.[23]

Promoting Human Rights Abroad

Since its first days of nationhood, U.S. policymakers have made advancing human rights abroad a cornerstone of U.S. foreign policy.[24] That commitment, however, has varied in intensity and strategy under different presidential administrations.[25] Although the U.S. Department of State claims that "the values captured in the Universal Declaration of Human Rights ... are consistent with the values upon which the United States was founded centuries ago," the United States concentrates on promoting certain rights, such as civil and political rights. Moreover, George W. Bush administration policymakers often conflate protecting human rights with "advancing freedom" and promoting democracy in other countries abroad.[26]

The United States uses a wide range of tools to advance its freedom agenda, including bilateral diplomacy, multilateral engagement, foreign assistance, reporting and public outreach, and economic sanctions.[27] George W. Bush administration officials relied on FTAs as an additional tool to export human rights.

Trade and Investment Overview

The United States is the world's largest single economy, and trade is an important engine of that growth. The U.S. exports and imports more goods than any other nation (whereas the EU is the world's largest trading bloc). However, the U.S. imports much more then it exports. In 2005, the U.S. trade deficit was $716 billion (6.4% of GDP), up from $611 billion (5.7% of GDP) the year before.[28] The United States has a relatively open trading regime, and protectionism is low in many sectors in which the U.S. producers are very competitive. However, the United States maintains relatively high tariffs on food, tobacco products, clothing, textiles, and footwear. The United States also maintains tariff quotas on beef imports, dairy products, sugar, peanuts, and cotton.[29] Developing country producers often find these tariff barriers particularly difficult to surmount.

The United States is deeply involved in the activities of the WTO. As noted in Chapter 1, U.S. policymakers played a major role in developing the ITO, GATT, and WTO.[30] Today trade officials frequently state that they consider the WTO "the core of international trade relations" and note that "multilateral trade negotiations are a stated priority," although it is not the only negotiating priority for these officials.[31] The United States is also an active litigant in the WTO's dispute settlement system.

Despite America's role establishing and leading the world trade regime, in recent years U.S. policymakers have taken two types of actions that may undermine the WTO system. First, U.S. trade officials have increasingly relied on unilateral (rather than multilateral) trade mechanisms under the WTO system to alter the trade practices of their trade partners. U.S. policymakers first used unilateral threats of retaliation (primarily via trade restrictions) in the 1980s to get its trade partners, particularly the Japanese, to change their trade practices. Scholars termed this approach "aggressive unilateralism." Today, the United States uses "aggressive unilateralism" to prod countries such as Ukraine and Russia to protect intellectual property. Many U.S. policymakers see this approach as a quick and effective alternative to dispute settlement under the WTO. However, others see these tactics as coercive and out of sync with international norms and law.[32]

Second, U.S. policymakers have devoted more time and effort to negotiating bilateral trade agreements (rather than focusing their trade liberalization efforts at the WTO). Soon thereafter, other nations followed suit. The U.S. focus on negotiating bilateral and regional trade agreements may also undermine the WTO (Table 6.1). In 2002, U.S. trade representative Robert Zoellick argued that by combining global regional and bilateral negotiations, "the United States is creating a competition for liberalization" at the bilateral, regional, and global levels. This competition would force other governments to make greater multilateral concessions. The Bush administration has made these FTAs the centerpiece of its trade negotiations.[33] Obviously, it is easier to negotiate bilateral and regional agreements with only one or five countries than it is to hammer out an agreement involving 151 countries. However, some officials (and many trade scholars) argue that such negotiations are trade diverting rather than trade creating. For example, in its report on U.S. trade barriers, the Brazilian government notes that it has lost trade to Mexico because of the North American Free Trade Agreement (NAFTA).[34] Alex Erwin, South Africa's former trade minister, claims that because of their varying and sometimes divergent rules, the growing plethora of bilateral trade agreements increases the compliance costs for small corporations, traders, and developing countries.

TABLE 6.1. *U.S. free trade agreements in effect or signed as of April 2007**

Name of agreement	Date signed or entered into force
U.S./Israel FTA	Entered into force September 1, 1985
U.S./Canada FTA	Implemented by P.L. 100–449 (September 28, 1988) Entered into force January 1, 1989
North American Free Trade Agreement (NAFTA)	Entered into force January 1, 1994
U.S./Jordan FTA	Entered into force December 17, 2001
U.S./Singapore FTA	Entered into force January 1, 2004
U.S./Chile FTA	Entered into force January 1, 2004
U.S./Australia FTA	Entered into force January 1, 2005
U.S./Bahrain FTA	Enter into force August 2006.
Pending FTAs	
U.S./Morocco FTA	Signed into law by President Bush August 17, 2004.
U.S/ Dominican Republic-Central America FTA (DR-CAFTA)	Signed on May 28, 2004. Not yet ratified by all member nations.
U.S./Oman FTA	Signed into law September 26, 2006.[35]
U.S./Peru Trade Promotion Agreement	Signed April 12, 2006, ratified by Peru, not yet ratified by United States
U.S./Colombia FTA	Signed February 27, 2006, not yet ratified.

Note: Table by Jan Cartwright; updated April 2007. The table does not include Malaysia, Panama, Korea, Thailand, and the UAE.

Thus, he likens these agreements to the equivalent of a tax on the trade of poor nations. Moreover, some observers see these bilateral and regional agreements as eroding the central principle of the GATT/WTO – nondiscrimination.[36] And not surprisingly, many policymakers and analysts blamed U.S. unilateralism, America's focus on bilaterals, and its unwillingness to compromise for the greater good for the collapse of the WTO Doha development round trade talks in June 2006. (The talks restarted in February 2007.)[37]

Like other industrialized countries, the United States has created several preference programs to help developing countries participate in international trade. The United States grants unilateral preferential tariff treatment to countries that qualify under the Generalized System of Preferences (GSP), the Caribbean Basic Economic Recovery Act (as amended CBTPA), the Andean Trade Preference Act (ATPA), and the African Growth and Opportunity Act (AGOA).[38]

The U.S. GSP program provides benefits for some 140 developing countries. The program encourages trade from poorer countries by providing incentives to U.S. firms to buy tariff-free products from GSP beneficiary countries.[39] GSP recipients must adhere to certain requirements, particularly related to workers' rights and the protection of intellectual property rights. The United States reserves the right to remove these benefits at the behest of U.S. firms or for a wide range of policy reasons.[40] The GSP program is not permanent, so policymakers can threaten its termination as leverage to change the behavior of GSP beneficiary countries. For example, in August 2006, U.S. Trade Representative Susan Schwab announced that U.S. officials would consider whether to limit, suspend, or withdraw the eligibility of some thirteen countries, including Brazil and India. Senator Charles Grassley, then chairman of the Senate Finance Committee, and Congressman Bill Thomas, then chairman of House Ways and Means (the two trade-writing committees), blamed these two countries for the collapse of the Doha Round of trade talks and had threatened not to renew the GSP program in general if the U.S. continued to provide the two countries with preferential treatment.[41]

The United States also provides considerable amounts of capacity-building assistance to developing countries. In 2004, the United States provided some $903 million in trade capacity-building funds. Some of these funds went to the World Bank, some to individual countries, and some to the WTO for technical assistance.[42] Unfortunately, due to budget constraints, these funds have been reduced in recent years.[43]

Linking Human Rights and Trade Agreements

U.S. policymakers have long relied on trade policy tools to change how its trade partners protect human rights. For example, in 1890, the United States banned the importation of goods manufactured by convict labor. In 1912, in response to Russian pogroms, the United States abrogated a commercial treaty with Russia. And, in 1930, Congress banned the importation of goods made by forced labor.[44] During the Clinton administration, the U.S. began to think creatively about how to provide incentives to policymakers to advance human rights. In 1998, the United States agreed to increase Cambodia's textile quotas if the

HOW TRADE POLICY IS DEVELOPED IN THE UNITED STATES AND WHERE HUMAN RIGHTS ENTERS THE DISCUSSION

The U.S. trade policymaking process begins when Congress grants authority to the executive to negotiate trade agreements. Under this authority (formerly called fast-track, now called trade promotion authority), when considering legislation approving and implementing a new trade agreement, Congress can simply approve or reject the legislation. But Congress must do so without amendment and within a fixed period of time.[45] Congress also maintains control of trade policy through resolutions and policy statements, legislative directives, and pressure that includes funding authorization, funding restrictions, informal advice, and congressional oversight.[46]

The Office of the U.S. Trade Representative (USTR) develops and coordinates trade policies and negotiations with other countries. USTR also resolves disagreements and frames issues for presidential decision.[47] But Congress has the ultimate authority to regulate trade with foreign nations. Thus, USTR not only must consult with other government agencies and the public but also must work closely with Congress. As it determines the sectors and countries with which it will negotiate, USTR also talks with representatives from other U.S. government agencies.[48] Senior U.S. government officials from seventeen agencies meet as the Trade Policy Staff Committee.[49] This committee not only makes decisions on trade but it also sponsors hearings to obtain public comment on various FTAs or issues.[50] *The public may express human rights concerns at this point.*

If these officials cannot reach agreement, the Trade Policy Review Group reviews options.[51] If still no agreement is found, executives in the White House (either the National Economic Council or the National Security Council) will decide.[52]

USTR is obligated to seek advice from the broader public and from some twenty-seven formal advisory committees comprising some 700 individuals. Each advisory committee is required to prepare a report on proposed trade agreements for the administration and Congress, which are then made available to the public on USTR's Web site. There are three tiers of trade policy advisors. The most important advisory body, the Advisory Committee for Trade Policy and Negotiations, is charged with considering trade policy issues in the context of the overall national interest.[53] The second tier includes four policy advisory committees appointed by USTR alone or in conjunction with other key departments such as Agriculture, Labor, and the Environmental Protection Agency. The third tier includes twenty-two sectoral and technical advisory committees, which focus on the trade needs of economic interests.[54] Most of the individuals on these advisory committees are political appointees, and they tend to come from groups with a vested commercial interest in trade.[55] In particular, the lower-level advisory committees are generally oriented to meet the needs of producers.[56] However, in recent years the U.S.

government began to include a broader cross section of views, including those of environmentalists and representatives of civil society.[57] *Although this structure is not organized to address broad issues that don't fit in such neat sectoral or economy wide boxes, this is another point where human rights considerations can enter the discussion.*

Once a trade agreement has been negotiated, Congress has strict procedures and timetables for reviewing and approving it.[58] Floor debate is limited to twenty hours in each chamber of Congress.[59] At least seventeen federal agencies are charged with monitoring and enforcing the trade agreements signed by the United States. The Congressional agency, the U.S. Government Accountability Office (GAO) claims that U.S. government agencies are overwhelmed by the sheer number of these agreements. GAO concluded that the U.S. government cannot maximize the benefits of its trade agreements because it cannot completely fulfill its monitoring and enforcement responsibilities.[60]

All U.S. trade policymaking must be done in a transparent manner and must comply with federal rulemaking procedures established under the Administrative Procedure Act and U.S. trade legislation. Agencies must seek comments and respond to them. Rulemaking notices are published in the Federal Register; final rules are published in the Code of Federal Regulations online.[61] USTR also posts background information, including the reports of advisory committees, on its Web site. But USTR's Web site is not interactive. And the United States, like most nations, conducts trade negotiations in secret.

As Figure 6.1 illuminates, policymakers as well as constituents can bring human rights concerns up during the policy formation, negotiation, and implementation process. But with the exception of labor rights, the U.S. government does not weigh the impact of a proposed trade agreement on human rights at home or abroad.[62]

Cambodian government effectively enforced its labor laws and worked with factory owners to protect the fundamental rights of its workers. The agreement came into effect on December 31, 2001. The agreement was possible because at that time, Cambodia was not a member of the WTO, and thus this policy did not violate most-favored nation principles. The ILO agreed to monitor working conditions and to make the results of its findings public.[63] The agreement was phased out in 2005, when the textile quotas ended.[64] However, using World Bank funds, the ILO continues to monitor labor rights in this sector through the "Better Factories Program. Consequently, the U.S. State Department has reported that workers rights for employees in this sector continue to improve. State Department observers note there has been some spillover into the economy as a whole, but in general, due to a lack of interest, funds, and expertise, the government does

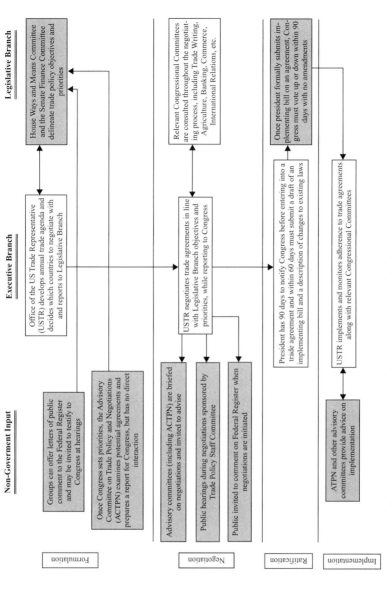

FIGURE 6.1. Charting the process. U.S. trade policy formation. Shaded boxes indicate some of the decision points where human rights can enter the process.

a poor job of protecting the labor rights of Cambodian workers.[65] Nonetheless, this agreement illuminates how incentives might be used to promote human rights without distorting trade.

U.S. policymakers are not reluctant to use sanctions to prod other governments to protect particular human rights. In 1986, Congress enacted comprehensive sanctions to push South Africa to end its system of apartheid.[66] On October 27, 1998, President Clinton signed the International Religious Freedom Act, which allowed the U.S. government to put in place sanctions against countries if they are determined to have engaged in or tolerated severe violations of religious freedom.[67] President Clinton also applied sanctions against Sudan under the 1977 International Emergency Economic Powers Act, citing Sudan's human rights violations. President Bush extended these sanctions in 2002.[68] After the United Nations Security Council prohibited all states from exporting weapons to Sierra Leone, Angola, and the Democratic Republic of the Congo, Congress passed the Clean Diamond Trade Act in April 2003. President Bush continued the ban on the importation of uncertified rough diamonds from Sierra Leone and Liberia.[69]

However, in contrast with many of their foreign counterparts, U.S. policymakers are comfortable using *unilateral* trade sanctions to defend human rights. For example, under the Helms–Burton Act, the United States maintains an embargo on Cuba because of the country's repression of political rights.[70] On January 7, 2003, Congress passed the Burmese Freedom and Democracy Act of 2003, noting that the Burmese government "continues egregious human rights violations against Burmese citizens." The Congress banned importation of any article that is a product of Burma, authorized the president to assist democracy activists, and called on the Secretary of State to report on the effect of the act upon Burma and the Burmese people.[71]

Congress also uses its ability to approve or disapprove normal trade relations as a tool to affect the human rights behavior of other countries. U.S. policymakers grant or have granted MFN status (or normal trade relations) to all members of the WTO or through bilateral compacts (such as friendship and commerce treaties or executive trade agreements). As of June 2006, the United States denies MFN tariff status to three countries: Cuba, Laos, and North Korea.[72] However, Congress has also twice modified the practice of providing such nondiscriminatory treatment by suspending MFN to countries and areas under communist control, in 1951 and 1962. (The United States justified this act for national security reasons.) In 1962, Congress modified this language to include "any country or area dominated by Communism."[73] However, in 1974, Congress required the president to restore nondiscriminatory treatment if he determines and reports to Congress that a country is not in violation of the requirements of the freedom of emigration (Jackson–Vanik) amendment or if he waives full compliance with such requirements under specified conditions.[74] In determining whether to grant MFN, policymakers consider how a country addresses other human rights issues beyond the right to emigrate.[75]

The United States also uses congressional hearings about permanent normal trade relations as a tool to bring attention to the extent to which some countries, such as Russia and Vietnam, protect human rights. Although this strategy provides no leverage on these countries, it does signal that the United States views protecting certain human rights (such as freedom of speech, and religious rights) as a priority for trade policymaking.[76]

Finally, as shown by the Harkin–Engel Protocol, members of Congress monitor human rights and actively develop trade-related legislation to address particular human rights issues. For example, after learning that U.S. technology was being used by repressive regimes in China and elsewhere in the world to censor Internet activity, Congressman Chris Smith introduced legislation to promote unrestricted access to information on the Internet.[77]

Current Areas of Tensions between U.S. Trade and Human Rights Priorities

Linking Trade and Labor Rights: An Activist Abroad While Indifferent at Home

On November 7, 2006, the earth moved for those individuals who follow the U.S. debate over trade and labor rights. After both houses of Congress changed hands from Republican to Democratic control, the leaders of the House Ways and Means and Senate Finance committees promised a new approach to trade policymaking. In March 2007, they offered the Bush Administration what they called "A Grand Bargain." The Bargain committed the Democrats to trying to win approval of Bush trade agreement priorities (various free trade agreements and if completed the Doha Round of WTO trade talks) if the administration agreed to major changes to key elements of the Bush administration approach to trade agreements.[78] While the "Grand Bargain" addressed a wide range of concerns about trade policy, the most important aspect of the proposal related to labor rights. Specifically, the Democrats called on the administration to require that all parties to future free trade agreements commit themselves to the core ILO labor standards rather than simply to enforce their own labor laws (as the Bush administration has required in earlier FTAs). The core labor standards include:

- freedom of association and the effective recognition of the right to collective bargaining;

- the elimination of all forms of forced or compulsory labor;
- the effective abolition of child labor;
- and the elimination of discrimination with respect to employment and occupation.

This proposed approach would commit the United States to adhere to the same standards that it asks its trading partners to provide and enforce. By so doing, the United States would acknowledge to its trade partners that it also has work to do to improve worker rights and to meet its obligations as a member of the ILO. But as of June 2007, the administration, many House Republicans, and Democrats could not find common ground on how to insert these provisions in pending FTAs. Administration officials and some Republicans claimed that some U.S. trade partners might challenge U.S. labor rights practices under the dispute settlement mechanism and thereby undermine U.S. sovereignty. Moreover, some Republicans members argued that the Democrats were using trade to change U.S. labor law.[79] However, according to the ILO, the U.S. committed to gradually realize these standards when it signed the ILO Declaration in 1998.[80]

This tug of war over how trade and labor rights should be linked is not new, but it has become an increasingly important issue in obtaining Congressional approval of trade agreements. The United States first included labor rights issues in a side agreement of NAFTA, during the presidency of George H. W. Bush (1988–1992). Although the Bush administration did the bulk of negotiating, NAFTA was completed under President William Jefferson Clinton. NAFTA, a trade agreement among the United States, Canada, and Mexico, provided a mechanism (the North American Agreement on Labor Cooperation [NAALC]) to investigate and discuss labor rights problems within any of the three participating nations. In addition, nongovernmental organizations, trade unions, business representatives, and other interested parties could submit complaints alleging noncompliance with the labor provisions to national administrative offices created in each of the three countries.[81] However, some U.S. labor and human rights advocates did not like the NAFTA approach to trade and labor rights because it required each party to enforce its own labor laws (the standards of which were often lower than internationally accepted core labor standards). Also, NAFTA's labor provisions were stipulated in side agreements rather than in the body of the trade agreement. These advocates wanted Congress to press the administration to take a more comprehensive, enforceable, and binding approach.

The Clinton administration negotiated the next major trade agreement after NAFTA, the U.S./Jordan FTA. In contrast to NAFTA, in this agreement the two parties agreed to place the labor rights provisions in the main text. The parties pledged to strive to ensure that domestic labor laws incorporated ILO principles, to effectively enforce domestic labor laws, and not to waive or derogate from those laws as an encouragement for trade or investment. These obligations were enforceable obligations subject to dispute settlement under the agreement. Although the AFL-CIO, a U.S. confederation of labor unions, described the labor rights commitments as "modest," it supported the agreement and fought for its congressional approval.[82]

But the Clinton administration left office before Congress considered the U.S./Jordan FTA, leaving the Bush administration to defend it before Congress. Many members of Congress wanted to quickly approve the agreement; they wanted to reward Jordan for its political moderation and its economic stewardship.[83]

Congress quickly divided on whether the Jordan model should become a template for future trade agreements or whether it went beyond the instructions Congress provided under trade promotion authority. For example, Senator Charles Grassley noted that the Jordan Agreement should not be a model for future trade agreements: "No one really knows what the 'Jordan Standard' is. In fact, when we held a hearing on the Jordan Free Trade Agreement on March 20, 2001, in the Senate Finance Committee, one of the most controversial issues raised was what the labor and environmental provisions of the Jordan Free Trade Agreement actually mean." He cited conflicting testimony of senior U.S. trade officials.[84] Some Republican members of Congress didn't like the idea that Jordan could challenge U.S. adherence to international labor standards, although such a challenge was unlikely. Moreover, these members didn't like the strong emphasis on labor rights within the agreement. Republican Senator Phil Gramm was particularly alarmed. He warned, "We are literally transferring a degree of American sovereignty in labor . . . areas to decision-making entities that will be beyond the control of the United States."[85]

These members demanded that the U.S. and Jordanian governments issue a side letter stating that the two countries did not anticipate a labor-related trade dispute.[86] Robert Zoellick, then U.S. Trade Representative, agreed to this strategy. The Jordanian Ambassador to the United States and the U.S. Trade Representative sent each other the exact same letter. It said, "I would expect few if any differences to arise between our two Governments over the interpretation or application of the Agreement. . . . In particular, my Government would not expect or intend to apply the Agreement's dispute settlement enforcement procedures to secure its rights under the Agreement in a manner that results in blocking trade."[87] But this step to appease the Republicans infuriated some Democratic members of the House Ways and Means Committee. In the House

Report on the Implementing Act of the Jordan FTA, they stressed, "We are disturbed by the precedent set by the exchange of letters." They noted that the letters were not binding commitments. It was clear that the administration and many Republicans were unwilling to accept trade sanctions as a tool to enforce labor obligations in trade agreements and they were registering their disagreement with that approach.[88] Despite these disagreements, in 2001, the Jordan FTA passed the U.S. Congress unanimously by voice vote.[89]

Yet Congress was quite clear that it wanted to use trade to advance labor rights abroad. In the Trade Promotion Act of 2002, Congress delineated labor obligations as *overall* trade negotiating objectives, *principal* negotiating objectives, and as *priorities to address U.S. competitiveness*.[90] Moreover, Congress stated that trade agreements negotiated under this law should require trade partners to effectively enforce their own labor laws; trade agreements should be designed to "strengthen the capacity of U.S. trading partners to promote respect for core labor standards, and to ensure that labor practices and policies do not arbitrarily or unjustifiably discriminate against U.S. exports."[91] Finally, the Act also asserted that, to maintain "United States competitiveness in the global economy," the president shall encourage cooperation between the WTO and the ILO, work to promote respect for core labor standards, and review the impact of future trade agreements on U.S. employment and labor markets.[92] With these provisions, Congress signaled that it would closely monitor how the executive handled labor rights concerns within trade agreements.[93]

Despite this explicit mandate, policymakers, business and labor leaders, and other members of civil society were and remain divided as to how to incorporate labor rights in trade agreements. Many Republican members of Congress were unenthusiastic about linking trade and labor rights.[94] Some business leaders argued that labor rights were nontrade issues and should be governed outside the trade agreement. Other business leaders agree that labor should be addressed in the context of trade, but they were unwilling to accept sanctions linked to labor standards, fearing that would alienate potential U.S. trade partners.[95] Labor and human rights organizations, in contrast, insisted those enforceable workers' rights provisions must be in the core of any agreements approved under fast track. And they stressed that such provisions should clearly delineate internationally accepted labor standards.[96] Many, but not all, Democrats agreed with that perspective, and they had public opinion behind them. Polling data revealed that most Americans polled want labor standards to be incorporated into trade agreements.[97] Americans saw this issue as one of morality. A June 2005 poll found that 75% of Americans agreed with the statement, "If people in other countries are making products that we use, this creates a moral obligation for us to make efforts to ensure that they do not have to work in harsh or unsafe conditions."[98]

Given these diverse perspectives, the George W. Bush administration found itself in a difficult position on labor rights. Like many Republicans in Congress, it was not enthusiastic about linking labor rights and trade agreements. But the USTR had to respond to the Congressional mandates (and, to a lesser extent, public concerns). The Bush administration decided to include labor rights within the body of trade agreements and make some but not all labor rights provisions enforceable under dispute settlement.[99]

Since 2002, the George W. Bush administration has developed several different approaches to promoting labor rights within its FTAs. These approaches recognize that every trade partner is different – some countries have inadequate labor laws and conditions, some countries do not do a good job of enforcing their laws, and other countries have minor labor law problems. But these models have not satisfied many individuals concerned with labor rights. For example, although USTR's Labor Advisory Committee for Trade Negotiations and Trade Policy (in 2002 comprising some 60 labor union leaders and a few academics) agreed that different countries have different labor rights conditions, they viewed every Bush administration FTA as a "back track from the minimal workers' rights provisions of the Jordan Agreement." The Labor Advisory Committee also stressed that under the Jordan agreement parties can bring a dispute regarding the other party's failure to comply with any provision of the labor chapter, including the commitments on nonderogation and ILO standards. However, under the Chile and Singapore agreements, "complaints regarding these two key commitments cannot be brought before dispute resolution at all. In fact, the only labor provision that is subject to dispute resolution in both agreements is the commitment to effectively enforce domestic laws . . . And while the dispute resolution procedures and remedies were identical for the labor environment, and commercial provisions of the Jordan FTA, the labor . . . enforcement provisions in the Chile and Singapore FTAs are both different from and weaker than the provisions for the enforcement of the agreements' commercial obligations." The Labor Advisory Committee recommended that Congress reject both agreements.[100]

The Bush administration countered that the Singapore and Chile labor provisions satisfy the TPA objective of making available equivalent procedures for all matters covered by the TPA principal negotiating objectives. USTR added that when monetary assessments are collected in labor disputes, the funds are to be used for appropriate labor initiatives designed to remedy the problem.[101]

But the Labor Advisory Committee was not assuaged. Since 2002, it has extensively reviewed every FTA and advised Congress to reject every agreement (Chile, Australia, Morocco, Central America, Dominican Republic, Bahrain, Oman, and Peru).[102] The Labor Advisory Committee was not alone in its criticism. Human Rights Watch called for enforcement parity for all trade agreement obligations and a more meaningful system of dispute settlement, in the belief that governments cannot effectively police each other on labor rights.[103]

Although the labor provisions in these FTAs were widely criticized in the United States, they received a more positive response from some U.S. FTA partners. Government officials from Jordan and Morocco recognized that U.S. labor demands gave them political cover to take politically difficult action and improve labor laws.[104] According to USTR, countries such as Chile, Morocco, Oman, and Bahrain have updated their laws to meet international standards. In July 2006, Oman's government issued a royal decree significantly reforming its labor laws and clarifying that unions will be free to operate without government interference. But the House Ways and Means Democrats stressed that the decree did not address areas in Oman's labor law that fall short of international standards.[105]

Although officials in America's FTA partner countries change their laws to meet U.S. expectations, they may not be willing or able to devote adequate resources to enforcement. In May 2006, the National Labor Committee of the United States documented substandard conditions in one-quarter of the 100 garment factories in Jordan. Most of the workers in these factories were guest workers from Bangladesh and China working without full pay in substandard conditions. U.S. trade officials told the Senate Finance Committee that if these allegations were true, they would violate Jordan's FTA commitments. However, these officials stressed that the United States would work with Jordan to address the issue before considering dispute settlement provisions in the FTA. The Jordanian minister of trade and industry told reporters that the country's inspection regime appeared to have "failed us miserably," but the government would work to ensure that violations of human rights, labor rights, or human trafficking do not reoccur on Jordanian soil.[106]

Under trade promotion authority, Congress set forth as a principal negotiating objective that the United States should help strengthen the capacity of its trade partners to promote respect for core labor standards. In this regard, Congress has authorized general trade capacity building assistance and has also provided specific funds for specific FTAs. But the George W. Bush administration repeatedly tried to cut the budget of the Bureau of International Labor Affairs, which directs labor rights capacity building.[107] Congress also shares some blame for not backing up promised aid with real money and expertise.[108] Nonetheless, members of Congress did convince the administration to agree to provide significant funds for capacity building linked to particular FTAs. For example, in agreements such as DR-CAFTA, the United States created trade capacity-building working groups. In these working groups, the United States' FTA partners specified their needs, and NGOs, firms, and governments in the United States specified what they could do to help.[109]

The United States also uses trade preference programs to promote labor rights linked to trade.[110] As noted earlier, GSP beneficiaries are required to protect U.S.-determined labor rights both in their laws and in practice. If these beneficiaries do not do so, their benefits may be reviewed and possibly removed.[111] But the United States rarely removes countries from the beneficiary list. For example, Bangladesh and Guatemala have been frequently reviewed for labor rights violations, but they have not lost their benefits.[112] According to scholars, Kimberley Ann Elliott and Richard Freeman, "workers' right conditionality works reasonably well in the GSP program because the target countries are mostly small and they perceive that denying U.S. demands will have higher costs than complying with them."[113] However, some analysts note that the United States uses these provisions in an inconsistent manner. For example, it is reluctant to use these provisions in countries where stable economic or strategic relationships are important U.S. foreign policy goals.[114]

The same FTAs that allow U.S. policymakers to contest labor standards abroad also provide mechanisms for the United States' FTA partners to criticize the labor rights practices in the United States which may distort trade. In general, these consultations have not led the United States to change policies.[115] However, in July 2004, the Department of Labor and Mexico's Foreign Relations Secretariat signed a joint declaration and two letters of agreement aimed at protecting and promoting the rights of Mexican migrant workers in the United States. The United States agreed to develop initiatives to improve compliance with and awareness of workplace laws and regulations protecting Mexican workers in North Carolina and other areas in the United States.[116]

American activism on labor rights abroad contrasts with Congressional attitudes about America's labor rights practices at home. U.S. performance on labor rights is mixed.[117] The International Confederation of Free Trade Unions (ICFTU) reported to the WTO that some 40% of all government workers, agricultural workers, domestic workers, and independent contractors are denied basic collective bargaining rights. Private sector employers often fight union organizing drives. Employers use the bankruptcy system to void collective bargaining agreements (for example, at auto parts maker Delphi) and to terminate pension plans. When employers act illegally, they rarely face penalties or an effective judicial system. The ICFTU stressed that the United States needs to ratify key ILO conventions to ensure the labor rights of its own people.[118] But many members of Congress are unwilling or uninterested in ensuring that the United States adopts and upholds the highest standards for workers. (Of course, this could change under a Democratic Congress and Executive.)

In sum, the United States promotes labor rights abroad with bilateral trade agreements. The countries that accept these agreements in some cases change some of their laws to meet internationally accepted standards and strive to enforce these laws. But many of America's FTA partners have a hard time enforcing their laws because of lack of resources, political will, or both.

As of November 2006, U.S. FTAs do not directly link trade benefits to compliance with all of the core international labor standards (they exclude non-discrimination). Instead, they require countries to effectively enforce their laws on the books.

As noted, the Democrats are trying to prod the U.S. to include adherence to all core ILO standards within trade agreements. But many Republican members of Congress insist that they will not accept an approach to linking trade and labor standards that binds the United States to adhere to ILO conventions that Congress has not agreed to or which subjects the United States to binding dispute settlement under the agreement.[119] They are not the only concerned parties. Growing numbers of governments are balking at labor rights conditions. In November 2006, Malaysia said it would resist U.S. pressure to include labor standards in the trade agreement.[120] The United States and South Korea were unable to find common ground on the treatment of North Korean workers in export processing zones that border the two Koreas in the FTA agreement finalized April 1, 2007. (South Korea maintains that the zones promote democratization and capitalism.)[121] Thus, Congress may continue to struggle to find ways to advance labor rights abroad while trying to mitigate the negative effects of globalization at home.

People Who Live in Glass Houses Won't Throw Stones: Exporting Transparency, Political Participation, and Due Process Rights with Trade Agreements

America's founders learned a valuable lesson from King George. If taxation (tariffs) without representation is tyranny, trade policies must be made by the people for the people (and in the U.S. case by democratically elected representatives).

The Founding Fathers took that lesson to heart. According to James Madison (former president and an author of *The Federalist Papers*), "A Popular

Government, without popular information, or the means of acquiring it, is but a Prologue to a Farce or a Tragedy; or perhaps both. Knowledge will forever govern ignorance: And a people who mean to be their own Governors, must arm themselves with the power which knowledge gives." Madison recognized that the U.S. democracy could not prosper if the public did not participate in decision making. He stressed that the only way that people can hold government accountable is through access to government information.[122]

U.S. policymakers argue that "transparency is the starting point for ensuring the efficiency, and ultimately the stability of a rules-based environment for goods crossing the border."[123] Thus, they make a business case for transparency. But U.S. policymakers also recognize that transparency can facilitate human rights, creating the virtuous circle delineated by Madison. Government institutions will not function effectively without feedback. Citizens cannot provide such feedback without information about what government is doing or without the ability to participate in policymaking.

According to the UNDP, democratic, transparent, and accountable governance can also yield other important human rights benefits. When institutions function badly, the poor and vulnerable tend to suffer the most because they often lack the resources to influence public policy. Transparent, accountable governance can foster democracy, capitalism, and political stability. Thus, by promoting transparency, the rule of law, and political participation, policymakers can promote many human rights.[124]

Although U.S. efforts to link trade and political participation are relatively new, the United States has been promoting transparency and due process rights in trade agreements since the end of World War II. Representatives of exporting interests in the United States became increasingly vocal about the wide range of trade barriers they encountered overseas and their inability to influence the use of these barriers. They were particularly concerned about British preferences and cartels, which many U.S. exporters saw as discriminatory and opaque.[125] Members of the House Special Committee on Postwar Economic Policy and Planning, the Colmer Committee, echoed these concerns.[126] Although they didn't describe their objectives as "promoting transparency," the architects of the postwar trade system determined that they must find ways to make trade rulemaking less opaque and more accountable. To succeed at that task, these officials recognized that they would need to work with their counterparts from other nations to set up rules governing how policymakers developed, published, and administered trade-related regulations. These rules and procedures were delineated in the GATT.

From 1948 to 1964, GATT contracting parties were required to promptly publish laws, regulations, and judicial decisions affecting imports and exports

(GATT Article X). In this way, exporting interests could learn about legal developments affecting trade and respond to them. GATT contracting parties gradually strengthened these notification requirements and members were also required to administer trade related laws, regulations, rulings, and agreements in a uniform, impartial, and reasonable manner.[127]

Today, the WTO has strong rules for transparency and due process. The WTO requires governments to make their trade laws and regulations transparent and public and encourages governments that cannot settle their disputes through bilateral discussions to submit them to binding dispute settlement under the WTO. According to the Canadian economist and former trade official Dr. Sylvia Ostry, the United States was the major force behind these provisions.[128] Under the negotiating rubric of trade facilitation, U.S. policymakers still work to promote transparency in trade regulation and administration at the WTO.[129]

However, in recent years, the United States has actively promoted transparency, due process, and public participation in trade policymaking with its FTAs.[130] The United States does not aim to promote transparency abroad as a means of promoting human rights per se. Yet it clearly links the two, stressing the importance of public access to information. Under the Bipartisan Trade Promotion Act of 2002, Congress required the Executive "to obtain wider and broader application of the principle of transparency through: increased and more timely public access to information regarding trade issues and the activities of international trade institutions; increased openness at the WTO and other international trade fora by increasing public access to appropriate meetings, proceedings, and submissions, including with regard to dispute settlement and investment; and increased and more timely public access to all notifications and supporting documentation submitted by parties to the WTO."[131] Congress also required trade officials to "achieve increased transparency and opportunity for the participation of affected parties in the development of regulations." The legislation also states that trade negotiators should "establish consultative mechanisms among parties to trade agreements to promote increased transparency in developing guidelines, rules, regulations and laws."[132] Finally, Congress wants negotiators to ensure that efforts to protect public health, labor, the environment or public safety are transparent and "do not arbitrarily or unjustifiably discriminate against United States exports or serve as disguised barriers to trade."[133]

All U.S. FTAs approved since 2002 have a chapter on transparency.[134] (There are transparency provisions in other chapters of these FTAs, such as the technical barriers to trade [TBT] chapters, but this book does not discuss them.) Although the language in these chapters varies from FTA to FTA, in general they set rules to facilitate the right of information. They require governments to publish, in advance, laws, rules, procedures, and regulations affecting trade, thereby giving "persons of the other party that are directly affected by an agency's process . . . a reasonable opportunity to present facts and arguments in support of their positions prior to any final administrative action." These agreements also have a section on review and appeal, designed to give each party a reasonable opportunity to support or defend their respective positions.[135]

Although the United States has been trying to promote transparency in trade regulations for over fifty years, U.S. efforts to promote public participation are relatively new (since 1992). The United States and its FTA partners first experimented with public participation provisions in NAFTA in *both the labor and environmental side agreements*. (This chapter focuses on the environmental provisions.) As part of that agreement, Mexico, Canada, and the United States created an international organization, the Commission for Environmental Cooperation of North America (CEC). The Commission includes a public advisory committee, comprised of five citizens from each of the three countries, to advise the Council (the Joint Public Advisory Committee).[136] It also set up a mechanism, the Citizen Submissions on Enforcement Matters, to enable members of the public from any one of the three countries to submit a claim when a government allegedly is not enforcing its environmental laws.[137] The Commission investigates the allegation and issues nonbinding resolutions. These investigations have occasionally led governments to change course. For example, according to a study of that process by a member of the Council, it led the Mexican government to promise remediation in the case of toxic pollutants abandoned at a lead smelter in Tijuana, and Mexico's president declared the Cozumel Coral Reef a protected area.[138]

The George W. Bush administration had two principal reasons to promote public participation with FTAs. First, they wanted to use trade agreements to encourage democracy, particularly in the Middle East, and to cement democracy in Central America.[139] They recognized that democracy could not simply be exported; some of their FTA partners needed help to strengthen democratic institutions, processes, and accountability.[140] Second, they acknowledged that these FTAs were often unpopular at home and abroad. By prodding its FTA partners to encourage their citizens to participate in and comment on trade policies, they hoped that trade policies, agreements, and institutions will be perceived as legitimate and eventually gain a base of public support in these nations.[141]

In September 2003, U.S. Trade Representative Zoellick asked his team working on environmental issues (the Trade and Environment Policy Advisory Committee [TEPAC]) to develop new strategies to foster public participation in trade agreements, akin to the environmental review process in the United States. Under the TPA, all proposed trade agreements undergo an environmental review process, which includes a process for public input. These reviews discuss how the partner government promotes the environment and informs the public about environmental laws and regulations.[142] He also tasked TEPAC to suggest ways to increase public involvement in matters regarding trade and the environment.[143] Meanwhile, Senator Max Baucus, ranking Democrat on the Senate Finance Committee, also pushed USTR to replicate and strengthen the citizens' submission process.[144] Baucus felt strongly that public dialogue is the best way to improve the environment.[145] USTR's advisors in TEPAC concurred, noting that "public participation helps ensure that an agreement's provisions operate as intended and greatly increases opportunities to . . . enhance capacity building and sustainable development efforts."[146]

Working with their counterparts in the Environmental Protection Agency and the Department of State, policymakers in USTR developed three models for public participation for the environmental chapters of FTAs. The first model, designed for FTA partners with strong records on sustainability and a robust democracy (such as Australia), had minimal public participation provisions in the environmental chapter. The second model was designed for countries with comparatively weak systems of environmental regulation and accountability or countries relatively new to democracy. The United States used this model for Chile, Bahrain, Oman, Morocco, and Singapore.[147] Under this model, the bilateral FTA partners set up an advisory committee, an Environmental Affairs Council, which would meet regularly and engage the public in discussion on the environment. The Council would seek appropriate opportunities for public participation in the development and implementation of cooperative environmental activities. In addition, each party should provide for the receipt and consideration of public communications on matters related to this chapter.[148] Policymakers also agreed to work with their FTA counterparts and environmentalists from their FTA partners to provide capacity-building assistance to support public participation.[149]

Senator Max Baucus played a major role in developing a third, more extensive, approach. In 2004, he called on USTR to put the public participation provisions directly in the trade agreement, to develop benchmarks and "ways to measure progress over time," and to find ways to encourage objective monitoring and scrutiny by the public.[150] The Central American/Dominican Republic Free Trade Agreement (DR-CAFTA) is USTR's first test of that model.

In February 2005, the United States and its six partners in DR-CAFTA agreed to establish a mechanism and secretariat that would allow the general public to submit petitions regarding the operation of the agreement's environmental provisions. If members of the public from any party to DR-CAFTA believe that any party is not effectively enforcing its environmental laws, they can make a new submission to this subbody, which reports to the Environmental Affairs Council established under the DR-CAFTA. The agreement also states that each party should review and respond to such communications in accordance with its own domestic procedures.[151] To develop a workable system, the United States agreed to fund the first year of the secretariat's work.[152]

In addition to setting up a complaint mechanism, USTR and trade and/or environmental ministries in each of the Central American Free Trade Agreement (CAFTA) countries reached out to their constituents on the environmental chapters. They held hearings, called for public comments, and published their new regulations on the Web and in print. Each environment ministry developed a Web site on environmental activities and outreach.[153] Under pressure from Senator Baucus and other members of Congress, USTR has agreed to replicate this model in other FTAs such as those with Colombia and Peru.[154] The draft Colombia FTA notes, "Each party shall ensure that judicial, quasi-judicial or administrative proceedings are available under its law to provide sanctions or remedies for violations of its environmental laws. Such proceedings shall be fair, equitable and transparent . . . and open to the public."[155] Article 18.6 of the Peru agreement notes, "each party shall promote public awareness of its environmental laws, including procedures for interested persons to request a Party's competent authorities to investigate alleged violations of its environmental laws." It also encourages and solicits public opinion on the environment and encourages the public to make submissions.[156]

In general, TEPAC has been enthusiastic about these approaches to encouraging greater public participation. But some members of TEPAC worried about the appropriateness of this approach, particularly in countries such as Bahrain and Oman. For example, three members of TEPAC stressed, "It is not enough to merely write about procedures for public dialogue in the agreement when the freedom to participate is so impaired by governmental interference. These concerns should be addressed."[157] The same three members have expressed similar concerns about the Oman environmental public participation provisions. They noted that the "Omani government's imposed interference with freedom of expression, freedom of assembly and other civil and political rights will make it difficult, if not impossible, for civil society to participate." They stressed that "public participation does not actually exist" in the country, citing the U.S. Department of State's 2004 country report on human rights practices in Oman. These members concluded, "Implementation of the public participation measures must be ensured. We believe it is essential that this issue be addressed firmly in the FTA or in a side letter. . . . American policy today is to foster democracy in Middle Eastern countries, and to make trade policy a partner in this process. This agreement can . . . advance that policy, or it can be seen as a tacit acquiescence in the very undemocratic practices we seek to have changed."[158]

USTR has tried to respond to these concerns about public participation provisions by providing training in environmental decision making. For example, it hired the Environmental Law Institute to provide training to set up accountable environmental institutions and processes in Morocco.[159] USTR officials told us that they plan to replicate this training in Bahrain and Oman. But these strategies may not assuage critics. The mere placement of participation provisions in trade agreements and the provision of training cannot magically stimulate democracy. Such an approach may not work in countries lacking a tradition of political participation or free speech. Moreover, it may appear to violate another country's sovereignty or cultural mores.

However, we found evidence that FTA negotiations may prod some policymakers to bolster their public outreach efforts during the negotiating process. For example, when Thailand entered into FTA negotiations with the United States, the Thai prime minister pledged to ensure greater public involvement in the Thai trade policymaking process.[160] USTR claimed that during the DR-CAFTA negotiations, El Salvador and Guatemala held their first public hearings on trade. Mexico has maintained public consultations on trade begun during NAFTA. Trade policymakers may be learning that because the policymaking process is so contentious, they must bring the public along by involving more citizens from the start.

In sum, U.S. efforts to promote transparency and due process rights, within the transparency chapters of the FTA (as well as in other chapters), aim to make America's FTA partners "glass houses" – open and transparent. Such steps certainly facilitate commerce, but citizens may also benefit from a government that is more open, accountable, and accessible. The U.S. government has evolved several different approaches to encouraging public participation. These provisions occur mainly in the environmental chapters of the FTAs as well as chapters on administration, transparency, and others. Policymakers have taken these steps in the belief that they will build greater public support for trade agreements and teach the habits of democratic governance. But U.S. policymakers have not fully considered how to use these provisions to improve human rights in countries where freedom of speech and participation are restricted.

An Unhealthy Approach to Protecting IPR and Access
to Affordable Medicines

In 2003, then U.S. Trade Representative Robert Zoellick wrote an op-ed attempting to clarify the U.S. government's position on the relationship between public health and trade. He noted, "The link between economic growth and public health could not be clearer. Improvements in public health are not only a consequence of economic growth, they also lay the foundation for it. As AGOA demonstrates, trade can drive economic growth, openness and opportunity, so as to improve people's lives and ameliorate poverty. As incomes grow, families and societies have the means to improve health."[161]

But many observers disagree with this assessment. They stress that under international human rights law, governments have an immediate obligation to ensure that their citizens have affordable access to the medicines they need, especially in times of public health crises. In particular, they criticize the United States for what they perceive as placing commercial interests over the public interest – by protecting the intellectual property rights of big pharmaceutical firms at the expense of public health. Critics also allege that the United States is forcing its bilateral trade agreement partners to accept stronger IPR standards than those stipulated in the WTO TRIPS agreement. Finally, they note that the United States does not weigh the views of public health advocates as it makes trade policy decisions at the intersection of trade and human rights. This section delineates how U.S. trade policymakers have responded to these concerns.

Critics of U.S. IPR and public health policies are building on a growing sentiment that the U.S. approach to IPR may undermine development in many countries around the world.[162] These critics allege that when developing country policymakers institute stronger protections for IPR, they drain scarce money and manpower from other important endeavors, such as education.[163] For example, the World Bank recently estimated that the United States would receive some nineteen billion dollars per year from developing countries as net rent transfers from the patent provisions of TRIPS.[164]

In recent years, HIV/AIDS advocates such as Act Up, consumer advocates such as Jamie Love of the Consumer Project on Technology, public health advocates such as Center for Policy Analysis on Trade and Health, and development advocates such as Oxfam have argued that U.S. multilateral and bilateral trade policies undermine not only development but also access to affordable medicines.[165] They note that the United States (working with Japan and other countries with strong pharmaceutical sectors) was the principal demandeur of including strong IPR protection in the GATT/WTO. After years of negotiations, these countries achieved the TRIPS agreement, which sets a minimum standard of IP protection requiring member states to grant monopoly patent rights on processes and products. According to Davinia Ovett of European NGO 3DThree, by demanding strong monopoly patent terms, "the TRIPS agreement enables patent owners to keep prices of medicines artificially higher for longer than previously, thereby affecting access to medicines ('affordability'), an inherent part of the realization of the right to health and the right to life."[166] Thus, these individuals claim that U.S. trade policy is effectively undermining the right to health of citizens in the developing world.

This human rights criticism of U.S. trade policy has gained increasing traction over the past several years. According to scholar Susan Sells, "The human rights rubric seeks to elevate the rights of patients over patents . . . In November 2005 the UN Committee on Economic, Social and Cultural Rights issued a General Comment highlighting the fact that intellectual property rights were limited in time and scope whereas human rights were timeless. While advocates of a human rights framing of access to health acknowledge that it is no panacea, they emphasize that it can offer a fresh perspective and catalyze overall efforts to ensure better access."[167]

However, at the same time that some policymakers, activists, and analysts have argued that the current (domestic and global) systems regulating IPR are a threat to development and human rights, U.S. business leaders and policymakers have found that their drug patents are increasingly vulnerable to theft by pirates, copiers, generic manufacturers, and "manufaketurers" of fake drugs.[168] The United States is by far the most assertive champion of the intellectual property provisions of trade agreements, even when America's trade partners argue that U.S. policies undermine their ability to provide access to affordable medicine or to protect indigenous knowledge.[169] U.S. assertiveness stems from a long-standing belief among policymakers that America's economic future is rooted in the global economic dominance of creative industries such as software, biotechnology, and entertainment.[170] These intellectual property–based industries represent the largest single sector of the U.S. economy.[171] To protect that future, U.S. policymakers work with their overseas counterparts to enforce IPR rules, seize counterfeit goods, pursue criminal enterprises involved in piracy and counterfeiting, and "aggressively engage our trading partners to join our efforts."[172]

In 2002, in recognition that the United States should not undermine access to medicines in times of public health emergencies, Congress called on the Bush administration to rethink its strategies for drug IPR protection. In the TPA, the principal negotiating objectives for the U.S. regarding trade-related intellectual property are to further promote adequate and effective protection of IPR through enforcement, "to secure, fair, equitable and nondiscriminatory market access opportunities for United States persons that rely on intellectual property protection; and, to respect the declaration on the TRIPS Agreement and Public Health adopted by the World Trade Organization."[173]

In response to these mandates, the United States tried to address public demands that TRIPS provisions should not stand in the way of measures necessary to protect public health. The USTR has issued press releases and fact sheets stressing that the United States is fully committed to helping countries experiencing public health crises to find real and comprehensive solutions to these situations.[174] In December 2002, it announced it would not challenge in a trade dispute any WTO member that breaks WTO rules in times of public health emergencies, although it also stressed that "the United States expects that all countries will cooperate to ensure that the drugs produced are not diverted from countries in need to wealthier markets."[175] In 2004, USTR stressed that the United States played an instrumental role in amending the WTO to "allow countries to override patent rights when necessary to export life-saving drugs."[176] The United States argues that its position on access to affordable medicines has been misunderstood. It notes that it was the first country to suggest that the poorest developing countries be allowed until 2016 to put pharmaceutical patents in place. Nonetheless, the fact sheet also stressed that "exceptions may be appropriate for health crises, but should not become the rule."[177]

However, the United States has not been so flexible regarding its unilateral trade policies. Under the Trade Act of 1974 (amended in 1988), the USTR is required to identify annually foreign countries that deny adequate and effective IPR protection or fair and equitable market access for "U.S. persons" who rely on intellectual property protection.[178] The United States obtains information from U.S. agencies, U.S. firms, and the public, and it publishes its results in an annual report, the Special 301 Report.[179] In its most recent report, USTR found problems in some fifty-two countries and placed them in three categories, the Watch List, the Priority Watch List, and Priority Foreign Country.[180] Countries placed on the Watch List simply receive a sort of warning that they are countries that do not sufficiently enforce IPR. Countries on the Priority Watch List receive assistance to help them address their IPR enforcement deficiencies. But if USTR designates a country as a Priority Foreign Country, policymakers have thirty days to decide whether to initiate an investigation. Such an investigation can lead to a new agreement or trade sanctions.[181]

This strategy of "naming and shaming" appears effective in the short run. Most countries on the list take steps to improve their IPR enforcement. But some countries, including the European Union, India, and Argentina, have been on the Special 301 Priority Watch List for longer than nine years. Clearly, this strategy does not always work to convince the citizens or policymakers in other countries to change their behavior. Moreover, it may alienate the very countries that the United States wants to convince of the importance of enforcement. For example, Ukrainian and Brazilian policymakers were furious that after they made real improvements in their IPR regimes, the report still cited them as key problem countries.[182]

Since 1984, the United States has also used its trade preference programs to provide disincentives to those countries with insufficient IPR protections. U.S. commercial interests can file petitions to withdraw GSP benefits from countries that do not meet certain criteria, including adequate IPR enforcement, and these petitions are then reviewed by an interagency committee. In August 2001, Ukraine lost its GSP benefits because of a long-standing failure to enforce IPR.[183]

Finally, the United States requires all countries that want to participate in a U.S. FTA to put in place IPR protections beyond those required in TRIPS. U.S. policymakers argue that TRIPS is a floor, not a ceiling, and, in that sense, reflects minimum international norms of IPR. In 2004, USTR's Advisory Committee on Intellectual Property noted, "the enforcement text is assuming increasing importance as countries improve their substantive standards of protection . . . the Committee also seeks to ensure that these standards of protection and enforcement keep pace with rapid changes in technology . . . The Committee seeks to establish strong precedents in these FTAs in order to raise the global level of protection and enforcement globally, nationally and in regional and multilateral agreements."[184]

Each U.S. free trade agreement has an IPR chapter. Although the provisions in these FTAs vary by country, all FTA IPR chapters include adherence to new Internet treaties, patent protection for plants and animals, and increased enforcement measures.[185] The United States insists that these FTAs *do* promote public health because "by protecting IP, FTAs, like the U.S.-Jordan FTA, encourage local pharmaceutical industries." Moreover, the United States has stressed that the FTAs contain the flexibility needed to address public health crises. Finally, it notes that agreements with Chile, Bahrain, CAFTA, and Morocco, do not contain any obligations with respect to compulsory licenses to address national health emergencies.[186]

However, some analysts allege that these more stringent IPR provisions will inhibit U.S. FTA partners' abilities ensure access to affordable medicines for their citizens. These critics cite, as an example, changes to Australia's IPR regime. Under chapter seventeen of the Australia/U.S. FTA, Australia agreed to make its IPR regime harmonious with that of the United States. Australia also agreed to make changes to its pharmaceutical benefits scheme, which was designed to ensure that all Australians had access to affordable medicines. In the name of transparency and effective regulation, Australia agreed to set up an independent review body, so that drug companies could resubmit requests to review drugs rejected by the scheme. But some analysts alleged that by so doing, Australia undermined its commitment to access to affordable medicines.[187] The UNDP came to a similar conclusion about CAFTA, noting that CAFTA's IPR provision "limits the ability of Central American governments to negotiate lower drug prices and could compromise the capacity of these governments to address public health concerns."[188] In 2004, Paul Hunt, the UN Commission on Human Rights Special Rapporteur on the right to physical and mental health, urged the United States and Peru to ensure that their FTA does not undermine access to affordable medicines.[189] The Health GAP, a U.S. NGO, alleged that the United States was using strong arm tactics to force its FTA partners to change their laws designed to increase access to affordable generic medicines. They note that the United States insisted that Guatemala revoke a law which expedited registration or marketing approval of generic equivalents of new medicines.[190]

The George W. Bush administration was determined to prove that its FTAs will not make it harder for America's FTA partners to ensure affordable access to medicines for their peoples. For example, it noted that "the Morocco FTA will not affect that country's ability to take measures necessary to protect public health or to use the WTO solution to import drugs." And USTR argues that "stronger patent and data protection increases the willingness of companies to release innovative drugs in free trade partners' markets, potentially increasing, rather than decreasing the availability of medicines."[191] In its fact sheet on the U.S./Thailand FTAs, it argued that "by eliminating the 10 percent tariff on medicines (which is not applied to AIDS drugs) the FTA should help lower the costs of drugs.[192]

Beginning in April 2004, all FTAs included a letter, "Understandings Regarding Certain Public Health Measures," signed by representatives of both governments. The letter says that the IPR provisions of the agreement "do not affect a Party's ability to take necessary measures to protect public health." This letter occurs in Morocco, Peru, DR-CAFTA, Colombia, Bahrain, and Oman FTAs.[193] But the letter did not assuage trade critics, who still claimed that these FTAs were undermining access to affordable medicines.

USTR has clearly struggled to put in place effective policies that balanced the interests of pharmaceuticals and public health needs. Although it has developed policies in concert with U.S. agencies charged with public health responsibilities such as the Food and Drug Administration (FDA), it has not solicited public health advice from outside experts. USTR's Intellectual Property Advisory Committee has no mandate to review how the agreement affects public health at home or abroad. In general, when the Advisory Committee has commented on public health issues, it has worried about manufakketure rather than on how a particular trade agreement might affect the right to health of its own citizens or that of their overseas counterparts.[194]

While many argue that the United States is too rigid on IPR issues, USTR's advisory committee on intellectual property thinks that the United States is not doing enough to meet the negotiating goals and objectives contained in the TPA. In its review of the U.S./Peru Trade Promotion Agreement Intellectual Property Provisions, it warned that these FTAs should set a baseline for all future FTAs, including a possible FTAA (Free Trade Agreement of the Americas). It also warned that the United States should insist, "In any future FTA negotiations with countries that have yet to implement fully their TRIPS obligations, they not only do so before the launch of the negotiations but also, where appropriate, provide a standstill specifically with respect to the approval of generic copies of pharmaceutical products."[195]

The U.S. approach to IPR and public health within its FTAs aroused public concern in the United States as well as abroad. For example, in 2004, ninety NGOs from the United States and abroad jointly signed a letter asking USTR Robert Zoellick "to uphold its Doha commitments and abandon the pursuit of 'TRIPS-plus'" provisions in free trade agreements, noting the health of millions was at stake.[196] But U.S. trade policymakers were not moved by guilt or by negative headlines. On July 12, 2004, the *New York Times* reported that members of Congress wanted to vote for the Australia/U.S. FTA, but were concerned about the effect of the IPR provisions upon local and state government entities.[197] Those provisions could make it harder for U.S. states and localities to negotiate with drug manufacturers to obtain price concessions on drugs.[198] Such concerns have only deepened over time. For example, in March 2007, when the Democrats proposed a new approach to trade policymaking, they recommended that trade agreements "re-establish a fair balance between promoting access to medicines and protecting pharmaceutical innovation."[199]

USTR's Intergovernmental Policy Advisory Committee, which consists of some thirty-five members representing states and other nonfederal government entities, suggested that state and local governments should be involved in consultations on the delivery and procurement of health care services and pharmaceutical products.[200] On October 7, 2005, Congressmen Rahm Emanuel, Charles B. Rangel, and Pete Stark wrote an impassioned letter to then U.S.

Trade Representative Rob Portman. They noted that "increasingly, provisions in our trade agreements have implications for . . . national health laws in both the United States and our trading partners." They asked him to establish an Assistant U.S. Trade Representative for Public Health with appropriate staffing and to include public health representatives on the Administration's trade advisory committees.[201] The USTR responded by posting a Federal Register announcement seeking public health nominees to several advisory committees. As of June 12, 2006, no appointments had been made.[202]

Thus, the U.S. government walks into the intersection of trade and public health with blinders on. Although policymakers argue that U.S. IPR policies promote access to affordable medicines, others see them as deliberately designed to undermine such access. The United States has a hard time reconciling its desire to protect the interests of its pharmaceutical industry with its equally important objective to ensure that people in the United States and abroad can obtain access to affordable medicines.[203] The United States has not developed an advisory structure or a strategy to develop policies that meet both objectives. As a result, many observers have concluded that American trade policy is imbalanced, favoring IPR holders over the general public.

Conclusion

President George W. Bush has argued that "free trade brings greater political and personal freedom," and, when the United States ships goods, it is "exporting freedom." However, the president cannot push this freedom agenda without the assent of Congress and U.S. trade partners.[204]

U.S. citizens have a long history of using trade policy and agreements to promote human rights. This activism reflects long-standing U.S. beliefs: that freedom of speech, thought, expression, religion, and association are priority human rights; that individuals have the right to own the fruits of their own ideas; that transparency and the rule of law are essential to both democracy and capitalism; and that government is best when it governs least and remains small and close to the people. However, U.S. policymakers don't agree on what human rights trade policy and agreements should promote or how trade agreements should be used to achieve human rights objectives.

U.S. policymakers behave differently at the intersection of trade and human rights than their overseas counterparts. Americans often conflate rights and freedoms and do not trust in a strong central government to provide rights such as access to basic services. Moreover, the United States government does not always behave as though human rights are universal and indivisible, as outlined in the Universal Declaration of Human Rights. Instead, the

United States uses trade policy to advance specific human rights in some of its trade partners.

U.S. policymakers believe that, in cases of egregious human rights abuse such as Burma, sanctions speak louder than words. The United States is quite willing to use trade to punish countries for their human rights practices. The huge U.S. market also allows U.S. policymakers to be more active at the intersection of trade and human rights. The United States frequently uses access to its market as an incentive to prod countries to improve their human rights laws and practices. Through its free trade agreements, it actively promotes particular human rights such as the right to information, public participation or labor rights. These links do prod changes in the interaction between citizens and policymakers. Yet in some countries where democracy is nascent or nonexistent, the U.S. effort to use trade to advance political participation may be inappropriate.

However, the United States does not always act to protect human rights with its trade policies. In fact, U.S. trade and human rights strategies often work at cross-purposes. U.S. trade policymakers argue that the United States is a leader in helping to provide access to affordable medicines abroad, thereby promoting the right to health. Yet to many observers, the United States appears more concerned with creating new international standards for IPR than with ensuring that all people have access to affordable medicines. And U.S. policymakers have not yet explored how trade decisions may affect access to affordable medicines at home.

The United States makes trade policy in a relatively transparent manner (although, like many other nations, it does not negotiate trade in the most transparent manner). However, in the United States, legislators as well as nongovernmental advisors have a major impact on particular trade policies. As in many countries, well-organized economic interests (whether protectionist or supportive of freer trade) often trump less-organized general interests. Moreover, although the U.S. government performs labor and environmental reviews of trade agreements, it has no capacity to examine how trade agreements might broadly affect other national policy goals such as promoting democracy or thwarting terrorism. One of USTR's key policy advisory committees, the Intergovernmental Policy Advisory Committee, warned that the United States must "broaden and deepen an informed non-partisan trade policy dialogue" to "serve to bridge the gaps between federal agencies' understanding of the varied state processes and socio-economic contexts."[205]

For two centuries, some Americans have dreamed that the United States would be a beacon for liberty and democracy for oppressed people everywhere.[206] The United States has, to some extent over the years, succeeded in that goal. For example, the U.S. Revolutionary War inspired revolutionary movements in Europe, and the U.S. civil rights movement helped inspire the black majority in South Africa to peacefully fight for their rights.[207] Today, however, many people no longer see the United States as a human rights paragon or as a model for their own country's behavior.[208] If the United States really wants to use trade policies to export those human rights values, it will need to think clearly and creatively about how to offset the imbalance between trade and human rights.

7

Conclusion

How to Right the Trade Imbalance

On October 21, 2003, a group of senior citizens from the U.S. state of Minnesota traveled to Canada, where they planned to commit a crime – to purchase prescription drugs. In the United States, it is illegal to reimport drugs from abroad.[1] But the price of prescription drugs in the United States has risen dramatically in recent years. So, instead of buying their medications at home, they bought their medicines at a licensed pharmacy in Winnipeg, Canada, where prescription drug prices are significantly lower. The next day, the seniors took the bus home. As the bus steered back onto U.S. territory, U.S. FDA agents boarded the bus and confronted the wily seniors.[2] Although the agents didn't confiscate the medicines, they used their position of authority to dissuade the seniors from making future trips.[3]

The United States does not regulate the price of drugs or subsidize drug costs for many Americans. Drug prices are high and rising.[4] Thus, many Americans buy their drugs on the Internet or, like the crafty seniors, buy drugs abroad.[5] They travel to countries where governments purchase drugs for their citizens or regulate the price of medicines. But U.S. pharmaceutical manufacturers argue that when governments, such as Canada, use their monopsony power to drive down the cost of drugs, these governments distort the market for drugs. These pharmaceutical manufacturers claim that the United States is the only country where they can charge market rates for the drugs they research, develop, and test. Thus, to pharmaceutical firms, the high prices are only fair, because they reflect the true costs of medicine.[6]

In recent years, however, some U.S. state governments have implemented "buying programs" to bargain down drug prices for their citizens. These statewide bulk purchasing programs resemble many of those same national purchasing programs that U.S. pharmaceutical firms condemn for undermining market forces abroad.[7]

After intense public protest, the U.S. government agreed to allow its citizens to purchase a three-month supply of imported drugs for personal use.[8] However, many U.S. citizens that desperately need lower-cost drugs have no access to the Internet and can't travel abroad. These Americans need a broader solution to gain access to affordable medicines.

At the same time that some Americans were trying to use trade to advance access to affordable medicines, on the other side of the globe, Indians were facing a different and more disturbing challenge at the intersection of trade and human rights. From 2001 to 2006, thousands of India's small farmers (more than 8,900 according to the Indian government) committed suicide. The farmers had given up on life because they could not longer provide for their families. Many such farmers had taken on substantial debt to buy genetically modified seeds and pesticides to produce commodities such as cotton and soy. They thought modern seeds and tools would make their farms more productive and thus they were willing to borrow from local lenders at exceptionally high interest rates. Alas, many of the farmers soon found they could not afford to pay off their debts with the money they earned from the sale of their crops. During this same period, the Indian government abandoned many farm subsidy programs and announced that it would no longer procure cotton from local farmers. It took these steps to comply with its WTO obligations. But for some Indian farmers, these pressures became overwhelming.[9] After local and global media reported on the farmers' plight and the disturbing surge in suicides, the Indian public demanded that the Indian government take action. In June 2006, the Indian government announced a series of measures to help the affected farmers.[10]

Some analysts blamed trade policies and the WTO for the farmers' suicides. They argued that by adhering to WTO rules, India had undermined the human rights of these farmers.[11] No doubt India's WTO commitments made it harder for India to subsidize these farmers and to shield them from foreign competition. However, the farmers' ability to achieve a sustainable livelihood cannot be directly attributed to trade policies and agreements. The farmers had little land, little education, and few, if any, opportunities to seek alternative employment. The farmers viewed agriculture as their only and best livelihood. Moreover, the local lenders were the only source of capital for many of these farmers. Finally, the Indian government failed to address the many challenges faced by its small farmers in an integrated and effective manner.[12]

*   *   *

Although the plights of U.S. senior citizens and of India's small farmers are worlds apart, their stories illuminate how policymakers behave at the intersection of trade and human rights. In general, policymakers struggle to balance their trade and human rights objectives. The United States has not developed effective public policies to ensure that all its citizens have access to affordable medicines. Although imports would help more Americans obtain a broader supply of affordable medicines, in the end, imports alone cannot address the failure of U.S. public policies to ensure universal access to medicines. Meanwhile, as India's small farmers struggled to compete in global markets, their problems such as access to credit, rising costs, and declining prices for commodities, became increasingly clear. Trade policies did not create the problems of India's small farmers, but they exacerbated them. Thus, some observers found it easy to attribute these problems to WTO rules.

What We Hope to Achieve with This Book

With this book, we aim to describe how policymakers behave at the intersection of trade and human rights. As we traveled the world to discuss this relationship, we learned that many policymakers, activists, and business leaders would like to find ways to achieve both trade and human rights objectives. But policymakers consistently told us they don't know how to do so effectively.

There are many reasons why policymakers struggle to expand trade and advance human rights. First, trade policies are becoming increasingly complex. Most countries not only belong to the WTO but also participate in a plethora of bilateral and/or regional trade agreements. Thus, they have multiple, different, and at times confusing trade priorities, policies, and objectives. Second, each nation has different human rights conditions, objectives, and policies. Each country's human rights priorities change over time, reflecting demographics, culture, and the country's political and economic situation. Third, in most countries, trade policymakers are not explicitly tasked to find ways to coordinate trade and human rights objectives (*a strategic problem*). Fourth, most governments have not developed channels to coordinate human rights and trade objectives and policies. Policymakers in the trade area have little interaction with those officials working to promote human rights at home or abroad (*a structural problem*). Finally, there has been very little research on how trade policies may affect human rights and how human rights policies may support trade (*an information problem*). Thus, policymakers, activists, scholars, and citizens walk into this juncture half-blind.

This book is an effort to open people's eyes to these issues and a call for further research. With greater understanding of this relationship, citizens and policymakers alike can work toward greater coherency between trade and human rights objectives. Over time, we believe greater understanding will help policymakers develop effective policies and prevent collisions at the intersection of trade and human rights. Policymakers may find it easier to balance trade and human rights objectives.

What We Found and Concluded

Our mode of analysis was to examine how policymakers in our case study countries *behaved* as they sought to reconcile incongruities between their trade policies and agreements and their domestic and international human rights policies and priorities. After completing extensive background research, we traveled to each case study country to meet with and interview policymakers, scholars, civil society and labor activists, and business leaders. In each country, we focused our analysis on particular examples that policymakers, activists, and business leaders shared with us. We acknowledge that these examples do not comprise a rigorous sample. Nonetheless, these case studies illuminate how policymakers think and behave when they perceive trade and human rights objectives may clash. Our findings are presented below.

Policymakers Generally View Trade as Human Rights Enhancing (but Not Always)

Policymakers from our case study countries, like those of most countries, see trade as an engine of growth. In general, they think that trade can help them progressively realize human rights. They believe that as trade agreements facilitate global market integration and economic efficiencies, these agreements will also promote an internationally shared rule of law for international transactions.[13] They argue that these same trade agreements can make it easier for their citizens (and others) to participate in the global economy and provide people with new skills and greater opportunities. And they accept the proposition that as nations get richer through trade, government officials will find it easier to ensure that they help their citizens (and others abroad) progressively realize human rights. In sum, many policymakers assume:

Trade → Economic growth → ↑ Overall human rights protection → ↑ Human welfare → ↑ Purchasing power → ↑Trade

But policymakers in many countries have not been able to convert trade-related economic growth into rising incomes, improved living standards, poverty reduction, and progressive realization of human rights.[14] They don't really know how to ensure that such growth will provide access to opportunities for more of their people, more of the time. As noted in Chapter 1, history is replete with examples of slavery, oppression, and human rights violations linked to trade. When confronted with potential conflicts, policymakers often respond to each situation in an ad hoc manner. And ad hoc solutions may not address the root causes of why trade policies and agreements, or trade in general, may undermine human rights:

> Trade policy → Perceived or actual inconsistency with human rights priority or obligation → Ad Hoc strategies to mitigate Problem → Continued trade

No Case Study Country Has Mandated Trade Policymakers to Ensure That Trade Policies and Agreements Protect Human Rights in General: The Signals Are Wrong

Under international law, state parties are supposed to do everything in their power to respect, promote, and fulfill human rights. However, most countries do not explicitly task their trade policymakers with ensuring that their trade policy decisions enhance human rights at home or abroad. *Until trade policymakers receive such a mandate, they will probably not weigh the human rights impact of their trade policies on either their citizens or those of their trade partners.*

In most countries, policymakers develop trade policies as if they are strictly commercial policies. They weigh the interests of their producers and consumers; they may include national security or political concerns, but these officials rarely introduce the interests of the global community into such deliberations. As a result, although policymakers are well aware of the human rights consequences of some of their trade decisions, they have few incentives to ensure that trade policies advance the thirty-some human rights outlined under the UDHR.

Nor are most policymakers given the responsibility to ensure that trade does not undermine specific human rights at home or abroad. The right to food provides a good example of this dilemma. The Commission on Human Rights has extensively examined the right to food, and the Special Rapporteur on the right to food, Jean Ziegler, has shown that despite these commitments, hunger and malnutrition persist throughout the world. Although the Universal Declaration of Human Rights does not explicitly set down a human right to food, it does delineate that everyone has the right to life and also states that everyone has a right to a standard of living adequate for the health and well-being of himself and his family, including food. States are not to take actions that deprive people of access to adequate affordable food. As a last resort, governments are required to provide adequate food to those people that cannot feed themselves.[15] Moreover, under international law, governments are obligated "to take into account... international legal obligations regarding the right to food when entering into agreements with other States or with international organizations."[16] However, we know of no government explicitly tasked by policymakers to develop trade compromises that promote *humankind's* right to food.[17]

Meanwhile, *national trade* policymakers are generally not charged to promote the right to food at home or abroad. In general, they develop their trade positions based on the interests of their agricultural producers and consumers and their national need to ensure food security, not on behalf of the world's hungry and poor. Although these officials increasingly recognize that the poor, especially the rural poor in the developing world, have little voice to influence national level trade policies, in general, they are not required under national law to ensure that trade policies promote the right to food and food security for the world's people.

WTO Rules Limit How and When Policymakers Can Promote Particular Human Rights

Many people believe that the WTO forces members to choose between trade rules and objectives and human rights rules and objectives. As a result, they claim that the WTO directly undermines human rights. But WTO rules make no explicit mention of human rights, and neither the WTO nor the GATT was in any way intended to address human rights questions. But WTO rules do limit how and when policymakers can use trade policy tools to protect human rights.

All members of the WTO must adhere to certain principles as they make trade policy. They must automatically extend the best trade conditions granted to one member to every other nation that belongs to the WTO. They must treat products of foreign firms in the same way they do products of local firms. Policymakers cannot discriminate between products originating in different countries nor between imported goods and like domestically produced goods. If member states don't adhere to these rules, they may find their trade policies subject to trade disputes at the WTO.

Within these strictures, countries have considerable flexibility under WTO rules to protect human rights at home or abroad. Member states can use trade waivers and exceptions to promote human rights abroad or at home. They occasionally bring up human rights during accessions and trade policy reviews. Furthermore, as we showed in the WTO chapter, human rights concerns have seeped into WTO and GATT negotiations, although many WTO members still see human rights concerns as "non-trade" issues.

Some people see the TRIPS agreement as compelling governments to make choices that can undermine their human rights responsibilities. However, members of the WTO have now amended the TRIPS agreement to make it clear that nations can use the public health exceptions to TRIPS in times of public health emergencies. That is an important start. But we found that many developing country policymakers believe that the TRIPS system does not sufficiently protect indigenous populations from the theft of their traditional knowledge and practices or from biopiracy of their indigenous plants, animals, and seeds. Members of the WTO should pay greater attention to these concerns.

Meanwhile, policymakers are acting at the national level to protect indigenous rights. The United Nations Development Programme has noted that a growing number of middle-income and developing countries are developing national legislation to reconcile disputes between public health and the rights of indigenous peoples. Argentina, India, Thailand, and South Africa have legislation legalizing compulsory licensing and parallel imports. Brazil has laws to prevent biopiracy, and India regulates exports of germ plasm and has created a national gene bank.[18]

Interestingly, we found that WTO membership may have some interesting side effects on promotion of particular human rights. To comply with WTO rules, all members must regulate in a transparent accountable manner and provide citizens and traders (whether individuals or companies) the opportunity to influence and participate in certain aspects of policymaking. WTO members have gradually modernized their administrative procedures or put new laws and regulations into place to meet these obligations. These "habits of good governance" may spill over to other aspects of the polity.

Every Country Is Concerned about Labor Rights

In all of the countries we visited, policymakers were concerned about their ability to maintain labor standards and encourage job creation. Some countries were quite creative. Brazil, for example, used "naming and shaming" to get business owners to stop exploiting labor but often found that disincentive was not harsh enough to eradicate the problem. South Africa and Brazil created social labels. But these inventive strategies could not guarantee sufficient numbers of new jobs, especially for citizens without skills. South Africa maintained its high labor standards even though that strategy appeared to make it harder for the country to encourage foreign investment and job creation for its relatively unskilled majority population. Meanwhile, European countries are under significant pressure to alter certain aspects of labor rights such as unemployment benefits and hiring/firing laws. But they are constrained by EU-wide budgetary rules and EU preferences for strong workplace protections.[19] Although the United States actively promotes its own vision of labor standards overseas, U.S. labor standards appear to be declining. Fewer workers have access to unions and companies are reducing worker benefits at the same time that growing numbers of jobs are moving overseas. However, the U.S. economy remains incredibly productive, workers are well paid, and every year many jobs are created. Although each country has made promoting labor rights at home and/or abroad a priority, none of our case study countries have figured out how to balance policies to attract investment and create and retain jobs while promoting core worker rights.

Many Countries Are Concerned about the Effects of Services Liberalization

Services trade liberalization can enhance human rights by providing more people with affordable and reliable access to services such as credit, water, health, electricity, and education. But if national governments do not effectively regulate the provision of these services, some of their citizens may not benefit. Prices may rise, corruption could increase, and citizens may be denied affordable access to services.

Services negotiations are an increasingly important component of bilateral and multilateral trade talks. In the Doha Round, all of our case studies made initial offers to open some of their service sectors to trade. However, many developing countries such as South Africa find it difficult to figure out which sectors to open to foreign investment and how such investment will affect access to essential human services such as electricity, water, or education. Many of these countries do not have adequate regulatory institutions in place to oversee service sectors such as banking or telecommunications.[20] These countries need guidance on how to regulate provision of services before they make decisions on what sectors to open up to trade. We believe this is an area where policymakers could greatly benefit from more research.

Trade and Human Rights Is a Two-Way Street

Much of this book has focused on how policymakers use trade policies to affect human rights abroad or devise domestic policies to address how trade may affect human rights at home. But we also believe that countries that protect human rights implicitly signal to traders and investors that they are good places to do business. (*We make no claims that investors respond to this message.*) The chart below compares several "subjective indicators of governance" designed to measure governance, human rights, and investor protections. Subjective indicators are expert opinions about a country. It compares country performance on the UNDP human development ranking (thus showing a country's performance on social, economic rights indicators) the World Bank Voice and Accountability Index (which aggregate free and fair elections, civil and political rights, freedom of the press, and other criteria), and, finally, the UNDP Subjective Indicators of Governance Polity Score (political participation, constraints on the executive, regulation of the executive).[21] We then compare these assessments to World Bank assessments of how friendly a country is toward doing business. (Again, Germany, Spain, and Lithuania are our EU proxies.) Obviously, rich countries tend to have strong institutions, protect human rights, and are, to varied degrees, good places to do business. These countries send a message that they view investments in their citizens, a deep commitment to human rights, and the rule of law as enabling conditions for investment. Some countries such as South Africa may be trying to send similar signals. The chart on p. 195 summarizes these indicators.

Scholars and development policymakers have theorized as to the meaning and rationale for such signals. To economist Dani Rodrik "a high-quality policy environment is one that sends clear signals to producers and investors, precludes rent-seeking, does not waste economic resources . . . and maintains social peace."[22] However, law professor Daniel A. Farber believes policymakers may be trying to signal judicial independence and thereby demonstrate a willingness or commitment to ensuring that all people – foreign and domestic – have the right to recognition before the law and equal protection of the law and to provide rights to effective judicial remedies. Farber argues that investors conclude that "the government that protects human rights is the government that is likely to protect foreign investor rights."[23]

The World Bank Global Governance Unit and Foreign Investment Advisory Service have begun to explore these relationships. The Bank notes that a growing number of governments now understand that good governance, including human rights protections, are essential to attract trade and investment.[24] As example, Cambodia used its textile trade arrangement with the United States to improve labor rights and by so doing was able to compete with other exporters such as China on textiles.[25] South Africa remains adamant that it will not relax its high labor standards as a strategy to attract more foreign investment. We believe that policymakers need further information on how protecting human rights can be an incentive for trade and investment.

Reflecting Different Human Rights Priorities and Global Economic and Political Status, Countries Use a Variety of Public Policies at the Intersection of Trade and Human Rights

There is no one right way to ensure that trade does not undermine policymakers' ability to help their citizens realize particular human rights. For example, although Brazil and South Africa are determined to ensure their citizens' right

CHART 1. *Better human rights practices lead to more trade and investment?*

Country name	UNDP Human Development Ranking (2005) Score delineates rankings among countries.	World Bank Ranking as country to do business in (2005) Score delineates rankings among countries.	World Bank Investor Protection Index (2005) Score delineates an average of indexes on a scale up to 10	World Bank Voice and Accountability (2002) Aggregate from a variety of sources including CIRI, Freedom House, scaled −2.5–2.5	UNDP Subjective Indicators of Governance Polity Score −10 to 10 (2000)
Norway	1	5	6.7	1.58	10
Canada	5	4	8.7	1.33	10
United States	10	3	8.3	1.24	10
Lithuania	14	15	5.3	1.00	10
UK	15	9	8	1.46	10
Germany	20	19	5.3	1.42	10
Spain	21	30	4.7	1.15	10
Brazil	63	119	5.3	.53	8
South Africa	120	28	8	1.17	9
India	127	116	6	.66	9
Cambodia	130	133	5.3	−0.77	2

Note: The country rankings on business come from the 2005 World Bank Doing Business Economy Rankings. http://www.doingbusiness.org/EconomyRankings/ The Doing Business database provides objective measures of business regulations and their enforcement. The Doing Business indicators are comparable across 155 economies. They indicate the regulatory costs of business and can be used to analyze specific regulations that enhance or constrain investment, productivity and growth. The Protecting Investors Index is an average of 3 indexes related to transparency, director liability and the ability of shareholders to sue for misconduct at http://www.doingbusiness.org/ExploreTopics/ProtectingInvestors/. The Human Development Ranking comes from the UNDP Human Development Report 2005, table 31, p. 320. The Polity scores come from the UNDP Human Development Report 2002, table A1.1 Subjective Indicators of Governance. The Voice and Accountability scores come from the World Bank Governance Indicators Dataset, which is an aggregate data set that builds on Freedom House and other sources.

to health (and specifically affordable medicines), Brazil has taken more of a leadership (and confrontational) role to achieve these goals through the WTO. To some degree this reflects the sophistication of Brazilian trade negotiators, as well as Brazil's willingness to use its economic and political clout to push for change. In South Africa, trade-related growth has accentuated inequalities among particular population groups. South African officials developed affirmative action programs or programs to create new opportunities for the poor. But some foreign investors perceive South Africa's approach as discriminatory. Press reports noted that the United States abandoned efforts to negotiate a free trade agreement with South Africa because investors were concerned about alleged "performance requirements" of South Africa's Black Economic Empowerment plan.

Nor is there one right way to use trade to advance human rights abroad. The United States and the European Union present contrasting approaches. The EU argues that human rights are universal and indivisible – that all rights are important and mutually dependent. Since 1995, all EU association agreements and partnership and cooperation agreements contain a clause stipulating that human rights must be protected to receive trade benefits. The signatories to the Cotonou Agreement – a trade and aid pact that links the European Union with seventy-eight developing countries in Africa, the Caribbean, and the Pacific – have agreed that their trade benefits are contingent on their human rights performance. If these countries don't adhere to provisions of the agreement, the EU can suspend trade concessions and reduce foreign aid. Nonetheless, the EU seems reluctant to use the power inherent in these agreements. It rarely suspends trade concessions; policymakers believe that the very process of dialogue can change hearts and minds and is more effective in the long run at building public and policymaker support for human rights.

In contrast, the United States focuses on *particular* rights in its bilateral trade agreements and GSP programs. It requires its FTA partners to make specific commitments on labor rights, IPR, and transparency/due process rights and political participation. Like the EU, the United States often backs up its human rights objectives with trade capacity-building programs. But the United States does not have a very strong commitment to fund such programs. As a result, the long-run efficacy of America's approach is unclear. This approach does little to stimulate grass roots support (on the demand side) for protecting labor or protecting individual rights to intellectual property among the citizens of America's FTA partners. Thus, U.S. strategies seem unlikely to create a demand for the enforcement of these particular human rights in other countries over the long term.

The two nations also contrast in their use of sanctions. The United States has a long tradition of using trade sanctions to change the behavior of other nations and is willing to act unilaterally. The EU is no fan of sanctions, but when it has no alternative, it tries to target the negative effects of sanctions on decision makers rather than the general populace.

Beyond the major industrialized powers, most countries are reluctant to use trade policies and agreements as a means of getting other nations to change their human rights practices. Instead, they work through the WTO system. Thus, Brazil and South Africa worked to amend WTO rules to ensure that countries could breach IPR rules in times of public health emergencies. Brazil, along with India, is leading global efforts to link the Convention on Biodiversity and WTO TRIPS rules. Building on UN sanctions, South Africa pressed the members of the WTO to ban trade in conflict diamonds and to promote trade in only those diamonds that had been certified through the Kimberley Process.

These different approaches to linking trade and human rights reflect a wide range of political, social, economic, and cultural factors as well as the degree of human rights emergency policymakers perceive. Richer societies are more likely to contest human rights abuses abroad. Moreover, richer societies are more likely to contest human rights abuses regarding the human rights they value. Thus, both the United States and the EU are willing to use trade sanctions against Burma, where civil and political rights have long been denied. But the United States and the EU part ways on Cuba, where the government provides access to education and health care but denies its citizens political freedoms. Finally, richer societies are more capable of defending as well as progressively realizing rights at home. But these differences can also be explained by a country's affinity toward using its power. The United States has dominated the world economy for almost a century and is not afraid to use that clout on behalf of powerful special interests (whether they are concerned about violations of immigration rights, as in the Soviet Union in the 1970s, or expropriation of property rights in Bolivia in the 21st century). The EU also believes that it has a special responsibility to promote human rights internationally, to draw attention to human rights problems, to raise human rights concerns, and to strengthen other countries' capabilities to protect human rights. But policymakers in many other countries do not perceive it is appropriate to intervene in the affairs of other nations, even in the most extreme cases of human rights abuse (as in Burma or Zimbabwe).

The Trade Policymaking Process May Undermine Human Rights

Many countries have not developed a trade policymaking process that is open, transparent, and accountable to all of their citizens. In general, trade policies are determined by senior government officials who are responsive to a small group of concerned citizens/business interests. In response to public concerns about globalization, every one of our case studies was trying to make trade policies more transparent and democratic. However, although the circle of people making trade policy was growing more inclusive, it remained small and insular. Nonetheless, in every case study country, policymakers and activists could and did introduce human rights concerns into the policymaking process (for example in U.S. efforts to thwart child labor). However, no country had established a formal advisory structure to examine how trade policies and agreements affected human rights outlined in the International Bill of Human Rights. Some countries such as Brazil and the United States had developed an advisory process to examine how trade might affect a particular human right. For example, Brazil had an infrastructure to examine how trade policies affected public health. The United States had an advisory group examining how trade may affect labor rights at home and abroad. U.S. policymakers had also agreed (but as of 2007 have not yet acted) to include public health advocates on their industry advisory committee on pharmaceuticals.

The United States Is an Outlier

As we note in the U.S. chapter, the United States actively uses trade to promote human rights. But its behavior differs from that of many other countries. First, the United States frequently acts on its own to promote particular human rights. Second, Congress has its own trade and human rights agenda, which can include acting on human rights issues without the involvement of the Executive. Third, policymakers in the executive and legislative branches frequently do not act as if human rights are universal and indivisible, as outlined in the Universal Declaration of Human Rights. In fact, the United States often acts in ways that undermine the notion that human rights are universal and indivisible. And finally, U.S. policymakers use trade policies and agreements to advance particular human rights that the United States views as important, including labor rights, administrative due process rights, and intellectual property rights. These American priorities may not be major priorities for other nations that are struggling to ensure adequate affordable food, education, credit, and basic services for their people. By pushing some but not all human rights, and linking them to access to its huge home market, the United States prods other countries to make *its* concerns (such as IPR protection) *their* concerns. Such a strategy may enhance some human rights at the expense of others and may appear insensitive.

U.S. willingness to lead on human rights efforts can be admirable, but it is also unfortunate. The United States likes to lead, but it doesn't always choose to cooperate, particularly when it has to work with institutions that many Americans distrust or disapprove of. Moreover, to be effective in promoting human rights, the United States must find ways to cooperate with other governments. Human rights can flourish only if citizens can increase the demand for human rights as well as the supply of institutions, law, policies, and skilled people to advance such rights.

We have singled out the United States because of its global economic and political influence. We believe the United States needs to develop objectives, a strategy, and an institutional structure to make its ad hoc approach to trade and human rights more coherent. But other nations also need to consider strategies to make their human rights and trade policies more harmonious and effective.

What We Recommend

With this book, we hope to help policymakers do a better job of governing globalization. If policymakers want to find ways to accommodate human rights concerns, they will have to rethink the objectives and process of trade policymaking. Frankly, there is no one policy solution that can guide government officials at the intersection of trade and human rights. As the UNDP has noted, "governments are charged in trade negotiations to pursue national interests, not global interests."[26] We would not purport to change that. However, below we outline seven recommendations that we believe will help policymakers weigh human rights criteria (domestic as well as international) as they make trade policy decisions.

Make a Policy Determination That Trade and Human Rights Can and Should Be Better Coordinated

In all of our case study countries, policymakers claimed that trade and human rights were top policy priorities. But these officials also admitted that trade and human rights policymakers rarely coordinate their efforts. As the Brazilian tire case illuminates, when government officials fail to harmonize their policies, they often stumble. Sometimes they waste time and resources on ineffective policy solutions or alienate their trade partners. In other examples, they may put citizens at risk or send confusing signals to market actors (as in export processing zones, where some governments may ignore violations of their own labor laws). Thus, it is in their citizens' interest (as well as the global community's) that human rights and trade officials find ways to communicate and develop strategies to coordinate their efforts. But policymakers we interviewed said they have no mandate to collaborate.

However, it seems the public is beginning to ask for such coordination. For example, in June 2006, the international polling firm GlobeScan and the Program on International Policy Attitudes (University of Maryland) surveyed some

21,000 people from twenty countries around the world on globalization issues. The poll revealed that on average some two-thirds of those polled favored more regulation of global companies to protect the rights of workers and consumers. Those polled also wanted policymakers to find strategies to increase the voice of citizens – large majorities of those polled said that "large companies have too much influence over our national government." Although the poll did not explicitly address the kind of global regulation those polled would support, clearly international trade is an area of global regulation that can affect the behavior of business across borders. As the public demands that trade policies enhance human rights, policymakers will respond.[27]

Reform the Trade Policymaking Process at the National Level: Involve Human Rights Advocates and Human Rights Policymakers

Policymakers should develop a regular channel for human rights concerns to enter into the policymaking process (see Figure 7.1). We recommend that when appropriate, policymakers consult with human rights advocates and human rights officials before they make trade policy decisions. They could, for example, set up a human rights policy advisory committee. With input from such a committee, government officials can begin to examine how trade is affecting (and/or how potential trade could affect) various human rights objectives and priorities at home and abroad, reflecting national norms and objectives. Moreover, within government, trade policy and human rights officials need to develop lines of communication and to learn how to work together. These reforms may slow down the public policymaking process, but they will make it more inclusive.

In Making Public Policy Decisions at the Intersection of Trade and Human Rights, Develop an Advisory Structure and Task Advisors to Ask the Right Questions

The commission or advisory committee described above should be charged with asking and answering some of the following questions. These questions are designed to ensure that trade policies achieve positive human rights outcomes, such as gains in voice, empowerment, or equity.[28] Although it may be impossible to predict human rights outcomes with certainty, policymakers should ask questions such as, but not limited to, the following:

1. How will this agreement/policy affect the most vulnerable groups at home and abroad? (*equity*)

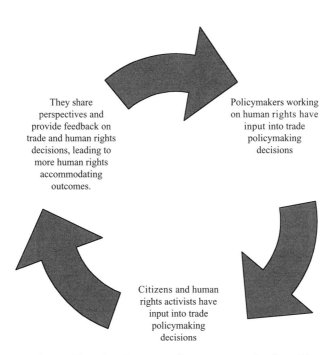

FIGURE 7.1. Making public policy decisions at the intersection of trade and human rights.

2. How will the agreement/policy impact our own government's ability, as well as that of our trade partners, to invest in or supply education, technology, and infrastructure, as well as social safety nets that permit economic flexibility? (*productivity and equity*)

3. Will this agreement/policy create fewer or greater opportunities for public speech and participation in national and global governance? (*voice and empowerment*)

4. Was the agreement developed and negotiated in a transparent accountable manner? (*voice*)

Create a Coalition of the Willing at the WTO to Bring Greater Attention to Human Rights and Trade

Although they have widely divergent human rights priorities and approaches, all of our case study countries are strong proponents of human rights. These countries are also influential trade players. They could achieve greater influence on both objectives by working collaboratively at the WTO to obtain greater clarity on trade and human rights issues. We recommend that this collaboration commit to three objectives:

1. These countries should ask the Secretariat to do a formal study on the relationship between WTO rules and human rights objectives. The Secretariat should publish its findings on the Web and organize a conference on these issues. The goal of this conference could be to help countries examine the relationship between their trade and human rights objectives.
2. These members should call on the WTO to appoint a staff person with human rights expertise as an ombudsman and liaison to international human rights bodies. This individual could be charged with pointing out potential conflicts between trade negotiations or member policies and human rights objectives and explaining these conflicts to WTO member state representatives in Geneva. This individual could also serve as a liaison to the UN's human rights bodies.
3. Finally, these governments could ask the WTO to set up a Working Group to examine specific human rights and trade issues. This Working Group could be given a mandate to explore, for example, two important but different topics: trade in conflict zones and export processing zones.[29]

Prod Firms to Make Human Rights a Business Priority

As corporations are the main agents of globalization, how firms act when they trade can have a huge impact on human rights. With their production and purchasing decisions, as well as political, financial, and philanthropic practices, multinational corporations can promote human rights or undermine these rights. But the human rights responsibilities of business in overseas markets are unclear. Although the Universal Declaration of Human Rights calls on all organs of society to protect and promote human rights, states are primarily responsible for advancing human rights. Professor John Ruggie of Harvard was tasked by the UN Secretary General to try to map out these responsibilities.[30] Until these responsibilities are clear, at every opportunity, policymakers should stress that they expect local firms to adhere to international human rights rules, that corporate codes of conduct should reflect international human rights standards, and that, as they trade, companies must adhere to these standards.[31]

Clarify the Relationship between Voluntary CSR Strategies that Promote Human Rights and WTO Rules

Policymakers in a growing number of countries recognize that they can use public policy to encourage more firms to promote human rights when they operate in nations with inadequate governance. Increasingly, these policymakers are relying on voluntary corporate social responsibility (CSR) initiatives.

TWO IMPORTANT ISSUES TO DISCUSS AT THE WTO

On Export Processing Zones

The WTO allows members to put in place EPZs to attract foreign investment and stimulate trade. Developing country policymakers have often exempted firms in these zones from certain fiscal or financial regulations and others do not require firms in their EPZs to comply with labor laws. As a result, workers in these EPZs often toil in substandard conditions and have little recourse to improve such conditions. The Working Group could be charged with developing strategies to ensure that member states do not undermine labor rights in these EPZs. A recent UNDP study found that although these EPZs stimulate exports, they do not appear to help workers gain new skills, and their impact on poverty reduction has been marginal.

On Business in Conflict Zones

WTO rules provide little guidance on trade in zones of conflict. When business operates in conflict zones, they may trade with nonstate actors that don't comply with international norms. In other instances such trade may perpetuate conflicts. Should the WTO develop procedures for such circumstances, especially if the UN has made a determination that trade contributes to human rights abuses? What role should the UN and its specialized human rights agencies play in WTO examinations of the relationship of conflict and human rights? Are trade waivers the best strategy for the members of the WTO to use in such circumstances?

These CSR initiatives include codes of conduct, auditing strategies, and reporting strategies.[32]

Many of the countries that want to promote CSR are finding ways to link CSR initiatives to trade policies. These governments are creating a new policy hybrid that links hard law (WTO or other trade agreement rules) and soft law (voluntary CSR initiatives). Such experimentation may encourage more companies to protect human rights as they operate overseas. However, some policymakers are concerned that such a new approach to public policy may distort trade.[33]

For example, several governments use procurement policies to promote CSR, but they don't know if their strategies violate WTO norms. Many WTO members use their procurement policies not only to buy needed goods and services but to also achieve other important policy objectives such as energy efficient production. The WTO requires governments to use procurement policies in a manner that does not distort trade. But although governments have adopted a wide range of approaches to procurement in the hopes of promoting global CSR, the WTO has not provided guidance regarding how members can do so. Member governments should not have to wait until another country or countries dispute these strategies to obtain greater clarity regarding whether these strategies distort trade.[34]

WTO member governments should also clarify when policymakers can use social labels to promote human rights. A growing number of governments, civil society groups, and business groups have partnered to develop labeling programs. However, opponents of such labeling allege that these labels could be trade distorting because they create barriers to trade based on a technical or qualitative requirement.[35] Some developing countries fear that these "stricter product standards" are *de facto* trade barriers. Moreover, trade measures based on how goods are made could challenge the WTO approach to "like products."[36]

To obtain clarity on how member states might use procurement policies and social labels, a WTO member should request that the WTO Secretariat research and publish findings on this issue for the members. There are many reasons why the WTO should provide such clarity. First, the WTO could add momentum to corporate efforts to act responsibly by green-lighting those strategies that do not distort trade. Second, a marriage of CSR and trade could strengthen the limited ability of trade agreements to promote global standards by helping to create a greater demand and supply for these standards in developing countries around the world. When socially responsible multinational companies require and then assist their suppliers in implementing better business practices, their suppliers learn how to operate efficiently in a more sustainable and a more humane manner. As these suppliers will not want to be undercut by less responsible competitors, they will likely become advocates for stronger regulation. Third, linking CSR initiatives and trade might also help create global market efficiencies. Consumers would receive more of the information they need to make socially responsible purchasing decisions, and in turn, investors would have the information they need to reward responsible companies.

Encourage Further Research

As noted in Chapter 1, scholars really know very little about how trade and trade agreements may affect particular human rights. Without these insights, policymakers may make inappropriate choices at the intersection of trade and human rights. For example, at this writing (June 2007) the George W. Bush administration would like to gain congressional approval for a bilateral free trade agreement with Colombia. Bush administration policymakers want to reward Colombia for its democratization, counterterrorism, and counter-narcotics efforts. However, since the mid-1980s, some 4,000 labor union leaders have been assassinated in Colombia. Labor and human rights activists in both countries don't want this trade agreement to go forward without Colombia adopting and enforcing stronger labor rights and taking steps to punish those citizens who murder labor union organizers.[37] Yet empirical evidence on the links between human rights and trade (see Chapter 1) might tell Congressional policymakers to forge ahead. In general, personal integrity rights tend to improve with expanded trade. However, these findings may be too preliminary. We want to encourage scholars from many disciplines to do further research on these topics and encourage both scholars and policymakers to ask and attempt to answer the right questions. In the long run, information and evidence will help policymakers make better choices.

Explore Human Rights Impact Assessments

Independent observers and policymakers have significant experience evaluating and critiquing the human rights performance of other countries. Governments, in contrast, are just beginning to launch independent national assessments of human rights. In 1996, the Brazilian government and NGOs developed a national action plan for human rights and, in 1997–1999, the government began to implement this plan.[38] However, we know of no government that has developed or implemented a strategy to evaluate the human rights impact of its previous or potential trade policies. Moreover, some governments cannot be trusted to do such an assessment fairly or transparently.

Policymakers are just beginning to explore how to use human rights impact assessments when they make trade policies and agreements. We believe that this process deserves encouragement and we hope that scholars and activists will engage in developing effective analytical tools and strategies.[39]

The United States and EU Should Collaborate on Labor Rights Questions

Both the European Union and the United States believe that trade should advance the rights of workers. If these two giants of global trade collaborate on labor rights objectives and projects, they are more likely to strengthen both public support and the governance capacity needed to protect labor rights in the developing world. This will not be easy. Both countries have effectively "branded" their approaches to trade and foreign aid, in the hopes that they will reap positive spillovers (such as better foreign relations) from these policies. Yet by collaborating, the United States and the EU will save money and recipient

Recommendations for policymakers to encourage greater coherence between their trade and human rights objectives and policies

Recommendation	Strategy
Make a policy determination that trade and human rights should be coordinated	Respond to public concerns; make strategies to address globalization more coherent.
Reform national trade policymaking process	Develop a channel for human rights concerns to enter the policymaking process. Set up an advisory system. Include human rights policymakers and advocates in the decision-making process.
Task advisors to weigh human rights concerns	Ask the right questions when making public policy decisions.
Create coalition of the willing at the WTO	Member states should jointly request the WTO to study the relationship between WTO rules and human rights rules; encourage the Director General to appoint a human rights liaison; and set up a working group to examine trade in conflict zones and export processing zones.
Encourage business to make human rights a business priority	Policymakers should send a consistent message that human rights are important and clarify their human rights expectations of international business.
Clarify relationships	Member states should request that WTO staff examine how social labeling and procurement policies can be designed so they do not distort trade.
Encourage and disseminate research	Ask scholars and human rights advocates to do research, test it, and disseminate it.
Explore human rights impact assessments	Governments and foundations should fund research and testing of human rights assessments.
US and EU labor rights collaboration	The two governments should work together to help their trade partners improve the demand for labor rights and increase the expertise of government officials to protect labor rights.

countries will avoid repetitive reporting requirements and other administrative costs. They can focus their efforts on the capacity-building efforts that they do best. Some scholars of development claim that, for example, the United States excels in areas such as promoting worker health, whereas the EU excels in helping other governments promote the rule of law.[40] We believe that if the EU and the United States collaborate to advance labor rights and trade, they are more likely to be effective at building both a demand for labor rights as well as a supply of laws, skills, and administrative expertise for labor rights in the developing world.

A Final Word

In this digital age, people are the principal wealth of nations. There is a growing consensus that those countries that protect and promote human rights are those countries that will achieve sustainable economic development. By investing in their people, countries will be better positioned to achieve growth and benefit from trade.[41] Trade policies and agreements can help policymakers achieve a broad range of human development objectives. Economic growth and more open markets may, over time, increase access to education, opportunities, and credit. For these reasons, policymakers that weigh human rights considerations as they develop trade policy are more likely to ensure that their constituents thrive at the intersection of trade and human rights.[42]

Interviews for Righting Trade, 2005–2007

South Africa

J. Daniel O'Flaherty, Executive Director; Matthew Michael Mullen, Project Director and Michael Lake, Deputy Director; United States South Africa Business Council, June 14th, 2005

Ted Craig, Senior South Africa Desk Officer, Department of State, Wednesday, June 22nd, 2005

Hema Odhav, Third Secretary for Public Diplomacy and Andre Groenewald, First Secretary Economic Affairs, South African Embassy, July 8th 2005

Michael Canham, First Secretary for Political Affairs Office, South African Embassy, July 13th 2005

Tony Carroll, Managing Director (and trade lawyer with expertise in South Africa) Manchester Trade Ltd, July 7th, 2005

Bill Jackson and Patrick Coleman, Directors for African Affairs, Office of the United States Trade Representative, July 7th, 2005

Bill Fletcher, President, The Trans-Africa Forum, June 27th, 2005

Whitney W. Schneidman, President, Schneidman and Associates International

Herbert Ross, Director of the NEPAD and Governance Program, and Nkululeko Khumalo, Senior Researcher, Development Through Trade Project, South Africa Institute for International Affairs (SAIIA), July 20th, 2005

Paul Graham, Executive Director, Institute for Democracy Alternatives in South Africa (IDASA), July 20th, 2005

Garth le Pere, Executive Director, Christi van der Westhuizen, Senior Researcher, Michelle Pressend, Senior Researcher for the Mulitlateral Programme, Institute for Global Dialogue, July 21st, 2005

Alan Tousignant, First Secretary Economic Affairs, U.S. Embassy in South Africa, July 21st, 2005

Roger D. Crawford, Executive Director, Government Affairs and Policy, Johnson and Johnson, July 25th, 2005

Peter Leon, Partner; Danie Smit, Candidate Attorney; Kevin Williams, Associate, Weber, Wentzel and Bowens, July 25th, 2005

Luanne Grant, Executive Director, American Chamber of Commerce in South Africa, July 26th, 2005

Neva Magketla, Fiscal, Monetary and Public Sector Policy and Tonya Van Meelis, Coordinator for Trade and Industry, COSATU (Congress of South Africa Trade Unions), July 26th, 2005

Gilbert Marcus and Wim Trengrove, Constitutional Human Rights Lawyers, July 26th, 2005

Loretta Ferris, Center for Trade Law, and Christof Heyns, Center for Human Rights, University of Pretoria, July 27th, 2005

Eric Watkins, South African Human Rights Commission, July 28th, 2005

Thabo Chauke, Deputy Director for the Americas, Department of Trade and Industry, July 28th, 2005

Ms. Nkensani, Policy Analyst, Department of Trade and Industry, Economic Research and Policy Analysis, July 28th, 2005

Tony Ehrenreich, Labor Representative, National Economic Development and Labor Council and COSATU- Cape Town, July 29th, 2005

Judge Dennis Davis, High Court of South Africa, West Cape Province and Professor, University of Cape Town, August 1st, 2005

Lawrence Edwards, Professor of Economics, University of Cape Town, August 2nd 2005

Philip Krawitz, CEO, Cape Union Mart, August 3rd, 2005

Trudi Hartzenberg, Director, Trade Law Center for South Africa (TRALAC), University of Stellenbosch, August 5th, 2005

Brazil

Welber Barral, Professor of International Law, University of Santa Catarina, Georgetown University, September 27th, 2005

Riordan Rhoett, Sarita and Don Johnson Professor and Director, Western Hemisphere Affairs, Johns Hopkins University School for Advanced International Studies (SAIS), October 18th, 2005

Flavio Marega, Counselor for the Trade Policy Desk, and Aluisio G. De Lima-Campos, Advisor, Embassy of Brazil, November 1st, 2005

Elio de Almeida Cardoso, First Secretary for Human Rights and Humanitarian Affairs, Brazilian Mission to the United Nations, November 1st, 2005

Silvio Albequerque e Silva, First Secretary for Human Rights, Brazilian Mission to the Organization of American States, November 2nd, 2005

Tatiana Lacerda Prazeres, Brazilian Agency for Industrial Development, November 7th, 2005

Fabio Martins Faria, Director, Secretariat for Foreign Trade (SECEX), Ministry of Development, Industry and Foreign Trade, November 8th, 2005

Aloisio Tupinamba Gomes Neto, Special Advisor, Chamber of Foreign Trade (CAMEX), Ministry of Development, Industry and Foreign Trade, November 9th, 2005

Carlos Henrique Fialho Mussi, Economist, Economic Commission for Latin America and the Caribbean, November 9th, 2005

Otavio Brandelli, Deputy Chief, and Henrique Choer Moraes, Secretary, Intellectual Property Division, Ministry of Foreign Affairs, November 9th, 2005

Igor Resende, Political Officer, Department for Social Issues, Ministry of Foreign Affairs, November 9th, 2005

Marcelo Della Nina, Coordinator General, Economic Organizations, Department of Economics, Ministry of Foreign Affairs, November 10th, 2005

Braz Baracuhy, Division of Agriculture and Raw Materials, Ministry of Foreign Affairs, November 10th, 2005

Haroldo de Macedo Ribeiro, Secretary for General Coordination of Disputes, Ministry of Foreign Affairs, November 10th, 2005

Murilo Vieira Komniski, International Advisor, Special Secretariat for Human Rights, Office of the Presidency, November 10th, 2005

Alberto do Amaral, Professor of International Law and Coordinator, University of Sao Paulo and the Institute for International Trade Law and Development, November 13th, 2005

Frederico Figuereido, Trade Program, Brazilian Institute for Consumer Defense, November 13th, 2005

Diego Zancan Bonomo and Frederico Arana Meira, International Negotiations Officers, International Relations and Foreign Trade Department, Federation of the Industries of the State of Sao Paulo (FIESP), November 15th, 2005

Juana Kweitel, Program Coordinator, Conectas and SUR Human Rights Journal, November 15th, 2005

Paulo de Mesquita Neto, Executive Secretary, Sao Paulo Institute Against Violence, November 15th, 2005

Rubens Antonio Barbosa, President and former Brazilian Ambassdor to the United States, Rubens Barbosa and Associates, November 15th, 2005

Itamar Batista Goncalves, Abrinq Foundation, November 16th, 2005

Kjeld Jakobsen, President, Social Observatory Institute, United Workers Confederation (CUT), November 16th, 2005

Caio Magri, Partnerships and Mobilization Manager, Ethos Institute for Business and Social Responsibility, November 17th, 2001

Denise Dora, Program Officer for Human Rights, Ford Foundation Brazil, November 21st, 2005

Europe

Claes Hammar and Lisa Svensson, Trade Counselor and Second Secretary, Embassy of Sweden, November 16th, 2005

Adeline Hinderer, European Commission, GATS Investment, November 23, 2005

Kim Eling, EC, External Relations, November 23, 2005

Poul Nyrup Rasmussen, Member of the European Parliament, President of the Party of European Socialists, PES, November 24, 2005

Jean-Francois Boittin, Minister Counselor, Trade and Economic Affairs, French Embassy, December 20th, 2005

Helge Hassold, Minister Counselor, Trade and Economic Affairs, German Embassy, December 29th, 2005

Zbigniew Kubacki and Andrzej Gdula, Minister Counselor Economic and Commercial Affairs, and Counselor for Economic Affairs, Polish Embassy, January 3rd, 2006

Dr. Steven Schneebaum, Greenberg Traurig (a law firm), January 9th, 2006

Dr. Esther Brimmer, Deputy Director and Director of Research, Center for Transatlantic Relations, Johns Hopkins SAIS, January 10th, 2006

Peter Horvath, Trade and Economic Affairs Counselor, Hungarian Embassy, January 18th, 2006

James Hughes, First Secretary, Trade Policy and Agriculture, UK Embassy, January 17th, 2006

Margriet Vonno, Economic Counselor, Embassy of the Netherlands, January 31st, 2006

Ambassador Hugo Paemen, Hogan and Hartson LLP, February 7th, 2006

Nikolaos Zaimis, Trade Counselor, European Commission Delegation to the United States, February 17th, 2006

Luis Morago, Director, Oxfam Brussels Office, February 17th, 2006

Lotte Leicht, Brussels Office Director, Human Rights Watch, February 28th, 2006

Anja-Susan Loercher, Lawyer/Trade Policy Advisor, Foreign Trade Association (FTA), March 14th, 2006

Paolo Garzotti, Co-ordination of WTO, OECD, Trade Related Assistance; GATT. 133, Committee at DG Trade of the European Commission, March 16th, 2006

Rupert Schlegelmilch, Head of Unit "Sustainable Development" (including Trade and Environment), Dialogue with Civil Society – Bilateral Trade Relations with China, Taiwan, Hong Kong, Macao, Mongolia at DG Trade of the European Commission, March 24th, 2006

India

V Venkateswara Rao, Commercial Counselor, Embassy of India

Bipul Chatterjee, Director, Center for International Trade, Economics and the Environment, Consumer Unity and Trust Society (CUTS), April 7th, 2006

Debashis Chakraborty, Assistant Professor, Indian Institute of Foreign Trade, April 10th, 2006

Dr. Vijaya Katti, Professor and Chairperson, Management Development Programs, Indian Institute of Foreign Trade, April 10th, 2006

Dr. Sachin Chaturvedi, Fellow, Research and Information System for Developing Countries, April 10th, 2006

D. Shyam Babu, Fellow, Rajiv Gandhi Institute for Contemporary Studies, Rajiv Gandhi Foundation, April 10th, 2006

Suhas Chakma, Director, Asian Center for Human Rights, April 11th, 2006

Prasenjit Bose, Economist, Communist Party of India, April 11th, 2006

Dr. Bibek Debroy, Secretary General, and Amir Ullah Khan, Deputy Secretary General, PHD Chamber of Commerce and Industry, April 12th, 2006

Dr. Ravi Shanker, Professor and Chairman (Graduate Studies), School of International Business, Indian Institute of Foreign Trade, April 12th, 2006

Dr. K. Rangarajan, Professor and Head, Centre for SME Studies, Indian Institute of Foreign Trade, April 12th, 2006

Dr. Biswajt Dhar, Professor and Head, Centre for WTO Studies, Indian Institute of Foreign Trade, April 12th, 2006

Dr. Biswajit Bag, Associate Professor, Indian Institute of Foreign Trade, April 12th, 2006

Dr. Rajiv Mehta, Member Secretary, Commission for Agricultural Costs and Prices, Ministry of Agriculture, Government of India, April 13th, 2006

Amita Joseph, Director General, Business and Community Foundation, April 13th, 2006

Amitabh Kundu, Dean, School of Social Sciences, Jawaharlal Nehru University, April 15th, 2006

Dr. Manoj Pant, Secretary, Center for International Trade and Development, School of International Studies, Jawaharlal Nehru University, April 17th, 2006

Rama V. Baru, Associate Professor, Center of Social Medicine and Community Health, School of Social Sciences, Jawaharlal Nehru University, April 17th, 2006

Dr. Amit Shovon Ray, Professor of Economics and Chairman, Center for International Trade and Development, School of International Studies, Jawaharlal Nehru University, April 17th, 2006

Dr. Laveesh Bhandari, Director, Indicus Analytics, April 18th, 2006

Dr. Arpita Mukherjee, Senior Fellow, Indian Council for Research on International Economic Relations, April 18th, 2006

Dr. Nagesh Kumar, Director General, Research and Information System for Developing Countries, April 18th, 2006

Mrs. Aruna Sharma, Joint Secretary, National Human Rights Commission, April 19th, 2006

Dr. Ramesh Chand, Acting Director, National Centre for Agricultural Economics and Policy Research, April 19th, 2006

Dr. Veena Jha, India Programme Coordinator, United Nations Conference on Trade and Development (UNCTAD), April 20th, 2006

United States

Jeffrey Krilla, Deputy Assistant Secretary, Bureau of Democracy, Human Rights and Labor, Department of State, United States Government, April 18th, 2006

Grant Aldonas, Center for Strategic and International Studies, former Undersecretary for International Trade, Department of Commerce, and head of the Department's International Trade Administration. Also former Staff Director, Senate Finance Committee, Unites States Government, April 19th, 2006

Victoria Espinal, Assistant US Trade Representative for Intellectual Property, Office of the USTR, United States Government, April 21st, 2006

Eric Biel, Senior Counsel, Human Rights First and former Senate Finance Trade Counsel, Washington, DC, April 24th, 2006

Chris Moore, Deputy Assistant Secretary of State for Economic Affairs, Department of State, United States Government, April 21st, 2006

Demetrius Marantis, Senate Finance Committee, United States Senate, April 27th, 2006

Hannah Royal, Legislative Assistant, Senator Sam Brownback, United States Senate, May 3rd, 2006

Thea Lee, Director of International Affairs, AFL-CIO, May 23rd, 2006

Chris Whatley, Director of International Programs, Council of State Governments, May 19th, 2006

Robert Stumberg, Professor, Georgetown University Law School, Washington, DC, May 24th, 2006

Douglas Bell, Deputy Assistant USTR for Europe and the Middle East, Office of the USTR, United States Government, May 29th, 2006

Aaron Rosenberg, Deputy Assistant USTR for Labor Rights, Office of the USTR, United States Government, June 2nd, 2006

Kimberley Ann Elliott, Senior Fellow, Institute for International Economics and Center for Global Development, June 2nd, 2006

Christine Bliss, Assistant USTR for Services, and Christopher Melly, Deputy USTR for Services, United States Government, June 5th, 2006

Jeff Schott, Senior Fellow, Institute for International Economics, Washington, DC, June 5th, 2006

Robert Vastine, President, Coalition for the Services Industries, June 5th, 2006

Laura Baughman, President, The Trade Partnership, June 7th, 2006

Michael Castellano, Senior Trade Counsel to Senate Minority Leader Harry Reid, United States Senate, June 9th, 2006

Ben Miller, Legislative Assistant, Congressman George Miller, United States Congress, June 9th, 2006

Alan Stayman, former Deputy Assistant Secretary for Territorial and International Affairs, Department of the Interior, United States Government, June 9th and 12th, 2006

Pete Leon, Legislative Director, Congressman Elliott Engel, United States Congress, June 14th, 2006

Mark Linscott, Assistant U.S. Trade Representative for the Environment, and Jennifer Prescott, Deputy Assistant US Trade Representative for the Environment, United States Government, August 2nd, 2006

Joe Ferrante, Trade and Environment Coordinator, Environmental Protection Agency, United States Government, August 8th, 2006

Brian Pomper, Senior Trade Counsel, Senate Finance Committee, United States Government, August 9th, 2006

Shara Aranoff, Vice Chair, International Trade Commission, United States Government, August 9th, 2006

Kay Alison Wilkie, International Policy Analyst, Empire State Development/NYS Department of Economic Development, August 9th, 2006

Notes

1. Introduction: The Struggle to Weigh Human Rights in Trade Policymaking

1. Geography as destiny has been a focus of many economists. See, for example, Paul Krugman's paper, "The Role of Geography in Development, at /www.worldbank.org/ html/rad/abcde/html/krugman.htm; and Barry Eichengreen, "Geography as Destiny: A Brief History of Economic Growth," *Foreign Affairs*, March/April 1998; at www.foreignaffairs.org/19980301fareviewessay1379barry-ei, last searched 9/13/2005.

2. Information on Bolivia from 2004 CIA Fact Book at http://www.theodora.com/wfb-current/bolivia/bolivia_government.html and Bolivia Web at http://www.boliviaweb. com/cities/cbba.htm, last searched 9/13/2005.

3. Fact Sheet, Right to Water, at www.cohre.org/water; last searched 9/10/2005. Privatization of water services means that the private sector can own a concession, a lease, provide services as a management firm, or it can own the concession outright in perpetuity.

4. World Health Organization and UNICEF, *Global Water Supply and Sanitation Assessment 2000 Report* (Geneva and New York: WHO and UNICEF, 2000) and World Health Organization, "Right to Water" (Geneva: WHO, 2003). In many countries, the right to water is guaranteed by the constitution. Yet over 1.1 billion people lack access to safe drinking water and the World Health Organization (WHO) estimates that some 2.4 billion people do not have adequate sanitation.

5. William Finnegan, "Letter from Bolivia: Leasing the Rain," posted 5/13/2005, at http://www.waterobservatory.org/library.cfm?refID=33711, last searched 9/10/2005. Finnegan notes that protest against international water privatization erupted in Indonesia, Pakistan, India, South Africa, Poland, and Hungary. Finnegan, 14. All last searched 4 /10/2005.

6. World Health Organization, "Right to Water," 28, and "Substantive Issues Arising in the Implementation of the International Covenant on Economic, Social and Cultural Rights," General Comment No. 15 (2002), and http://www.unhchr.ch/tbs/doc.nsf/ (Symbol)/a5458d1d1bbd713fc1256cc400389e94? Opendocument, last searched 12/05/2005.

7. The Bolivian government did not want to break the deal with the consortium, because they feared it would undermine the confidence of foreign investors in Bolivia's economic management. But as the riots dragged on, military police were called in. Bolivian

Indians joined the water protestors and the government became increasingly afraid that the country's Indian majority might revolt. The police killed one young man. The government informed the company that the contract was revoked. Ultimately the old public utility was returned to control. The new board of directors vowed to treat water as a "social good," but service remains poor. The pros and cons of privatization and the right to water are discussed at http://www.africanwater.org/ppp_new_main.htm and http://www.africanwater.org/ppp_debate.htm.

8. John Hilary, "GATS and Water: The Threat of Services Negotiations at the WTO," Save the Children: 2003, 7–8. Increasingly experts believe local utilities must be strengthened and then monitored rather than privatized. See Elisabeth Malkin, "At World Forum, Support Erodes for Private Management of Water," *New York Times*, 3/29/06, at http://www.nytimes.com/2006/03/20/international/americas/20water.html?ex=1300510800&en=f0bf520329e8e3a7&ei=5088&partner=rssnyt&emc=rss and Monte Reel, "Turning the Taps Back to the States," *Washington Post*, 3/26/06, http://www.washingtonpost.com/wp-dyn/content/article/2006/03/26/AR2006032600861.html.

9. Patricia Ranald, "Australian Government Concedes That Water Does Not Belong in Trade Agreements," http://www.tradeobservatory.org/headlines.cfm?refID=76604, last searched 9/10/05.

10. http://www.releases.gov.nl.ca/releases/2001/just/1018n05.htm. Canada has put forth the following position. With regards to water distribution services, Canada will ensure that nothing in the FTAA undermines the ability of governments to deliver potable water. In Canada, drinking water is currently delivered to citizens by municipal, regional or provincial governments, either directly by these governments or through procurement by these governments of water distribution services. In the FTAA negotiations, Canada will continue to ensure, using the approach that was taken in the NAFTA, that our international trade obligations preserve this right. Water in its natural state is a natural resource and is not a good for the purposes of trade agreements. Only when water has been transformed into a good does it become subject to trade disciplines dealing with trade in goods. With respect to water distribution services, the Government of Canada is committed to ensuring that Canada's international trade obligations, including those for government procurement, continue to clearly preserve the ability of Canada to deliver drinking water to its citizens either as a public service or by means of government procurement. http://www.international.gc.ca/tna-nac/FTAA/services-en.asp, both last searched 4/11/2007.

11. For a good overview of these trade issues, see Scott Vaughan, "Privatization, Trade Policy and the Question of Water," Les Seminaires de L'iddri, no. 9, p. 23. The WTO fact sheet , "GATS: Fact and Fiction-Misunderstandings and Scare Stories," is at http://www.wto.org/english/tratop_e/serv_e/gats_factfiction8_e.htm, last searched 4/11/2007.

12. Claudia H. Deutsch, "There's Money in Thirst," *New York Times*, 10/10/2006, C5.

13. The UNDP has noted that although services liberalization offers many benefits to the poor, liberalization is best managed through national strategies, not through multilateral trade rules. UNDP, *Human Development Report*, 2005, 136.

14. On July 27, 2007, the WTO General Council approved the accession of Tonga. Once Tonga's government ratifies the deal, it will become WTO member 151 30 days after it informs the WTO of such ratification.

15. The *New York Times* recently summarized the contradictions in arguments that subsidies hurt smaller, poorer farmers and help rich farmers in the industrialized world. The article concludes that economists agree that "developing countries could help themselves greatly by liberalizing their own agricultural markets. Poor countries often heavily protect their farms and support vast uncompetitive agricultural sectors, drawing investment and labor into farming when it could be better used elsewhere. Eduardo Porter, "Ending Aid to Rich Farmers May Hurt the Poor One," *New York Times*, 12/18/2005, 4.

16. Carlos Manuel Vazquez, "Trade and Human Rights – Past, Present, and Future," *Journal of International Economic Law* 6(4) (2003), 797–839.

17. Alan Riding, "A Global Culture War Pits Protectionists against Free Traders," *New York Times*, 2/5/2005, A19; Armand Mattelart, "Cultural Diversity Belongs to Us All," *Le Monde*, 11/15/2005, mondediplo.com/2005/11/15unesco.

18. When President George Bush and Australian Prime Minister John Howard met at the White House in July, 2005, Bush and Howard agreed that they would "work together to reinforce the need for China to accept certain values as universal." But the two men disagreed on how to press China on complex human rights issues such as religious freedom or the right to information. Their differences became front page news in Australia. Australian officials sought to downplay these differences by categorizing them as "temporary arguments." "President Welcomes Prime Minister of Australia to the White House," www.whitehouse.gov/news/releases /2005/07/20050719.html; The Australian press reported that a Chinese diplomat who defected to Australia, Chen Wonglin, described how China wanted to woo Australia away from the United States. Mr. Chen has detailed how China wants Australia to play a role – like France – of saying no to the United States and that China is using the leverage of trade to keep Australia quiet on human rights and other sensitive issues. Mr. Chen also says his former political masters believe that Foreign Minister Downer has indicated that the ANZUS treaty wouldn't automatically cause Australia to join the United States in a future military defense of Taiwan. Australian reporters seemed to see the conference as signaling wide differences about when and how to press China on human rights during trade negotiations. Washington reporters didn't seem to see it the same way. See Jason Koutsoukis, "Bush Presses PM on Rights in China," The Age, 7/21/2005, at http://www.theage.com.au/news/national/bush-presses-pm-on-rights-in-china/2005/07/20/1121539030537.html?oneclick=true. For a summary of Australian editorial opinion, see Tom Regan, "Australia Sidesteps US over China," CS Monitor Online, at www.csmonitor.com/2005/0721/dailyUpdate.html. For the view from Washington, see Bill Sammon, "Bush Skirts Military Questions," *Washington Times*, 7/21/2005 at washingtontimes.com/national/20050719-103116-5937r.htm and Richard McGregor, "Hu Aims to Defuse Rising Tension with the US," *Financial Times*, 9/2/2005, at news.ft.com/cms/s/312427e8-1bdf-11da-9342-00000e2511c8.html. The bickering continued in 2006. Steven R. Weisman, "Rice and Australian Counterpart Differ About China," *New York Times*, 3/17/2006, A8.

19. Peter Temin, "Mediterranean Trade in Biblical Times." MIT Department of Economics Working Paper) 3–12: March 2003, 8, 14–16. This interesting study attempts to meld economics and archeology. Also see Clarence H. Wagner, Jr., "Commerce in the Bible, Israel: Crossroads of the East," at www.bridgesforpeace.com;publications/ dispatch/everydaylife/ last searched 8/25/2005.

20. Pirates wanted people more than goods because they could sell poor people as slaves and rich people for ransom.

21. Douglas A. Irwin, *Against the Tide: An Intellectual History of Free Trade* (Princeton: Princeton University Press, 1996), 14–16.

22. Gary Clyde Hufbauer *et al.*, *Economic Sanctions Reconsidered: History and Current Policy*, 2nd ed. (Washington, DC: IIE, 1990), 4.

23. Douglas A. Irwin, *Against the Tide* (Princeton: Princeton University Press, 1996), 14–16, quotations on p. 21.

24. Susan Ariel Aaronson, *Taking Trade to the Streets: The Lost History of Global Efforts to Shape Globalization* (Ann Arbor: University of Michigan Press, 2001), 36, 44.

25. As economist Dani Rodrik has noted, when government officials take steps to meet their trade obligations, they improve many long-standing patterns of government behavior. Trade reform "sets new rules and expectations regarding how . . . policy choices are made and implemented, establishes new constraints and opportunities . . . , creates a new set of stakeholders while disenfranchising the previous ones, and gives rise to a new philosophy . . . on what development policy is all about." Dani Rodrik, "Trade Policy Reform as Institutional Reform," August 2000, available on his Web site http://ksghome.harvard.edu/~drodrik/papers.html. Also see his "Getting Institutions Right," at same location.

26. Joel R. Paul, "Do International Trade Institutions Contribute to Economic Growth and Development?" *Virginia Journal of International Law* 44 (2002), 23, 53–55.

27. However, the benefits of trade may not be broadly shared and inequality may increase. David Dollar and Art Kraay, "Trade, Growth and Poverty," Poverty Research working Paper 2615, Washington DC, World Bank., 2001 and Dollar and Kraay, "Growth is Good for the Poor,"*Journal of Economic Growth* 7(3) (September), 195–225.

28. Kimberley Ann Elliott and Richard B. Freeman, *Can Labor Standards Improve Under Globalization?* (Washington, DC: IIE, 2003), 16; and Steven Charnovitz, "The Influence of International Labour Standards on the World Trading System: A Historical Overview," *International Labour Review* 126(5) (Sept–Oct.): 565–584.

29. David L Richards *et al.*, "Money with a Mean Streak? Foreign Economic Penetration and Government Respect for Human Rights in Developing Countries," *International Studies Quarterly* 45 (2001), 219–239; David L. Richards and Ronald D. Gelleny, "Business Friendly or Friendly Business: Examining the Impact of Government Respect for Human Rights on Foreign Economic Penetration in Developing States," unpublished paper, provided by authors; and Shannon Blanton and Robert G. Blanton, "Trade and Human Rights: Beyond the Spotlight," unpublished paper, provided by the authors.

30. D. Kaufmann A. Kraay and M. Mastruzzi, "Governance Matters IV: Governance Indicators for 1996–2004," at /www.worldbank.org/wbi/governance/pubs/govmatters4.html; World Bank *Doing Business in 2004: Understanding Regulation* (Oxford: Oxford University Press, 2004); Kapstein, Ethan, "Behavior Foundations of Democracy and Development" Center for Global Development Working Paper, #52, December 2004; and Dani Rodrik *et al.*, "Institutions Rule: The Primacy of Institutions over Geography and Integration in Economic Development," *Journal of Economic Growth* 9(2): 131–165, 2002.

31. The Cingranelli and Richards Human Rights Dataset contains standards-based quantitative information on government respect for 13 internationally recognized human rights for 195 countries, annually from 1981 to 2003. It is designed for use by scholars

and students who seek to test theories about the causes and consequences of human rights violations, as well as policymakers and analysts who seek to estimate the human rights effects of a wide variety of institutional changes and public policies including democratization, economic aid, military aid, structural adjustment, and humanitarian intervention. See ciri.binghamton.edu/. For a bibliography of scholarship using the data set, see http://ciri.binghamton.edu/bibliography.asp. For an example of how that data has been used, see Ifie M. F. Okwuje, "Human Rights and Globalization, Is It Time to Take This Relationship in a New Direction," unpublished paper prepared for the American Political Science Association 2004 conference, 9/2/2004, provided by the author.

32. Amartya Sen, *Development as Freedom* (Oxford: Oxford University Press, 1999).

33. Robert Barro, *Determinants of Economic Growth* (Cambridge, MA; MIT Press, 1997), 67.

34. UNDP, *Human Development Report* 2000 (New York: Oxford University Press), 2000, iii.

35. WTO Consultative Board, *The Future of the WTO: Addressing Institutional Challenges in the New Millennium* (Geneva: WTO, 2004), 10.

36. UNDP, *Human Development Report*, 2005, 73.

37. A. Alessina and R. Perott, "The Political Economy of Growth: A Critical Survey of the Recent Literature," *World Bank Economic Review* 8(3) 1994: 351–371AU: year?. On the link between the quality of institutions and growth see J. Aron, "Growth and Institutions: A Review of the Evidence," *World Bank Research Observer* (New York: Oxford University Press, 2000); 15(1), 99–135.

38. Daniel Kaufmann, "Human Rights and Development: Towards Mutual Reinforcement," prepared for Human Rights and Governance: The Empirical Challenge, NYU University Conference, 3/1/2004, p. 10–12.

39. D. Kaufmann, A. Kraay, and M. Mastruzzi, "Sustained Macroeconomic Reforms, Tepid Growth: A Governance Puzzle in Bolivia?" in D. Rodrik, ed., *In Search of Prosperity* (Princeton, NJ: Princeton University Press, 2003). In Bolivia, citizens/consumers of public services perceived that they couldn't influence the management of public services and saw these managers as disinterested and corrupt.

40. Economists are often skeptical concerning the economic effects of various forms of human rights: some think protecting basic human rights can make the legal system less efficient and that extensive social rights are incompatible with market economies. Lorenz Blume and Stefan Voigt of the University of Kassel, Germany, argue that basic human rights are a precondition for other kinds of rights such as property and civil rights and that they are thus efficiency-enhancing. They identify four different groups of rights and asked what effects they have on welfare and growth. They estimate their effects on investment in both physical and human capital and overall productivity. Basic human rights have indeed a positive effect on investment, but do not seem to contribute to productivity. Social or emancipatory rights, in turn, are not conducive to investment in physical capital but do contribute to productivity improvements. They also found that none of the four groups of rights ever has a significant negative effect on any of the economic variables here included. The research was published as University of Kassell Working Paper, No.67/ 04. Also see Randall Peerenboom, "Show Me the Money: The Dominance of Wealth in Determining Rights Performance in Asia," *Duke Journal of Comparative and International Law* 15 (2004), 75–152 and Daniel A. Farber, "Rights as Signals," Boalt Hall, UCB School of Law.

41. Louis Henkin, "Human Rights: Ideology and Aspiration, Reality and Prospect," in Samantha Power and Graham Alison, eds., *Realizing Human Rights: Moving From Inspiration to Impact* (New York: St. Martins: 2000), 5; and Esther Brimmer, *The United States, the European Union, and International Human Rights Issues* (Washington, DC: Center for Transatlantic Relations, Johns Hopkins University Press, 2002), 2.

42. Henkin, "Human Rights," 3–4.

43. Percy Bidwell, *The Invisible Tariff: A Study of the Control of Imports into the United States* (New York: Council on Foreign Relations, 1939), 111–115.

44. The speech www.classbrain.com/artteenst/publish/printer_four_freedoms_speech. shtml, last searched 7/26/2005.

45. Henkin, "Human Rights," 4–9.

46. www.udhr.org/index.htm, last searched 8/10/2006.

47. Henkin, "Human Rights, 10–12.

48. Ernest-Ulrich Petersmann, "The WTO Constitution and Human Rights," *Journal of Economic Law*, 19 (2000). 12.

49. In the Western political tradition human rights are held to be inalienable; they are necessary for freedom and they belong to all humans. If a right is inalienable, it cannot be bestowed, granted, or sold. But rights can also be nonderogable: they cannot be limited in times of national emergency. "Certain rights . . . may never be suspended or limited, even in emergency situations." They include the rights to life, to freedom from torture, to freedom from enslavement or servitude, to recognition as a person before the law, and to freedom of thought, conscience, and religion. "Fact Sheet," www.unhchr.ch/html/menu6/2/fs2.htm

50. These covenants were drafted by committees under the UN. The members of the UN then committed and member states were invited to become parties. Covenants, conventions, and protocols are international agreements, binding on the states that become parties to them by procedures indicated in the particular treaty. See "Fact Sheet," http://www.unhchr.ch/html/menu6/2/fs2.htm

51. James Nickel, "Human Rights," *The Stanford Encyclopedia of Philosophy* (Fall 2006), Edward N. Zalta, ed., forthcoming. http://plato.stanford.edu/archives/fall2006/ entries/rights-human/, last searched 7/30/2006.

52. The International Bill of Rights includes the Universal Declaration of Human Rights; the International Covenant on Economic, Social, and Cultural Rights; and the International Covenant on Civil and Political Rights; as well as the Optional Protocol to the International Covenant on Civil and Political Rights and the Second Optional Protocol to the International Covenant on Civil and Political Rights, which are aimed at the abolition of the death penalty "Fact Sheet, International Bill of Human Rights," last searched 2/12/06. http://www.unhchr.ch/html/menu6/2/fs2.htm

53. OECD. Patents and Innovation Trends and Policy Challenges, 2004. www.dklevine .com/archive/refs41222470000000000502.pdf., quoted in Rafael Pastor, "The Impact of Free Trade Agreements on Intellectual Property Standards in a Post-TRIPS World," 4/4/2006, at http://www.bilaterals.org/article.php3?id_article=4311#nb25. Also see fn. 99 for further criticism.

54. Vasquez, "Trade Sanctions and Human Rights," 803; Sarah H. Cleveland, "Human Rights Sanctions and International Trade: A Theory of Compatibility," *Journal of International Law* 133 (2002), 188–189. However, nations still continue to use force to enforce human rights with UN approval (e.g., in Kosovo).

55. **Obligations of the Parties to the International Covenant on Civil and Political Rights**

    Art. 2: (1) respect and ensure the rights recognized in the Covenant (2) take the necessary steps to adopt such laws or other measures as may be necessary to give effect to the rights recognized in the present Covenant (3) (a) ensure that any person whose rights or freedoms recognized in the Covenant are violated shall have an effective remedy (b) ensure that any person claiming such a remedy shall have his right determined by competent judicial, administrative or legislative authorities and to develop the possibilities of judicial remedy (c) ensure that the competent authorities enforce such remedies when granted.

    Art. 4: (1) In time of public emergency States Parties may take measures derogating from their obligations under the Covenant to the extent strictly required by the exigencies of the situation, provided that such measures are not inconsistent with their other obligations under international law and do not involve discrimination solely on the ground of race, colour, sex, language, religion or social origin. (2) No derogation from articles 6 (right to life), 7 (right to prevention of torture), 8 (paragraphs 1 and 2 on right to abolition of slavery, slave-trade and servitude), 11 (right to liberty of movement), 15 (right to non-retro-active penal code), 16 (right to recognition before the law) and 18 (right to freedom of thought, conscience, and religion) may be made.

    Art. 5: (1) No State, group or person has to right to engage in any activity aimed at the destruction of any of the rights and freedoms recognized by the Covenant or at their limitation to a greater extent than is provided for in the Covenant.

    Remaining Parties to the International Covenant on Civil and Political Rights (countries that have signed but not ratified the covenant).

    Andorra (signed 2002), Antigua and Barbuda, Bahamas, Bahrain, Bhutan, Brunei, China (signed 1998), Comoros, Cook Islands, Cuba, Fiji, Guinea-Bissau (signed 2000) Holy See, Lao People's Democratic Republic (signed 2000), Indonesia, Kiribati, Malaysia, Maldives, Marshall Islands, Mauritania, Micronesia, Myanmar, Nauru (signed 2001), Niue, Oman, Pakistan, Palau, Papua New Guinea, Qatar, Saint Kitts and Nevis, Saint Lucia, Samoa, Sao Tome and Principe (signed 1995), Saudi Arabia, Singapore, Solomon Islands, Tonga, Tuvalu, United Arab Emirates, Vanuatu.

56. **Obligations of the Parties to the International Covenant on Economic, Social and Cultural Rights**

    Art. 2: (1) Take steps, individually and through international assistance and co-operation, especially economic and technical, to the maximum of its available resources, with a view to achieving progressively the full realization of the rights recognized in the Covenant by all appropriate means, including particularly the adoption of legislative measures. (3) Developing countries, with due regard to human rights and their national economy, may determine to what extent they would guarantee the economic rights recognized in the Covenant to non-nationals.

    Art. 4: State Parties may subject rights in the Covenant only to such limitations as are determined by law and only in so far as this may be compatible with the nature of these rights and solely for the purpose of promoting the general welfare in a democratic society.

    Art. 5: (1) No State, group or person has the right to engage in any activity aimed at the destruction of any of the rights or freedoms recognized in the Covenant, or at their limitation to a greater extent than is provided for in the Covenant.

Remaining Parties to International Covenant on Economic, Social and Cultural Rights (countries that have signed but not ratified this covenant).
Andorra, Antigua and Barbuda, Bahamas, Bahrain, Belize (2000), Bhutan, Botswana, Brunei, Comoros, Cook Islands, Cuba, Fiji, Haiti, Holy See, Indonesia, Kiribati, Malaysia, Maldives, Marshall Islands, Mauritania, Micronesia, Mozambique, Myanmar, Nauru, Niue, Oman, Pakistan, Palau, Papua New Guinea, Saint Kitts and Nevis, Saint Lucia, Samoa, Sao Tome and Principe (signed 1995), Saudi Arabia, Singapore, South Africa (signed 1994), Tonga, Tuvalu, United Arab Emirates, United States of America (signed 1977), Vanuatu.

57. Susan Ariel Aaronson, *Trade and the American Dream* (Lexington: University of Kentucky Press, 1996), 23–33. This book was the first archival history of the development of the ITO and the GATT, using U.S. and British archives. On August 14, 1941 the United States and Britain jointly released the Atlantic Charter "to make known certain common principles . . . on which they base their hopes for a better future for the world." The Atlantic Charter is at usinfo.state.gov/usa/infousa/facts/democrac/53.htm. The Declaration by the United Nations built on the Atlantic Charter. It was signed by the United States of America, the United Kingdom of Great Britain and Northern Ireland, the Union of Soviet Socialist Republics, China, Australia, Belgium, Canada, Costa Rica, Cuba, Czechoslovakia, Dominican Republic, El Salvador, Greece, Guatemala, Haiti, Honduras, India, Luxembourg, Netherlands, New Zealand, Nicaragua, Norway, Panama, Poland, South Africa, Yugoslavia. These nations agreed to the principles expressed in the Atlantic Charter and to work to defeat the Tripartite Pact. See http://www.ibiblio.org/pha/policy/1942/420101a.html, both last searched 1/15/06.

58. Committee on Ways and Means, U.S. House of Representatives, "Report on the Havana Charter for An International Trade Organization," May 1994, pp. 58–61, discusses Article 2. It states that Members accept the view that unemployment is an international issue and when ignored can lead to depression. Article 7 of Chapter II relates to labor standards ("fair labor standards").

59. Steve Charnovitz, "The Moral Exception in Trade Policy," *Virginia Journal of International Law* 689(38) (1998), 8, 13 at www.worldtradelaw.net/articles/charnovitzmoral .pdf. For example, the British banned trade in slaves in 1807 for moral reasons. The United States established a "moral embargo" in 1940, which applied to airplanes and aviation gasoline against any country whose government bombed civilians. These earlier policies established clear precedents that trade could be banned or sanctioned in the interest of protecting human rights at home or abroad.

60. See Aaronson, *Trade and the American Dream*, and *Rubber Manufacturers Association*, "Pro's and Cons of the ITO," 1/10/1950. Opponents alleged it was hypocritical, dealt with the symptoms of trade and employment ills rather than the ills, affects sovereignty, and will lead to socialism, summarized p. 12., 99; and William Diebold Jr., "The End of the ITO," Princeton, Essays in International Finance, no. 16, October, 1952, 9–28.

61. Aaronson, *Trade and the American Dream*, 115–131.

62. When the ITO came to the U.S. Congress for approval, members were preoccupied with domestic conditions (inflation and shortages) and international conditions (the spread of communism, the invasion of Korea, and economic problems in Europe). The ITO was not a top priority for President Harry S Truman or the members of the U.S. Congress. Ibid. 4–5. The battle quote is from Paul G. Hoffman, *Peace Can Be Won* (Garden City, NY: Doubleday, 1951), 87.

63. Robert E. Hudec, *The GATT Legal System and World Trade Diplomacy* (New York: Praeger, 1975), 356, no. 3. Moreover, members of Congress were not enthusiastic devotees of the GATT. They were willing to accept it as a set of rules governing trade, but they were not willing to accept GATT as a treaty organization (which could require the United States to change some of its domestic policies and regulations). Congress consistently authorized a GATT disclaimer when it renewed the president's authority to negotiate under GATT. It noted that congressional approval of the act should not be construed as denoting approval or disapproval of the GATT.

64. Aaronson, *Taking Trade*, 54–55, fn, 110–113. The footnotes delineate documents in the U.S. National Archives Record Group 364.1, Records of the Office of the United States Trade Representative.

65. Thomas W. Zeiler, *Free Trade, Free World: The Advent of GATT* (Chapel Hill: University of North Carolina Press, 1999), 138. In 1951, the U.S. suspended benefits to GATT members that were in the Communist block including Czechoslovakia and China. China withdrew from the GATT in 1950.

66. Aaron Forsberg, "The Politics of GATT Expansion: Japanese Accession and the Domestic Political Context in Japan and the United States, 1948–1955," *Business and Economic History* 27(1) (1998), 185–195; and Aaronson, *Taking Trade* 69, 80–82.

67. The WTO is now conducting its first round, but it is really the ninth round of trade talks. The Geneva negotiations were 1947, Annecy, 1949; Torquay, 1950–1951; Geneva, 1955–1956; Dillon, 1959–1962; Kennedy Round, 1963–1967, Tokyo Round, 1973–1979; and, finally, the Uruguay Round, 1986–1993, which led to the creation of the WTO.

68. GAO, "Current Issues in US Participation in the Multilateral Trading System," GAO/NSIAD-85–118, 8/23/1985, 1–10; and William R. Cline, "Introduction and Summary," in William R. Cline, ed., *Trade Policy in the 1980s* (Washington, DC: IIE, 1983), 1–53.

69. http://www.wto.org/english/docs_e/legal_e/ursum_e.htm#General.

70. The Marrakesh Agreement Establishing the World Trade Organization is at www.wto.org/english/res_e/booksp_e/analytic_index_e/wto_a

71. Ibid. The agreement establishing the World Trade Organization (WTO) calls for a single institutional framework encompassing the GATT, as modified by the Uruguay Round, all agreements and arrangements concluded under its auspices and the complete results of the Uruguay Round. Its structure is headed by a Ministerial Conference meeting at least once every two years. A General Council oversees the operation of the agreement and ministerial decisions on a regular basis. This General Council acts as a Dispute Settlement Body and a Trade Policy Review Mechanism, which concern themselves with the full range of trade issues covered by the WTO, and has also established subsidiary bodies such as a Goods Council, a Services Council, and a TRIPS Council. The WTO framework ensures a "single undertaking approach" to the results of the Uruguay Round – thus, membership in the WTO entails accepting all the results of the Round without exception. Alan Riding, "Months of Risk, Moments of Isolation, Now Boasts of Triumph," *New York Times*, 12/15/1993, D19.

72. The sections below refer to GATT 1994, not other agreements of the WTO such as TRIPS or GATS.

73. Vasquez, "Trade Sanctions," 810.

74. www.wto.org/english/thewto_e/minist_e/min01_e/brief_e/brief16_e.htm; Robert Howse, "Human Rights in the WTO: Whose Rights, What Humanity?" Comment on

Petersman, at http://www.ejil.org/journal/Vol13/No3/art2.html, last searched 8/30/2006; and Steve Charnovitz, "The Moral Exception in Trade Policy," *Virginia Journal of International Law* 38, 689,(Summer: 1998) www.worldtradelaw.net/articles/ charnovitzmoral.pdf, last searched 12/10/2005.

75. Article XXI provides that: Nothing in [the GATT] shall be construed:
    (a) to require any contracting party to furnish any information the disclosure of which it considers contrary to its essential security; or
    (b) to prevent any contracting party from taking action which it considers necessary for the protection of its essential security interests
        (i) relating to fissionable materials or the materials from which they are derived;
        (ii) relating to the traffic in arms, ammunition and implements of war and to such traffic in other goods and materials as is carried on directly or indirectly for the purpose of supplying a military establishment;
        (iii) taken in time of war or other emergency in international relations; or
    (c) to prevent any contracting party from taking any action in pursuance of its obligations under the United Nations Charter for the maintenance of international peace and security. Article XXI was determined to ensure that governments could take care of real security interests.

76. According to legal scholar Joel Trachtman, "Scholars debate whether WTO panels or the Appellate Body are mandated to apply non-WTO international law as law. They generally agree that non-WTO international law cannot form the basis of claims in the WTO dispute settlement system, but disagree as to whether such law can form the basis of defense to claims. They also agree that certain non-WTO international law may be used in interpreting the WTO agreements." Personal communication, Professor Joel P. Trachtman, Professor of International Law, Fletcher School, Tufts University, and Member of Our Advisory Committee, 10/28/2005. He is also a member of editorial boards of *American Journal of International Law*, *European Journal of International Law*, and *Journal of International Economic Law*.

77. www.customs.gov/ImageCache/cgov/content/import/commericial_5fenforcement/ rough_5fdiamonds_2edoc/v1/rough_5fdiamonds.doc.

78. These reports often examine developments over time. At: http://www.state.gov/g/ drl/rls/hrrpt/2003/27768.htm; http://hrw.org/english/docs/2005/06/08/china11103.htm; http://web.amnesty.org/web/ar2002.nsf/asa/china?Open, all last searched 8/30/2006.

79. Article XIII of the World Trade Agreement establishing the WTO, at www.jus.uio.no/ lm/wta.1994/index.html, last searched 12/10/2005; and Membership, Alliances and Bureaucracy, http://www.wto.org/english/thewto_e/whatis_e/tif_e/org3_e.htm, last searched 2/06/06. Nations can decide not to apply GATT or WTO rules to a particular country at the time of accession; this is called nonapplication.)

80. During this debate, Congress changed the name of the MFN review to normal trade relations or NTR. Several members perceived that although most favored nation was the long-standing diplomatic term, it implied that the country under consideration got special benefits, rather than normal benefits.

81. See WTO and China, at www.uschina.org/public/wto and Ways and Means Subcommittee on Trade, "United States China Trade Relations and Renewal of China's Most-Favored Nation Status, 104th Congress, 2nd session, July 11, 1996, 4; and Business Coalition for US China Trade, "China PNTR: Advancing American Values, 4/26/2000, at www.uschina.org/public/wto/usavalues.html.

82. Decision on Measures Concerning the Possible Negative Effects of the Reform Programme on Least Developed and Net Food-Importing Developing Countries, at www.wto.org/english/docs_e/legal_e/ursum_e.htm#General.

83. http://www.wto.org/english/tratop_e/dda_e/dohaexplained_e.htm#agriculture http://www.wto.org/english/tratop_e/dda_e/dda_e.htm; and http://www.wto.org/english/tratop_e/dda_e/dohaexplained_e.htm; both last searched 8/12/2006.

84. The Millennium Development goals, are described at www.un.org/millenniumgoals/.

85. The UN Office of the High Commissioner for Human Rights tried to bring this forward at the Cancun Ministerial of the WTO, UNHCR, Paper prepared for the 5th WTO Ministerial Conference in Cancun, at www.unhcr.ch/html/menu2/trade/index.htm Peter Woike, former Executive Vice President, IFC, has been very forceful about these issues. The IFC, an arm of the World Bank, includes human rights in its performance standards. See conference on "Human Rights and Development: Towards Mutual Reinforcement," NYU Law School, 3/1/2004; and ILO (International Labor Organisation, "A Fair Globalization: Creating Opportunities for All," at www.ilo.org/public/english/wcsdg/.

86. Press Release, IFC, "IFC and ILO Team Up to Improve Working Conditions in Global Supply Chains," 8/21/2006.

87. For examples of scholarship, see www.worldtradelaw.net/articles.htm#trachtman. This site has links to a wide range of scholarly papers. Also see Robert Howse and Makau Matua, "Protection Human Rights in a Global Economy: Challenges for the World Trade Organization" (Montreal: Rights and Democracy, 2000), 4–6, at www.rightsanddemocracy.org.

88. http://www.ohchr.org/english/issues/globalization/trade/index.htm; and http://ap.ohchr.org/documents/dpage_e.aspx?s=115

89. www.ohchr.org/english/issues/globalization/trade/ last searched 9/20/05. It has prepared papers on human rights and trade generically, on the right to health, nondiscrimination and other topics. ap.ohchr.org/documents/dpage_e.aspx?s=115, last searched 9/10/05.

90. The study yielded a new book, Thomas Cottier, Joost Pauwelyn, and Elisabeth Burgi, Eds., *Human Rights And International Trade* (Oxford: Oxford University Press, 2006). This book examines the theoretical framework of the interaction between the disciplines of international trade law and human rights, by focusing on seven case studies, ranging from freedom of expression and anti-trust rules, to the fight against trade in conflict diamonds and the UN's new convention on tobacco control.

91. For Joost Pauwelyn, see www.asil.org/insights/2004/11/insight041117.html; Steve Charnoviz, "The WTO and the Rights of the Individual," chapter in *Trade Law and Global Governance* (London: Cameron May, 2002). An attorney from the WTO has also contributed to this discussion, see Gabrielle Marceau's excellent article, "WTO Dispute Settlement and Human Rights," *European Journal of International Law* 13(4) (2002). 753–814

92. For an example of an activist's report, see publications on www.ciel.org Web page or www.oxfam.org.

93. For example, from civil society, see www.3dthree.org; www.rightsanddemocracy.org; and www.panos.org.uk.

94. www.3dthree.org/en/pages.php?IDcat=6

95. Alan I. Marcus and Howard P. Segal, *Technology in America: A Brief History* (San Diego: Harcourt Brace, 1989), 42–43. The U.S. Constitution granted Congress the power "to promote the progress of science and the useful Arts, by securing for limited Times to Authors and inventors the exclusive Right to their respective Writings and Discoveries."

96. A copyright provides protection for literary and artistic works such as books, musical compositions and cinematographic works. A patent protects an invention by giving the inventor the right to exclude others from making, using, or selling a new useful, non obvious invention during a specific term. Trademarks are words, phrases, logos or other graphic symbols used by manufacturers or merchants to identify their goods and distinguish them from others. Other types of intellectual property include trade secrets, industrial designs and geographic indicators such as cognac, champagne, or Idaho potatoes.

97. The TRIPS agreement covers: how nations should give adequate protection to intellectual property rights; how countries should enforce those rights; how to settle disputes on intellectual property between members of the WTO; and special transitional arrangements during the period when the new system is being introduced The TRIPS agreement took effect on January 1, 1995. Developed countries were given one year to ensure that their laws and practices conform with the TRIPS agreement. Developing countries and (under certain conditions) transition economies were given five years, until 2000. Least-developed countries have 11 years, until 2006 – now extended to 2016 for pharmaceutical patents. If a developing country did not provide product patent protection in a particular area of technology when the TRIPS agreement came into force (January 1, 1995), it had up to 10 years to introduce the protection. But for pharmaceutical and agricultural chemical products, the country had to accept the filing of patent applications from the beginning of the transitional period, although the patent did not need to be granted until the end of this period. If the government allowed the relevant pharmaceutical or agricultural chemical to be marketed during the transition period, it had to – subject to certain conditions – provide an exclusive marketing right for the product for five years, or until a product patent was granted, whichever was shorter. Proponents of the TRIPS agreement argued that it would create a framework which encourages domestic innovation, and by protecting foreign IPR holders, gave them incentives to invest in production and research in the developing world. http://www.wto.org/english/thewto_e/whatis_e/tif_e/agrm7_e.htm, last searched 4/18/2006.

98. Pastor, "The Impact of Free Trade Agreements," www.bilaterals.org/article.php3?id_article=4311, and NA, "Patently Problematic," *The Economist*, 9/14/2002, www.economist.com/science/displayStory.cfm?story_id=1325219; See as example Civil Society Report on Intellectual Property, Innovation and Health," http://www.policy network.net/main/index.php; and Commission on Public Health, Innovation and Intellectual Property Rights 'Public Health, Innovation, and Intellectual Property Rights, 4/3/2006, http://www.who.int/intellectualproperty/ documents/thereport/en/index.html, both searched 5/18/2006; and "How Poor Countries can Avoid the Wrongs of Intellectual Property Rights," *The Economist*, 9/14/02, www.economist.com/science/displaystory.cfm?story_id+1325360. For a scholarly overview of these issues, see Carsten Fink and Keith E. Maskus, *Intellectual Property and Development: Lessons From Recent Economic Research* (Washington, DC: World Bank and Oxford University Press, 2005), 1–13.

99. Fact Sheet: TRIPS and Pharmaceutical Patents: Obligations and Exceptions, at www.wto.org/english/tratop_e/trips_e/factsheet_pharm02_e.htm, last searched 12/05/2005;

100. WTO Press Release, "Members OK Amendment to Make Health Flexibility Permanent," www.wto.org/english/news_e/pres05_e/pr426_e.htm, last searched 12/10/2005.

101. Emilie M. Hafner-Burton, "Trading Human Rights; How Preferential Trade Agreements Influence Government Repression," *International Organization*, 59 (2005), 593–629; and Emilie M. Hafner-Burton, "Forum Shopping for Human Rights: The Politics of Preferential Trade," presented at APSA, at www.apsanet.org, last searched 12/10/2005.

2. The World Trade Organization and Human Rights: Providing Some Power to the People Some of the Time

1. Jonathan Watts, "Field of Tears," *The Guardian*, 9/16/2003, http://www.guardian.co.uk/wto/article/0,2763,1042865,00.html, last searched 3/30/2007.

2. Under trade liberalization, Korean farmers found it difficult to compete with imported rice. Bae Keun-Min, "Local Farmers Alert over Additional Market-Opening in International Year of Rice," *Korea Times*, http://times.hankooki.com/lpage/biz/200402/kt2004020519420711860.htm 4020519420711860.htm; and Donald Greenlees, "South Korea Farmers Wary over Rice Deal," *International Herald Tribune*, http://www.iht.com/articles/2005/12/12/business/wtorice.php; both last searched 12/27/2005.

3. John Vidal and David Munk, "Farmer Who Got Hearing by Paying the Ultimate Price," *The Guardian*, 9/12/20003, http://www.guardian.co.uk//article/0,2763,1040297,00html, last searched 12/27/2005.

4. Bae Keun-Min, "WTO Talks, Farmers Buy Time for Restructuring," *Korea Times*, 9/15/2003, http://times.hankooki.com/lpage/nation/200309/kt2003091519092811950.htm; NA, "South Korean Activist Kills Himself, Others Injured in Cancun Protest," *Agence France Press*, 9/11/2003, http://www.commondreams.org/headlines03/0911-06htm; "Suicide Highlights Plight of Farmers," Focus on the Global South, http://www.focusweb.org/content/view/153/36/; all last searched 12/29/2005.

5. Rights and Democracy, "Globalization and Human Rights: Policy Seminar," 10/19/2000, http://www.ichrdd.ca/english/commdoc/publications/globalization/policy Seminar Globali . . . , last searched 12/14/2004; Oxfam, "Cut the Cost, Patent Injustice: How World Trade Rules Threaten the Health of Poor People," http://www.oxfam.org.uk/what_we_do/issues/health/patent_injustice.htm, last searched 1/20/2006; and more recent criticisms from a wide range of groups are summarized at http://www.tradeobservatory.org/, last searched 2/04/2006. From the United Nations, see Office of the High Commissioner for Human Rights, "Human Rights and Trade," 5th WTO ministerial conference, Cancun, Mexico, 9/10–14/2003.

6. International Federation for Human Rights, "Report, The WTO and Human Rights," No. 320/2, 11/2001, p. 3.

7. We are grateful to our advisor, Professor Joel P. Trachtman, for these comments (and to anonymous reviewers for similar comments for Aaronson's article for *World Trade Review*).

8. See Universal Declaration of Human Rights at http://www.un.org/Overview/rights.html. On participating in public affairs, see Article 25 of the International Covenant on Civil and Political Rights (ICCPR). It has been interpreted by General Comment No. 25 (1996) articles 13 and 17. The Human Rights Committee, the

treaty body monitoring the implementation of the ICCPR has interpreted the right to participate as including participation in "All aspects of public administration, and the formulation and implementation of policy at the international, national, regional, and local levels." Also see 3DThree, "Policy Brief on Intellectual Property, Development and Human Rights: How Human Rights Can Support Proposals for a World Intellectual Property Organization (WIPO) Development Agenda," Policy Brief 2, 2/2006, p. 5, at www.3dthree.org/en/page.php?IDpage=27.

9. General Agreement on Tariffs and Trade 1994 includes: (a) Understanding on the Interpretation of Article II: 1 (b) (b) Understanding on the Interpretation of Article XVII; (c) Understanding on Balance-of-Payments Provisions; (d) Understanding on the Interpretation of Article XXIV; (e) Understanding on the Interpretation of Article XXV; (f) Understanding on the Interpretation of Article XXVIII; (g) Understanding on the Interpretation of Article XXX. GATT 1994 incorporates the GATT 1947 provisions (except for the Protocol on Provisional Application). We do not discuss the Agreement on Sanitary and Phytosanitary Measures; Agreement on Textiles and Clothing; Agreement on Technical Barriers to Trade; Agreement on Trade-Related Investment Measures; Agreement on Implementation of Article VI; Agreement on Implementation of Article VII; Agreement on Preshipment Inspection; Agreement on Rules of Origin; Agreement on Import Licensing Procedures; the Agreement on Subsidies and Countervailing Measures; or the Agreement on Safeguards. usinfo.org/law/gatt/toc.htmllast searched 8/10/2006.

10. Michael J. Trebilcock, "Trade Policy and Labour Standards: Objectives, Instruments and Institutions," Law and Economics Research Paper No. 02–01, http://ssrn.com/abstract_id=307219; Lance A. Compa and Stephen F. Diamond, eds., *Human Rights, Labor Rights and International Trade* (Philadelphia: University of Pennsylvania Press, 1996); Steve Charnovitz, "The Influence of International Labour Standards on the World Trading Regime," http://www.geocities.com/charnovitz/ilo.htm, last searched 2/6/2003; Steve Charnovitz, "The World Trade Organization and Social Issues," *Journal of World Trade* 28(5) (1994), 17–33; and M. Mehra, ed., *Human Rights and Economic Globalisation: Directions for the WTO* (London: Global Publications Foundation and International NGO Committee on Human Rights in Trade and Investment, 1999).

11. Economist Jagdish Bhagwati believes that human rights were not and cannot be part of the WTO's purview. Jagdish Bhagwati, "Introduction," in Jagdish Bhagwati and Robert Hudec, *Fair Trade and Harmonization* (Cambridge, MA: MIT Press, 1996), 1.

12. Professor Maria Green describes this debate as using the WTO to enforce human rights or using human rights to regulate the WTO (and other trade regimes). Maria Green, "Comments: Integrating Enforcement of Human Rights Laws with Enforcement of Trade Laws: Some Baseline Issues," 4/5–6/2004. Also see Hoe Lim, "Trade and Human Rights: What's at Issue?" E/C 12/2001/WP.2, pp. 4–5, http://www.unhchr.ch/tbs/doc.nsf/o/907f88e4d28e4cb9c1256a63003069fd?Opendocument, last searched 1/6/2006; and Joost Pauwelyn, T. Cottier, and Elisabeth Burgi, *Human Rights and International Trade* (Oxford: Oxford University Press, 2005).

13. Caroline Dommen, "Raising Human Rights Concerns in the World Trade Organization: Actors, Processes and Possible Strategies," *Human Rights Quarterly* 24(1) (2002), 3.

14. Ernst-Ulrich Petersmann, "Time for a United Nations 'Global Compact' for Integrating Human Rights into the Law of Worldwide Organizations: Lessons from European

Integration" *European Journal of International Law* 13 (2002) 624, 655–659. Law Professor Robert Howse has an interesting response to Petersmann. Robert Howse "Human Rights in the WTO: Whose Rights, What Humanity? Comment on Petersmann," *European Journal of International Law* 13 (2002), 651–660.

15. Gabrielle Marceau, "WTO Dispute Settlement and Human Rights," paper prepared for the joint meeting of the American Society of International Law and the World Trade Forum on "International Economic Law and Human Rights," 8/13–14/2001; and Salman Bal, "International Free Trade Agreements and Human Rights: Reinterpreting Article XX of the GATT," *Minnesota Journal of International Trade* 10(62) (Winter 2001) 62–108.

16. Layna Mosley and Saika Uno, "Racing to the Bottom or Climbing to the Top? Economic Globalization and Collective Labor Rights," unpublished paper in possession of author; Layna Moseley, "Varieties of Capitalists? Economic Globalization and Labor Rights in the Developing World," unpublished paper in possession of author, presented at the Southern Political Science Association, 1/5–7/2006; Emilie M. Hafner-Burton and Kiyoteru Tsutsui, "Human Rights in a Globalizing World: The Paradox of Empty Promises," *American Journal of Sociology* 110 (2005), 1373–1411; David Cingranelli, "Democratization, Economic Globalization, and Workers' Rights," in Edward McMahon and Thomas Sinclair, eds., *Democratic Institutional Performance: Research and Policy Perspectives* (New York: Praeger, 2002); Rhonda Callaway and Julie Harelson-Stephens, "The Weakest Link? Debunking the Direct Link between Trade and Basic Human Needs," paper at ECPR Joint Sessions, "The Systematic Study of Human Rights Violations," Turin, Italy, 3/22–27/2002; and Clair Apodaca, "Global Economic Patterns and Personal Integrity Rights after the Cold War," *International Studies Quarterly* 45 (2001), 634–647. Many of these articles (but not the book chapters) are available for download at http://www.rightingtrade.org and www.hrt.projectspaces.com.

17. Mary Comerford Cooper, "International Organizations and Democratization: Testing the Effect of GATT/WTO Membership," Asia Pacific Research Center (April 2003), p. 15, http://www.kenan-flagler.unc.edu/KI/kiWashington/humanRightsAndTrade/hrtLibrary.cfm.

18. We use "diktat" in the sense of authoritative decree imposed unilaterally. See http://dictionary.reference.com/search?r=10&q=diktat, last searched 11/06/2006. Examples where people presume WTO "diktat" include Otieno Amisi, "Hong Kong Trade Talks Failed: Behind the Scenes at the World Trade Talks," *Kenya Times Magazine*, 12/30/2005, http://www.timesnews.co.ke/30dec05/magazine/magazine2.html, last searched 12/30/2005; and Pat Buchanan, *The Great Betrayal: How American Sovereignty and Social Justice Are Being Sacrificed to the Gods of the Global Economy* (Boston: Little Brown, 1998), 17–19.

19. http://www.wto.org/english/thewto_e/minist_e/min99_e/english/book_e/stak_e_6thm, last searched 1/04/2006.

20. Settling disputes is the responsibility of the Dispute Settlement Body (the General Council in another guise), which consists of all WTO members. The Dispute Settlement Body has the sole authority to establish "panels" of experts to consider the case, and to accept or reject the panels' findings or the results of an appeal. It monitors the implementation of the rulings and recommendations, and has the power to authorize retaliation when a country does not comply with a ruling. If a nation doesn't like a decision, it can refuse to comply and accept retaliation, it can compensate the

affected parties or it can change the contested policy. Understanding Dispute Settlement, http://www.wto.org/English/thewto_e/whatis_e/tif_e/disp1_e.htm, last searched 11/2/2006.

21. Hoe Lim, "Trade and Human Rights: What's at Issue?" E/C 12/2001/WP.2, pp. 4–5, http://www.unhchr.ch.

22. Ernst-Ulrich Petersmann, "Time for Integrating Human Rights into the Law of Worldwide Organizations," Jean Monnet Working Paper 7/01, 15, Lim, 4–5, http://www.unhchr.ch. In the notes linked to the International Bill of Rights, we discuss which countries have signed and which have not signed the two covenants.

23. In 1989, the General Assembly called for the convening of a world meeting that would review and assess progress made in the field of human rights since the adoption of the Universal Declaration of Human Rights and identify obstacles and ways in which they might be overcome. The members met at Vienna, Austria, in 1993 and agreed to work harder to integrate human rights and ensure that human rights were advanced at the national, regional, and international levels. The Vienna Declaration on Human Rights declares (Article 27), "Every State should provide an effective framework of remedies to redress human rights grievances or violations." Article 35 calls for "The full and effective implementation of United Nations activities to promote and protect human rights must reflect the high importance accorded to human rights by the Charter of the United Nations and the demands of the United Nations human rights activities, as mandated by Member States." The World Conference on Human Rights calls on regional organizations and prominent international and regional finance and development institutions to assess also the impact of their policies and programs on the enjoyment of human rights. UN General Assembly, "Vienna Declaration and Plan of Action," 7/12/1993, http://www.unhchr.ch/huridocda/huridoca.nsf/(Symbol)/A.CONF.157.23.En?OpenDocument.

24. On context, see Petersmann, "Time for," 658–659; On UN High Commissioner Reports, see /www.ohchr.org/english/issues/globalization/trade/index.htm; and http://ap.ohchr.org/documents/dpage_e.aspx?su=11&s=60, all last searched 8/12/2006.

25. http://www.wto.org/english/thewto_e/whatis_e/tif_e/fact1_e.htm, last searched 1/04/2006. According to the Web site, the members of the WTO agree to gradually remove regulations or policies that distort trade between domestic and foreign producers. They also agree to inform their citizens and firms (the people and entities that trade) about the WTO's rules. Finally, they agree to provide these individuals and firms with information about how they should conform to these rules.

26. Remarks of Law Professor Steve Charnovitz at a Brooklyn Law Conference, "The Globalization of Economic Human Rights," http://www.geocities.com/charnovitz/brooklyn.htm, last searched 1/26/2005.

27. WTO Analytical Index; Technical Barriers to Trade: Agreement on Technical Barriers to Trade, http://www.wto.org/english/res_e/booksp_e/analytic_index_e/tbt_01_e/htm#top.

28. Several countries, including Brazil, India, Bolivia, Colombia, Cuba, Dominican Republic, Ecuador, Peru, Thailand, and others, have come to recognize that the TRIPS agreement does not protect traditional or indigenous knowledge, which is often passed from one family member or tribal member to another and is not written down or protected under modern rules. Policymakers from these countries fear that industrialized country pharmaceutical and agricultural companies plan to use and

adapt indigenous knowledge, such as that relating to medicinal plants (for example, aloe and taxol) without compensating the true owners of such knowledge. As a result, they want to amend TRIPS to make it consistent with the Convention on Biological Diversity (CBD). They have proposed that TRIPS should require patent applicants to disclose the country of origin of genetic resources and traditional knowledge used in the inventions, evidence that they received "prior informed consent" (a term used in the CBD), and evidence of "fair and equitable" benefit sharing. Policymakers from these countries argued that their indigenous knowledge would otherwise be patented without their citizens reaping the economic benefits of such knowledge. In recognition of this perspective, members of the WTO agreed to review Article 27.3(b), which deals with patentability or nonpatentability of plant and animal inventions, and the protection of plant varieties. Broadly speaking, part (b) of paragraph 3 (i.e., Article 27.3(b)) allows governments to exclude some kinds of inventions from patenting (that is, plants, animals, and "essentially" biological processes [but microorganisms and nonbiological and microbiological processes have to be eligible for patents]). However, plant varieties have to be eligible for protection either through patent protection or a system created specifically for the purpose (*sui generis*) – or a combination of the two, http://www.wto.org/english/tratop_e/trips_e/art27_3b_background_e.htm. At Doha, members agreed that the TRIPS Council should evaluate the relationship between the TRIPS agreement and the CBD, as well as the protection of traditional knowledge and folklore, but these talks have made little progress, and many developing countries are frustrated by the slow pace. These countries have demanded that TRIPS be amended to require disclosure on sources of origin of biological material and traditional knowledge. However, in over five years of discussion, they have not reached any agreement. Several countries, including Bolivia, have mentioned this problem in their trade policy reviews. At the Hong Kong ministerial in December 2005, members agreed to continue this work and to report on it. See http://www.wto.org/english/tratop_e/trips_e/art27_3b_background_e.htm; WT/MIN(05)/W/3/Rev.2 18 December 2005, Doha Work Programme, Ministerial Declaration, at http://www.wto.org/english/thewto_e/minist_e/min05_e/final_text_e.htm; and Trade Policy Review, Bolivia, WT/TPR/M/154, 1/16/2006, 16.

29. During accession, a working party delineates principles for joining the WTO and then bilateral talks begin between the prospective new member and individual countries. These talks cover tariff rates and specific market access commitments, as well as other policies in goods and services. The new member's commitments are to apply equally to all WTO members. Once the working party has completed its examination of the applicant's trade regime and the parallel, bilateral market access negotiations are complete, the working party finalizes the terms of accession. These appear in a report, a draft membership treaty ("protocol of accession"), and lists "schedules" of the member-to-be's commitments. The final package, consisting of the report, protocol, and lists of commitments, is presented to the WTO General Council or the Ministerial Conference. If a two-thirds majority of WTO members votes in favor, the applicant is free to sign the protocol and to accede to the organization. In many cases, the country's own parliament or legislature has to ratify the agreement before membership is complete. "How to Join the WTO: The Accession Process," http://www.wto.org/english/thewto_e/whatis_e/tif_e/org3_e.htm, last searched 1/6/2006.

30. Arvind Subramanian and Shang-Jin Wei, "The WTO Promotes Trade, Strongly but Unevenly," NBER Working Paper No. 10024 (October 2003); and Michael Tomz, Judith Goldstein, and Douglas Rivers, "Membership Has Its Privileges: The Impact of GATT on International Trade," p. 18.

31. Human Rights Watch, on Macedonia, see http://www.hrw.org/doc?t=europe&c=macedo; on tensions among ethnic minorities, see http://hrw.org/english/docs/2005/01/13/macedo9875.htm discusses; Human Rights Watch describes human rights violations as "pervasive in Saudi Arabia," http://hrw.org/english/docs/2006/01/18/saudia12230.htm; Human Rights Watch said human rights declined drastically in Nepal, http://hrw.org/english/docs/2006/01/18/nepal12256.htm, and human rights worsened in 2005 in Cambodia, http://hrw.org/english/docs/2006/01/18/cambod12269.htm and http://hrw.org/english/docs/2006/01/18/cambod12269.htm; all last searched 2/10/2006.

32. Working Party on the Accession of Cambodia, Report of the Working Party on the Accession of Cambodia, WT/ACC/KHM/21, 8/15/2003, 7, #34–37, and 25 no. 124 on standards and TBT, 27, 30 (Action Plans).

33. "Accession of the Kingdom of Cambodia," WT/MIN (03)/18, 9/11/2003.

34. Working Party on the Accession of Saudi Arabia, WT/ACC/SAU/61, p. 94, #296 and #297; on transparency and public comment, 96, 304.

35. Ibid., 96, #301–#304.

36. "Report of the Working Party on the Accession of the Kingdom of Nepal to the World Trade Organization," WT/ACC/NPL/16, 8/28/2003; and "Report of the Working Party on the Accession of the Former Yugoslav Republic of Macedonia," WT/ACC/807/27, 8/26/2002.

37. The working party report describes how Vietnam will bring its domestic laws and regulations in line with WTO practices. See Daniel Pruzin, "WTO Circulates Final Working Party Report on Vietnam Accession; Vote Set for October 26," *Daily Report for Executives*, No 205, 1024/2006. Vietnam has made public pronouncements that it will try to improve human rights conditions. NA, "Twelve Years to Free Markets, Pledges Vietnam on Joining WTO," http://www.rfa.org/english/news/politics/2006/11/10/vietnam_WTO/, Radio Free Asia, 11/10/2006, last searched 11/11/2006.

38. Article IIIV, Note by the Secretariat, MTN.GNG/NG7/2/30 November 6, 1987, at, http://www.wto.org/gatt_docs/English/SULPDF/92030084.pdf, last searched 8/10/2006.

39. http://www.wto.org/English/docs_e/legal_e/ursum_e.htm#General, last searched 8/10/2006.

40. The United States used nonapplication in the case of Romania (WT/L/11) (this was withdrawn); Mongolia (WT/L/203); Kyrgyz Republic (WT/L/318-withdrawn); Georgia; Armenia (WT/L/385); and Moldova (WT/L/395). Peru and El Salvador used nonapplication for China (but this was probably not based on human rights). Member states can rescind a nonapplication decision.

41. WTO, "Accession of Vietnam: Invocation by the United States of Article XII of the Marrakesh Agreement Establishing the World Trade Organization with respect to Viet Nam," WT/L/668, November 7, 2006; Daniel Pruzin, "WTO Circulates; and Rangel Sees Little Opposition to Vietnam, Calls For Preference Extensions," *Inside U.S. Trade*, 11/8/2006. Congress is approved permanent normal trade relations. At that point, the United States will withdraw its invocation of nonapplication. But on November 13,

the bill did not achieve the necessary two-thirds votes needed for approval. Amy Tsui, "Daily Report for Executives: House Will Not Take Up Permanent NTR for Vietnam until After Bush Visit to APEC," 11/15/2006.

42. U.S. policymakers wanted to prevent communist countries from joining the GATT, arguing that these nations did not protect political rights, this became a problem when original members Czechoslovakia and Cuba turned communist. GATT moved by consensus, and the other contracting parties wanted these nations to remain in the GATT. In 1951, Congress passed a law forbidding the U.S. government from providing commercial concessions to the Soviet Union or any Soviet bloc country. The United States revoked Czechoslovakia's tariff benefits, but no nation challenged this violation of MFN. Both Cuba and Czechoslovakia remained GATT/WTO members (until 1993 when Czechoslovakia became two countries, the Czech Republic and Slovakia). Aaronson, *Trade and the American Dream* 35, 82–83, and Thomas H. Zeiler, *Free Trade, Free World: The Advent of GATT* (Chapel Hill: University of North Carolina Press, 1999), 122, footnote 48.

43. For a good overview, see Joost Pauwelyn, "WTO Compassion or Superiority Complex? What to Make of the WTO Waiver for Conflict Diamonds," *Michigan Journal of International Law* 24 (2003), 1184–1191.

44. http://www.kimberleyprocess.com. Also see WTO, "Waiver Concerning Kimberley Process Certification Scheme for Rough Diamonds," Decision of May 15, 2003. WT/L/518, 5/27/2003.

45. WTO members are allowed to waive an obligation in exceptional circumstances under the approval of three-fourths of the members. Procedures for waivers, http://www.wto.org/english/docs_e/legal_e/11-25_e.htm, last searched 1/06/2006. See update in Global Witness, "An Independent Commissioned Review Evaluating the Effectiveness of the Kimberley Process, Submitted to the Ad Hoc Working Group on the Review of the Kimberley Process 2006," at www.globalwitness.org. Update on Kimberley Members, http://www.kimberleyprocess.com/site/participants.html, last searched 4/12/2007.

46. The certification scheme imposes stringent requirements on all participants to guard against conflict diamonds entering legitimate trade. Participants are required to implement internal controls, as outlined in the Kimberley Process Certification Scheme document, and all shipments of rough diamonds must be accompanied by a Kimberley Process Certificate. Participants can only trade with other participants who have met the minimum requirements of the certification scheme; http://www.kimberleyprocess .com:8080/site/?name=background&PHPSESSID=c450045836888a0cfbde43c8ef 3a290c

47. Foreign Affairs and International Trade Canada, Press Release, "Pettigrew Welcomes WTO Waiver for Kimberley Process Certification Scheme," 5/22/2003, http://w01 .international.gc.ca/MinPub/Publication.asp?publication_id=380114&Language=E, last searched 8/10/2006.

48. For an update on these waivers, see http://www.wto.org/english/thewto_e/gcounc_e/ meeting_july06_e.htm.

49. WTO High Level Symposium on Trade and Development Geneva, 17–18 March 1999. Background document Development Division World Trade Organization, "Developing Counties and the Multilateral Trading System: Past and Present, Background Note by the Secretariat," http://www.wto.org, last searched 2/10/2006.

50. According to law professor John H. Jackson, scholars presumed it was authorized by the Tokyo Round Understanding. John L. Jackson, *The World Trading System: Law and Policy of International Relations*, 2nd ed. (Cambridge, MA: MIT Press, 1998), 164, 323.

51. http://www.wto.org/English/res_e/booksp_e/analytic_index_e/wto_agree_02_e.htm# index969230, and http://www.wto.org/English/res_e/booksp_e/analytic_index_e/wto_ agree_01_e.htm#index124599, last searched 8/14/2006.

52. The Status of Trade Preferences in the WTO, http://www.fao.org/DOCREP/ 004/Y2732E/y2732e08.htm, searched 8/12/2006.

53. EU Generalised System of Preferences, http://europa.eu.int/rapid/pressReleasesAction .do?reference=IP/05/..., last searched 2/17/2006.

54. http://www.devstud.org.uk/publications/papers/conf01/conf01raffer.doc -; and Bridges, "EU-ACP Cotonou Waiver Finally Granted," http://www.ictsd.org/weekly/01-11- 15/story2.htm, both last searched 2/15/2006.

55. WTO, "Least-Developed Country Members Obligations under Article 70.9 of the TRIPS Agreement With Respect to Pharmaceutical Products, Decision of 8 July, 2002," WT/L/478, 7/12/2002.

56. Pauwelyn, "WTO Compassion or Superiority Complex?

57. Lim, p. 6; and Jackson, pp. 175–179. The text of Article XX is at http://www.wto .org/english/docs_e/legal_e/gatt47_02_e.htm#articleXX; also, Gudrun Monika Zagel, "WTO and Human Rights: Examining Linkages and Suggesting Convergence," *IDLO Voices of Development Jurists Paper Series* 2(2) (2005), 12. Zagel notes that governments have used Article XX paragraphs (b) (protection of human, animal, or plant life or health) and (g) (measures relating to the conservation of exhaustible human resources) to justify a trade ban but have rarely applied the other articles. Also see Lim, "Trade and," p. 6.

58. GATT 1994, Article XX, the chapeau.

59. This provision of the article was not tested in dispute settlement until 2003, in a dispute related to a ban on Internet gambling. See Zagel, "WTO and Human Rights," p. 13, footnote 37, when Antigua and Barbuda requested consultations with the United States regarding measures applied by central, regional, and local authorities in the United States that affected the cross-border supply of gambling and betting services. The panel found the use of the provision justified as long as it did not violate existing trade obligations or discriminate among domestic/foreign providers. Nations might use a public morals exception to protect the rights of women or children (Internet pornography). But these articles contain a necessity test that requires that measures pass a "weighting and balancing test," to see if a measure is necessary to achieve the intended goal and the trade impact of the challenged measure. Governments should implement the least-trade-restrictive means to reach the goal (whether product labeling or an import ban). But law professor Joost Pauwelyn believes that "by broadly interpreting the per se prohibited market access restrictions exhaustively listed in Article XVII of the GATS, the Appellate Body has considerably expanded the reach of GATS prohibitions ... to include also substantive qualitative regulations ... This may well mean that ... the validity of scores of domestic services regulations ... are threatened." See Joost Pauwelyn, "WTO Softens Earlier Condemnation of U.S. Ban on Internet Gambling But Confirms Broad Reach into Sensitive Domestic Regulation," *ASIL Insight*, 4/12/2005, 222.asil.org/insights/2005/04/insights050412.html, last searched 7/20/2006.

60. See Zagel, 12, footnote. 32; and Lim, "Trade and," 7. Also, Farkhanda Mansoor, "The WTO versus the ILO and the case of child labour," *Web Journal of Current Legal Issues* [2004] 2 WJCLI, webjcli.ncl.ac.uk/2004/issue2/mansoor2.html#top, last searched 1/06/2006.

61. Office of the UN High Commissioner for Human Rights, "Human Rights and World Trade Agreements: Using General Exception Clauses to Protect Human Rights," p. 6.

62. Gabrielle Marceau, "WTO Dispute Settlement and Human Rights," and Salman Bal, "International Free Trade Agreements and Human Rights," 62–108.

63. Some scholars allege that "in the Shrimp/Turtle case, the Appellate Body of the WTO confirmed that import restrictions may be justifiable under WTO law for protecting human rights values." However, the Appellate Body did not link the notion of conservation of exhaustible natural resources to human rights values." The case is U.S.-Import Prohibition of Shrimp and Shrimp Products, Report of the Appellate Body, WT/DS58/AB/R (October 12, 1998). The quote is from Howse, "Human Rights in the WTO," p. 6, footnotes 9, 10, 8–10; and Consultative Board to the Director-General Supachai Panitchpakdi, "The Future of the WTO," 2004, pp. 52–53.

64. Article XXI provides that:Nothing in [the GATT] shall be construed

   (a) to require any contracting party to furnish any information the disclosure of which it considers contrary to its essential security interests; or

   (b) to prevent any contracting party from taking action which it considers necessary for the protection of its essential security interests

      (i) relating to fissionable materials or the materials from which they are derived;

      (ii) relating to the traffic in arms, ammunition and implements of war and to such traffic in other goods and materials as is carried on directly or indirectly for the purpose of supplying a military establishment;

      (iii) taken in time of war or other emergency in international relations; or

   (c) to prevent any contracting party from taking any action in pursuance of its obligations under the United Nations Charter for the maintenance of international peace and security. Article XXI was determined to ensure that governments could take care of real security interests.

65. Over the past several years, U.S. and/or multilateral sanctions have been placed on several significant oil-producing countries, including Iran, Iraq, Libya, Sudan, and Syria. In addition, North Korea has faced energy sanctions by the European Union and the United States, while Cuba and Burma (Myanmar) remain subject to comprehensive U.S. trade sanctions, including energy, http://www.eia.doe.gov/emeu/cabs/sanction.htm, last searched 1/06/2006.

66. U.S. Department of State, "Report on U.S. Trade Sanctions against Burma," 4/28/2004, http://www.state.gov/p/eap/rls/rpt/32106.htm, last searched 8/14/2006. Prior to 2003, the United States had placed a ban on new investment in Burma, a ban on arms sales to Burma, limits on humanitarian assistance to Burma, and a "no" vote on any loan or assistance to Burma by international financial institutions. In 2003, the United States put in place a broad range of new sanctions in place including a ban on all imports from Burma, a ban on the export of financial services by U.S. persons to Burma, and an asset freeze on certain named Burmese institutions. The United States also expanded existing visa restrictions to include the managers of state-owned

enterprises and their immediate family members. The State Department also produces an annual report on the human rights situation in Burma. In 2003, the report
noted that the Government's extremely poor human rights record had worsened, particularly highlighting the premeditated, government-sponsored, May 2003 attack on
Aung San Suu Kyi and her supporters, in which government-affiliated agents killed
as many as 70 pro-democracy activists. The report also noted that citizens of Burma
still do not have the right to change their government, and that security forces continued to commit extrajudicial killings and rape, forcibly relocate persons, use forced
labor, and have reestablished forced conscription of the civilian population into mili-
tia units. Other annual reports detail U.S. concerns for the situation in Burma in
such areas as trafficking in persons, international religious freedom, and the control of
narcotics.

67. The Generalized System of Preferences, http://europa.eu.int/comm/trade/issues/
global/gsp/index_en.htm, last searched 4/24/06.

68. Article 16 of the 2005 Council Regulation on GSP.

69. Lorand Bartels, "Conditionality in GSP Programmes – The Appellate Body Report in
European Communities: Conditions for Granting of Tariff Preferences to Developing
Countries and Its Implications for Conditionality in GSP Programmes" in Thomas
Cottier, Joost Pauwelyn, and Elisabeth Bürgi Bonanomi, eds., *Human Rights and
International Trade* (New York: Oxford University Press, 2005), 468–472.

70. Lorand Bartels, "Conditionality in GSP Programmes – The Appellate Body Report in
European Communities: Conditions for Granting of Tariff Preferences to Developing
Countries and Its Implications for Conditionality in GSP Programmes" in Cottier
et al., eds., "*Human Rights and International Trade* 468–472. In late 2001 the EC
added Pakistan to the list of countries that received additional tariff preferences under
the arrangement regarding the combat of drug production and trafficking.

71. Request for the establishment of a panel by India, WT/DS246/4, 9 December 2002,
p. 2. India considered that the tariff preferences accorded by the European Community under the special arrangements, (i) for combating drug production and
trafficking and (ii) for the protection of labour rights and the environment, create undue difficulties for India's exports to the European Community, including for
those under the general arrangements of the European Community's GSP scheme,
and nullify or impair the benefits accruing to India under the MFN provisions of
Article I:1 of the GATT 1994 and paragraphs 2(a), 3(a), and 3(c) of the Enabling
Clause. The European Community is in the process of modifying its GSP program,
http://www.wto.org/english/tratop_e/dispu_e/cases_e/ds246_e.htm.

72. *Bridges Weekly Trade News Digest*, "India Challenges EU GSP Scheme on Environment and Labour Standards," /www.ictsd.org/weekly/03-01-15/story3.htm; and *Bridges
Weekly*, "DSB: India Wins Landmark EU-GSP case," 11/5/2003, www.ictsd.org/
weekly/03-11-05/story1.htm, both last searched 8/15/2006. Also see Robert Howse,
"India's WTO Challenge to Drug Enforcement Conditions in the European Community Generalized System of Preferences: A Little Known Case with Major Reper-
cussions for "Political" Conditionality in US Trade Policy," *Chicago Journal of International Law* 4 (2003), 386; and Robert Howse, "Back to Court After Shrimp/Turtle?
Almost but not Quite Yet: India's Short Lived Challenge to Labor and Environmental
Exceptions in the European Union's Generalized System of Preferences," *American
University International Law Review* 18(1333) (2003), 1333–1381.

73. India referred to paragraphs 2(a), 3(a), and 3(c) of the Clause. These provisions stipulate that 2(a): "Preferential tariff treatment accorded by developed contracting parties to products originating in developing countries in accordance with the Generalized System of Preferences (defined as the establishment of 'generalized, non-reciprocal and non-discriminatory preferences' beneficial to developing countries)"; 3(a): "Any differential and more favorable treatment provided under this clause shall be designed to facilitate and promote the trade of developing countries and not to raise barriers to or create undue difficulties for the trade of any other contracting parties"; 3(c): "Any differential and more favorable treatment provided under this clause shall in the case of such treatment accorded by developed contracting parties to developing countries be designed and, if necessary, modified, to respond positively to the development, financial and trade needs of developing countries." See http://www.worldtradelaw.net/tokyoround/enablingclause.pdf, last searched 4/24/2006.

74. See http://www.worldtradelaw.net/tokyoround/enablingclause.pdf, last searched 4/24/2006.

75. India had demonstrated that the European Communities' Drug Arrangements are inconsistent with Article I:1 of GATT 1994; that the European Communities has failed to demonstrate that the Drug Arrangements are justified under paragraph 2(a) of the Enabling Clause[.] The Panel also concluded that the European Communities had "failed to demonstrate that the Drug Arrangements are justified under Article XX(b) of GATT 1994" Finally, the Panel concluded, pursuant to Article 3.8 of the *Understanding on Rules and Procedures Governing the Settlement of Disputes* (the "DSU"), that "because the Drug Arrangements are inconsistent with Article I:1 of GATT 1994 and not justified by Article 2(a) of the Enabling Clause or Article XX(b) of GATT 1994, the European Community has nullified or impaired benefits accruing to India under GATT 1994." WT/DS246/R; http://www.wto.org/english/tratop_e/dispu_e/cases_e/ds246_e.htm.

76. http://www.wto.org/english/tratop_e/dispu_e/cases_e/ds246_e.htm, last searched 4/24/2006.

77. http://www.wto.org/english/tratop_e/dispu_e/cases_e/ds246_e.htm.

78. European Commission, Communication from the Commission to the Council, the European Parliament and the European Economic and Social Committee – Developing Countries, International Trade and Sustainable Development: the Function of the Community's Generalised System of Preferences (GSP) for the Ten-Year Period from 2006 to 2015, COM(2004)461 final, 7/07/2004, Brussels; and http://www.wto.org/english/tratop_e/dispu_e/cases_e/ds246_e.htm.

79. Robert Howse, "India's WTO Challenge," 386–387.

80. Lorand Bartels, "Conditionality in GSP Programmes," 482.

81. Lorand Bartels, "Conditionality in GSP Programmes," 484.

82. Ibid.

83. Professor Trachtman cites the Appellate Body Report, Mexico – Tax Measures on Soft Drinks and Other Beverages, WT/DS308/AB/R (March 6, 2006). E-mail, Professor Joel Trachtman, The Fletcher School of Law and Diplomacy, Tufts University, to S. Aaronson, 8/16/2006. The WTO reported the case in this way: On March 16, 2004, the United States requested consultations with Mexico concerning certain tax measures imposed by Mexico on soft drinks and other beverages that use any sweetener other than cane sugar. On June 10, 2004, the United States requested the establishment of a

panel. On October 7, 2005, the Report of the Panel was circulated to Members. The Panel found several violations of GATT 1994. On December 6, 2005, Mexico notified its decision to appeal to the Appellate Body certain issues of law dealt with in the Panel report and certain legal interpretations developed by the Panel. On March 6, 2006, the Appellate Body Report was circulated to Members. The Appellate Body found that the Panel did not err in rejecting Mexico's request that it decline to exercise jurisdiction. In addition, the Appellate Body upheld, albeit for different reasons, the Panel's finding that Mexico's measures do not constitute measures "to secure compliance with laws or regulations" within the meaning of Article XX(d) of the GATT 1994 because that provision does not permit WTO Members to take measures that seek to secure compliance by another Member with that other Member's international obligations. http://www.wto.org/english/tratop_e/dispu_e/cases_e/ds308_e.htm

84. Gabriel Marceau, "WTO Dispute Settlement and Human Rights," p. 2. Also see work of Joel Trachtman, "The Domain of WTO Dispute Resolution," *Harvard International Law Journal* (1999); Joost Pauwelyn, "The Role of Public International Law in the WTO: How Far Can We Go?" *American Journal of International Law* (2001); Joel Trachtman, "Trade and . . . Problems," *European Journal of International Law* (1998), 9.

85. Joost Pauwelyn, "WTO Compassion or Superiority Complex? What to Make of the WTO Waiver for 'Conflict Diamonds,'" *Michigan Journal of International Law*: 4 (2003), 1177–1207.

86. On India-EU, see http://www.wto.org/english/tratop_e/dispu_e/cases_e/ds246_e.htm.

87. The largest trading nations must be reviewed every two years, the next sixteen are reviewed every four years, and others are reviewed every six years. The WTO system allows developing countries a longer period between reviews.

88. Donald B. Keesing, *Improving Trade Policy Reviews in the World Trade Organization* (Washington: IIE, 1998), 1, 12. The GATT had some fifty-seven reviews from 1989 to 1994.

89. Trade Policy Review, Egypt, WT/TPR/M/150, July 26 and 28, 2005, Comments of the Representative of Egypt, 3, Discussant comments, 6–7, European comments, 7, Japan, 8, United States, 9, China, 12 (especially on SPS and TBT).

90. Trade Policy Review, Romania, WT/TPR/M/155/Add.1, 1/18/2006, p. 15.

91. Trade Policy Review, Bolivia, WTO/TPR/M/154/Add.1, 1/16/2006, p. 37.

92. Trade Policy Review, Ecuador, "Draft Minutes of Meeting," WT/TPR/M/148, #93.

93. Trade Policy Review, People's Republic of China, WT/TPR/M/161, 6/6/2006, p. 1–2 and final comments #181, p. 5. On comments of Uribe, see, #13, 18, p. 3. On China's investment in lifting people out of poverty, #25, 27, 28, 29, pp. 4–5.

94. WT/TPR/M/161, Comments of the U.S. Representative on transparency #40, 42, public comment, #41, IPR, 40; Comments of India on transparency especially on SPS, #62, New Zealand, #58, Canada, #78, Norway on a lack of transparency especially on SPS, #80, EC on transparency, #96, Singapore on transparency, #110, WT/TRP/M/161, Concluding remarks, #185, Switzerland on IPR, #44; Japan on IPR, #51, Korea, #60, Norway, #79.

95. WT/TPR/M/161, #95. China's response on transparency, #146, 147. The US urged China to "consider a system seeking public comment on all measures," #148, but China responded that "the transparency obligation did not cover the whole drafting process." It also added however, that it had published the draft Property Rights law and sought public comments, #149, response of the representative from Cuba, #118.

96. WT/TPR/M/161, Concluding remarks, #178, #179. Surprisingly, member states never discussed labor rights in China.

97. Trade Policy Review, European Communities, WT/TPR/G/136, pp. 10–11, paragraphs 33–39. Trade Policy Review, European Communities WT/TPR/M/136/Add.1, Question 1 of Australia.

98. Trade Policy Review, European Communities WT/TPR/M/136/Add.1, Question 1 of Australia.

99. In 1998, the 175 members of the ILO agreed on four "fundamental principles and rights at work" that all countries, regardless of their level of development, should respect and promote. Kimberley Ann Elliott and Richard B. Freeman, *Can Labor Standards Improve Under Globalization?* (Washington: IIE, 2003), 8–9; and Robert Howse, "The World Trade Organization and the Protection of Workers' Rights," *Journal of Small and Emerging Business Law* 131 (1999), 2–3.

100. Howse, "The World Trade Organization and the Protection of Workers' Rights," 131, Guide to WTO Law and Practice, 491; http://www.wto.org/english/res_e/boosp_e/analytic_index_e/gatt19.

101. Steve Charnovitz, "The Influence of International Labour Standards on the World Trading Regime," 9 FN 41, http://www.geocities.com/charnovitz/ILO.htm, last searched 2/06/2006. The Leutwiller Report is titled *Trade Policies for a Better Future*. Proposals for Action, GATT, Geneva, March 1985, p. 29.

102. Concluding remarks of the Chairman of the Trade Negotiations Committee of the Multilateral Trade Negotiations of the Uruguay Round at Marrakesh, GATT Doc. MTN.TNC/MIN (94)/6 (April 15, 1994).

103. Press Briefing Trade and Labor Standards, http://www.wto.org/english/thewto_emin96_3/labstand.htm.

104. Singapore Ministerial Declaration, 12/13/1996, http://www.wto.org/english/thewto_e/minist_e/min96_e/wtodec_e.htm. "We renew our commitment to the observance of internationally recognized core labour standards. The ILO is the competent body to set and deal with these standards, and we affirm our support for its work in promoting them. We believe that economic growth and development fostered by increased trade and further trade liberalization contribute to the promotion of these standards. We reject the use of labour standards for protectionist purposes, and agree that the comparative advantage of countries, particularly low-wage developing countries, must in no way be put into question. In this regard, we note that the WTO and ILO Secretariats will continue their existing collaboration."

105. WTO, "Trade and Labour Standards: Subject of Intense Debate," http://www.wto.org/english/thewto_e/minist_e/min99_3/english/abo; National Intelligence Council (CIA), "Prospects for WTO Trade Negotiations after Seattle: Foreign Strategies and Perspectives," 5/1/2000, http://www.cia.gov/nic/confreports_worldtrade.html; Pascal Lamy, "World Trade Organisation Ministerial Conference in Seattle Appraisal and Prospects," http://europa.eu.int/comm/archives/commission_1999_2004/lamy/speeches_articles/spla08_en.htm; and "EU=LDC Themes, Social, Environmental and Welfare Aspects of Trade-Research," labour standards background at http://62.58.77.238/themes/socialwelfare/socialwelfare_research1.php, all searched 2/12/2006.

106. Roger Downey, "Clinton Throws Brick: Shatters Chance for WTO Unity," *Seattle Weekly*, http://www.seattleweekly.com/news/9949/features-downey.html, last searched 1/16/2006.

107. Charavarthi Raghavan, "Clinton Uses Demonstrations to Push Labor Standards," Third World Network, 12/2/1999, http://www.twnside.org.sg/title/clinton-cn.htm, and "WTO Response to Clinton Proposal," http://www.npr.org/templates/story/story.php?storyId=1067395. It was seen as damaging to the WTO, to developing countries and to U.S. leadership in the WTO, http://www.heritage.org/Research/InternationalOrganizations/EM639.cfm

108. Hoe Lim, "Trade and," pp. 12–14.

109. According to a World Bank Discussion Paper, policymakers presume that lax labor standards attract investment. Takayoshi Kusago and Zafiris Tzannatos, "Export Processing Zones: A Review in Need of an Update," Social Protection Discussion Paper No. 9802, 1/1998, p. 23, http://www.worldbank.org.

110. United Nations Development Programme, "Human Development Report," p. 124, footnote 28, at http://hdr.undp.org/reports/global/2005/pdf/HDR05_chapter_4.pdf, last searched 1/13/2006.

111. http://www.wto.org/english/tratop_e/scm_e/subs_e.htm. A subsidy, according to the WTO, contains three basic elements: (i) a financial contribution (ii) by a government or any public body within the territory of a member, (iii) which confers a benefit. All three of these elements must be satisfied in order for a subsidy to exist. Multilateral disciplines are the rules regarding whether or not a subsidy may be provided by a member. They are enforced through invocation of the WTO dispute settlement mechanism. Countervailing duties are a unilateral instrument, which may be applied by a member after an investigation by that member and a determination that the criteria set forth in the SCM Agreement are satisfied. Also see WTO Secretariat, "Special and Differential Treatment for Least-Developed Countries: Note by the Secretariat," WT/COMTD/W/135, 10/5/2004, pp. 2 and 14.

112. Trade Policy Review of El Salvador, WT/TPR/M/111, February 3 and 5, 2003, pp. 10–11.

113. WTO, Trade Policy Review Body, Report by the United States, 12/17/2003, WT/TPR/G/126. See Section 100, "WTO ministers renewed their commitment to the observance of internationally recognized core labor standards in the 2001 Doha Ministerial Declaration. Recognizing that there is a connection between labor standards and trade issues, we believe that the subject of implementation of core labor standards is relevant for TPRM reviews. In reviews of other countries, the United States has raised questions about the application of core labor standards. In that spirit, we are including, in this statement, relevant information on U.S. labor law and practice as it relates to fundamental workers' rights." Also see sections 97 and 98, which describe U.S. objectives regarding labor rights: "The labor-related overall U.S. trade negotiating objectives are threefold. First, to promote respect for worker rights and rights of children consistent with the core labor standards of the International Labor Organization (ILO). TPA defines core labor standards as: (1) the right of association; (2) the right to organize and bargain collectively; (3) a prohibition on the use of forced or compulsory labor; (4) a minimum age for the employment of children; and (5) acceptable conditions of work with respect to minimum wages, hours of work, and occupational safety and health. Secondly, to strive to ensure that parties to trade agreements do not weaken or reduce the protections of domestic labor laws as an encouragement for trade. And finally, to promote the universal ratification and full compliance with ILO Convention 182 – which the United States has ratified – concerning the elimination of the worst forms of child labor. . . . " The principal trade negotiating objectives in TPA include, "for labor, the provision that a party to a trade agreement with the United

States should not fail to effectively enforce its labor laws in a manner affecting trade. TPA recognizes that the United States and its trading partners retain the sovereign right to establish domestic labor laws, and to exercise discretion with respect to regulatory and compliance matters, and to make resource allocation decisions with respect to labor law enforcement. To strengthen the capacity of our trading partners to promote respect for core labor standards is an additional principal negotiating objective, as is to ensure that labor, health or safety policies and practices of our trading partners do not arbitrarily or unjustifiably discriminate against American exports or serve as disguised trade barriers. A final principal negotiating objective is to seek commitments by parties to trade agreements to vigorously enforce their laws prohibiting the worst forms of child labor."

114.   India wished to draw attention to the view of ministers, both at Singapore and at Doha, that while they were committed to the observance of internationally recognized core labour standards, the competent body to set and deal with labour standards was the ILO. It was clear, therefore, that the WTO was not competent to deal with this matter. The representative of India recalled the mandate of the Trade Policy Review Mechanism (TPRM) exercise and stated that it could not be used as an open forum to discuss non-trade issues or address issues not discussed elsewhere in the WTO. Venezuela joined the representative of India in his assessment that it was not pertinent to discuss labour issues in the context of the TPRM. Discussion of those issues belonged in the ILO. WTO, Trade Policy Review, Minutes of Meeting, 1/14–1/16, WT/TPR/M/12615 March 2004.

115.   Madani, "A Review," p. 17.

116.   Richard H. Steinberg, "Institutional Implications of WTO Accession for China," February 1999, http://brie.berkeley.edu/~briewww/publications/WP110.pdf, last searched 1/10/2006, pp. 5, 6, 8.

117.   Other recent accessions have not included similar language designed to ensure that the country applies the rule of law to all of its environs, including special/foreign trade zones or EPZs. We examined a number of accession documents for countries that use EPZs as a means of stimulating trade and investment. See, for example, Accession of the Republic of Panama, WT/ACC/PAN/21, 10/11/1996, and Accession of the Hashemite Kingdom of Jordan, WT/ACC/Jor/35, 12/1999, both at http://www.wto.org. None included information on administration of trade agreements, special economic zones, or transparency. See also accessions, noted in footnotes 64–68, of Cambodia, Nepal, Macedonia, and Saudi Arabia.

118.   WTO, "Accession of the People's Republic of China, Decision of 10 November 2001," WT/L/432, (A) 1, 2, http://www.wto.org.

119.   Ibid., Sections (B), (C), 3.

120.   Jamil Anderlini, "Lamy Backs Inclusion of Standards for Workers," South China Morning Post, 12/13/2005. Lamy never endorsed including labor standards in the WTO. The headline is misleading.

121.   Consumers may benefit from access to cheaper more efficiently produced food. Smaller producers may benefit from new markets, creating jobs and economic growth. But small farmers in the developing world may not be able to benefit from trade liberalization per se. These farmers may not be able to produce at the quality level required in the highly regulated markets of the United States and Europe. In addition, should they fail to make a livelihood competing in global markets, they may flood urban areas in search of new income, bringing down wages for other relatively poor people in their

home countries, or moving overseas in search of a better life. Thus, trade liberalization may not increase access to food or food security or ensure that small farmers can earn enough to provide for their families.

122. To ensure food security, a food system should be characterized by (i) the capacity to produce, store and import sufficient food to meet basic needs for all; (ii) maximum autonomy and self-determination (without implying self-sufficiency), which reduces vulnerability to international market fluctuations and political pressures; (iii) reliability, such that seasonal, cyclical and other variations in access to food are minimal; (iv) sustainability, such that the ecological system is protected and improved over time; and (v) equity, meaning, as a minimum, dependable access to adequate food for all social groups."Jostein Lindland, OECD, "Non-Trade Concerns in a Multifunctional Agriculture: Implications for Agricultural Policy and the Multilateral Trading System, COM?AGR/CA/TD/TC/WS(98)124, http://www1.oecd.org/agr/trade/ws98-124.pdf. In November 2004, the FAO issued voluntary guidelines for governments to help their people progressively achieve the right to food. in the context of food security. http://www.fao.org/docrep/meeting/009/y9825e/y9825e00.htm, both last searched 8/12/2006.

123. The Commission on Human Rights has extensively examined the right to food, and the Special Rapporteur on the right to food, Jean Ziegler, has noted that despite these government commitments, hunger and malnutrition persist throughout the world. 3D3, "Planting the Rights Seed: A Human Rights Perspective on Agriculture Trade and the WTO," Backgrounder No. 1, 3/2005, 4. As a last resort, governments are required to provide adequate food to those people that cannot feed themselves.

124. Commission on Human Rights, "Economic, Social and Cultural Rights: The Right to Food: Report Submitted by the Special Rapporteur on the Right to Food, Jean Ziegler, in accordance with Commission on Human Rights Resolution 2003/25, E/Cn.42004/10, 2/9/2004, 6–8.

125. "Phase 1 'Non-trade' Concerns: Agriculture Can Serve Many Purposes," http://www .wto.org/English/tratop_e/agric_e/negs_bkgrnd11_nontrade_e.htm, last searched 8/12/2006.

126. Rights & Democracy, "Implementing the Human Right to Food: Domestic Obligations and the International Trade in Agriculture, Report of an Inter-sessional Workshop Held September 11, 2003 in Cancun, Mexico," http://www.ichrdd.ca/english/ commdoc/publications/globalization/Food/foodRightReportOct2003.html, p. 5, last searched 3/3/2005.

127. Members noted, "It is recognized that during the reform programme least-developed and net food-importing developing countries may experience negative effects with respect to supplies of food imports on reasonable terms and conditions. Therefore, a special Decision sets out objectives with regard to the provision of food aid, the provision of basic foodstuffs in full grant form and aid for agricultural development." Decision on Measures Concerning the Possible Negative Effects of the Reform Programme on Least-Developed and Net Food-Importing Developing Countries said, "It is recognized that during the reform programme least-developed and net food-importing developing countries may experience negative effects with respect to supplies of food imports on reasonable terms and conditions. Therefore, a special Decision sets out objectives with regard to the provision of food aid, the provision of basic foodstuffs in full grant form and aid for agricultural development. It also refers to the possibility of assistance from the International Monetary Fund and the World Bank with respect to

the short-term financing of commercial food imports. The Committee of Agriculture, set up under the Agreement on Agriculture, monitors the follow-up to the Decision," http://www.wto.org/english/docs_e/legal_e/ursum_e.htm#General.

128. WTO, Committee on Agriculture, G/AG/NG/W/36/Rev.1, 11/9/2000, 2, 4. See especially Discussion Paper Six, presented by Norway, "The Need for Flexibility in National Policy Design to Address Non-Trade Concerns," G/AG/NG/W/36 Rev.1, 60.

129. Ibid., Discussion Paper Three, Food Security and the Role of Domestic Agriculture Production," Presented by Japan and the Republic of Korea, "Summary and Conclusions," in G/AG/NG/W/36/Rev.1.

130. Doha WTO Ministerial 2001: Ministerial Declaration, WT/MIN (01)/Dec/1; and http://www.wto.org/english/tratop_e/dda_e/dohaexplained_e.htm.

131. Under the Agreement on Agriculture, members can freely use trade measures with minimal impact on trade – they are in a "green box" ("green" as in traffic lights). They include government services such as research, disease control, infrastructure and food security. They also include payments made directly to farmers that do not stimulate production, such as certain forms of direct income support, assistance to help farmers restructure agriculture, and direct payments under environmental and regional assistance programmes. Governments can also make certain direct payments to farmers where the farmers are required to limit production (sometimes called "blue box" measures), certain government assistance programmes to encourage agricultural and rural development in developing countries, and other support on a small scale ("de minimis") when compared with the total value of the product or products supported (5% or less in the case of developed countries and 10% or less for developing countries). http://www.wto.org/english/thewto_e/whatis_e/tif_e/agrm3_e.htm

132. International Institute for Sustainable Development, "Non-Trade Concerns in the Agricultural Negotiations of the World Trade Organization," Spring 2003, IISD Brief No. 1, 3–4, www.iisd.org, last searched 8/12/2006.

133. Oxfam: US Blocking Trade Deal at the WTO," July 28, 2004, at http://www.oxfam .org.uk/press/releases/wto_280704.htm, last searched 3/30/2007.

134. /www.ustr.gov/assets/Document_Library/Fact_Sheets/2004/asset_upload_file784_6153 .pdf?ht=http://www.ustr.gov/Document_Library/Press_Releases/2004/September/ WTO_Panel_Issues_Mixed_Verd ict_in_Cotton_Case.html?ht=

135. IISD, "Non-Trade Concerns," 3–4.

136. UNDP, "Asia Pacific Development Report 2006, 51.

137. IISD, "Non-trade Concerns," 3, Asia-Pacific Human Development Report, 74.

138. E/CN.4/2004/10, 9–10.

139. The Director General of the WTO, Pascal Lamy decided to suspend the negotiations after talks among six major members broke down on Sunday 23 July. http://www.wto.org/english/news_e/news06_e/mod06_summary_24july_e.htm.

140. WTO, "DG Lamy: Time Out Needed to Review Options and Positions," 7/27/2006, http://www.wto.org/english/news_e/news06_e/tnc_dg_stat_24july06_e.htm

141. http://www.wto.org/english/tratop_e/dda_e/tnc_e.htm

142. This section builds on the scholarship of Professor Steve Charnovitz. Steve Charnovitz, "The WTO and the Rights of the Individual," *Intereconomics* (March/April 2001), http://ssrn.com/abstract = 282021. The article shows how WTO rules guarantee rights to individuals.

143. Interpretation and Application of Article 1 of the WTO Agreement on Safeguards, http://www.wto.org/english/res_e/booksp_e/analytic_index_e/safeguards_02_e.htm#. It

notes "Competent authorities are required to seek out pertinent information.... The focus of the investigative steps mentioned in Article 3.1 is on 'interested parties,' who must be notified of the investigation, and who must be given an opportunity to submit 'evidence,' as well as their 'views,' to the competent authorities. The interested parties are also to be given an opportunity to 'respond to the presentations of other parties.' The Agreement on Safeguards, therefore, envisages that the interested parties play a central role in the investigation and that they will be a primary source of information for the competent authorities."

144. Agreement on Technical Barriers to Trade, http://www.wto.org/english/res_e/booksp_e/analytic_index_e/tbt_01_e.htm#p. It says, when introducing new standards, members shall "publish a notice in a publication at an early appropriate stage"; notify other members at an early appropriate stage, when amendments can still be introduced and comments taken into account; provide to other members particulars or copies of the proposed technical regulation and, whenever possible, identify the parts which in substance deviate from relevant international standards; allow reasonable time for other members to make comments in writing, discuss these comments upon request, and take these written comments and the results of these discussions into account.

145. Article 11 provides the importer with the right to appeal against a valuation determination made by the customs administration for the goods being valued. Appeal may first be to a higher level in the customs administration, but the importer shall have the right in the final instance to appeal to the judiciary. Text of Interpretive Note to Article XI, http://www.wto.org/english/res_e/booksp_e/analytic_index_e/cusval_02_e.htm #article11A, last searched 1/06/2006.

146. For example, members could choose who would represent them, the Dispute Settlement Body would closely examine legislative histories, and the rules of dispute settlement would be clear and transparent, http://www.wto.org/english/res_e/booksp_e/analytic_index_e/dsu_09_e.htm#articleXXIXA, last searched 1/17/2006.

147. The WTO Secretariat noticed that, in Thailand, import licensing for various items remains opaque. The government still uses procurement to provide markets for domestic suppliers. Trade Policy Review, Thailand, WT/TPR/S/123, 10/15/2003, p. ix.

148. Charnovitz, "The WTO and the Rights of the Individual," p. 21.

149. Article X, GATT 1994, http://www.wto.org/english/res_e/booksp_e/analytic_index_e/gatt1994_04_e.htm#articleXA, last searched 1/16/2006.

150. Paragraph 2, (a) General 319, GATT Analytical Index, http://www.wto.org/english/res_e/booksp_e/analytic_index_e/gatt1994_04_e.htm#articleXA.

151. "Trade Policy Reviews, Ensuring Transparency," http://www.wto.org/english/thewto_e/whatis_e/tif_e/agrm11_e.htm and http://www.wto.org/english/thewto_e/whatis_e/tif_e/agrm11_e.htm.

152. Trade Policy Review Malaysia, WT/TPR/S/156, p. 16. The Malaysian government has established advisory committees comprised of representatives of the business sector, academia, and NGOs (see p. 20).

153. USTR, "2005 Report to Congress on the Extension of Trade Promotion Authority," p. 6, http://www.ustr.gov/Document_Library/Reports_Publications/2005/2005_TPA_Report/Section_Index.html?ht= and CAFTA National Action Plans, and http://www.ustr.gov/Trade_Agreements/Bilateral/CAFTA/Trade_Capacity_Building/Section_Index.html, last searched 1/06/2006.

154. Trade Policy Review, El Salvador, WT/TPR/M/111, February 3 and 5, 2003, 5, 14. Remarks of the European Union, 7.
155. Trade Policy Review, Romania,WT/TPR/M/155/Add.1, 1/18/2006, 3–4.
156. Trade Policy Review, Romania, WT/TPR/M/155, Nov. 28–30, 2005, "Minutes of Meeting."
157. Trade Policy Review, Bolivia, WT/TPR/M/154. Remarks of Colombian representative, 8–9, echoed by the representative of Turkey, 17–18.
158. Ibid., representative of Uruguay, 17, European Union, 22–23.
159. We note, however, that if governments use limited money to improve the judiciary system to create special courts to protect intellectual property but do not provide sufficient funds for education or other public goods, the positive benefits may be limited or negative.
160. The CIRI Human Rights Data Set contains standards-based quantitative information on government respect for thirteen internationally recognized human rights for 195 countries annually from 1981 to 2003. The variable measures the extent to which citizens enjoy freedom of political choice and the legal right and ability in practice to change the laws and officials that govern them.
161. The WTO ambassador from Rwanda was speaking on behalf of the African group and referred to U.S. President George W. Bush's speech on the Terry Schiavo case. Ms. Schiavo was kept on life support for years, although brain dead. The U.S. Congress intervened in the case when her husband sought to take her off life support. Sangeeta Shashikant, "Heated Discussions As Trips and Health Deadline Is Missed," South North Development Monitor SUNS #5772, 4/4/2005, http://www.cptech.org/ip/wto/tsuns04042005.html, last searched 12/29/2005.
162. Statement of the Human Rights Caucus on the Occasion of the Sixth Ministerial Conference of the WTO, 12/10/2005, http://www.globalizacija.com/doc_en/e0064dok.htm, last searched 1/6/2006.

3. South Africa: In the "Rainbow Nation" Trade and Human Rights Are Anything but Black-and-White

1. We are grateful to Julie Maupin of Yale University, who contributed to the research and prepared an early draft of this chapter.
2. "My Son Died of AIDS: Mandela," 1/12/2006, www.southafrica.info/mandela/mandela-son.htm; "Mandela Shares in Grief of Khoza Family," http://46664.tiscali.com/; and "AIDS: Mandela Calls for Leadership," 7/16/2004, last searched 3/27/06.
3. Andre Brink, "Leaders and Revolutionaries, Nelson Mandela, The Time 100: The Most Important People of the Century," http://www.time.com/time/time100/ leaders/profile/mandela.html, "Notable Dates in AIDS Epidemic," Forbes, http://www.forbes.com/business/feeds/ap/2006/03/27/ap2624941.html "Mandela's Eldest Son Dies of AIDS," at news.bbc.co.uk/1/hi/world/ africa/4151159.stm; Craig Timberg, "Mandela Says AIDS Led to Death of Son: Health Activists Praise Ex-President's Openness," http://www.washingtonpost.com/wp-dyn/articles/A52781-2005Jan6.html; and "My Son Died of AIDS: Mandela, 1/12/2006, http://www.southafrica.info/mandela/mandela-son.html; all searched 3/24/07.
4. Mandela, "South Africa's Future Foreign Policy," *Foreign Affairs* November/December 1993, 86.

5. Alan Whiteside and Clem Sunter, *AIDS: The Challenge for South Africa* (Cape Town: Human and Rosseau, 2000). They argue that many South Africans deny the epidemic exists and others believe it exists but they can't do anything about it. On problems encountered by policymakers dealing with AIDS, see Alexander G. Higgins, "Bid to Give AIDS Drugs to Poor Nations Lag," AP, http://www.philly.com/mld/philly/living/health/14204524.htm. The article notes that the United Nations has been unable to meet its target of providing retrovirals to the 3 million needy persons, but the number of people treated has risen dramatically and prevented some 300,000 deaths.

6. Moyiga Nduru, "PanAfrica: Somber Outlook on AIDS," Interpress Service, 3/24/2006, http://allafrica.com/stories/200603260004.html, last searched 3/27/2006 .AIDS Foundation of South Africa, 2004/2005 Annual Report, http://www.aids.org .za/admin/news/uploadpics/annual2005_small.jpg; and AIDS Foundation South Africa, "Current Situation, Trends and Challenges," http://www.aids.org.za/hiv.htm, all last searched 3/26/2006.

7. Channing Arndt and Jeffrey Lewis, "The Macro Implications of HIV/AIDS in South Africa." Paper prepared for the International AIDS Economics Network (IAEN) Symposium on "The Economics of HIV/AIDS in Developing Countries" held in Durban, South Africa on July 7–8, 2000, available online at: http://www.worldbank .org/afr/wps/wp9.pdf

8. A National AIDS Convention of South Africa was established in 1992 and the new ANC government accepted its strategy for fighting AIDS in 1994. But policymakers disagreed over how much to spend on AIDS, whose responsibility AIDS was, whether antiretroviral drugs worked, whether women who were raped deserve medicines, and other issues. The government presumed that the public would protect themselves from infection, but women often cannot. See AIDS Foundation South Africa, http://www.aids.org.za/hiv.htm; for a government defense of its actions questioning the medical science on AIDS, see http://www.gcis.gov.za/docs/publications/govt_aids.htm

9. HIV/AIDS in South Africa, http://www.avert.org/aidssouthafrica.htm, last searched 9/1/2006.

10. According to the South Africa Health Review of 2000, electricity was not available at all fixed public clinics; 20% of these clinics had no telephone, and 12.5% of the country's satellite clinics used rainwater for water. The most recent health review is at http://www.hst.org.za/generic/29, last searched 3/24/07. For a more recent update on the government's response, see AIDS Foundation South Africa, http://www.aids.org.za/ hiv.htm, last searched 3/24/2007.

11. Department of State, Country Report, South Africa, 12; and http://www.aids.org .za/hiv.htm

12. David Barnard, "In the High Court of South Africa, Case No. 4138/98: The Global Politics of Access to Low-Cost AIDS Drugs in Poor Countries," *Kennedy Institute of Ethics Journal* 12(2) (2002), 159–174

13. "The Cruellest Curse: AIDS Makes Most of South Africa's Other Problems Seem Trivial," *The Economist*, 2/22/2001, at http://economist.com/surveys/displaystory.cfm?story_id=E1_VTDGGR, last searched 3/24/07. Also see Sharon LaFraniere, "U.N. Envoy Sharply Criticizes South Africa's AIDS Program," 10/25/2005, at http://query.nytimes.com/gst/fullpage.html?sec=health&res= 9C01E4D8103FF936A15753C1A9639C8B63, searched 3/24/07.

14. Lawrence K. Altman, "U.N. Official Assails South Africa on its Response to AIDS," *New York Times*, 8/19/2006, A3.

15. Declaration on the TRIPS agreement and Public Health, available at http://www.wto.org/english/thewto_e/minist_e/min01_e/mindecl_trips_e.htm. WTO members declared, "We agree that the TRIPS Agreement does not and should not prevent members from taking measures to protect public health. Accordingly, while reiterating our commitment to the TRIPS Agreement, we affirm that the Agreement can and should be interpreted and implemented in a manner supportive of WTO members' right to protect public health and, in particular, to promote access to medicines for all."

16. World Trade Organization, Trade Policy Review for the Southern African Customs Union, report by the Secretariat, WT/TPR/S/114/ZAF, A4-218-220.

17. Mariette Le Roux, "Loans to Zimbabwe An Insult," 9/27/2005, at http://www.int.iol.co.za/index.php?set_id=1&click_id=84&art_id=qw1127820781822B253, last searched 10/21/2005; and "South Africa Confirms Ongoing Zim Loan Talks," Mail and Guardian Online, 9/27/2005 at http://www.mg.co.za/articlePage.aspx?articleid=252031&area=/breaking_news/breaking_news__national/

18. Robert K. Massie, *Loosing the Bonds: The United States and South Africa in the Apartheid Years* (New York, Doubleday, 1997), 294.

19. Gary Clyde Hufbauer, Jeffrey J. Schott, and Kimberley Ann Elliott, *Economic Sanctions Reconsidered: Supplemental Case Histories*, 2nd ed. (Washington, DC: Institute for International Economics, 1990), Case 62-2, *UN v. South Africa*, pp. 227–238. Although these sanctions certainly impeded the country's economic performance during this period, they alone did not end apartheid.

20. We are grateful to our advisory committee member, Maria Green, for reminding us of this point.

21. http://www.southafrica.info/ess_info/sa_glance/constitution/constitution.htm, last searched 8/1/2006. The constitution notes, for example, that everyone has the right to an environment that is not harmful to their health or well-being, and to have the environment protected, for the benefit of present and future generations, through reasonable legislative and other measures.

22. South African Constitution, Bill of Rights, Section 39, Interpretation, http://www.concourt.gov.za/site/yourrights/thebillofrights.htm, last search 3/24/2007.

23. See *Government of the Republic of South Africa v. Grootbroom and Others*, South African Constitutional Court Case CCT 11/00. Full text available online: http://www.constitutionalcourt.org.za/uhtbin/hyperion-image/S-CCT11-00

24. Department of State, Country Reports, South Africa, 2005, 10.

25. Department of State, Country Reports on Human Rights Practices, South Africa, 2005; see in particular pp. 1, 10–11; and Human Rights Watch, Overview, South Africa, http://hrw.org/english/docs/2006/01/18/safric12309.htm. Also see Michael Wines, "A Highly Charged Rape Trial Tests South Africa's Ideals, The Defendant: Old-School Zulu," *New York Times*, 4/10/2006, A3.

26. Section 8 of the South African Constitution binds all organs to the state to enforce human rights. "A provision of the Bill of Rights binds a natural or a juristic person if, and to the extent that, it is applicable, taking into account the nature of the right and the nature of any duty imposed by the right." http://www.concourt.gov.za/site/theconstitution/english.pdf. See Danwood Mzikenge Chirwa, "Socio-Economic

Rights Project, University of the Western Cape," *ESR Review* 3(3) (2002), at http://www
.communitylawcentre.org.za/Projects/Socio-Economic-Rights/, last searched 3/24/
2007; and Interview with South African Constitutional Court Lawyers, Gilbert Marcus
and Wim Trengrove, the Island Group, Midrand, South Africa 7/27/2005.

27. A major court case called *Government of the Republic of South Africa and Others
v. Grootboom and Others*; the Constitutional Court held that, in the context of the
right to adequate housing, there exists a negative obligation upon the state and all
other entities . . . to desist from preventing or impairing the right to access to adequate housing. The court also suggested that it is not only the state but also private actors that are responsible for the provision of houses. See Danwood Mzikenge
Chirwa, "Non-State Actors Responsibility for Socio Economic Rights: The Nature
of Their Obligations under the South African Constitution," at https://www.up.ac.za/
dspace/bitstream/2263/1096/1/mwebe_h_1.pdf, last searched 3/24/2007.

28. For a discussion of these rights, see "Report on the Seminar on Privatisation of Business Services, Democracy and Human Rights, University of the Western Cape,"
October 2–3, 2003, and Dr. Susan Booysen, "The Effect of Privatization and Com-
mercialisation of Water Services on the Right to Water: Grassroots Experience in
Lukhanji and Amahlati," August 2004, both available online at http://www.community
lawcentre.org.za/, last searched 3/24/2007.

29. In 2001, the South Africa Human Development Report noted "37.7 percent of the
country's 11.2 million households were deprived of 'good' access" to many of these
services." South Africa Human Development Report, 2003, p. 98, available online at
http://www.undp.org.za/Nhdr2003/chap05.pdf

30. Eric Watkins, Deputy Director of the Economic and Social Rights Unit, South African
Human Rights Commission, interview 7/28/2005, and Peter Leon, Partner at Weber
Wentzel Bowens, interview 7/26/2005. Also, Shola Olowu, "Young South Africans."

31. The most prominent of the state-owned enterprises that were privatized are Telkom
(telecommunications), Spoornet (transport and freight), Portnet (port operations), and
Eskom (energy).

32. South Africa did not make offers in many public sector areas. It also listed several
MFN exemptions. See GATS/SC/78 and Suppl. 1–3. It committed to telecommunications, finance, and business and professional services. http://www.wto.org/english/
tratop_e/serv_e/serv_commitments_e.htm, last searched 8/27/2006.

33. South African Constitution, Chapter 2, Bill of Rights, Section 25(3). available online
at www.info.gov.za/documents/constitution/index.htm

34. See "Land Reform in South Africa", http://www.deneysreitz.co.za/news/news.asp?
ThisCat=3&ThisItem=398; and NA, "SA Land Expropriation to Start Soon,"
Mail and Guardian Online, http://www.mg.co.za/articlePage.aspx?articleid=263484&
area=/breaking_news/breaking_news_national/ both last searched 4/12/2006. By
March 2004 the Department of Land Affairs had handed a total of 810,292 hectares of
land to claimants. 48,825 restitution claims involving 122 292 households were settled
between 1995 and March 2004, with 662 307 people benefiting from the programmed.
South Africa, Department of Trade and Industry, "Fair Price for Land Reform,"
www.southafrica.info/doing_business/economy/fiscal_policies/landreform-policy.htm

35. John Reed, "South Africa Plans to Accelerate Programme of Land Reform," *Financial
Times*, 2/04/2006.

36. Sipho Sibanda, "Land Reform and Poverty Alleviation in South Africa," Paper Presented at the SARPN Conference on Land Reform and Poverty Alleviation in Southern Africa," http://www.oxfam.org.uk/what_we_do/issues/livelihoods/landrights/downloads/sastudy.rtf, and South Africa, Department of Trade and Industry, "Fair Price for Land Reform," www.southafrica.info/doing_business/economy/fiscal_policies/landreform-policy.htm both last searched 8/23/2006. As of October 25, the government agreed to fast track land reform. http://za.today.reuters.com/news/NewsArticle.aspx?type = topNews&storyID=2006-10-25T121027Z_01_BAN543813_RTRIDST_0_OZATP-SAFRICA-BUDGET-LAND-20061025.XML

37. Nelson Mandela, "South Africa's Future Foreign Policy," 97.

38. Khulekani M. Dube, "Overview: South Africa's Foreign Policy in Africa," 9/1/2003, at http://www.ai.org.za/electronic_monograph.asp?ID=1, last searched 3/24/2007.

39. The TRC is based on the Promotion of National Unity and Reconciliation Act, No. 34 of 1995. As of 2006, the Commission is no longer active. The Web site is http://www.doj.gov.za/trc/

40. Mark L. Wolf, "Truth and Reconciliation Commission: Quality of Mercy," http://www.racematters.org/truthreconciliationcomm.htm. Although some members of the African National Congress demanded Nuremberg-style trials of white officials, these officials were leery to relinquish power without a general amnesty. In 1998, the Truth and Reconciliation Commission issued a report detailing a horrible history of human rights violations by the government. It also documented comparable crimes committed by some members of the A.N.C., including Winnie Mandela. The report made recommendations concerning reparations and the prosecution of officials who had not received amnesty. But the report was widely criticized. Also see Helena Meyer Knapp, "Truth and Reconciliation Commissions: Traumatic Community Legacies Can Be Healed," http://diac.cpsr.org/cgi-bin/diac02/pattern.cgi/public?pattern_id=528; Center for the Study of Violence and Reconciliation, South Africa, http://www.csvr.org.za/projects/truthcom.htm; Roger Cohen, "A South African Model for Reconciling in Iraq," *New York Times*, 3/11/2006.

41. See South Africa Conference Web site, http://www.racism.gov.za/host/index.html; World Conference Web site, http://www.un.org/WCAR/coverage.htm, response to conference at http://www.adl.org/durban/default_intro.asp; and http://www.npr.org/programs/specials/racism/index.html; all last searched 4/06/06.

42. Michael Wines, "South Africa Lowers Voice on Human Rights," *New York Times*, 3/27/2007, http://www.nytimes.com/2007/03/24/world/africa/24africa.html?ex=1332388800&en=2f58d3b7c646fe94&ei=5088&partner=rssnyt&em=rss.

43. Chris Landsberg, "Promoting Democracy: The Mandela-Mbeki Doctrine," *Journal of Democracy* 11(3) (2000), 109; and Human Rights Watch Africa Report, http://www.hrw.org/wr2k3/africa.html, last searched 11/10/2005.

44. Landsberg, "Promoting Democracy," 114.

45. See Southern African Migration Project, SAMP Migration Policy Briefs, http://www.queensu.ca/samp/sampresources/samppublications/. The government limits immigration of unskilled workers to South Africa, encouraged the immigration of certain skilled workers or those who can create job opportunities. See Visas and Consular, South African High Commission, New Delhi, http://www.indconjoburg.co.za/, last searched 3/24/2007.

46. Ministry of Foreign Affairs Strategic Plan, 2005–2008, p. 18 (vision) and Remarks of Minister Zuma 10. The Strategic Plan is available online at http://www.dfa.gov.za/department/stratplan05-08.pdf, last searched 10/20/05

47. CIA, "South Africa, World Fact book," https://www.cia.gov/cia/publications/factbook/geos/sf.html, and South Africa, "Economy Overview," http://www.southafrica.info/doing_business/economy/econoverview.htm

48. South Africa is not only self-sufficient in virtually all major agricultural products, but is also a net food exporter. Farming remains vitally important to the economy and development of the southern African region. Since 1994, the government has been working to develop small-scale farming to boost job creation. South Africa is the world's top exporter of avocados, tangerines and ostrich products, the second-biggest exporter of grapefruit, third-biggest exporter of plums and pears, and fourth-biggest exporter of table grapes. Farming contributes some 8 percent to the country's total exports. The largest export groups are wine, citrus, sugar, grapes, maize, fruit juice, wool, and deciduous fruit such as apples, pears, peaches and apricots. http://www.southafrica.info/overview/english/agriculture-english.htm, last searched 8/24/2006.

49. The country provides a wealth of statistics at http://www.thedti.gov.za/econdb/raportt/IMFTradeSOUTH percent20AFRICATrade.html; last searched 11/05/2005.

50. South Africa: Economic Structure, *The Economist*, available online: http://www.economist.com/countries/SouthAfrica/profile.cfm?folder=Profile-Economic percent20Structure.

51. *Financial Times*, "South Africa," 6/12/2006, http://www.ft.com/reports/southafrica2006, last searched 8/22/2006.

52. South Africa, "Economy Overview," http://www.southafrica.info/doing_business/economy/econoverview.htm; and http://www.southafrica.info/doing_business/economy/success/financial-times.htm, both last searched 8/22/2006.

53. *The Gazette* serves as South Africa's official publication for national policy and legislation notification.

54. "Green papers," in South African government parlance, refer to raw policy proposals in their early stages which the government floats to test the waters of public opinion and obtain initial reactions to a new policy idea. Based on public reaction to the green paper, the government may choose to either drop the idea altogether or to refine it further and reissue it as a "white paper." White papers outline more serious policy proposals. They stand a greater chance of becoming official government policy. The feedback solicitation process for white papers is therefore generally more formal in nature. Because the stakes are higher, many civil society organizations that provide no input at the green paper stage will comment in defense of their interests at the white paper stage.

55. This step helps fulfill the Constitutional mandate for policymaking coordination between the national and provincial levels.

56. The aim of the National Economic Development and Labor Council (NEDLAC) is to make economic decision making more inclusive and to promote the goals of economic growth and social equity. It is funded by the Department of Labor, but the Departments of Trade and Industry, Finance, and Public Works are also centrally involved in NEDLAC; http://www.nedlac.org.za/.

57. While some civil society groups focus on labor rights, others have examined how trade may affect specific rights (such as the right to health) or specific groups of people such

as children or HIV/AIDS victims. Some of the most influential NGOs include the South African Institute for International Affairs (SAIIA), the Trade Law Center at the University of Stellenbosch (TRALAC), the University of Pretoria Faculty of Law, the Department of Economics at the University of Cape Town, the Institute for Global Dialogue, the South Africa Foundation, and the Free Market Foundation.

58. The Department of Trade and Industry was restructured in March 2000 to better assist South African enterprises trying to enter the global marketplace and to help it work better with the Department of Foreign Affairs. Marie Muller, "South Africa's Economic Diplomacy: Constructing a Better World for All?" *Diplomacy & Statecraft*, vol. 13, no. 1 (March 2002), 13–18.

59. Aaron Griffiths, "Annotated Bibliography on South Africa's Trade Policy and the WTO," February 2002, 1–2, www.gapresearch.org/governance/South percent20Africa percent20Trade percent20Bibliog.pdf, last searched 8/22/2006.

60. http://www.southafrica.info/doing_business/sa_trade/agreements/traderelations.htm, last searched 11/5/2005. Barbara Kalima-Phiri, "South Africa's Trade Policy," 8/23/2005, at http://www.sarpn.org.za/documents/d0001613/index.php; and WT/TPR/S/114/ZAF, p. A4-227.

61. For extensive statistics, including South Africa's economic background and bilateral trade overview, see http://www.agoa.info/index.php?view=country_info& country=za#, last searched 10/21/2005.

62. An overview of SACU's internal and external trade policy by the WTO (WT/TPR/S/114 24; March 2003) is at http://www.wto.org/english/tratop_e/tpr_e/tp213_e.htm.

63. The 1969 SACU agreement is available online at http://www.tralac.org/scripts/ content.php?id=3031, last searched 10/21/2005.

64. The poorer countries in SACU are more dependent on a limited number of products, including basic agriculture, mining, and quarrying (WT/TRP/S/114, p. vii).

65. Under the World Bank's classification scheme, Lesotho is classified as a least-developed country, entitling it to special preferences under the WTO system; Namibia and Swaziland are lower-middle-income countries, and Botswana and South Africa are both upper-middle-income countries. For more on the World Bank's classifications by GDP, see World Bank 2004 GNIPC (Gross National Income Per Capita) table, available online at: http://www.worldbank.org/data/databytopic/GNIPC.pdf, last searched 10/21/2005 and WT/TPR/S/114, p. vii.

66. WT/TPR/S/114 Annex 4, p. A4–228. Available at http://www.wto.org/english/tratop_ e/tpr_e/tp213_e.htm

67. In his speech, he focused on market access for African workers as well as products; a mechanism should be established in the WTO that provides African countries with "flexibility" not to implement specific rules, if the rationale is properly motivated. This should be understood as operationalising the principle of special and differential treatment, and targeted capacity building should assist in meeting this obligation. He also called for governments to review and revise WTO agreements from a development perspective. A specific example of direct relevance and great importance for Africa is a review of Article 24. Article 24 requires signatories of FTAs to eliminate trade barriers on substantially all their bilateral trade flows. This is not in the interest of Africa as it will cause trade diversion and transfer tariff revenues. This is anti-development and an example of policy incoherence. Moreover, he noted that more effective financial and technical cooperation will need to address any erosion of preferences that will occur as a result of the Doha Round and regional arrangements.

Such "compensation" should be designed to encourage sustainable diversification and to cushion any negative socio-economic effects of the reform process. Moreover, preferences need to be improved to make them meaningful. Finally, he stressed that African countries require expanded trade capacity to more effectively address supply constraints: the so-called aid for trade programme, which spans trade capacity building, enhancing competitiveness as well as action in importing countries to both assist African exports penetrate markets and to raise the returns accruing to Africa. Mandisi Mpahlwa, "Keynote Speech," South Africa's National Consultative Conference for the 6th WTO Ministerial Conference," 10/27/2005, http://www.sarpn.org.za/documents/d0001683/index.php, last searched 8/22/2006.

68. "U.S. Formula Invites Developing Country Criticism," *Inside U.S. Trade*, 10/14/2005, 19.

69. "Hope for Hong Kong WTO Talks," 10/28/2005, at http://www.southafrica.info/what_happening/news/news_international/wto-281005.htm, last searched 8/27/2006; also see http://weekly.ahram.org.eg/2005/767/in4.htm.

70. NA, "India, S.Africa urge rich nations to cut farm subsidies," The Hindu News Update Service, 10/02/2006 http://www.hindu.com/thehindu/holnus/001200610021926.htm; and Catherine Maddox, "African Aid Ministers Urge End to US Cotton Subsidies," news.voa.com, both last searched 10/25/2006.

71. "Bush Administration to Explore Flexibilities in SACU FTA," *Inside U.S. Trade*, 10/14/2005, 3

72. "US Drops FTA with SACU, Starts Trade and Investment Work Program," *Inside U.S. Trade*, 4/21/2006, 4.

73. The Ministry of Foreign Affairs illuminated their desire to strengthen trade with developing nations in their Strategic Plan 2005–2008, p. 12. "We shall continue to work with like-minded countries in order to extend the global space for freedom and progressive change. We are strengthening our work through South-South co-operation, especially through the IBSA forum as well as NAM and AASROC and deepening our commitment to extending trade relations in these regions. Part of our engagement is in the form of an ongoing dialogue amongst and within the entire African Diaspora to redress power relations, to defeat poverty and to stop the marginalization of Africa and the African in the world." http://www.dfa.gov.za/department/stratplan05-08.pdf, last searched 10/20/2005.

74. Herbert Ross, Director of NEPAD and Governance program at South African Institute of International Affairs, commented on this strategic move. Interview with SAIIA 7/20/2005. In the March 2004 edition of his program's newsletter, *eAfrica*, Steven Gruzd openly remarks "India, Brazil and South Africa aspire to converge in Southern pact to rival North's dominance." *eAfrica newsletter* 2 (2004), available online at: http://www.saiia.org.za/print.php?sid=231, last searched 10/21/2005. The Director General of the Department of Foreign Affairs commented on South Africa's need to foster greater South-South ties in order to restore balance between the North and the South in the May 20, 2004 address at the South African Institute of International Affairs, available online at http://www.saiia.org.za/modules.php?op=modload&name=News&file=article&sid=341, last searched 10/21/2005.

75. "AIDS Makes Most of South Africa's Other Problems Seem Trivial," *The Economist*, http://www.economist.com/surveys/printerfriendly.cfm?story_id=510668. South Africa's Bill of Rights includes, in the Labour Relations Section, (1) "Everyone

has the right to fair labour practices" and (2) "every worker has the right to form and join a trade union, to participate in the activities and programmes of a trade union; and to strike." The Basic Conditions of Employment Act of 1997 is equally strong.

76. Department of State, Country Reports, South Africa, 2005, 16.

77. South Africa National Labour Relations Act No. 66 of 1995 (last amended in 2002), available at http://www.labour.gov.za/act/index.jsp?legislationId=5540&actId=7608, last searched 10/21/2005.

78. South Africa's labor legislation at http://www.labourguide.co.za/legislation.htm; on cost of labor relative to capital, see "Jobless and Joyless: A Survey of South Africa," *The Economist*, 24 of February, 2001. http://www.economist.com/surveys/displaystory.cfm?story_id = E1_VTDGRV

79. WT/TPR/S/114/ZAF, p. A4-218.

80. South Africa Human Development Report, Appendix, Table 11, Wage Share by Industry, United Nations Development Programme (UNDP), available at http://www.undp.org.za/NHDR2003/chap12.pdf, last searched 10/21/2005. The Textiles and Apparel industry in South Africa has historically had (and currently has) the highest wage share (wages relative to nominal gross value added at factor cost) of all secondary South African industries (80 percent in 2002).

81. Although some high-skilled sectors, such as personal services, and other tertiary sector industries are performing quite well in South Africa, industries that are low skilled and labor intensive continue to suffer from increased competition from cheaper markets elsewhere. With the end of the Multi-Fiber Agreement quota in January 2005, the issue of textiles is a popular one in South Africa – widely and heatedly debated. The textiles discussion came up in the majority of conducted interviews, despite the fact that other sectors employ a greater percentage of the population. For that reason alone, we highlight the textile sector argument in depth in this chapter.

82. Total employment in textiles declined from 3.3% in 1996 to 2.8% of the formal labor sector in 2002. South Africa Human Development Report, Appendix, Table 4, available online at http://www.undp.org.za/NHDR2003.htm Industry Share of total employment (percent) (1970–2002), p. 240. The same is true for other historically strong high-employment sectors, such as manufacturing, mining, and metals. All sectors have experienced decreases in share of total employment percentages since 1996.

83. Interview with Neva Makgetla and Tanya Van Meelis, Congress of South African Trade Unions, Johannesburg, 7/26/2005.

84. SA, China Sign Key Textile Deal, 6/22/2006; http://www.southafrica.info/what_happening/news/news_international/china-130606.htm, last searched 3/24/2007.

85. Oxfam UK, "Trading Away Our Rights, Women Working Global Supply Chains" at http://www.oxfam.org.uk/what_we_do/issues/trade/trading_rights.htm, last searched 4/12/2006.

86. Interview with Thabo Chauke, Trade Negotiator for the Americas, Department of Trade and Industry, Government of South Africa, 7/28/2005.

87. According to Thabo Chauke, Trade Negotiator for the Americas of the Department of Trade and Industry, "It is clear from economic theory that with liberalization there are always winners and losers. The question is how to compensate the losers in such a way as to make the liberalization beneficial to the economy as a whole." Interview with Thabo Chauke, 7/28/2005.

88. For more information on the skills development levy, see the 2003 Amended Skills Development Act at http://www.labour.gov.za/act/index.jsp?legislationId=5976&actId=7310, last searched 2005.

89. Shaun Benton, "Parastatal Spending Spree," 2/6/2006, http://www.southafrica.info/doing_business/economy/asgi_sa/asgisa060206.htm; and Boost Skills, Boost Growth: Mbeki, 2/6/2006, http://www.southafrica.info/ess_info/sa_glance/government/stateofnation2006-skills.htm, last searched 8/22/2006.

90. http://www.proudlysa.co.za

91. Ayesha Kajee, "Made in China, Made Scared in a Textile Mill in Africa," http://www.saiia.org.za/modules.php?op=modload&name=News&file=article&sid=515; and NEDLAC, "Global Review of Eco-Labels: Implications for South Africa, Phase Two Report," January 2003.

92. See the 2004 Democratic Alliance General Election Manifesto, p. 9, available online at http://www.da.org.za/da/Site/Eng/campaigns/2004/misc percent5Cmanifesto.doc, last searched 10/21/2005.

93. Both Trudi Hartzenberg of the Trade Law Center and Lawrence Edwards of the University of Cape Town commented on the infeasibility of the two-tier strategy, though they both commended the government for acknowledging and proactively working to address the unemployment. Trudi Hartzenberg interview 8/3/2005 and Lawrence Edwards interview 8/2/2005.

94. Investors See SA with "Fresh Eyes," 7/06/2005, http://www.southafrica.info/doing_business/investment/imcmission-europe.htm; and Foreign Direct Investment Soars, 4/5/2006, http://www.southafrica.info/doing_business/investment/fdi-m&a2006.htm, In April 2006, the government reported that mergers and acquisitions in South Africa increased 63% from 2004 to 2005.

95. According to Statistics SA's latest Labor Force Survey, this represents a marked increase of 5.7% to 12.3 million formal sector jobs following sluggish growth in previous years. The increase in the year to end September 2004 was only 1.9%, whereas over a longer period, from September 2001 to September 2005, job gains in the labor market were just over 1 million (1,120,000). Despite this growth in employment, an increase in the country's economically active population meant South Africa's unemployment rate was virtually unchanged at 26.7% in September 2005, as against 26.2% in September 2004. "Economic Growth Creating Jobs,"1/30/2006, http://www.southafrica.info/doing_business/businesstoday/economy_update/employment-300106.htm, last searched 8/24/2006.

96. http://www.safrica.info/doing_business/sa_trade/importing/open.htm, last searched 11/9/2005.

97. http://www.southafrica.info/doing_business/trends/empowerment/ and http://www.safrica.info/doing_business/sa_trade/importing/open.htm, last searched 10/05/2005.

98. Ibid.

99. These ethnic classifications are distinctly South African. They originated under the apartheid regime of the National Party and were perpetuated and institutionalized through many apartheid-era policies. The terms *black* and *African* typically refer to the dark-skinned descendants of the northern and central African peoples who migrated down to South Africa in previous centuries, including the Xhosa and Zulu peoples. The Sotho-Tswana, Ndebele, and several other less populous groups are also referred to as *black*. The word *coloured* is used to denote people of lighter skin who are typically either of mixed race or descended from the original inhabitants of South Africa, the

Khoisan and Khoikhoi peoples. Cape Malays – descendants of slaves from Malaysia, Indonesia, Polynesia, and other proximate regions – are also often termed *coloured* for purposes of statistical tracking. Finally, the term *Indian* refers to both voluntary immigrants from India and descendants of Indian slaves who were brought to South Africa by the Dutch East Indies Company and other commercial and governmental powers during colonial times. We are grateful to Julie Maupin for this analysis.

100. Thabo Chauke interview, 7/28/2005.
101. Act No. 53, 2003, of the Parliament of South Africa: Broad Based Economic Empowerment Act 2003. Published in the *Government Gazette, Cape Town,* 463 (25899) (2004). Available at http://www.dti.gov.za/bee/BEEAct-2003-2004.pdf; and the DTI, "The Codes of Good Practice on Broad Based Black Economic Empowerment: Phase One," *A Guide to Interpreting the Codes,* 2005, 4.
102. http://www.dti.gov.za/bee/codes/3_20code000.pdf; BEE Codes Clear Confusion, 12/5/2005; http://www.joburg.org.za/business/bee.stm; http://www.workinfo.com/BEE/index.htm, all last searched 8/24/2006.
103. DTI, "The Codes," 11; and Renée Bonorchis, "BEE Codes Pose a Challenge," *Business Report,* 11/2/2005, http://www.busrep.co.za/index.php?fArticleId=2976280, last searched 8/24/2006.
104. For more information on the rules and stipulations of BEE compliance, see section 3.5 of the comprehensive BEE strategy, available online at http://www.beeonline.co.za/, last searched 10/21/2005 and DTI, "The Codes," 4–11.
105. On positive responses, see South African Migration Project, Media Coverage of Empowerment Charter Debate, http://www.queensu.ca/samp/Mining/Media.htm, last searched 4/11/2006; and Nicky Oppenheimer, "A Fairer Society Needs Faster Growth," *Financial Times,* 8/25/2003.
106. In our interviews, South Africans expressed concern that the BEE had simply created new black elite to accompany the white elite. Some well-known black businessmen have made millions off of multiple BEE deals, but the vast majority of blacks continue to own no capital whatsoever. For example, interview with Philip Krawitz, CEO of Cape Union Mart, Cape Town, 8/3/2005; and Address by COSATU President Wille Madisha, speech delivered at the Harold Wolpe Memorial Seminar, 8/6/2005, available at http://www.cosatu.org.za/speeches/2005/wm20050608.htm, last searched 10/21/2005.
107. John Etkind, "Cracking the BEE Codes," *Business in Africa Online,* 7/19/2006, http://www.businessinafrica.net/economy/678540.htm
108. Hamilton, "Is Black Economic Empowerment?"
109. U.S. Department of State, 2006 Investment Climate Statement, South Africa, http://www.state.gov/e/eeb/ifd/2006/62034.htm. However, another survey found that the BEE was less important then positive economic conditions. It argued that the BEE supports an emerging middle class and thus is a net contributor to foreign investment. Empowerdex, "The Effects of Black Economic Empowerment on Foreign Direct Investment (FDI), June 2005, www.empowerdex.co.za/downloads/BEE percent20and percent20FDI percent20June percent202005.pdf – both last searched 8/26/2006.
110. Tumi Makgetla, "Foreign Firms Fret Over BEE," *Mail and Guardian Online,* 8/25/2006, http://www.mg.co.za/articlePage.aspx?articleid=262340&area=/insight/insight__economy__business/, last searched 8/25/2006.
111. Jacqui Pile "Sectoral Charters, Reward or Risk?" *Financial Mail,* 3/4/2005 /free. financialmail.co.za/projects05/topempowerment/stories/hbee.htm, last searched 8/24/2006.

112. Tumi Makgetia, "Foreign Firms Fret Over BEE," *Mail and Guardian Online*, 8/25/2006.
113. U.S.-South Africa Business Council interview, 6/14/2005; and Luanne Grant, American Chamber of Commerce in South Africa interview, 7/26/2005. The validity of this claim has not yet been established. While the equity ownership provision does require a transfer of ownership, it does not do so without compensation. Indeed, the BEE instructs firms to sell 25% of their companies to black owners at "fair market value." For details, see Code 000 (Broad-Based Black Economic Empowerment Framework), Statement 100 (The Role of Equity Ownership in Broad-Based Economic Empowerment), Section 3.9.
114. Luanne Grant interview, 7/26/2005.
115. Both Luanne Grant, Executive Director of the American Chamber of Commerce of South Africa, and Dan O'Flaherty, Senior Vice President of the U.S.-South Africa Business Council, asserted that this is the position of many U.S. and international businesses. Luanne Grant interview, 7/26/2005, and USSABC interview, 6/14/2005. Also interview with Roger Crawford, Executive Director of Government Affairs and Policy, Johnson & Johnson South Africa, Midrand, 7/25/2005.
116. Johnson & Johnson executive Roger Crawford explained that his company has a non-negotiable policy of maintaining 100% integrated ownership of all of its subsidiaries, both foreign and domestic. Thus, he argued "if black South Africans want to buy 25 percent of its shares, they are free to do so via the New York Stock Exchange." Interview with Roger Crawford, 7/25/2005.
117. Dr. Jim Harris, The Free Market Foundation of Southern Africa, 2/28/2006, http://www .freemarketfoundation.com/ShowArticle.asp?ArticleType=regulation&ArticleID= 1162
118. Jonathan Clayton, "ANC Ready to Scrap Rules on Investment," 1/31/2006, http:// business.timesonline.co.uk/article/0,19609-2017041,00.html; Jonathan Clayton, "Changes will Allow Blacks to Capitalize on Gains," 11/7/2006; and business. timesonline.co.uk/tol/business/markets/africa/article627629.ece.
119. However, the South African government is not a member of the WTO Plurilateral Government Procurement Agreement (GPA) and thus it does not violate GPA rules. It could affect national treatment in services that South Africa has made offers in, such as banking. Under the WTO's national treatment principle, South Africa cannot apply one set of standards to its domestic companies while applying a different standard to foreign companies, even if that standard is lower. See Albert. H. Cho and Navroz K. Dubash, World Resources Institute, "Will Investment Rules Shrink Policy Space for Sustainable Development? Evidence from the Electricity Sector, South Centre," Working Papers 16, December 2003; and South Bulletin 51, "Services Train in a Headlong Rush," 2/15/2003.
120. DTI, "The Codes of Good Practice: Phase One," 2005, chs. 5–6, code 100, "Measurement of the Ownership Element of Broad-Based Black Economic Empowerment," 22–24.
121. BEE Codes to be simplified, 7/12/2006, www.southafrica.info/doing_business/ trends/empowerment/bee-codes-120706.htm, last searched 8/24/2006.
122. Draft codes were created to accommodate multinational companies operating in South Africa. The codes distinguish between three types of multinationals – multinationals headquartered in South Africa, multinationals that used to be headquartered in South

Africa and businesses that were never headquartered in South Africa. Multinationals have the following options in fulfilling the ownership element of the scorecard. They can sell equity in South African operations; assets in South African operations; equity in their offshore businesses – applicable to a South African multinational; or equity equivalents. An equity equivalent is a public programme approved by the DTI involving a value contribution to the South African economy. Lerato Buhlebuyeza Mathopo and Greg Nott, "Africa: A Clearer Future," *Legal Week*, 10/25/2006, http://www.legalweek.com/ViewItem.asp?id=31219.

123. Hamilton, "Is Black Economic Empowerment"; Shola Olowu, "Young South Africans Empowerment Dream," BBC News, 4/23/2004, http://news.bbc.co.uk/1/hi/business/3652201.stm; and WT/TPR/S/114/ZAF, p. A4-248.

124. United Nations Development Programme, South Africa Human Development Report, 2003, ch. 2, p. 28, at http://www.undp.org.za/NHDR2003.htm, last searched 3/24/3007.

125. South Africa Human Development Report, ch. 2, pp. 26–27; and AIDS Foundation South Africa, http://www.aids.org.za/hiv.htm

126. "Cruellest Curse: AIDS Makes Most of South Africa's Other Problems Seem Trivial," *The Economist*, 2/22/2001, at http://www.economist.com/surveys/displaystory.cfm?story_id=E1_VTDGGR last searched 10/1/2005. ILO and Kaiser Foundation statistics from Barnard, "In the High Court," p. 160.

127. South Africa Human Development Report, AHD, ch. 2, p. 30 and note 35.

128. Michael Wines, "Mandela, Anti-AIDS Crusader, Says Son Died of Disease," *New York Times*, 1/7/2005 and "4664: 1 Minute for AIDS in Africa," http://query.nytimes.com/gst/fullpage.html?res=9D03E0DD1139F934A35752C0A9639C8B63&sec=health&spon=&pagewanted=print, last searched 3/24/2007.

129. Wines, "Mandela, Anti-AIDS Crusader, Says Son Died of Disease," *New York Times*, 1/7/2005 and "4664: 1 Minute for Aids in Africa," http://www.southafrica.info/mandela/46664.htm, last searched 3/24/2007

130. According to the AIDS Foundation South Africa, the burden of care and support has fallen on the family members in impoverished rural communities. In these communities, "awareness is spread or ignorance reinforced." AIDS Foundation South Africa, "Current Situation, Trends and Challenges," http://www.aids.org.za/hiv.htm. Also see Bruce Greenberg, "Women from South Africa AIDS Support Group Speak in Washington," usinfo.state.gov/gi/archive/2006/march/16-305342.html and AIDS Foundation South Africa, "Current Situation, Trends and Challenges," http://www.aids.org.za/hiv.htm, all last searched 3/26/2006. The South African government has frequently revised its approach to AIDS treatment, and in late October 2006, Deputy President Phumzile Mlambo-Ngcuka was appointed head of a new interministerial committee on HIV/AIDS, sidelining Health Minister Manto Tshabalala-Msimang who has had an especially bitter relationship with activists in the past. Wendell Rouf, "South African Ministry Devising New AIDS Battle Plan," 10/26/2006, http://www.alertnet.org/thenews/newsdesk/L26547447.htm, last searched October 26/2006.

131. Lawrence K. Altman, "UN Official."

132. Medicines Amendment Act (1997), Section 10 (Insertion of Section 15.C in Act 101 of 1965). The Medicines Amendment Act is available online at http://www.doh.gov.za/docs/legislation/acts/1997/act90.pdf, last searched 10/21/2005.

133. Medicines Amendment Act (1997), Section 10 (Insertion of Section 15.C in Act 101 of 1965). The amendment instituted the following new procedures: (a) not withstanding anything to the contrary contained in the Patents Act, 1978 (Act No. 57 of 1978) determine that the rights with regard to any medicine under a patent granted in the Republic shall not extend to acts in respect of such medicine which has been put onto the market by the owner of such medicine, or with his or her consent; (b) describe the conditions on which any medicine which is identical in composition, meets the same quality standard and is intended to have the same proprietary name as that of a medicine already registered in the Republic but which is imported by a person other than the person who is the holder of the registration certificate of the medicine already registered and which originates from any site of manufacture of the original manufacturer as approved by the council in the prescribed manner, may be imported; and (c) prescribe the registration procedure for, as well as the use of, the medicine referred to in paragraph (b). The Medicines Amendment Act is available online at http://www.doh.gov.za/docs/legislation/acts/1997/act90.pdf, last searched 10/21/2005.
134. The Pharmaceutical Manufacturers Association and Others v. The President of the Republic of South Africa and Others, case no: 4183/98, High Court of South Africa (Transvaal Provincial Division).
135. SA Constitution, Section 25 (1): "No one may be deprived of the right to property except in terms of law of general application, and no law may permit arbitrary deprivation of property."
136. Mark Heywood, "Debunking 'Conglomo-talk': A Case Study of the *Amicus Curiae* as an Instrument for Advocacy, Investigation and Mobilization." This paper was prepared for presentation at "Health, Law and Human Rights: Exploring the Connections, An International Cross-Disciplinary Conference Honoring Jonathan M. Mann," September 29–October 1, 2001, Philadelphia, PA. Available online at http://www.law.wits .ac.za/cals/pub-jnl.htm Heywood is the head of the AIDS Law Project at the Centre for Applied Legal Studies, University of the Witwatersrand, Johannesburg.
137. April 30, 1999, USTR 301 report on South Africa, annotated at http://www .cptech.org/ip/health/sa/sa301-ap99.html, last searched 11/05/2005.
138. WT/TPR/S/114/ZAF, p. A4-226.
139. Zackie Achmat, TAC Chairperson to President Thabo Mbeki, Minister of Health Manto Tshabalala-Msimang, and Parliament, 3/14/2001, at http://www.cptech.org/ ip/health/sa/tacsag03142001.html, last searched 3/24/2007.
140. Although the case and affiliated campaign brought significant attention to the high cost of drugs, it did not solve the larger problem of ensuring affordable accessible medicine for the world's poor. Oxfam and its allies gathered signatures on a petition demanding changes to intellectual property rules so that the poor could get access to the medicines they need to survive plagues and diseases. It encouraged investors to pressure the drug companies and develop a strategy to lower drug prices. And they called on governments to reevaluate the rules. In Doha, Qatar, when WTO members agreed to launch a new round of trade talks, participating nations agreed that developing countries could use the public health safeguards in the TRIPS to improve access of the poor to medicines. However, they did not agree that these countries could violate TRIPS and import cheap generic drugs. Thus, this trade approved solution still did not ensure that the poor in the developing world could receive the medicines their citizens needed. Many developing countries do not have the capacity to produce drugs and would have had to

import them. A trade solution cannot solve this problem, which can only be addressed when drug manufacturers produce drugs for the diseases of the poor and find ways to produce them cheaply through economies of scale and scope. In the interim, some foundations and donors are pooling their funds to subsidize drug purchases and delivery systems in the poorest countries. Oxfam, "Cut the Cost, Patent Injustice: How World Trade Rules Threaten the Health of Poor People," 8–9; at http://www.oxfam.org.uk/; and Kevin Watkins, Senior Policy Advisor, Oxfam, "Trade Globalization and Poverty Reduction: Why the Rules of the Game Matter," Seminar on World Trade and Poverty, Carnegie Endowment, 7/2/2002.

141. South Africa has opted for a waiver from TRIPS obligations at the WTO regarding public health under the July 8, 2002, Decision of the General Council of the WTO, which states "obligations of least-developed country Members under paragraph 9 of Article 70 of the TRIPS Agreement shall be waived with respect to pharmaceutical products until 1 January 2016." See http://www.wto.org/english/tratop_e/trips_e/art70_9_e.htm for more information.

142. Khomanani – the government campaign to prevent the spread of diseases such as AIDS. https://www.healthinsite.net/corporate/ last searched 3/24/2007.

143. Republic of South Africa Department of Foreign Affairs, Strategic Plan 2005–2008, Part One: Message from the Minister of Foreign Affairs, Dr. N. C. Dlamini Zuma, p. 10, published on the Department of Foreign Affairs Web site at http://www.dfa.gov.za/department/stratplan05-08.pdf, last searched 10/19/2005.

144. U.S. Department of State Country Reports on Human Rights Practices 2004 at http://www.state.gov/g/drl/rls/hrrpt/2004/41627.htm last searched 3/24/2007

145. Under the guise of land reform, Robert Mugabe's government in Zimbabwe has evicted 700,000 people from their homes, creating a vast refugee crisis (with many of the refugees fleeing to South Africa) and engendering a hunger epidemic. For more information, see Human Rights Watch report "Clear the Filth: Mass Evictions and Demolitions in Zimbabwe," September 11, 2005, at http://www.hrw.org; and Michael Wines, "In Zimbabwe, Homeless Belie Leader's Claim," *New York Times*, 11/13/2005, 1, 8. On the response of business, see "Jobless and Joyless," http://www.economist.com/surveys/displaystory.cfm?story_id=E1_VTDGRV.

146. Interview with Tom Tieku, Ph.D. candidate, University of Toronto, and expert in regional politics of Africa, 11/11/2005.

147. The State Department Report on Human Rights in South Africa criticizes South Africa for its treatment of refugees. See http://www.state.gov/g/drl/rls/hrrpt/2004/41627.htm for more details, last searched 10/21/2005. Also see Charlayne Hunter-Gault, "South Africa Absorbs Zimbabwean Refugees," http://www.npr.org/templates/story/story.php?storyId=9269300, and Zim Refugees Pour into South Africa," http://www.int.iol.co.za/index.php?set_id = 1&click_id = 68&art_id=vn20070404112133660 C519174, both last searched 4/7/2007.

148. Department of State, Country Report, South Africa; and Human Rights Watch, "Living on the Margins: Inadequate Protection for Refugees and Asylum Seekers in Johannesburg," http://www.hrw.org/reports/2005/southafrica1105/index.htm, last searched 4/12/2006.

149. Dumisani Muleya, "Southern Africa: SADC Confirms Zim a Trouble Spot," *Zimbabwe Independent*, 8/25/2006, http://allafrica.com/stories/200608250371.html, last searched 8/25/2006.

150. Rob Crilly, "Mugabe Gets Backing, But Neighbors Call for Changes," 3/30/2007, at http://scotlandonsunday.scotsman.com/topics.cfm?tid=1559&id=492172007; NA, "SA has Strong Words for Mugabe," 24.com, http://www.news24.com/News24/South_Africa/Politics/0,9294,2-7-12_2090644,00.html; and Brendan Boyle, "Southern Africa: South Africa Fails Zimbabwe," *Sunday Times (Johannesburg)*, OPINION section 8/20/2006, http://allafrica.com/stories/200608210449.html.

151. Wines, "South Africa," http://www.nytimes.com/2007/03/24/world/africa/24africa.html?ex=1332388800&en=2f58d3b7c646fe94&ei=5088&partner=rssnyt&emc=rss.

152. Herbert Ross and Nkululeko Khumalo of the South African Institute for International Affairs (SAIIA) expressed disapproval of this policy in an interview with the author, as did Christi van der Westhuizen of the Institute for Global Dialogue and Judge Dennis Davis of the High Court of South Africa, Western Cape Province. Interviews with Herbert Ross, Head of the NEPAD and Governance Program, and Nkululeko Khumalo, Trade Facilitation Project Manager, Development through Trade Project, South African Institute of International Affairs (SAIIA), Johannesburg, 7/20/2005. Interview with Garth le Pere, executive director; Michelle Pressend, senior researcher, Multilateral Programme; and Chrisi van der Westhuizen, senior researcher; Institute for Global Dialogue (IGD), Pretoria, 7/21/2005. Interview with Judge Dennis Davis, Judge for the High Court of South Africa, Western Cape, Cape Town, 8/1/2005. Judge Davis also teaches law, including international and human rights law, at the University of Cape Town.

153. Michael Canham interview, 7/13/2005.

154. Thabo Chauke interview, 7/28/2005.

155. Khulekani M. Dube, "South Africa's Foreign Policy in Africa," 3–4.

156. In May 2000, De Beers's representatives gave written testimony on conflict diamonds before the U.S. House Subcommittee on Africa, Global Human Rights, and International Operations. Their testimony stated, "De Beers knows all too well the deleterious effects that conflict and political instability often have on potential large-scale investors.... Having spent hundreds of millions of dollars on advertising its product, De Beers is deeply concerned about anything that could damage the image of diamonds as a symbol of love, beauty and purity." Dick Durham, "De Beers Sees Threat of Blood Diamonds," http://www.cnn.com; http://cnnstudentnews.cnn.com/2001/WORLD/africa/01/18/diamonds.debeers/, last searched 9/29/2005. However, some analysts see the Kimberley Process as a way for De Beers to gain greater control over the market. See Mongo Sugot, "Making a Killing: Conflict Diamonds Are Forever," http://www.publicintegrity.org/bow/report.aspx?aid=152, last searched 9/29/2005.

157. Tracey Michele Price, "The Kimberley Process: Conflict Diamonds, WTO Obligations, and the Universitality Debate," *Minnesota Journal of Global Trade*, 12, 1 (Winter 2003), 1. According to Price, conflict diamonds mainly originate in Angola, Sierra Leone, and the Democratic Republic of the Congo, but they are often smuggled into neighboring African countries.

158. On the Kimberley Process, Diamond Facts.org, http://www.diamondfacts.org/ and https://mmsd1.mms.nrcan.gc.ca/kimberleyprocess/qa_e.asp, both last searched 3/29/2007.

159. Several of these critiques are at http://www.globalpolicy.org/security/issues/diamond/ngoindex.htm; last searched 9/20/2005.

160. Press release, "Diamond Development Initiative Begins," 8/15/2005, at http://www .globalpolicy.org/security/issues/diamond/2005/0815ddi.htm, last searched 8/26/2006.

161. Amnesty International, "Kimberley Process: An Amnesty International Position Paper," http://web.amnesty.org/library/index/engpol300242006, June 21st 2006, last searched 8/16/06.

162. Press release, "Diamond Development Initiative Begins," 8/15/2005, at http://www .globalpolicy.org/security/issues/diamond/2005/0815ddi.htm last searched 9/29/2005.

163. Address by Premier Mbhazima Shilowa, Commonwealth Investment Forum, 10/10/2005, at http://www.gpg.gov.za/docs/sp/2005/sp1010.html

164. Republic of South Africa Department of Foreign Affairs, Strategic Plan 2005– 2008, "Part One: Message from the Minister of Foreign Affairs," Dr. N. C. Dlamini Zuma, p. 9, published on the Department of Foreign Affairs Web site at http://www.dfa.gov.za/department/stratplan05-08.pdf, last searched 10/19/2005.

4. Brazil: Creating New Rules of the Road

1. We are grateful to Philip Van der Celen, who participated in the extensive background and field research for this chapter.

2. Joao R. Martins Filho *et al.*, "Brazilian Military under Cardoso: Overcoming the Identity Crisis," *Journal of Interamerican Studies and World Affairs* (Fall 2000), at www.findarticles.com/p/articles/mi_qa3688/is_200010/ai_n8907460/pg_1; and "Brazilian Military," http://www.globalsecurity.org/military/world/brazil/army.htm, both last searched 11/20/2006.

3. Carlos DeJuana, "Dengue Mosquito Becomes Brazil's Public Enemy No. 1," Reuters, 3/1/2002, http://www.heatisonline.org/contentserver/objecthandlers/index .cfm?id=3891&method=full, last searched 12/26/2005.

4. NA, "Brazilians Take Strong Steps to Fight a Deadly Mosquito," *Boston Globe*, 3/10/2002, p. A8, http://www.heatisonline.org/contentserver/objecthandlers/ index.cfm?id=3891&method=full, last searched 3/22/2006.

5. Resolução No. 258, de 26 de Agosto de 1999 of the National Council on the Environment details the environmental and health dangers of disposed and rotting tires. The resolution is available online at http://www.mma.gov.br/port/conama/res/ res99/res25899.html; last searched 3/22/2006. See also the updated 2005 resolution, http://www.mma.gov.br/port/conama/processos/83C56F5F/ PropResolAPROMACPneu.pdf, last searched 3/29/2006.

6. NA, "President of IBAMA (Brazilian Institute for the Environment) Goes to the STJ (Superior Tribunal of Justice) against Importation of Used Tires," Ambiente Brazil, 12/4/2003, available online at http://www.mma.gov.br/ascom/ultimas/ index.cfm?id=814, last searched 3/22/2006.

7. NA, "President of IBAMA (Brazilian Institute for the Environment) Goes to the STJ (Superior Tribunal of Justice) against Importation of Used Tires," Ambiente Brazil, 12/4/2003, available online at http://www.mma.gov.br/ascom/ultimas/ index.cfm?id=814, last searched 3/22/2006. The untreadable tires are sometimes used as base materials in construction or other industries.

8. Basel Convention on the Control of Transboundary Movements of Hazardous Wastes and Their Disposal, available online at http://www.basel.int/, last searched 3/29/2006.

9. http://www.abip.com.br/site/guerra/gue_1992.php, last searched 3/28/2006.

10. CONAMA Resolution 258/99 adopted on 8/26/1999, available in Portuguese at http://www.abip.com.br/abip/guerra/gue_resolucao.php. See also "Brazil, the Battle over Used Tires," http://www.tierramerica.net/2003/1222/iecobreves.shtml, last searched 3/22/2006.

11. Portaria 9/25/2000 Article 39, Portaria No. 17, 12/1/2005, available online at http://www.mma.gov.br/conama/res/reso5/res36005.xml, last searched 3/22/2006.

12. Uruguay vs. Brazil, MERCOSUR Ad Hoc Arbitration Tribunal, available online at http://www.MERCOSUR.int/msweb/principal/contenido.asp, last searched 3/22/2006.

13. Adriana Franzin, "Forced to Import Used Tires from Europe, Brazil Appeals to the WTO," *Brazzil Magazine*, 7/27/2005, http://brazzilnews.com/content/view/3350/49/, and "Brazil, the Battle over Used Tires," both last searched 12/26/2005.

14. "Brazil Mandates Tire Disposal," *Recycling Today*, 7/5/2001, http://www.sdbmagazine.com/articles/article.asp?Id = 2903&SubCatID=18&CatID=6, last searched 8/30/2006. Almost 40,000 cases of dengue had been officially registered in Rio de Janeiro state, the worst-hit area, in 2002. The number of cases in January alone in the state was the worst in a decade. AP, "Brazilians Take Strong Steps to Fight a Deadly Mosquito." On the spread of dengue fever, see Capsule Report, "Dengue Fever: An Environmental Plague for the New Millennium," No 2, 1999, at. http://heatisonline.org/contentserver/objecthandlers/index.cfm?id=3891&method=full, and Mary Wilson, "Emerging Infections: Dengue and Beyond," Harvard School of Public Health, http://drclas.fas.harvard.edu/revista/articles/view/423, both searched 12/26/2005.

15. Decreto No. 3.919, de 14 de Setembro de 2001, available online at http://www.presidencia.gov.br, last searched 3/29/2006.

16. Portaria No. 17 of December 1, 2003 of the Secretariat of Foreign Trade of the Brazilian Ministry of Development, Industry and International Commerce that prohibits the issuance of import licenses for retreaded tyres. http://www.desenvolvimento.gov.br/arquivo/legislacao/portarias/secex/2003/prtSECEX17_2003.pdf
    <http://www.desenvolvimento.gov.br/arquivo/legislacao/portarias/secex/2003/prtSECEX17_2003.pdf>

17. WTO Document WT/DS332/4, "Brazil – Measures Affecting Imports of Retreaded Tires: Request for the Establishment of a Panel by the EC," 11/18/2005, at http://www.wto.org. "Brazil – Measures Affecting Imports of Retreaded Tires," and WT/DS332/1/G/L/741, 6/23/2005, http://www.wto.org/english/tratop_e/dispu_e/cases_e/ds332_e.htm. The European Union cites the law as inconsistent with Articles I:1, III:4, XI:1, and XIII:1 of GATT 1994.

18. Adriana Franzin," Forced to Import Used Tires from Europe, Brazil Appeals to the WTO," *Brazzil Magazine*, 7/27/2005, http://brazzilnews.com/content/view/3350/49/, and "Brazil, the Battle over Used Tires," both last searched 12/26/2005; http://www.tierramerica.net/2003/1222/iecobreves.shtml. On the dispute panel, see http://www.wto.org/english/news_e/news06_e/dsb_20jan06_e.htm and http://www.wto.org/english/tratop_e/dispu_e/cases_e/ds332_e.htm, last searched 1/26/2006.

19. WTO Document WT/DS332, Brazil – Measures Affecting Imports of Retreaded Tires, First Written Submission of Brazil, June 8, 2006.

20. Interview with Haroldo de Macedo Ribeiro, Secretary of General Coordination of Disputes, Economics Division, Ministry of Foreign Affairs, 11/12/2005. Also, see Fabio Morisini, "The Case of the Tires: Regional Preferences and Environmental

Questions," *Pontes Newsletter* 1(4), (2005), available online at http://www.ictsd.org/monthly/pontes.htm, last searched 1/11/2006.

21. WTO Decision, WT/DS332/4, p. 245, at www.wto.org/english/news-e.htm; and the response of Brazil, www.mre.sov.br/portugues/imprensa/nota_detalhe3.asp?ID_RELEASE = 4441; both last searched 6/12/2007. Several NGOs submitted briefs supporting Brazil's position. See http://www.hsus.org/about_us/humane_society_international_hsi/international_trade_policy_and_capacity_building/hsi_supports_brazil_at_WTO.html, last searched 8/20/ 2006.

22. Interviews with Aloisio Gomez Neto, Special Advisor, Chamber of Foreign Trade (CAMEX), Ministry of Development Industry and Foreign Trade, 11/9/2005; Carlos Henrique Filho Mussi, Economist, Economic Commission for Latin America and the Caribbean (ECLAC), 11/9/2005; Riordan Rhoett, Sarita and Don Johnston Professor and Director for Western Hemisphere Affairs, Johns Hopkins University–SAIS, 10/ 2005.

23. "Speech of Minister Azeredo da Silva in the Open Session of the 32nd General Assembly of the United Nations in 1977," *The Word of Brazil in the United Nations*, Alexandre de Gusmao Foundation, Ministry of Foreign Affairs, 1995. For more information on Brazilian behavior in the Human Rights Commission, see Jose Augusto Lindgren Alves, "Os Direitos Humanos como Tema Global [Human Rights as a Global Issue]" (Sao Paulo: Perspectiva, Alexandre de Gusmao Foundation, Study Series, 1994), pp. 87–104.

24. Economist Intelligence Unit, "Brazil," Country Profile 2005, pp. 4–5, http://www.eiu.com/schedule.

25. Economist Intelligence Unit, "Brazil," Country Profile 2005, pp. 5–7.

26. Luiz Carlos Bresser Pereira, "Brazil," in John Williamson, ed., *The Political Economy of Policy Reform* (Washington DC: IIE, 1994), pp. 338–339, 340–353.

27. The Constitution of the Federal Republic of Brazil, last searched 3/8/2006. http://www.senado.gov.br/sf/legislacao/const/, last searched 3/22/2006. Brazil's constitution includes rights such as the right to "development," a "healthy environment," and collective rights amongst the human rights protected. The term "collective rights" refers to the rights of peoples to be protected from attacks on their group identity and group interests. The most important such collective right is often said to be the right of self-determination.

28. Economist Intelligence Unit, "Brazil," Country Profile 2005, pp. 5–7.

29. Economist Intelligence Unit, "Brazil," Country Profile 2005, pp. 5–7.

30. "Brazil Blocks Gun Ban," Associated Press, 10/23/2005, http://www.foxnews.com/story/0,2933,173154,00.html, last searched 3/22/2006.

31. Biography, "Luiz Inácio Lula da Silva," at http://www.answers.com/topic/luis-inacio-lula-da-silva, last searched 3/7/2006.

32. NA, "Brazil Refuses $40M in U.S. AIDS Grants to Protest Policy Requiring Groups to Condemn Commercial Sex Work," http://www.medicalnewstoday.com/medicalnews.php?newsid=23744 and http://news.bbc.co.uk/2/hi/americas/4513805.stm, both last searched 3/6/2006.

33. U.S. Department of State, "Country Reports on Human Rights Practices 2004: Brazil," http://www.state.gov/g/drl/rls/hrrpt/2005/61718.htm, last searched 3/22/2006.

34. Human Rights Watch, "Brazil: Human Rights Overview," http://hrw.org/english/docs/2006/01/18/brazil12204.htm.

35. Interviews with Dr. Paulo de Mesquita Neto, Executive Director, Sao Paulo Institute against Violence, 11/16/2005; Juana Kweitel, Programs Coordinator, Conectas Direitos Humanos, 11/15/2005; Frederico Figueiredo, Trade Program, Brazilian Institute for Consumer Defense, 11/13/2005. For more information, see http://lanic.utexas.edu/la/region/hrights/, last searched 3/10/2006. Also see Human Rights Report, 2002–2005, at http://www.global.org.br/docs/relatoriodefensores2005ingles.pdf.

36. The gap between Brazil's rich and poor is increasing. In the 2005 World Human Development Report, Brazil was ranked the fourth-most-unequal economy in the world in 2004. See the UN Human Development Report indices for more details, http://hdr.undp.org/reports/global/2005/pdf/HDR05_HDI.pdf.

37. Establishing a National Programme for Human Rights was a recommendation of the 1993 Declaration and Action Programme of Vienna, http://www.unhchr.ch/huridocda/huridoca.nsf/(Symbol)/A.CONF.157.23.En?OpenDocument, last searched 3/22/2006. See also "Foreign Affairs and Human Rights: Brasil in the UN Human Rights Commission," Programa de Acompanimento de Politica Externa em Direitos Humanso, Informe 1, April 2005, pp. 18–20.

38. See the National Programme for Human Rights, available online in English at http://www.planalto.gov.br/publi_04/COLECAO/NATPROI.HTM, last searched 1/23/2006.

39. The National Programme for Human Rights (PNDH) II was released on 5/13/2002, via presidential decree 4.229, both available online at the Special Secretariat for Human Rights site, http://www.planalto.gov.br/sedh/.

40. The Special Secretariat for Human Rights was created via law 10.683, 5/20/2003. For more information, see http://www.planalto.gov.br/sedh/ and Paulo Sergio Pinheiro, "Human Rights: Introduction," available online at http://www.mre.gov.br/cdbrasil/itamaraty/web/ingles/polsoc/dirhum/apresent/index.htm, last searched 2/8/2006.

41. Brazilian Federal Constitution, Title I, Article IV, available online at http://www.v-brazil.com/government/laws/titleI.html, last searched 3/22/2006. The principles guiding international relations include (1) national independence, (2) the prevalence of human rights, (3) self-determination of the people, (4) nonintervention, (5) equality between states, (6) defense of peace, (7) peaceful conflict resolution, (8) repudiation of terrorism and racism, and (9) cooperation of people for the progress of humanity.

42. Paulo Sergio Pinheiro, "Human Rights," Ministry of Foreign Affairs, available online at http://www.mre.gov.br/ingles/politica_externa/temas_agenda/direitos_humanos/introducao.asp, last searched 1/12/2006. Brazil is a signatory to the most important international treaties on human rights, both under the auspices of the United Nations and of the Organization of American States. They include the International Agreement on Civil and Political Rights; the International Agreement on Economic, Social, and Cultural Rights; the Convention against Torture and Other Cruel, Inhuman, or Degrading Punishment or Treatment; and the American Convention on Human Rights. Brazil has not put forward reservations in respect to any of these treaties. Brazil played an important part in the preparation and realization of the World Conference on Human Rights in Vienna in 1993, where it chaired the committee that drafted the Declaration and the Action Programme, which were

unanimously adopted by the conference on 6/25/1993. In 1996, Brazil assumed the presidency of the 52nd Meeting of the UN Human Rights Commission.

43. Jose Miguel Vivanco, Executive Director of Americas Division, Human Rights Watch, "Letter to President Lula da Silva," 2/2/2004. Available online at http://www.hrw.org/english/docs/2004/02/02/brazil7309_txt.htm, last searched 1/23/2006.

44. From "Foreign Affairs and Human Rights, Brazil in the UN Human Rights Commission," Informe 1, 4/2005. For information on Brazil's proposal to reform the UN Human Rights Commission, see http://www.ohchr.org/English/bodies/chr/docs/61chr/speeches/brazil15march.pdf.

45. Jose Miguel Vivanco, Executive Director of Americas Division, Human Rights Watch, "Letter to President Lula da Silva," 2/2/2004. Available online at http://www.hrw.org/english/docs/2004/02/02/brazil7390_txt.htm, last searched 1/23/2006.

46. Jose Miguel Vivanco, Executive Director of Americas Division, Human Rights Watch, "Letter to President Lula da Silva," 2/2/2004. Available online at http://www.hrw.org/english/docs/2004/02/02/brazil7390_txt.htm, last searched 1/23/2006. See also Special Statement of Nilmario Miranda, Special Secretary for Human Rights in Brazil, 61st Session of the Commission on Human Rights, 3/15/2005, http://www.ohchr.org/English/bodies/chr/docs/61chr/speeches/brazil15march.pdf.

47. Conectas, "Foreign Affairs and Human Rights: Brazil in the UN Human Rights Commission," Programa de Acompanimento de Politica Externa em Direitos Humanos, Informe 1, 4/2005, available online at http://www.pnud.org.br/seguranca/reportagens/index.php?id01=1502&lay=jse, last searched 8/30/2006

48. In both 1998 and 2005, Brazil presented reform proposals to the United Nations Human Rights Commission, both of which suggested that the United Nations create a global reporting system to monitor the human rights situations in countries around the world, in order to have a multilateral and objective system that could serve as a "thermometer of the global human rights situation in order to serve as a map for the work of the Human Rights Commission." See "Foreign Affairs and Human Rights: Brazil in the UN Human Rights Commission," Programa de Acompanimento de Politica Externa em Direitos Humanso, Informe 1, 4/2005, pp. 18–20.

49. As it occurs for all projects submitted to the UN Human Rights Commission during a regular session, the presenting country must hold prior consultations with the other member states to garner support. Without this lobbying, it is very improbable that a country would risk proposing a resolution. The Brazilian delegation to the UN Human Rights Commission held a meeting (informal consultations on the draft resolution "Human Rights Global Report") on 3/21/2005. But due to pressure from the EC countries, the United States, and Canada, other meetings or proposals were given priority. See "Foreign Affairs and Human Rights: Brazil in the UN Human Rights Commission," Programa de Acompanimento de Politica Externa em Direitos Humanos, Informe 1, 4/2005, pp. 18–20.

50. Economist Intelligence Unit, "Brazil," Country Profile 2005.

51. For elaboration on the elements of "Custo Brazil," see the World Bank Country Assessment Report for Brazil, "Introduction," available online at http://wbln0018.worldbank.org/LAC/LACInfoClient.nsf/d29684951174975c85256735007fef12/4dc168b98b512dc385256df700548474/$FILE/Annex%205.pdf, last searched 3/22/2006.

52. For statistics and ratings on Brazil's competitiveness, see "Doing Business in Brazil," http://www.doingbusiness.org/ExploreEconomies/Default.aspx?economyid=28, last searched 3/18/2006.

53. For more information see 2005 Investment Climate Statement: Brazil, U.S. Department of State, http://www.state.gov/e/eeb/ifd/2005/41988.htm, or the OECD Economic Survey of Brazil: 2005, available online at http://www.oecd.org/document/52/0,2340,en_2649-34599-34415156_1_1_1_1,00.html, last searched 1/23/2006. For statistics on informal sector employment, see the following ILO Report, http://www.ilo.org/public/english/bureau/stat/download/comp1a.pdf, last searched 3/16/2005.

54. Economist Intelligence Unit, "Brazil," Country Profile 2005, pp. 5–7. See Maria de Lourdes Rollemberg Mollo and Alfredo Saad-Filho, "The Neoliberal Decade: Reviewing the Brazilian Economic Transition," available online at http://netx.u-paris10.fr/actuelmarx/m4mollo.htm#_edn1, last searched 8/30/2006.

55. Fabio S. Erber, "Presentation of the Brazilian Industrial Policy," 2005, http://www.iadb.org/intal/aplicaciones/uploads/ponencias/Foro_LAEBA_2005_01_Erber.pdf.

56. WTO Document WT/TPR/S/140, 2005, "Trade Policy Review for Brazil, Section II: Trade Policy and Investment Regimes," paragraph 46, p. 25.

57. For a historical overview, see Sylvia Ostry, "The Future of the World Trading System: Beyond Doha," John. J. Kirton and Michael J. Trebilcock, eds. *Hard Choices, Soft Law* (Aldershot: England: Ashgate, 2004), 201, 203, which highlights Brazil's role as the leader of the developing world. Also see Chakravarthi Raghavan, "Rulings Against Brazil and India Set WTO Bias Issues," /www.twnside.org.sg/title/bias-cn.htm; "Brazil Celebrating WTO Victories Against US/EU," *Brazzil Magazine*, 9/4/2004 http://www.brazzilmag.com/content/view/131/41/, last searched 8/20/2006.

58. Kenneth Rapoza, "Brazil and the WTO: Leader of the Pack," *World Press Review*, 9/25/2003, http://www.tel3advantage.com/index.aspx?AgentNumber=866196&CID=1871; Gumisai Mutume," Hope Seen in the Ashes of Cancun," *Africa Recovery* 17(3) (2003), 3, http://www.un.org/ecosocdev/geninfo/afrec/vol17no3/173wto.htm, all last searched 8/20/2006.

59. Balakrishnan Rajagopal, "A Floundering WTO, Part II," Yaleglobal, 3/23/2006; http://yaleglobal.yale.edu/display.article?id=7164; Ed Gresser, "A Floundering WTO-Part I," 3/21/2006, http://yaleglobal.yale.edu/display.article?id=7153; CAFOD, Policy Brief, The Cancun Ministerial Meeting, "What Happened? What Does it Mean for Development?" www.cafod.org.uk/archive/policy/cancunanalysis20030924.shtml#4; Christina R. Sevilla, Can the U.S. and Brazil Spur Free Trade in the Americas? *In the International Interest*, http://www.inthenationalinterest.com/Articles/Vol3Issue1/Vol3Issue1Sevilla.html, all last searched 8/20/2006.

60. WTO document WT/TPR/S/140.

61. WTO Document: WT/TPR/S/140, "Trade Policy Review: Brazil, Trade and Investment Policy Regime," pp. 17–22.

62. Until 1994, trade policies were developed by one agency – the Carteira de Comercio Exterior do Banco do Brasil (CACEX). CACEX officials barely consulted with the Congress or even officials from other government agencies.

63. The Chamber of Foreign Trade (CAMEX) is responsible for the formulation and changes of the tariff and for its approval. The CAMEX also comprises an Executive Management Committee, in which representatives from other ministries and agencies,

an Executive Secretariat, and a Private Sector Consultative Council (CONEX) comprising twenty representatives of the private sector participate.

64. WTO Document WT/TPR/140/S, "Trade Policies and Practices by Measure." Also reiterated in an interview with Aluisio Gomes Neto, Deputy Director, Chamber of Foreign Trade (CAMEX), Ministry of Development, Industry and Foreign Trade (MDIC), Government of Brazil, 11/9/2005.

65. WTO Document: WT/TPR/S/140, Trade Policy Review: Brazil, Trade and Investment Policy Regime, pp. 17–22. Brazil has a large number of laws, provisional measures, decrees, and resolutions governing foreign trade, which sometimes overlap and make it difficult to understand Brazil's trade policy. This body of legislation is amended frequently with provisional measures (MPs) issued by the President. Regulations are also changed constantly, mainly through the use of Ministerial Acts (Portarias). Provisional measures are permitted under Article 62 of the Constitution, and are used to legislate on issues considered to be of importance and urgency; they are issued by the President and become effective upon publication. Provisional measures are analysed by Congress upon enactment; they should be voted on within 60 days, renewable once for the same period, failing which, they lapse. They have the same legal status as ordinary laws. Many laws in Brazil originate as provisional measures. An amendment to the Constitution was introduced in 2001 to prevent the proliferation of provisional measures. The amendment expressly prohibited the regulation by provisional measures of several matters, and extended the examination period by Congress from thirty to sixty days. Legislative decrees, which are administrative in nature, enact congressional deliberations on matters of its competence. Legislative decrees are approved by a simple majority in Congress and do not need the sanction of the President; they are the legal instrument through which international treaties and conventions are internalized. Legislative decrees have the same legal status as ordinary laws.

66. Marconi Article, Trade Policy Making in Brazil, May 2005, available at: http://www.lse.ac.uk/collections/internationalTradePolicyUnit/Events/May2005/ IADBPaperofMarioMaroconini.doc "Interestingly, [formal public participation in negotiations] started with the advent of FTAA. stakeholders. The Ministry of External Relations thus created the *Secretaria Nacional da ALCA – SENALCA* (National FTAA Secretariat) with the attribution of congregating representatives from other ministries and government agencies, as well as *guests* from civil society. In addition to the umbrella SENALCA, the government would create thematic groups around negotiating issues – also a first in Brazil's trade policy. The FTAA was therefore the ground-breaking motivation for Brazil to revamp and overhaul the manner it went about trade policymaking. Since then, a similar construct has been put into place for the MERCOSUR-European Union negotiations –SENEUROPA, and for WTO-related matters – *the Grupo Interministerial de Trabalho sobre Comércio Internacional de Mercadorias e Serviços* (GICI). MERCOSUR has its own formal consultative process, undertaken by the *Fóro Consultivo Econômico e Social* (Economic and Social Consultative Forum). The system that exists today for consultations is a result of this FTAA-driven process and some of the changes introduced along the way – particularly since the beginning of the Lula Government."

Negotiation divisions are typically divided into regions or themes. Although the MRE also houses the human rights department and the "social issues" department, our interviews indicated that they rarely speak with or coordinate with one another. However, the MRE negotiating sections have set up "advisory councils" to involve business, civil society, and labor on specific on-going negotiations. These include councils for the FTAA (SENALCA); the EU (SENEUROPA); WTO-related matters (GICI); and MERCOSUR. It is important to note that the Economic and Social Consultative Forum of MERCOSUR is the ONLY formal and institutionalized public-private consultation. That said, although these consultative groups are forums in which human rights issues can enter the discussions, they are more advised on negotiations decisions made within CAMEX than consulted on future negotiations. The MRE does not discuss strategy with these groups, and the groups are typically uninformed about *how* the government goes about formulating its various positions

67. Mario Marconi, "Trade Policymaking Process in Brazil," 3/2/2005. Some civil society and business groups believe that the government is not really interested in their ideas, but instead created these advisory councils to legitimize proposed policy measures. Also, several interviewees expressed this frustrations, including (1) Diego Zancan Bonomo and Frederico Meira, International Negotiators, International Relations and Foreign Trade Department, Federation of the Industries of the State of Sao Paulo, 11/16/2005; (2) Frederico Figuereido, International Trade Projects, Brazilian Institute for Consumer Defense, 11/13/2005; (3) Juana Kweitel, Programs Coordinator, Conectas: Human Rights, 11/15/2005; (4) Caio Magri, Partnerships and Mobilizations Manager, Ethos Institute for Business and Social Responsibility, 11/17/2005; and (5) Paulo de Mesquito Neto, Executive Secretary, Sao Paulo Institute against Violence, 11/15/2005.

68. MERCOSUR is incorporated in the Latin America Integration Association (LAIA) legal regime as Economic Complementarity Agreement No. 18. A major characteristic of LAIA's economic complementarity agreements is that they have to be open for accession by any LAIA country.

69. WTO/TPR/S/140, "Trade Policy Review: Trade and Investment Policy Regimes," pp. 34–37. Framework agreements are partial-scope agreements that lay the foundation for a future free trade agreement.

70. Brazilian trade with Arab nations has been growing, http://www.anba.com.br/ ingles/noticia.php?id=10415, last searched 3/22/2006; on Iran, http://www.kishtpc. com/global_Brazil1.htm.

71. Marc Bossuyt, "The Adverse Consequences of Economic Sanctions on the Enjoyment of Human Rights," Economic and Social Council, E/CN.4/Sub.2/2000/33, 6/21/2000, pp. 58–61.

72. Jose Miguel Vivanco, Executive Director of Americas Division, Human Rights Watch, "Letter to President Lula da Silva," 2/2/2004. Available online at http://www.hrw.org/ english/docs/2004/02/02/brazil7390_txt.htm, last searched 1/23/2006.

73. Ibid. Also see http://www.ictsd.org/weekly/03-02-27/story3.htm, last searched 3/10/2006.

74. Interviews with Aloisio Gomes Neto, Deputy Director, Chamber of Foreign Trade (CAMEX), Ministry of Development, Industry and Foreign Trade (MDIC), Government of Brazil, 11/9/2005, and Marcelo Della Nina, General Coordinator of Economic Organizations, Economic Department, Ministry of Foreign Affairs, 11/10/2005.

75. Interviews with policymakers and negotiators at the Ministry of Development, Industry and Foreign Trade and the Ministry of Foreign Affairs indicated that they have

traditionally felt little pressure to address human rights concerns within the trade policymaking process, due in large part to the history of trade policymaking in Brazil. These interviews include Flávio Marega, Counselor to the Trade Policy Desk and Aluisio G. de Lima-Campos, Embassy of Brazil, 11/1/2005; Fabio Martins Faria, Director, Secretariat of Foreign Trade, Ministry of Development, Industry and Foreign Trade, 11/8/2005; Aloisio Gomez Neto, Deputy Director, Chamber of Foreign Trade, Ministry of Development Industry and Foreign Trade, 11/9/2005. Marcelo della Nina (Coordinator General of Economic Organizations, Economics Department, Ministry of Foreign Affairs), Haroldo de Macedo Ribeiro (Secretary, General Coordination of Disputes, Ministry of Foreign Affairs), and Braz Baracuhy (Division of Agriculture and Raw Materials, Ministry of Foreign Affairs) were all interviewed on 11/19/2005.

76. See Treaty Establishing a Common Market, 3/26/1991, UN Doc. A/46/155 (1991), reprinted in 30 I.L.M. 1041(1991).

77. Ushuaia Protocol on Commitment to Democracy in MERCOSUR, The Republic of Bolivia and the Republic of Chile 24 July 1998 http://www.ohchr.org/english/law/compilation_democracy/mercosurprot.htm, last search 3/22/07

78. For the full text of the speech of the Brazilian Delegation on behalf of MERCOSUR at the 55th UN General Assembly, see http://www.un.int/brazil/speech/00d-mercosul-human-rights-2610.htm, last searched 1/23/2006.

79. Interview with Alberto do Amaral, director at IDCID and professor of international trade law at the University of Sao Paulo, 11/13/2005.

80. Project Performance Asset Report: Brazil, First and Second AIDS and STD Control Projects, The World Bank, April 27, 2004, p. 9; available online at: http://lnweb18.worldbank.org/OED/oeddoclib.nsf/DocUNIDViewForJavaSearch/DA1801C961D8F41785256E8B0055A79E/$file/ppar_28819.pdf.

81. Theo Smart, "Brazil's HIV/AIDS Programme Is a Model for the Rest of the World, but the Cost of Second-Line Therapies and the Spread of HIV-1C Could Spell Danger for the Future," HIV & AIDS Treatment in Practice #53, Center for HIV/AIDS Information, University of California San Francisco, 8/18/2005, available online at http://hivinsite.ucsf.edu/InSite?page=pa-hatip-53, last searched 1/15/2006.

82. World Bank Profile, "Improving Healthcare and Quality of Life for People Living with HIV/AIDS in Brazil," available online at http://web.worldbank.org/WBSITE/EXTERNAL/COUNTRIES/LACEXT/BRAZILEXTN/0,,contentMDK:20754486~pagePK:141137~piPK:141127~theSitePK:322341,00.html, last searched 1/15/2005; and "Representative Waxman Statement on Brazilian Compulsory License Dispute," lists.essential.org/pipermail/ip-health/2005-June/008087.html; last searched 3/10/2006.

83. Law 9.313, Presidency of the Republic, Casa Civil, Subchefia para Assuntos Juridicos, 11/13/1996.

84. Press accounts and related documents on these negotiations can be found at http://www.cptech.org/ip/health/c/brazil/#US/Brazil, last searched 3/10/2006.

85. Committee on Government Reform, Minority Staff, Special Investigations Division, "Trade Agreements and Access to Medications under the Bush administration," 6/2005, p. 3, at http://oversight.house.gov/Documents/20050609094902-11945.pdf searched 3/22/2007.

86. Compulsory licensing can be defined as the governmental granting of a license to a manufacturer other than the patent holder to produce and sell a product.

87. Translation of the Brazilian patent law is at http://www.araripe.com.br/law9279eng. htm#patente; Gary G. Yerkey and Daniel Pruzin, "United States Drops WTO Case against Brazil over HIV/AIDS Patent Law," WTO Reporter, 6/26/2001, at http://www. cptech.org/ip/health/c/brazil/bna06262001.html.

88. Brazil, "Presidential Decree on Compulsory Licensing," http://www.cptech/org/ip/ health/c/brazil/PresDecree.html, last searched 3/5/2006. The presidential decree defined public interest as, among others, "public health, nutrition, protection of the environment, as well as those of primordial importance to the technological or social and economic development of this country."

89. For extensive background on the history on drug prices, negotiations, and compulsory licensing in Brazil, see http://www.cptech.org/ip/health/c/brazil/, last searched 3/17/2006.

90. Stephen Buckley, "Brazil Becomes Model in Fight against AIDS: Government, Activists Team to Defy Epidemic through Distribution of Drugs," *Washington Post*, 9/17/2000, p. A22; and Kristen Jill Kresge, "Brazil's Model Approach," IAVI Report, http://www.iavireport.org/Issues/Issue9-3/RioReport.asp, last searched 3/8/2006.

91. See documents and news articles on Brazil at http://www.cptech.org/ip/health/ c/brazil/#US/Brazil, last searched 3/10/2006.

92. Industrial Property Law of 1996. Text available online at: http://www.trt02.gov.br/ geral/tribunal2/Legis/Leis/9279_96.html (in Portuguese) searched 3/22/2007. The patent provisions in the law permit Brazilian companies to manufacture patented products inside the country within three years of patent approval or else risk a government override of the patent and government to allow third-party manufacture or importation of the product from the cheapest international source.

93. See documents and news reports at http://www.cptech.org/ip/health/c/brazil/#US/ Brazil, last searched 3/29/2005.

94. Statement of Jose Serra, Minister of Health to the 2001 USTR 301 Report, 5/3/2001, http://www.cptech.org/ip/health/c/brazil/serra05032001.html, last searched 3/22/2006.

95. NA, "The Drug Companies vs. Brazil: A Threat to Public Health," Oxfam Great Britain, 2001, http://www.oxfam.org.uk/what_we_do/issues/health/drugcomp_brazil. htm, last searched 3/22/2006. Brazil presented a resolution to the UN Human Rights Commission on the right to access to affordable medicines in the context of the HIV/AIDS pandemic. The motion was supported by fifty-two nations, with a single abstention – the United States.

96. WT/DS199/4 G/L/454 IP/D/23/Add.1.

97. Ibid.

98. The Doha Declaration on the TRIPS Agreement and Public Health, available online at http://www.wto.org/english/thewto_e/minist_e/min01_e/mindecl_trips_e.htm, last searched 3/28/2006.

99. Decreto de 21 de Agosto de 2001, Presidency of the Republic, Ministry of the Casa Civil. This group includes representatives from several ministries, including Agriculture; Science and Technology; Culture; Development, Industry and International Trade; Justice; Foreign Relations; Health; Civil House of the Presidency; and the Environment.

100. "New Anti-HIV Drug Deal for Brazil," http://news.bbc.co.uk/1/hi/world/americas/ 3281683.stm; "PhRMA Statement on Protecting Patent Rights in Brazil," http://lists.

essential.org/pipermail/ip-health/2005-July/008126.html;   http://www.cptech.org/ip/
health/c/brazil/#US/Brazil, all searched 3/8/2006.

101. 2005 Special 301 Report, Priority Watch List, USTR, p. 1, available online at http://
www.ustr.gov/assets/Document_Library/Reports_Publications/2005/2005_Special_301/
asset_upload_file519_7649.pdf. While USTR lauds Brazil for continued improvements
in protecting IPR and claims that it is "one of the largest global markets for legitimate
copyright products," they also contend that "high levels of piracy still exist and warrant
Brazil's continued placement on the Priority Watch List in 2005."

102. IIPA Brazil GSP Review Extension 2005, http://www.iipa.com/pressreleases/
IIPA%20Brazil%20GSP%20IPR%20Review%20April%20Extension%2004042005.pdf,
last searched 3/22/2006.

103. Federal Register Vol. 71, No. 9 / Friday, January 13, 2006 / Notices Available online at
http://a257.g.akamaitech.net/7/257/2422/01jan20061800/edocket.access.gpo.gov/2006/
pdf/06-368.pdf, last searched 3/22/2006.

104. Press/350/Rev.1, "Decision Removes Final Patent Obstacle to Cheap Drug
Imports," 8/30/2003, available online at http://www.wto.org/english/news_e/pres03_e/
pr350_e.htm, last searched 3/22/2006.

105. "Members OK Amendment to Make Health Flexibility Permanent," http://www.wto.
org/english/news_e/pres05_e/pr426_e.htm. It was lauded by the WHO. Statement
of the World Health Organization at the World Trade Organization Ministerial, 12/10/2005, at http://lists.essential.org/pipermail/ip-health/2005-December/
008850.html, last searched 3/10/2006.

106. NA, "Banking on Generic Drugs," 9/19/2004, http://www.pharmabiz.com/article/
detnews.asp?articleid=23456&sec . . . , last searched 3/8/2006; and NA, "Generic Drugs
in Brazil Are a Hard Pill for Big Pharma to Swallow," 1/16/2006, http://wharton
.universia.net/index.cfm?fa=viewArticle&id=1086&la . . . , last searched 3/9/2006.

107. NA, "Generic Drugs in Brazil Are a Hard Pill for Big Pharma to Swallow," 1/16/
2006,   http://wharton.universia.net/index.cfm?fa=viewArticle&id=1086&la . . . ,   last
searched 3/9/2006.

108. Ibid. Interview with Octavio Brandelli, Deputy Chief, and Henrique Choer de Moraes,
Division of Intellectual Property, Ministry of Foreign Affairs, Government of Brazil,
11/11/2005.

109. According to Brazilian health minister Humberto Costa, in 2005 the Brazilian Government paid $2,600 annually for each dose of the AIDS drugs lopinavir and riton-
avir. See comments of U.S. Congressman Henry A. Waxman, on Brazilian Compulsory License Dispute, 7/28/2005, http://lists.essential.org/pipermail/ip-health/2005-
June/008087.html; last searched 3/10/2006.

110. An Interview with Otavio Brandelli and Henrique Choer Moraes, Intellectual Property
Department, Ministry of Foreign Affairs, 11/2005. They indicated that this is a major
controversy that spurred Brazil to tackle this more forcefully at the international level.
Questions of biodiversity, biopiracy, and trade have been discussed in Brazil for many
years, particularly since the Rio Earth Summit in 1992.

111. Jose Augusto Bezerra, "A Cienca do Sapo," *GloboRural Magazine*, available online at:
http://revistagloborural.globo.com/GloboRural/0,6993,EEC821951-1484-6,00.html.

112. Interview with Otavio Brandelli and Henrique Choer Moraes, Intellectual Property
Department, Ministry of Foreign Affairs, 11/2005. The University of Kentucky Research

Foundation registered five patents between 1999 and 2003 with technology derived from the *kambo*, including patents numbers WO0222152, US 6380164, US 6294519, and two patents under WO9956766, http://www.biopirataria.org/patentes_kambo.php

113. See a Sciencia do Sapo, http://www.biopirataria.org/patentes_kambo.php

114. An Interview with Otavio Brandelli, Deputy Chief, and Henrique Choer Moraes, Secretary, Division of Intellectual Property, Ministry of Foreign Affairs, 11/9/2005.

115. Indigenous people in Brazil, http://www.socioambiental.org/pib/english/orgsi/amazo.shtm#t5 and http://www.state.gov/g/drl/rls/hrrpt/2005/61718.htm.

116. U.S. Department of State, "Human Rights Report, Brazil," http://www.state.gov/g/drl/rls/hrrpt/2005/61718.htm

117. Although *The Economist* lauds the government for trying to protect these rights, Amnesty International criticized the government's lack of a clear indigenous policy and noted that indigenous people continued to be victims of attacks, killings and other forms of discrimination. The report noted that the government's failure to demarcate indigenous territories contributed to violence, racial discrimination, and other human rights abuses. NA, "Brazil's Indians, Land Wars," 2/2/2006, at http://www.economist.com/displayStory.cfm?story_id=5473510, and Amnesty International, "Foreigners in Our Own Country, Indigenous Peoples in Brazil," http://web.amnesty.org/library/index/engamr190022005, both last searched 3/10/2006.

118. Rain forest Web portal. Brazil, the largest country in South America, has perhaps the best opportunity remaining to save large tracts of tropical rain forest. Although Brazil has lost approximately 58% of its frontier forests (large tracts of relatively undisturbed old growth forest), the country still has over 772,200 square miles of frontier forest, among the largest amount of any country worldwide. See http://www.rainforestweb.org/Rainforest_Regions/South_America/Brazil/, and http://www.mongabay.com/saving_brazils_forests.html, last searched 3/10/2006.

119. Brazil, "Land and Resources," http://www.countriesquest.com/south_america/brazil/land_and_resources.htm, last searched 3/6/2006; and Water and Indigenous Peoples, http://www.wateryear2003.org/en/ev.php-URL_ID = 5550&URL_DO = DO_TOPIC&URL_SECTION=201.html, last searched 3/10/2006.

120. U.S. Department of State, "Human Rights Report, Brazil," http://www.state.gov/g/drl/rls/hrrpt/2005/61718.htm.

121. Water and Indigenous Peoples, http://www.wateryear2003.org/en/ev.php-URL_ID = 5550&URL_DO = DO_TOPIC&URL_SECTION=201.html.

122. See "Biopiracy in the Amazon – An Introduction," http://www.amazonlink.org/biopiracy/index.htm.

123. The Convention on Biodiversity text is available online at http://www.biodiv.org/convention/articles.asp. The objectives of the Convention, to be pursued in accordance with its relevant provisions, are the conservation of biological diversity, the sustainable use of its components and the fair and equitable sharing of the benefits arising out of the utilization of genetic resources, including by appropriate access to genetic resources and by appropriate transfer of relevant technologies, taking into account all rights over those resources and to technologies, and by appropriate funding.

124. Although 188 countries are parties and 168 have signed the Convention on Biodiversity, the United States remains reluctant. Although the United States signed the Convention on Biodiversity in 1993, it never became party to the convention. Most other major

trading powers have signed and either accepted or ratified the agreement in their governments. Japan has not ratified the agreement, but it has been accepted. See http://www.biodiv.org/world/parties.asp for a complete list of parties and signatories, last searched 3/22/2006.

125. David Greer and Harvey Brian, *Blue Genes: Sharing and Conserving the World's Aquatic Biodiversity*; EarthScan IDRC; 2004, http://www.idrc.ca/en/ev-67656-201-1-DO_TOPIC.html.

126. "Biopiracy: Plain Dealing or Patent Theft," International Development Research Center, Canada, http://www.idrc.ca/en/ev-67656-201-1-DO_TOPIC.html, last searched 3/10/2006.

127. Since the establishment of the Council for TRIPS in the WTO in 1999, member states have submitted more than thirty communications related to the issue. WTO Document IP/C/W/420, "The Relationship between the TRIPS Agreement and the Convention on Biological Diversity (CBD)," Checklist of Issues, 3/2/2004.

128. WTO Document WT/MIN(01)/DEC/1, "Doha Ministerial Declaration," paragraphs 12, 19, and 47. Paragraph 19 of the 2001 Doha Declaration says the TRIPS Council should also look at the relationship between the TRIPS Agreement and the UN Convention on Biological Diversity and at the protection of traditional knowledge and folklore.

129. WTO Document IP/C/W/420, "The Relationship between the TRIPS Agreement and the Convention on Biological Diversity (CBD)," Checklist of Issues, 3/2/2004; and http://www.wto.org/English/tratop_e/trips_e/art27_3b_background_e.htm. The TRIPS agreement allows members to provide patents over biological resources (plants, animals, and micro-organisms). Currently, the TRIPS agreement contains no provisions preventing biopiracy acts, in which a person may claim patent rights in one country over genetic resources that are under the sovereignty of another country. In particular, the TRIPS agreement contains no provisions ensuring the prior informed consent of the owners of the biological resources used in the invention. The agreement also contains no provisions allowing a member's claims to enforce its national regimes for fair and equitable sharing of benefits from the patenting of its own genetic resources in another country.

130. See WTO Document IP/C/W/429/Rev.1, "Elements of the Obligation to Disclose the Source and Country of Origin of the Biological Resources and/or Traditional Knowledge Used in an Invention," Submission from Brazil, Cuba, Ecuador, India, Pakistan, Peru, Thailand, and Venezuela, 9/27/2004.

131. An interview with Otavio Brandelli, deputy chief, and Henrique Choer Moraes, secretary, Division of Intellectual Property, Ministry of Foreign Affairs, 11/9/2005.

132. For background, see http://www.wto.org/english/tratop_e/trips_e/art27_3b_background_e.htm, last searched 3/22/2006.

133. WTO Documents IP/C/W/434, Article 27.3(b), "Relationship between the TRIPS Agreement and the CBD, and the Protection of Traditional Knowledge and Folklore," Communication from the United States, 11/26/2004; and *Bridges Weekly*, http://www.ictsd.org/weekly/04-12-08/story1.htm. See also, "Contracts-Based System Provides Better Protection for Biological Diversity," Doha Development Agenda Policy Brief, Office of the United States Trade Representative, available online at www.ustr.gov.

134. Brazil and India have responded "if anything, the communication has provided evidence of why the proposed disclosure requirements would be the best way of achieving the objectives of ensuring that the implementation of the TRIPS Agreement does not undermine...the objectives of the Convention on Bio Diversity." WTO Document IP/C/W/443, "The Relationship between the TRIPS Agreement and the CBD and the Protection of Traditional Knowledge: Technical Observations on Issues Raised in a Communication by the US (IP/C/W/434)," Submission from Brazil and India, 3/18/2005.

135. WTO Document WT/MIN(05)/DEC, "Doha Work Programme," Ministerial Declaration, paragraph 39.

136. "Final GMO Panel Limits Application of MEAs in Future WTO Disputes," *Inside U.S. Trade*, October 13, 2006.

137. WIPO Document IIM/1/4, "Proposal to Establish a Development Agenda for WIPO: An Elaboration of Issues Raised in Document WO/GA/31/11," Inter-Sessional Intergovernmental Meeting on the Development Agenda for WIPO, 4/6/2005. Specifically, it would like the WTO to weigh the costs and benefits generated by IPR protection and to examine the issue of technical cooperation from a broader perspective – in which countries are helped to frame intellectual property legislation that responds to their specific needs – guaranteeing wider transparency and participation in the discussions and ensuring that the intellectual property system effectively fosters innovation and technological development.

138. http://www.cptech.org/ip/wipo/pcda/

139. "Brazil Gets Tough on Bio-Pirates," http://forests.org/articles/reader.asp?linkid=43332.

140. U.S. Department of State, Human Rights Report, Brazil, 2005, http://www.state.gov/g/drl/rls/hrrpt/2005/61718.htm, last searched 3/29/2006.

141. Paulo Prada, "Poisonous Tree Frog Could Bring Wealth to Tribe in Brazilian Amazon," *New York Times*, 5/30/2006, http://www.nytimes.com/2006/05/30/business/worldbusiness/30frogs.html?pagewanted = 1&ei = 5070&en = 4f1f1de32277b393 &ex=1149739200&emc=eta1.

142. Michael Smith and David Voreacos, "Slaves in Amazon Forced to Make Material Used in Cars (Update2)," *Bloomberg News*, 12/2006, available online at: http://www.bloomberg.com/apps/news?pid = 20601109&refer=home&sid=a4j1VKZq34TM, last searched 11/13/2006.

143. "Anais da Oficina Trabalho Escravo: Uma Chaga Aberta," World Social Forum, 1/25/2003, ILO Office in Brazil, 2003. Some civil society groups, such as the Pastoral Land Commission, claim that number is much higher (upwards of 40,000).

144. Project Document, "Combating Forced Labor in Brazil," ILO Office in Brazil, http://www.oitbrasil.org.br/tbesc_english/brasil/projetos/documento.htm.

145. Combating Forced Labor in Brazil, http://www.oitbrasil.org.br/tbesc_english/brasil/projetos/documento.htm. See also, for example, U.S. Department of State, Human Rights Report, Brazil, 2004, http://www.state.gov/g/drl/rls/hrrpt/2004/41751.htm.

146. http://www.ilo.org/dyn/declaris/DECLARATIONWEB.DOWNLOAD_BLOB?Var_DocumentID=3466

147. See ILO-Brasilia Office http://www.oitbrasil.org.br/tbesc_english/brasil/documentos/documentos.php); and Armand F. Pereira: "Toward integrated action against sexual exploitation and other forms of forced labor and related trafficking: Links between labor markets and migration – An ILO perspective (Box 2: Combating forced labor

and sexual exploitation and trafficking in Brazil)", unpublished paper presented to the Canadian Parliament, Ottawa, October 28, 2006, in possession of authors.

148. Portaria No. 540, October 15, 2004, available online (in Portuguese), http://www.mte .gov.br/noticias/conteudo/5773.asp See also http://www.ilo.org/public/portugue/region/ ampro/brasilia/trabalho_forcado/brasil/iniciativas/lista_suja.pdf; and interview with Armind Pereira, Washington Director, ILO, 11/20/2006.

149. See http://www.reporterbrasil.com.br/listasuja/index.php?lingua=en 8/19/2006.

150. Juliana Andrade, "Slave Labor in Brazil Might Reach as Much as 40,000," *Brazzil Magazine*, 11/24/2004, www.brazzilmag.com/content/view/7974/54/, last searched 3/10/ 2006; http://www.social.org.br/relatorioingles2005/relatorio009.htm, last searched 3/29/ 2006.

151. Information available online at: www.reporterbrasil.com.br, last searched 3/29/2006.

152. U.S. Department of State, Human Rights Report, Brazil, 2005, http://www.state.gov/ g/drl/rls/hrrpt/2005/61718.htm.

153. U.S. Department of State, Human Rights Report, Brazil, 2005, http://www.state.gov/g/ drl/rls/hrrpt/2005/61718.htm.

154. See the lista suja for more information. Available online at http://www.reporterbrasil .com.br/listasuja/index.php, searched 3/22/2007.

155. National Pact against Slave Labor available online at http://www.ethos.org.br/_ Rainbow/Documents/PactoNacionalMinuta02_05.pdf, last searched 3/22/2006.

156. Ibid.

157. See the National Pact against Slave Labor, available online at http://www.ethos.org.br/_ Rainbow/Documents/PactoNacionalMinuta02_05.pdf, 3/22/2006.

158. Visit http://www.ethos.org.br for more information on the history of the National Pact. Before the Pact came into force in 2005, Ethos and ILO held several meetings to educate and involve business and civil society. Representatives from such sectors as petroleum and gas, combustible and lubricant distributors, the food industries, supermarkets, meat exporting industry, vegetable oil, and textile industries. They all participated in the development of the National Pact.

159. Commitments include continual efforts to define the challenges and goals that shape the enforcement of the Pact; define and implement penalties such a commercial restrictions against companies or employers using slave labor; support social reintegration of previously forced workers into the local economy; support education and capacity building programs for vulnerable groups or previously forced workers; support and demand the government fulfill its obligations under the National Plan for the Eradication of Slave Labor; monitor the implementation of the National Pact and National Plan as well as reaching proposed goals and publicly releasing the results; systematize and disseminate information about the program in order to promote the adoption of this program in other countries. Visit http://www.ethos.org.br for more information.

160. Internationally recognized labor standards in Brazil, "Report for the WTO General Council Review of Trade Policies of Brazil," International Confederations of Free Trade Unions (ICFTU), available online at http://www.icftu.org/ www/pdf/clsbrazilenglish2004.pdf.

161. For an overview of Brazil's legal framework on child labor, see http://www.brasilemb .org/social_issues/social_child_labor.shtml, last searched 3/22/2006.

162. Interview with Caio Magri, Partnerships and Mobilizations Manager, Ethos Institute for Business and Social Responsibility, Sao Paulo, Brazil, 11/18/2005.

163. "A Global Alliance against Forced Labor: Global Report under the Follow-Up to the ILO Declaration on Fundamental Principles and Rights at Work," 2005, International Labor Conference, 93 Session.

164. WTO Document WT/TPR/S/140.

165. "A Brazil Fit for Children: Brazilian Society and the MDGs for Children and Adolescents," Child-Friendly Monitoring Network, 8/2004.

166. U.S. Department of State, Human Rights Report, Brazil, 2005, http://www.state.gov/g/drl/rls/hrrpt/2005/61718.htm. See also http://www.brasilemb.org/social_issues/social_child_labor.shtml.

167. These data were provided by Armand F. Pereira drawn from official government figures analyzed in ILO-Brasilia's national supplement to the ILO's Global Report: "A Future Without Child Labour" (Geneva, 2002).

168. Legal Framework to Combat Child Labor, http://www.brasilemb.org/social_issues/social_child_labor.shtml, last searched 3/22/2006.

169. See www.abrinq.org.br for more information on the history of Abrinq Foundation. See also, Ministry of Justice, National Council for the Rights of the Child and Adolescent (CONANDA), State of the Child and Adolescent, https://www.planalto.gov.br/ccivil_03/Leis/L8069Compilado.htm, last searched 3/22/2007.

170. See Empresa Amiga Da Crianca Network for a full list of committed companies by region, http://www.abrinq.org.br/ http://www.fundabrinq.org.br/portal/alias__abrinq/lang__pt-BR/tabid__343/default.aspx, last searched 3/22/2006.

171. Abrinq Foundation 2004 Annual Report, p. 25.

172. Abrinq Foundation 2004 Annual Report, p. 27.

173. This was indicated in the study "Corporate Social Responsibility: The Brazilian Consumer's Perception," http://www.akatu.net/cgi/cgilua.exe/sys/start.htm?tpl=section_tipo1&url=http://www.akatu.net/areas/publicacoes/inc_conteudo_publicacoes.asp.

174. "Discovering the Conscious Consumer: A New Vision of Brazilian Reality," 2004, http://www.akatu.net/cgi/cgilua.exe/sys/start.htm?tpl=section_tipo1&url=http://www.akatu.net/areas/publicacoes/inc_conteudo_publicacoes.asp.

175. "A Brazil Fit for Children: Brazilian Society and the MDGs for Children and Adolescents," Child-Friendly Monitoring Network, 8/2004, p. 103.

176. Child Friendly President Plan, 2003, available online at http://sistemas.fundabrinq.org.br/biblioteca/acervo/1629_pac.ra.pdf, last searched 3/22/2007.

177. Ibid. Practically the entire R$875 million budget of the PPAC is allocated to Bolsa Crianca Cidada (income transfer program linked to school attendance) and the Jornada Escolar Ampliada (expanded school day program).

178. See Patrick Del Vecchio, "Child Labor in Brazil: The Government Commitment," 5/2005, http://usinfo.state.gov/journals/ites/0505/ijee/delveccio.htm; "Foreign Labor Trends: Brazil, Child Labor," United States Bureau of International Labor Affairs, http://www.dol.gov/ILAB/media/reports/flt/brazil-2002.htm#d16. See also the ILO report "The End of Child Labor: Within Reach; Global Report under the Follow-Up to the ILO Declaration on the Fundamental Principles and Rights at Work," International Labor Conference, 95ᵗʰ Session 2006. Report available online: http://www.ilo.org/declaration.

179. The WTO now has done a case study on trade and access to medicines in Kenya. http://www.wto.org/english/res_e/booksp_e/casestudies_e/case19_e.htm, last searched 8/20/2006.

180. NA, "Brazil's Foreign Policy, A Giant Stirs," *The Economist*, 6/10/2004, http://www.economist.com/world/la/displayStory.cfm?story_id=2752700; and William Greider and Kenneth Rapoza, "Lula Raises the Stakes," *The Nation*, 11/13/2003, at http://www.thenation.com/doc/20031201/greider, both last searched 8/21/2006.

181. Center for International Environmental Law, "The Brazil-Retreaded Tires Case: Background Paper – March 2006," www.ciel.org or accessible at http://www.trade-environment.org/page/theme/tewto/tyrescase.htm, last searched 9/1/2006.

182. Marconini, "Trade Policy-Making," 7, 10–12.

5. The European Union: The Behemoth Is Not a Dinosaur

1. We are grateful to Philip Van Der Celen, who did much of the research for this chapter and developed an initial draft.

2. France has been going through some hard times in recent years. Molly Moore, "After Job Law Fiasco, France Retreats on Other Fronts," *Washington Post*, 4/21/2006, p. A14; and Richard Bernstein, "Political Paralysis: Europe Stalls on Road to Economic Change," *New York Times*, 4/14/2006, at http://select.nytimes.com/gst/abstract.html?res=F50C17FF3D5B0C778DDDAD0894DE404482&n=Top%2fReference%2fTimes%20Topics%2fPeople%2fB%2fBernstein%2c%20Richard, last searched 3/29/2007. Chirac was actually the second world leader to propose an international convention to protect and promote cultural diversity. Canadian officials proposed a New International Instrument on Culture Diversity (NIICD). This new international instrument would set out clear ground rules enabling Canada and other countries to maintain policies that promote their culture, while respecting the rules governing the international trading system and ensuring markets for cultural exports. In other words, this new approach would recognize that cultural goods and services have a greater role in society than other products or services. See Pierre Pettigrew, "Minister for International Trade," Notes for an Address, "Culture and Trade," http://w01.international.gc.ca/MinPub/Publication.asp?publication_id=378494&Language=E; Chirac's first proposal is at http://www.un.org/events/wssd/statements/franceE.htm, both last searched 3/30/2006.

3. Australia, Nicaragua, Honduras, and Liberia abstained. Molly Moore, "UN Body Endorses Cultural Protection: U.S. Objections Are Turned Aside," *Washington Post*, 10/21/2005, http://www.globalpolicy.org/globaliz/cultural/2005/1021body.htm, last searched 4/06/2006.

4. Emma Clark, "Why Europe Feels Left Out in the Cold," BBC News, http://news.bbc.co.uk/1/hi/business/2052405.stm, last searched 5/12/2006. We use the term "freer trade," as there is no such thing as free trade, a point made to Susan Aaronson by John Leddy, one of the original architects of the GATT.

5. In 1999, the Canadian and French Governments pushed UNESCO to prepare a declaration on cultural diversity containing several major policy principles, which, as a formal text, should be submitted to the General Conference of the Organization for approval, http://www.vivoscuola.it/us/dlllsn3095/present/fix/Undecl_e.pdf.

6. http://portal.unesco.org/culture/en/ev.php-URL_ID = 26320&URL_DO = DO_TOPIC&URL_SECTION = 201.html, last searched 3/30/2006.

7. http://untreaty.un.org/English/guide.asp#conventions. According to the European Union, the Convention would allow governments "to take into account cultural diversity when developing other policies, by ensuring that cultural policies support fair access to both local cultures and other world cultures." Europa press release, "Adoption of a UNESCO Convention on Cultural Diversity," 2/10/2005, last searched 4/3/2006.

8. http://europa.eu.int/comm/culture/portal/action/regulations/reglem_1_en.htm, last searched 4/3/2006. Article 27(1) of the UNDHR enshrines the right to cultural participation. The EU Charter has been proclaimed but it will only become law when/ if it is ratified by the EU member states.

9. Europa press release, "Adoption of a UNESCO Convention on Cultural Diversity," 2/10/2005, http://europa.eu.int/rapid/pressReleasesAction.do?reference= MEMO/05/387.

10. Hugh Schofield, "U.S. Isolated over 'Protectionist' UN Culture Convention," *Agence France Presse*, 10/21/2005. A 2005 poll of Europeans found that although most Europeans think globalization has a positive effect on "cultural exchanges," the Greeks and the French were the most skeptical. Herve Boulhol, "How Europeans See Globalization," IXIS, 5/2/2005, No. 2005–155, 3, 5.

11. For an analysis of this phenomenon, see Jessica C. E. Chenow-Hect, "A European Considers the Influence of American Culture," http://usinfo.state.gov/journals/itgic/ 0206/ijge/gienowhecht.htm and http://www.culturalpolicy.org/pdf/CulturalDiplomacy .pdf, both last searched 4/06/2006.

12. Europa press release, "Adoption of a UNESCO Convention on Cultural Diversity," 2/10/2005, http://europa.eu.int/rapid/pressReleasesAction.do?reference= MEMO/05/387; and Note from the Presidency to the Delegations, 5778/05, "Code of Conduct Between the Council, the Member States and the Commission on the UNESCO Negotiations on the draft Convention on the protection of the diversity of Cultural Contents and Artistic Expressions," 5/31/2006. Also see Annex 1–3. These documents spell out the responsibility of the EU presidency, the European Commission, and the member states regarding the negotiations. The annexes delineate member state concerns about this process of sharing negotiating authority. These documents reveal that the negotiations and the procedure for the negotiations were controversial among EU member states. We are grateful to our advisor, John Morijin, for pointing this out. E-mail, John Morijin to Susan Aaronson, 5/31/2006.

13. http://www.unesco.org/culture/industries/trade/html_eng/question17.shtml. The GATT has a cultural exception relating to cinematographic films. The GATT also maintains a general exception for measures designed "to protect national treasures of artistic, historic or archaeological value." All other cultural goods are subject to GATT disciplines. Also see "Idees De France, Is There Room for a Cultural Exception," http://www.ideesdefrance.fr/Is-There-Room-for-Cultural.html, last searched 4/06/2006.

14. Frances Williams, "U.S. Stands Alone over Cultural Diversity Treaty," *Financial Times*, 10/20/2005.

15. Raymond J. Ahearn, "U.S.-European Union Trade Relations: Issues and Policy Challenges," CRS Issue Brief for Congress, IB 10087, 6/9/2003, 11.

16. For an overview of the EU perspective on this issue, see http://trade-info.cec.eu.int/ wtodispute/show.cfm?id=176&code=2, last searched 4/29/2006.

17. Some members are agriculture-oriented and labor-intensive countries (Greece, Portugal, and Spain); others are services-oriented, capital-intensive, and high-wage countries (for example, Belgium, the United Kingdom, the Netherlands, and Germany). Some of the newer members such as Hungary and the Slovak Republic are moving toward a more technology- and skill-intensive economy, whereas others, such as Latvia and Lithuania, remain natural resource and labor intensive. WTO, "Trade Policy Review, European Communities, Report by the Secretariat," WT/TPR/S/136, 6/23/2004, 2–3.

18. WTO, "Trade Policy Review, Report by the European Communities," WT/TPR/G/136, 10/1/2004, 5.

19. See http://europa.eu.int/constitution/ratification_en.htm, last searched 5/04/2006.

20. George Parker, "EU Leaders Likely to Leave Constitution on Ice," *Financial Times*, 4/28/2006.

21. The European Community (EC) was originally founded on 3/25/1957 by the signing of the Treaty of Rome under the name of European Economic Community. The 'Economic' was removed from its name by the Maastricht treaty of 1992. It refers to the economic union of the members.

22. http://hrw.org/wr2k2/europe21.html; John Ward Anderson, "Belgians Seek Roots of Racist Crimes," *Washington Post*, 5/20/2006; Christopher Hitchens, "Holland's The Caged Virgin: Holland's Shameful Treatment of Ayaan Hirsi Ali," 5/8/2006, http://www.slate.com/id/2141276/#ContinueArticle; Quentin Peel, "Hirsi Ali Exposes Dutch Divide," *Financial Times*, 5/17/2006, http://www.religionnewsblog.com/ 14677/ayaan-hirsi-ali-exposes-dutch-divide, all last searched 5/17/2006.

23. http://hrw.org/english/docs/2004/03/22/eu-letter032204.pdf; http://hrw.org/english/docs/2002/05/10/eca3916.htm; http://www.hrw.org/backgrounder/eca/eu0107/ http://hrw.org/wr2k2/europe21.html; and in particular, Kenneth Roth, "Filling the Leadership Void: Where is the European Union?" in *World Report 2007*, hrw.org/wr2k7/essays/introduction/index.htm, all last searched 3/30/2007.

24. The Treaty Establishing the European Coal and Steel Community (1951), the Treaty Establishing the European Atomic Energy Community (1957), and the Treaty Establishing the European Economic Community (1957). These treaties were designed to integrate economic activities.

25. Arts. 6(1) and (2) of the Treaty on European Union. See Official Journal of the European Communities, Consolidated Version of the Treaty on European Union, 12/24/2002, C325/5-181.

26. Art. 7 of the Treaty on European Union. See Official Journal of the European Communities, Consolidated Version of the Treaty on European Union, 12/24/2002, C325/5–181. The Nice European Council Meeting in December 2000 inserted this article in the Treaty on European Union after far-right parties gained power in Austria in January 2000.

27. Philip Alston and J. H. H. Weiler, "An 'Ever Closer Union' in Need of a Human Rights Policy: The European Union and Human Rights," 1999, Jean Monnet Working Paper No.1, Harvard Law School, 7–9.

28. These rights also include the right of every EU citizen to petition the European Parliament (Art. 21 of the Treaty Establishing the European Community (the Treaty of

Rome); the right to apply to the European Ombudsman (Art. 21 of the treaty establishing the European Community); the right of every EU citizen to write to any of the EU institutions or bodies in any of the twenty official languages and have an answer in the same language (Art. 21 of the Treaty Establishing the European Community); the right of every EU citizen to access to European Parliament, Council and Commission documents, subject to certain the principles and the conditions (Art. 255 of the Treaty Establishing the European Community). See Official Journal of the European Communities, Consolidated Version of the Treaty Establishing the European Community, 12/24/2002, C325/33-184

29. Philip Alston and J. H. H. Weiler, "An 'Ever Closer Union' in Need of a Human Rights Policy: The European Union and Human Rights," 1999, Jean Monnet Working Paper No.1, Harvard Law School, 7–9.

30. The Charter also recognizes social rights and principles beyond traditional worker rights. For example, it stipulates that workers have a right to information and consultation within the undertaking (Art. 27), protection in the event of unjustified dismissal (Art. 30), social security and social assistance (Art. 34), health care (Art. 35), and access to services of general economic interest (Art. 36) such as transport, energy, and communication services. See Official Journal of the European Communities, Charter of Fundamental Rights of the European Union, 12/18/2000, C364/01-C364/22.

31. Under Art. 11 (1) of the Treaty on European Union, one of the five objectives of the Common Foreign and Security Policy is to develop and consolidate democracy and the rule of law, and respect for human rights and fundamental freedoms. Art. 177 (2) of the Treaty establishing the European Community stipulates that contributing to the respect of human rights and fundamental freedoms as well as the consolidation and development of democracy and the rule of law is a general objective of the European Community's development cooperation policy. Finally, Art.181a of the Treaty Establishing the European Community stipulates that developing and consolidating democracy and the rule of law as well as respecting human rights and fundamental freedoms are general objectives to economic, financial, and technical cooperation with third countries outside the framework of the European Community development policy. Art. 181a thus extends the objective of promoting human rights to all forms of cooperation with third countries. See *Official Journal of the European Communities*, Consolidated Version of the Treaty on European Union, 12/24/2002, C325/5–181, and Official Journal of the European Communities, Consolidated Version of the Treaty Establishing the European Community, 12/24/2002, C325/33-184.

32. European Commission, "Implementation of the Commission Communication on the EU's Role in Promoting Human Rights and Democratisation in Third Countries," SEC(2004)1041, Brussels, 3–4; and EU Human Rights Report, 32–35.

33. European Parliament, Council, Commission, "Joint Statement," C46/15; European Commission, "The European Union's Role," 16.

34. The European Initiative for Democracy and Human Rights was created in 1994 by the European Parliament. It provides some 100 million euros, available annually under Chapter B7–70 of the budget to support human rights, democratization, and conflict prevention activities. These activities are carried out primarily in partnership with NGOs and international organizations. In 2004, the amount available for the activities of the EIDHR totalled 125 million euros, covering two budget lines: 19 04 03 (ex

B7–701): development and consolidation of democracy and the rule of law; respect for human rights and fundamental freedoms; 19 04 04 (ex B7-702), support for the activities of international criminal tribunals and the International Criminal Court. See http://europa.eu.int/comm/europeaid/projects/eidhr/eidhr_en.htm#eidhrstrategy, last searched 3/29/2006

35. The Copenhagen European Council in June 1993 stipulated that the candidate country (1) achieve stability of institutions guaranteeing democracy, the rule of law, human rights, and respect for and protection of minorities; (2) have a functioning market economy as well as the capacity to cope with competitive pressure and market forces within the Union; and (3) have the ability to take on the obligations of membership including adherence to the aims of political, economic, and monetary union. See European Council in Copenhagen, Conclusions of the Presidency, 6/21–22/1993, 14.

36. See http://europa.eu.int/comm/enlargement/financial_assistance/index_en.htm, last searched 3/23/2006.

37. European Commission, "Communication from the Commission to the Council and the European Parliament: The European Union's Role in Promoting Human Rights and Democratization in Third Countries," 5/08/2001, COM (2001) 252 final, Brussels, 8.

38. WT/TPR/G/136, 7.

39. The European Commission is the central executive body for the European Union. It has the power to initiate and propose legislation and common policies. The Commission also works to ensure that all members of the European Union implement EU legislation. The staff of the European Commission is organized into different departments, known as Directorates General (DGs). Each of these Directorates General is responsible for specific tasks or policy areas. DG Trade includes the external trade administration of the European Commission. It is responsible for conducting trade negotiations and ensuring compliance by third countries with international trade agreements.

40. Telephone interview with Anja Lörcher, trade policy advisor, Foreign Trade Association (FTA), Washington, DC, 3/14/2006.

41. The Article133 Committee derives its name from the legal basis for EU trade policy. The European Union's decision-making process for international trade agreements is governed by articles 133 and 300 of the European Community Treaty. Agreements concerning trade in goods, services and commercial aspects of intellectual property rights are negotiated and concluded on the basis of Art. 133. Art. 300 covers the general European Community Treaty rules for the conclusion of international agreements. See Official Journal of the European Communities, Consolidated Version of the Treaty Establishing the European Community, 12/24/2002, C325/33-184.

42. Ahearn, "Trade Policymaking."

43. Interview with Jean-Francois Boittin, Minister Counselor, Trade and Economic Affairs, French Embassy, Washington, DC, 12/20/2005. Interview with Helge Hassold, Minister Counselor, Trade and Economic Affairs, German Embassy, Washington, DC, 12/29/2005. Interview with Zbigniew Kubacki and Andrzej Gdula, Minister Counselor, Economic and Commercial Affairs, and Counselor for Economic Affairs, Polish Embassy, Washington, DC, 1/03/2006.

44. World Wildlife Fund, "A League of Gentlemen: Who Really Runs EU Trade Decision-Making?" November 2003, WWF-UK, Surrey, 8.

45. Interview with Nikolaos Zaimis, trade counselor, European Commission Delegation, Washington, DC, 2/17/2006.

46. Issues on which the Committee of Permanent Representatives could not agree are put as "B-points" for discussion on the Council's agenda; the ones on which the Committee of Permanent Representatives found an agreement are adopted as "A-points" without any further debate. The Council can, in theory, decide by qualified majority voting, but, in practice, the EU ministers also aim to reach a consensus. Interview with Ambassador Hugo Paemen, co-chairman of the European-American Business Council's Board of Directors and former EU ambassador to the United States, Hogan & Hartson LLP, Washington, DC, 2/07/2006. Qualified majority voting (QMV) is a voting procedure used by the Council of the European Union. The General Affairs and External Relations Council is one of the nine configurations in which the Council of the European Union meets. According to the procedure, each member state has a fixed number of votes. The number allocated to each country is roughly determined by its population, but progressively weighted in favor of smaller countries. To pass a vote by QMV, the proposal has to be supported by 232 out of the total of 321 votes (72.27%), it has to be backed by a majority of member states, and the countries supporting the proposal must represent at least 62% of the total EU population.

47. http://ue.eu.int/showPage.asp?id=388&lang=en, last searched 2/13/2006.

48. Art. 133 and Art. 300 of the Treaty Establishing the European Community. See Official Journal of the European Communities, Consolidated Version of the Treaty Establishing the European Community, 12/24/2002, C325/33-184.

49. The commissioners meet every Wednesday in Brussels, Belgium. During the European Parliament's plenary sessions, their meeting is held on Tuesday in Strasbourg, France. In addition to its regular weekly meeting, the Commission may, when necessary, decide to hold special sittings. The meetings are not public, and all discussions are confidential. However, the agendas and minutes of previous meetings are made available in the register of Commission documents. Importantly, the Commission does not take most of its decisions during its meetings: the Commission decides mainly by written procedure. A decision project or draft is circulated between all commissioners who can make comments or ask for changes during the time frame given. The decision is adopted when no comments have been given. See http://europa.eu.int/comm/atwork/collegemeetings/index_en.htm, last searched 2/16/2006.

50. Raymond J. Ahearn, "Trade Policymaking in the European Union: Institutional Framework," CRS RS21185, 3/27/2002, 3. Each member state has a different number of votes determined by a weighting system based on population and other factors. Five member states and twenty-six votes are necessary to block a decision.

51. However, international agreements that set up an institutional structure, have budgetary implications or establish an association involving reciprocal rights and obligations do require the assent of the European Parliament's by virtue of Art. 300(3) and Art. 310 of the current Treaty Establishing the European Community. See Official Journal of the European Communities, Consolidated Version of the Treaty Establishing the European Community, 12/24/2002, C325/33-184.

52. See, for example, Peter Mandelson, "Strengthening the Lisbon Strategy: The Contribution of External Trade to Growth and Competitiveness in Europe," Speech at High Level Seminar on the Lisbon Agenda, Stockholm, Sweden, 2/15/2005, 1.

53. Lisbon European Council, Presidency Conclusions, 3/23–24/2000, 2.

54. Since 2000, the European Union has not achieved an average annual growth rate of 3%. The overall employment rate for the EU-25 was 63% in 2003, which is significantly below the target level of 70% set by the Lisbon Agenda for 2010. See European Commission, Commission Staff Working Document in support of the Report from the Commission to the Spring European Council, 3/22-23/2005, on the Lisbon Strategy of economic, social and environmental renewal, 01/28/2005, SEC(2005)160, Brussels, 9, 11.

55. The youngest age group (0–14) in the European Union will decline by 11%from 2000 to 2015 and continue to do so by 6%until 2030. The age group above 65 years will increase by 22% between 2000 and 2015 and by a further 27% until 2030. The population over 65 years compared to the population of working age (that is, the dependency ratio) will increase from 25% in 2002 to 30% in 2015 and 40% in 2030. European Commission, "Commission Staff Working Document," 10.

56. European Commission, Communication from the President in Agreement with Vice President Wallström, Strategic Objectives 2005–2009, Europe 2010: A Partnership for European Renewal – Prosperity, Solidarity and Security, 1/26/2005, COM(2005)12 final, Brussels.

57. Peter Mandelson, "Strengthening the Lisbon Strategy: The Contribution of External Trade to Growth and Competitiveness in Europe," 2/15/2005, Speech at the High Level Seminar on the Lisbon Agenda, Stockholm, Sweden, 5. Peter Mandelson, "Europe's Global Trading Challenge and the Future of Free Trade Agreements," 9/26/2005, Speech at the Foreign Policy Centre Debate, Brighton, United Kingdom, 1.

58. "ECB Board Nominee Warns Against Protectionism in Europe," 4/20/2006, http://www.financialexpress-bd.com/index3.asp?cnd=4/20/2006&section_id=22& newsid=22117&spcl=no;Wearden, "HP: Protectionism Wont Save Europe's Jobs," *CNET News*, 1/23/2004, http://news.com.com/HP+Protectionism+wont+save+ Europes+jobs/2100-1022_3-5146154.html; and Mark Landler and Paul Meller, "Grappling With Protectionism across Europe," *International Herald Tribune*, 3/14/2006, http://www.iht.com/articles/2006/03/14/business/protect.php.

59. Peter Mandelson, "Free Trade Is Not the Enemy of Decent Work," 5/10/2006, http://ec.europa.eu/comm./commission_barroso/mandelson/speeches_, last searched 5/12/2006.

60. The Perspectives on Trade and Poverty Reduction Survey of the German Marshall Fund was conducted between September 16, 2005, and October 3, 2005, in the United States, France, Germany, the United Kingdom, Italy, and Poland. The pollsters interviewed a random sample of approximately 1,000 Europeans. The results of the survey showed that 67% of the European respondents held a favorable view of international trade. However, 74% of the French, 65% of the Italians, 59% of the Germans, and 51% of the Polish population feared that international trade decreases total jobs in their countries. Sixty-nine percent of European respondents found that trade liberalization mostly benefits multinational companies, not ordinary people or small companies. See German Marshall Fund, "Perspectives on Trade and Poverty Reduction – A Survey of Public Opinion: Key Findings Report 2005," October 2005, Washington, DC, 5, 8–9, http://www.gmfus.org/doc/Final%20Survey%20Report%201205.pdf, last searched 3/29/2005.

61. German Marshall Fund, "Perspectives on Trade," 8–9.

62. World Trade Organization, Trade Policy Review, report by the European Communities, WT/TPR/G/136, 8.

63. European Commission, Communication from the Commission to the Council and the European Parliament – Trade and Development: Assisting Developing Countries to Benefit from Trade, 9/18/2002, COM (2002)513 final, Brussels, 10–11.

64. http://europa.eu.int/comm/trade/issues/global/development/index_en.htm last searched 1/29/2006

65. Peter Mandelson, "European Parliament Hearings – Answers to Questionnaire for Commissioner Designate Mr. Peter Mandelson (Trade) – Part B (Specific Questions), Brussels, at http://www.europarl.eu.int/hearings/commission/2004_comm/pdf/speca_mandelson_en.pdf, last searched 1/16/2006, and Peter Mandelson, "Opening Statement for European Parliament Hearing," 10/04/2004, Brussels, http://ec.europa.eu/commission_barroso/mandelson/speeches_articles/sppm001_en.htm, last searched 3/31/2007

66. WTTPR/G/136, 9.

67. European Commission, "Trade and Development," 13.

68. http://europa.eu.int/comm/trade/issues/bilateral/regions/mercosur/index_en.htm, last searched 3/28/2006; http://europa.eu.int/comm/trade/issues/bilateral/regions/gcc/index_en.htm, last searched 3/28/2006.

69. See http://europa.eu.int/comm/trade/issues/bilateral/regions/gcc/index_en.htm, last searched 4/24/2006. The members of the Gulf Cooperation Council are Saudi Arabia, Kuwait, Bahrain, Qatar, United Arab Emirates, and Oman. The 2006 Freedom House survey of political rights and civil liberties in the world labels Qatar, Saudi Arabia, Oman, and United Arab Emirates as "not free." It labels Kuwait and Bahrain as "partly free." See http://www.freedomhouse.org/uploads/pdf/Charts2006.pdf, last searched 4/24/2006.

70. The Council of the European Union agreed in June 2002 to open negotiations with Iran which would cover political aspects as well as a trade and cooperation agreement. This Agreement should, once concluded, put Iran's trade and cooperation relations with the European Union on a contractual basis. The negotiations were launched in Brussels in December 2002, http://ec.europa.eu/comm/trade/issues/bilateral/countries/iran/index_en.htm, last searched 5/20/2006. On using trade as an incentive to get Iran to abandon its nuclear program, see Rory Watson, "Iran Ready to Abandon Nuclear Plans for Trade Deal," http://www.timesonline.co.uk/article/0,,3-1359563,00.html; and "EU Renews Trade Talks with Iran," http://www.timesonline.co.uk/article/0,,3-1359563,00.html.

71. European Commission, "The European Union's Role," 9.

72. European Commission, "Communication from the European Commission on the Inclusion of Respect for Democratic Principles and Human Rights in Agreements between the Community and Third Countries," 5/23/1995, COM (95)216, 8.

73. European Parliament, "Council, Commission, Joint Statement by the Council and the Representatives of the Governments of the Member States meeting within the Council, the European Parliament and the Commission on European Union Development Policy: "The European Consensus," 2/24/2006, Official Journal of the European Union, C46/2. European Commission, Communication from the Commission to the Council and the European Parliament – The European Community's Development Policy, 4/26/2000, COM (2000)212 final, Brussels, 27.

74. Interview with Jean-Francois Boittin, Minister, former Counselor Trade and Economic Affairs, French Embassy, Washington, DC, 12/20/2005; Interview with Helge Hassold, minister counselor, trade and economic affairs, German Embassy, Washington, DC, 12/29/2005; and Interview with James Hughes, first secretary of trade policy and agriculture, British Embassy, Washington, DC, 1/17/2006.

75. European Commission, "Communication from the Commission to the Council, the European Parliament and the Economic and Social Committee – Promoting Core Labour Standards and Improving Social Governance in the Context of Globalisation," COM (2001)416 final, Brussels, 13–16.

76. European Union, Human Rights Report, 2005, 58.

77. Under its General System of Preferences (GSP), the European Union grants products imported from GSP beneficiary countries either duty-free access or a tariff reduction, depending on which GSP arrangements a country enjoys. It is implemented following cycles of ten years, for which general guidelines are drawn up. Guidelines for the period 2006–2015 were adopted in 2004. Based on these guidelines, a new GSP scheme was adopted on 6/27/2005, through Council Regulation No. 980/2005. It applies from 1/1/2006 to 12/31/2008. The provisions concerning the GSP-Plus have already been applied from 1/7/2005. See http://europa.eu.int/comm/trade/issues/global/gsp/index_en.htm, last searched 1/29/2006.

78. The Generalized System of Preferences, http://europa.eu.int/comm/trade/issues/global/gsp/index_en.htm, last searched 4/24/2006.

79. The European Union plans to gradually reduce duties on bananas, rice and sugar. See http://europa.eu.int/comm/trade/issues/global/gsp/eba/index_en.htm, last searched 1/29/2006.

80. A country is "dependent and vulnerable" when the five largest sections of its GSP-covered exports to the Community represent more than 75% of its total GSP-covered exports. In addition, GSP-covered exports from that country must represent less than 1% of total EU imports under GSP. The core international human and labor rights conventions that have to be ratified and implemented by the beneficiary country include the International Covenant on Civil and Political Rights; the International Covenant on Economic, Social, and Cultural Rights; the International Convention on the Elimination of All Forms of Racial Discrimination; the Convention on the Elimination of All Forms of Discrimination Against Women; the Convention Against Torture and other Cruel, Inhuman, or Degrading Treatment or Punishment; the Convention on the Rights of the Child; the Convention on the Prevention and Punishment of the Crime of Genocide; the ILO Conventions on Minimum Age for Admission to Employment (No. 138), Prohibition and Immediate Action for the Elimination of the Worst Forms of Child Labor (No. 182), Abolition of Forced Labor (No. 105), Forced Compulsory Labor (No. 29), Equal Remuneration of Men and Women Workers for Work of Equal Value (No. 100), Discrimination in Respect of Employment and Occupation (No. 111); Freedom of Association and Protection of the Right to Organize (No. 87) and Application of the Principles of the Right to Organize and to Bargain Collectively (No. 98); and the International Convention on the Suppression and Punishment of the Crime of Apartheid. The international conventions related to environment and governance principles that have to be ratified and implemented by the beneficiary country include the Montreal Protocol on Substances That Deplete the Ozone Layer the Basel Convention on the Control of Transboundary Movements of Hazardous Wastes

and Their Disposal; the Stockholm Convention on Persistent Organic Pollutants; the Convention on International Trade in Endangered Species; the Convention on Biological Diversity; the Cartagena Protocol on Biosafety; the Kyoto Protocol to the UN Framework Convention on Climate Change; the UN Single Convention on Narcotic Drugs; the UN Convention on Psychotropic Substances; the UN Convention against Illicit Traffic in Narcotic Drugs and Psychotropic Substances; and the UN Convention Against Corruption.

81. http://europa.eu.int/comm/trade/issues/global/gsp/pr211205_en.htm, last searched 2/28/2006.

82. http://europa.eu.int/comm/external_relations/human_rights/torture/guideline_en.htm, last searched 3/23/2006.

83. Official Journal of the European Communities, Council Regulation (EC) No. 1236/2005 of 6/27/2005 concerning trade in certain goods which could be used for capital punishment, torture or other cruel, inhuman or degrading treatment or punishment, 7/30/2005, L200/1–L200/19.

84. http://mineco.fgov.be/protection_consumer/social_label/home_nl.htm and http://europa.eu.int/comm./employment_social/emplweb/csr-matrix?c...SA8000 is a way for retailers, brand companies, suppliers, and other organizations to maintain just and decent working conditions throughout the supply chain, http://www.sa-intl.org/SA8000/SA8000.htm.

85. http://europa.eu.int/comm/employment_social/emplweb/csr-matrix/csr_topic_allcountries_en.cfm?field=15, last searched 5/06/2006.

86. Art. 21 of the Universal Declaration of Human Rights.

87. United Nations Development Programme, Bureau for Development Policy, "Right to Information: Practical Guidance Note," 7/2004, 1–5.

88. Jennifer Mitchell, "The European Union's "Democratic Deficit: Bridging the GAP between Citizens and EU Institutions," http://www.eumap.org/journal/features/2005/demodef/mitchell. According to the European Union, "It is often said that the EU's decision-making system is too remote from ordinary people, who cannot understand its complexities and its difficult legal texts. The EU is trying to overcome this 'democratic deficit' through simpler legislation and better public information, and by giving civil society (see above) a greater say in European policymaking." See http://europa.eu.int/abc/eurojargon/index_en.htm, last searched 4/12/2006.

89. See as an example, EOS Gallup Europe, Flash EB-159-2, "The Future European Constitution," Eurobarometer, http://europa.eu.int/comm/public_opinion/index_en.htm, last searched 4/21/2006.

90. It is important to note that EU member states have their own systems for consulting civil society as they make trade policy.

91. Art. 214 of the Treaty Establishing the European Community. See Official Journal of the European Communities, Consolidated Version of the Treaty Establishing the European Community, 12/24/2002, C325/33–184. It is not the only committee that does not have formal recorded voting.

92. Raymond J. Ahearn, "Trade Policymaking in the European Union: Institutional Framework," 3/27/2002, CRS Report for Congress, The Library of Congress, Washington, DC, 4, http://fpc.state.gov/documents/organization/9189.pdf, last searched 4/07/2006.

93. Official Journal of the European Union, Council Decision of 3/22/2004 adopting the Council's Rules of Procedure, 4/15/2004, L106/25.

94. The Parliament reviews those agreements that set up an institutional structure, have budgetary implications, or establish an association involving reciprocal rights and obligations, such as Association Agreements and Partnership and Cooperation Agreements. Art. 300 (3) and Art. 310 of the Treaty Establishing the European Community. See Official Journal of the European Communities, Consolidated Version of the Treaty Establishing the European Community, 12/24/2002, C325/33-184.

95. Art. 214 of the Treaty Establishing the European Community. See Official Journal of the European Communities, Consolidated Version of the Treaty Establishing the European Community, 12/24/2002, C325/33-184.

96. Peter Mandelson, European Parliament Hearings – Answers to Questionnaire for Commissioner Designate Mr. Peter Mandelson (Trade) – Part B (Specific Questions), Brussels, 2, http://www.europarl.eu.int/hearings/commission/ 2004_comm/pdf/speca_mandelson_en.pdf, last searched 1/16/2006.

97. Art. 133(6) of the Treaty Establishing the European Community. See Official Journal of the European Communities, Consolidated Version of the Treaty Establishing the European Community, 12/24/2002, C325/33-184.

98. Ministry of Foreign Affairs of Denmark, Dealing with EU Matters in Denmark, 4/05/2006, http://www.um.dk/en/menu/EU/DealingWithEUMattersInDenmark/, last searched 4/11/2006; on Britain, Department of the Clerk of the House, "The European Scrutiny System in the House of Commons: A Short Guide for Members of Parliament by the Staff of the European Scrutiny Committee," 6/04/2005, http://www.parliament.uk/documents/upload/TheEuroScrutinySystemintheHoC.pdf, last searched 4/12/2006. House of Lords, Briefing: Scrutinizing European Legislation – The European Union Committee, 7/2005, http://www.parliament.uk/ documents/upload/HofLBpEULeg.pdf, last searched 4/11/2006; and on France, The Delegation for the European Union, 1/01/2006, http://www.assemblee-nationale. fr/english/european-delegation.asp, last searched 3/31/2007

99. For example, the German Parliament is regularly briefed. (For example, members of Parliament also belonged to the German delegation to the WTO ministerial meeting in Hong Kong. The Parliament regularly receives reports on major WTO meetings and informal meetings of the EU trade ministers.) It also exercises influence through motions introduced by the parliamentary groups. However, reports about meetings of the 133 Committee are not sent to the Parliament; rather, a status report on the current state of the negotiations of the Doha Round is provided every two months (available on the Web site of the Ministry of Economics and Technology). E-mail, Helge Hassold to Philip Van Der Celen, 4/25/2006. Mr. Hassold handles trade for the German Embassy in Washington, DC.

100. Interview with Ambassador Hugo Paemen, former EU ambassador to the United States and co-chairman of the European-American Business Council's Board of Directors, Hogan & Hartson LLP, Washington, DC, 7/02/2006.

101. Committee on Industry, External Trade, Research and Energy of the European Parliament, Report on Openness and Democracy in International Trade, 10/11/2001, Final A5–0331/2001, 11

102. Committee on Industry, External Trade, Research and Energy of the European Parliament, Report on Openness and Democracy in International Trade, 11.

103. Robin Ratchford, "Democratizing the EU's Trade Policy Making: The Commission's Perspective," Trócaire, Policy Roundtable on Democratizing the EU's

Trade Policy Making, 11/7/2003, Georgian Suite, Buswells Hotel, Dublin, Ireland, http://www.trocaire.org/policyandadvocacy/eupresidency/tradeseminarreport.htm, last searched 3/01/2006. As of 3/30/2007, however, the report was no longer available at the site.

104. Committee on Petitions, "MEPs Press Council of Ministers to Open Its Doors," 2/23/2006, http://www.europarl.eu.int/news/expert/infopress_page/021-5511-54-2-8-902-20060220IPR05479-23-02-2006-2006–false/default_en.htm, last searched 4/11/2006.

105. Committee on Civil Liberties, Justice and Home Affairs, Improving Transparency of the EU Institutions, 2/23/2006, http://www.europarl.eu.int/news/expert/infopress_page/019-5504-53-2-8-902-20060220IPR05472-22-02-2006-2006–false/default_en.htm, last searched 4/11/2006.

106. http://www.europa.eu.int/comm/trade/issues/global/csd/dcs_proc.htm, last searched on 12/29/2005.

107. The organizations that have a seat in the Contact Group include Network Women in Development Europe (WIDE), Association of European Chambers of Commerce and Industry (EUROCHAMBRES), Bureau Européen des Unions de Consommateurs (BEUC), Comité des Organisations Professionnelles Agricoles de l'Union Européenne & Comité Général de la Coopération Agricole de l'Union Européenne (COPA-COGECA-COPA-COGECA), Coopération Internationale pour le Développement et la Solidarité (CIDSE), Eurocommerce (retail and wholesale sector), Eurogroup for Animal Welfare (EUROGROUP), European Economic and Social Committee (EESC), European Trade Union Confederation (ETUC), Foreign Trade Association (FTA), SOLIDAR (umbrella organization of social and economic justice NGOs), European Services Forum (service sector), Union of Industrial and Employers' Confederations of Europe (UNICE, and World Wildlife Fund (WWF).

108. Sophie Meunier, "Trade Policy and Political Legitimacy in the European Union," *Comparative European Politics* 1 (2003), 83.

109. Trocaire, "Democratising the EU's Trade Policy Making," Remarks of Robin Ratchford, Deputy Head of Unit within DG Trade with responsibility for Sustainable Development and Dialogue with Civil Society, http://www.trocaire.org/policyandadvocacy/eupresidency/tradeseminarreport.htm.

110. Sophie Meunier, "Trade Policy," 83. The Issue Groups have covered topics such as trade and health, trade in services, trade and agriculture, trade and environment, trade and sustainable development, investment, competition, trade-related intellectual property rights, WTO reform and transparency, access to medicines, geographical indications (GIs), biodiversity, food safety, market access, and development.

111. Some EU officials told us that these discussions influenced EU trade policy on essential medicines, but NGOs told us they felt they had little influence on trade policy.

112. The EUR-Lex portal on the European Union became available in June 2001 for access to the Official Journal. The minutes of meetings of the College of the European Commissioners have been available on the Internet since January 2002. A public register of Commission documents has been available online since June 2002. The Council online register contains references to documents produced from 1999 onwards. Some documents can be displayed directly; others must be requested from the Council's document-access service.

113. http://trade-info.cec.eu.int/consultations/index.cfm, last searched 5/6/2006. The Web site invited public comments on several issues including rules of origin marking,

U.S./EU economic partnerships, and the sustainability impact assessment of trade policies.

114. http://ec.europa.eu/comm./trade/issues/bilateral/countries/chinapro8, last searched 5/12/2006.

115. Christina Deckwirth, "The EU Corporate Trade Agenda: The Role and Interests of Corporations and Their Lobby Groups in Trade Policy-making in the European Union," 11/2005, Seattle to Brussels Network, Brussels/Berlin, 14–16 at http://www.s2b-network.org/s2bnetwork/download/EU_corporate_trade_agenda.pdf.pdf?id = 96, last searched 4/12/2006; and SUSTRA Network, Policy Brief Paper Based on the Conclusions of the SUSTRA seminar on "Vested Interests and Trade Policy Reforms," 1/22–23/2004, Foundation for International Environmental Law and Development, London, 2, http://www.agro-montpellier.fr/sustra/publications/policy_briefs/policy-brief-VI.pdf, last searched 4/12/2006.

116. Telephone interview with Luis Morago, director of the Brussels office of Oxfam, Washington, DC, 2/17/2006.

117. World Wildlife Fund, "Civil Society and Trade Diplomacy in the 'Global Age' – The European Case: Trade Policy Dialogue between Civil Society and the European Commission," 9/2002, WWF European Policy Office, Brussels, 14.

118. Flash EB No. 151b, "Europa Poll on Globalization," 10/8–16/2003. See pp. 45–47, 65–67.

119. Ibid., 66.

120. Ibid., 95.

121. Boulhol, "How Europeans See Globalization," 5–6, quotation p. 7.

122. Jack Straw, foreign secretary of the United Kingdom, president of the Council of the European Union, "Preface," "EU Annual Report on Human Rights," 2005, 6.

123. Neil Buckley, "Self-Confident State Re-enters World Stage," *Financial Times*, Special Report FT Russia, 4/21/2006, 1, 3; Glenn Kessler, "Rice Warns against Russian Gas Monopoly," *Washington Post*, 4/26/2006, A21; and European Union, Annual Report on Human Rights, 2005, 104.

124. Council of the European Union, "EU Annual Report," quotation on p. 103, the situation is described on pp. 103–105.

125. Lionel Beehner, "Backgrounder: Energy's Impact on EU-Russian Relations," Council on Foreign Relations, 1/10/2006, http://www.cfr.org/publication/9535/energys_impact_on_eurussian_relations.html, last searched 5/23/2006.

126. http://ec.europa.eu/justice_home/doc_centre/external/russia/doc_external_russia_en.htm, last searched 5/12/2006.

127. EU/Russia agreements are at http://www.consilium.europa.eu/cms3_Applications/applications/Accords/searchp.asp?cmsid = 297&party = RU&pname=Russia&lang=EN&doclang=EN; last searched 5/12/2006.

128. European Union, Annual Report on Human Rights, 2005, 28, 105.

129. The European Union has included a human rights clause in the Europe Agreements (Bulgaria and Romania); the EU-Turkey Association Agreement; the Cotonou Agreement with the seventy-nine ACP countries; the Association Agreements with the Mediterranean countries (Tunisia, Israel, Morocco, Jordan, Egypt, Algeria, Lebanon, and the Palestinian Authority); the Stabilisation and Association Agreements with the Balkan countries (the Former Yugoslav Republic of Macedonia and Croatia); the Political Dialogue and Cooperation Agreements with the Andean Community (Bolivia, Colombia, Ecuador, Peru, and Venezuela); the Political Dialogue and

Cooperation Agreements with the five Central American States (Costa Rica, Panama, Honduras, Nicaragua, and El Salvador); the EU-Chile Association Agreement; the EU-Mexico Economic Partnership, Political Coordination and Cooperation Agreement (Global Agreement); the Partnership and Cooperation Agreements (Armenia, Azerbaijan, Georgia, Kazakhstan, Kyrgyzstan, Moldova, Russia, Turkmenistan, Ukraine, and Uzbekistan); the Trade and Cooperation Agreements (Laos and South Korea); the Cooperation Agreements (ASEAN [Brunei, Indonesia, Malaysia, Philippines, Singapore, Thailand, and Vietnam], Pakistan, Sri Lanka, Bangladesh, Nepal, Vietnam, and Cambodia); and EU-South Africa Trade, Development, and Cooperation Agreement.

130. The Cotonou Agreement (2000) provides for nonreciprocal preferential access to the European Union during an interim period from 2001 to 2007. These unilateral preferences will then be replaced by reciprocal Economic Partnership Agreements establishing FTAs between the European Community and individual ACP countries. Formal EPA negotiations started in September 2002. Since October 2003, regional negotiations have been launched with the six regions: West Africa, Central Africa, Eastern and Southern Africa, the Southern African Development Community, Caribbean, and the Pacific.

131. European Commission, Communication from the European Commission on the Inclusion of Respect for Democratic Principles and Human Rights in Agreements between the Community and Third Countries, COM(95)216, 5/23/1995, 3.

132. Other "appropriate measures" under the human rights clause include: alteration of the contents of cooperation programmes or the channels used, reduction of cultural, scientific and technical cooperation programmes, postponement of a Joint Committee meeting, suspension of high-level bilateral contacts, postponement of new projects, refusal to follow up partner's initiatives, and suspension of cooperation. See European Commission, "Inclusion of Respect for Democratic Principles," 9.

133. Togo (1998 and 2004), Niger (1996 and 1999), Guinea Bissau (1999 and 2004), Comoros Islands (1999), Haiti (2000), Ivory Coast (2000 and 2001), Fiji (2000), Liberia (2001), Zimbabwe (2002), Central African Republic (2003), Guinea-Conakry (2004), Uzbekistan (2005). See Andrew Bradley, "An ACP Perspective and Overview of Article 96 Cases," *ECDPM Discussion Paper 64D*, 7/01/2005, Maastricht, 3; http://www.europa.eu.int/comm/external_relations/cfsp/sanctions/measures.htm, last searched on 4/24/2006.

134. Since 1995, the European Union has imposed "appropriate measures" on Togo (since 1998), Haiti (since 2001), Liberia (since 2002), Zimbabwe (since 2002), Guinea-Conakry (since 2005), and Uzbekistan (since 2005). See Andrew Bradley, "An ACP Perspective," 3; and http://www.europa.eu.int/comm/external_relations/cfsp/sanctions/measures.htm, last searched on 4/24/2006

135. Emilie M. Hafner-Burton, "Trading Human Rights," 610–611.

136. European Parliament – Committee on Foreign Affairs, Report on the Human Rights and Democracy Clause in European Union Agreements (2005/2057[INI]), Final A6–0004/2006, 1/23/2006, 17.

137. Amnesty International – EU Office, "Ten Years of EUROMED: Time to End the Human Rights Deficit," *Amnesty International – EU Office*, 11/21/2005, Brussels, http://web.amnesty.org/library/index/engIOR610232005?open&of=eng-312, last searched, 4/21/2006.

138. Amnesty International – EU Office, "Ten Years of EUROMED."

139. European Parliament – Subcommittee on Human Rights, "Public Hearing on Human Rights in Cambodia, Laos and Vietnam," 4/14/2005, http://www.europarl.eu .int/news/expert/infopress_page/015-281-255-09-37-902-20050913IPR00280-12-09-2005-2005-false/default_en.htm, last searched 4/24/2006.

140. http://europa.eu.int/comm/external_relations/cfsp/sanctions/index.htm, last searched 4/24/2006.

141. Council of the European Union, Basic Principles on the Use of Restrictive Measures (Sanctions) (10198/1/04 REV1), PESC 450, 06/07/2004, Brussels, 3.

142. European Commission, "Inclusion of Respect for Democratic Principles," 8; and e-mail, 9/06/2005, Charles Whiteley to Susan Aaronson. Charles Whiteley is currently first secretary in the Political, Economic, Trade, Press, and Economic Section at the Delegation of the European Commission to Bangladesh, but previously he worked on human rights questions in Brussels.

143. Fidelius Schmid and Daniel Dombey, "EU to Freeze Belarus President's Assets," *Financial Times*, 5/15/2006.

144. Council of the European Union, Guidelines on Implementation and Evaluation of Restrictive Measures (Sanctions) in the Framework of the EU Common Foreign and Security Policy, (15114/05 PESC 1084 FIN 275), 12/02/2003, Brussels, 6.

145. Hadewych Hazelzet, "Carrots or Sticks? EU and U.S. Reactions to Human Rights Violations in the Nineties and Beyond," 7/2004, http://cadmus.iue.it/dspace/ bitstream/1814%20/2838/2/HHazelzetThesisJune03.pdf, last searched 4/1/2007.

146. Art. 301 of the Treaty Establishing the European Community. See Official Journal of the European Communities, Consolidated Version of the Treaty Establishing the European Community, 12/24/2002, C325/33-184.

147. Art. 301 of the Treaty Establishing the European Community. See Official Journal of the European Communities, Consolidated Version of the Treaty Establishing the European Community, 12/24/2002, C325/33-184.

148. Telephone interview with Lotte Leicht, director of the Brussels office of Human Rights Watch, 2/28/2006, Washington, DC.

149. European Parliament – Committee on Foreign Affairs, "Report on the Human Rights and Democracy Clause," 16.

150. European Parliament, European Parliament Resolution on the Human Rights and Democracy Clause in European Union Agreements (2005/2057[INI]), 2/14/2006, P6_TA-PROV(2006)0056, Strasbourg, 3.

151. European Parliament Resolution on the Annual Report on Human Rights in the World 2005 and the EU's Policy on the Matter, (2005/2203(INI), 5/18/2006, at http://www.europarl.europa.eu/sides/getDoc.do?pubRef = -//EP//TEXT+TA+P6-TA-2006-0220+0+DOC+XML+V0//EN&language=EN, both last searched 7/18/2006.

152. Human Rights Watch, Christian Solidarity Worldwide, and International Crisis Group, "No Trade Agreement for Turkmenistan – Joint Letter," 3/20/2006, http://hrw.org/ english/docs/2006/03/20/turkme13040.htm, last searched 4/24/2006; and Bruce Pannier, "Turkmenistan: Proposed EU Deal Sparks Criticism," *Radio Free Europe-Radio Liberty*, 10/28/2006, at http://www.rferl.org/featuresarticle/2006/04/4ba8501a-fa0c-4f0f-b639-b894ed9b0c36.html.

153. Human Rights Watch, "EU: Stop Trade Pact with Turkmen Regime – Use Leverage with Brutal Government," 3/21/2006, http://hrw.org/english/docs/2006/03/21/ turkme13044.htm, and http://www.rferl.org/featuresarticle/2006/04/4ba8501a-fa0c-4f0f-b639-b894ed9b0c36.html, last searched 5/18/2006. For Human Rights Watch's

description of conditions in Turkmenistan, see http://hrw.org/english/docs/2006/01/18/turkme12244.htm, last searched 5/23/2006.

154. European Union, "Guidelines on Human Rights Dialogues," http://ec.europa.eu/comm/external_relations/human_rights/doc/ghd12_01.htm, last searched 5/19/2006.

155. EU Human Rights Report, 32–35.

156. European Commission, "Communication from the European Commission to the Council and the European Parliament – The European Union's Role in Promoting Human Rights and Democratisation in Third Countries," COM(2001)252 final, 5/08/2001, Brussels, 3.

157. The Committee on Generalised Preferences assists DG Trade in its work. This Committee is composed of representatives of member states. The procedure for withdrawal is usually initiated by a complaint from an EU member state or any third party having an interest in the case. Before opening an investigation, preliminary consultations take place between DG Trade and the Generalized Preferences Committee in order to determine whether there is sufficient evidence for a case. If so, DG Trade will start an investigation. Where the DG Trade considers that its findings justify a temporary withdrawal because of serious and systematic violations of the rights referred to in the 1998 ILO Declaration on Fundamental Principles and Rights at Work (freedom of association and the effective recognition of the right to collective bargaining, the elimination of all forms of forced or compulsory labor, the effective abolition of child labor, the elimination of discrimination in respect of employment and occupation), it will monitor and evaluate the situation in the beneficiary country concerned for a period of six months. If, by the end of that period, the country has not made the required commitment to take the necessary measures to conform, DG Trade will submit an appropriate proposal to the General Affairs and External Relations Council (who decides by qualified majority). Where the Council decides for temporary withdrawal, such decision will enter into force six months after it was taken, unless it is decided before then that the reasons justifying it no longer prevail; http://europa.eu.int/comm/trade/issues/global/gsp/gspguide.htm, last searched 4/25/2006.

158. Guy Ryder, Emilio Gabaglio, and Willy Thys, "Request for Investigation into Violation of Freedom of Association in Belarus under the Procedures of the European Union GSP," 1/27/2003, http://www.icftu.org/displaydocument.asp?Index=991217051, last searched 4/25/2004. In January 2003, the International Confederation of Free Trade Unions, the European Trade Union Confederation (ETUC) and the World Confederation of Labor (WCL) alerted the European Commission to systematic and serious violations of freedom of association and the right to collective bargaining in Belarus.

159. European Commission, "Commission Staff Working Document – Implementation of the Commission Communication on the EU's Role in Promoting Human Rights and Democratisation in Third Countries," SEC(2004)1041, 07/30/2004, Brussels, 9. On withdrawing trade benefits, see NA, "EU to Withdraw Trade Preferences from Belarus, as It Fails to Reform Labor Rights," AP, 6/15/2007.

160. The European Community contracts with external consultants to conduct Sustainable Impact Assessments for DG Trade. The consultants study indicators such as real income, employment, and fixed capital formation; equity, poverty, health, and education; and biological diversity, environmental quality, and natural resource stocks. Negotiators are supposed to use these assessments to develop capacity building

programs linked to trade policies. The European Union launched the first assessment in 1999 in view of the new WTO round of negotiations. As of this writing, the European Union has performed such assessments for the Doha Development Agenda negotiations; for the negotiations with the African, Caribbean, and Pacific (ACP) countries; with Mercosur; and with the Gulf Cooperation Council (GCC) countries. See http://europa.eu.int/comm/trade/issues/global/sia/index_en.htm, last searched 1/29/2006.

161. Mariann Fischer Boel, Member of the European Commission Responsible for Agriculture and Rural Development, Europa Lecture, "European Agricultural Policy in a Changing Environment," 3/6/2006.

162. The German Marshall Fund found that 45% of Europeans feel that it is acceptable to subsidize domestic farmers even though developing country farmers suffer. But 21% more agreed when they were told EU farmers would close without subsidies. Twenty-eight percent found trade-distorting agricultural subsidies unacceptable in either circumstance. German Marshall Fund, "Perspectives on Trade and Poverty Reduction," 18.

163. Boel, 2; and Trans Atlantic Consumer Dialogue, "Towards Fairer Food and Agricultural Markets," 4/19//2005, Germany Embassy to the United States, http://www.tacd.org/events/meeting7/agriculture_report.htm.

164. Becker, "Agricultural Support" 4–5.

165. http://ec.europa.eu/comm/agriculture/capreform/index_en.htm, last searched 4/27/2006.

166. Boel, "European Agricultural," 4.

167. http://www.ers.usda.gov/briefing/EuropeanUnion/, last searched 5/04/2006.

168. http://europa.eu.int/comm/budget/library/publications/budget_in_fig/dep_eu_budg_2006_en.pdf, last searched 4/28/2006; and Gregory S. Becker, "Agricultural Support Mechanisms in the European Union: A Comparison with the United States," 7/31/2002, RL30753, 2, 4.

169. "European Farming – Why the European Union Retains its Strange Fondness for Farm Subsidies," *The Economist*, 12/08/2005, at http://topics.developmentgateway.org/foodsecurity/rc/ItemDetail.do~1053968, last searched 3/30/2007; and Tom Wright, "France Digs in Heels on Farm Subsidies, *International Herald Tribune*, 10/20/2005, www.iht.com/articles/2005/10/20/business/wto.php, both last searched 3/30/2007.

170. "European Farming – Why the European Union Retains its Strange Fondness for Farm Subsidies," *The Economist*, 12/08/2005, at http://www.economist.com/research/articlesBySubject/displayStory.cfm?story_ID=5278374&subjectid=478044. France's Europe Minister, Catherine Colonna, has made clear that the reforms agreed on "cannot be changed until 2013."

171. Christine Lagarde, "Big Cuts in Farm Tariffs Are No Solution to Poverty," *Financial Times*, 11/21/2005.

172. Interview with Zbigniew Kubacki and Andrzej Gdula, Minister Counselor Economic and Commercial Affairs and Counselor for Economic Affairs, Polish Embassy, Washington, DC, 1/03/2006.

173. Anthony Browne, "Blair Stands Alone on Rebate But With Friends on Reform," *The Times*, 6/13/2005.

174. Becker, "Agricultural Support Mechanisms," 5.

175. http://www.wto.org/english/thewto_e/thewto_e.htm#intro, last searched 5/04/2006.

176. These nations had agreed to continue the reform process (Article 20 of the Agriculture Agreement). "Members agree that negotiations for continuing the process will be initiated one year before the end of the implementation period, taking into account" their experience, effects of reduction commitments, "non-trade concerns, special and differential treatment to developing-country Members, and the objective to establish a fair and market-oriented agricultural trading system, and the other objectives and concerns mentioned in the preamble to this Agreement; and what further commitments are necessary to achieve the above mentioned long-term objectives," http://www.wto.org/english/tratop_e/agric_e/negoti_e.htm.

177. http://www.wto.org/english/tratop_e/agric_e/negs_bkgrnd22_cancun_e.htm; and Larry Elliott *et al.*, "Blow to World Economy as Trade Talks Collapse," *The Guardian*, 9/15/2003.

178. According to the WTO Web site, the framework also stresses that the balance of the outcome will only be found at the end of the negotiations – a balance both between agriculture and other subjects (the "single undertaking"), and within agriculture itself. The three pillars are connected, part of the whole deal, and must be balanced equitably, the text says. The introduction also reiterates issues such as development and non-trade concerns. The framework includes a short paragraph on "monitoring and surveillance": this will be improved by amending Article 18 of the Agriculture Agreement, to "ensure full transparency," including prompt and complete notifications on market access, domestic support and export competition. Developing countries' concerns on this will be addressed.

179. See, as an example, Boel, "European Agricultural Policy," 6; "Agriculture Modalities: Deadlines Missed, Eyes Now at Cancun," *Bridges Weekly Main Page* 7(12), 4/2/2005, http://www.ictsd.org/weekly/03-04-02/story1.htm; "EU Holding Talks Hostage," Fin24 (a South African newspaper), http://www.fin24.co.za/articles/int_economy/display_article.asp?ArticleID=1518-1785_1851878, all last searched 5/3/2006.

180. Oxfam International, "Making Trade Work for Development in 2005 – What the EU Should Do," *Oxfam Briefing Paper* 75, May 2005, http://www.oxfam.org.uk/what_we_do/issues/trade/downloads/bp75_eu_2005.pdf?m=234&url=http://www.oxfam.org.uk/what_we_do/issues/trade/downloads/bp70_sugar.pdf, last searched 4/26/2006.

181. Oxfam International, "Stop the Dumping! – How EU Agricultural Subsidies are Damaging the Livelihoods in the Developing World," *Oxfam Briefing Paper* 31 (October 2002), http://www.oxfam.org.uk/what_we_do/issues/trade/downloads/bp31_dumping.pdf, last searched 4/28/2006.

182. Canadian farmers believe EU subsidies have led to overproduction, depressed prices, and a farm income crisis. National Farmers Union, "The Farm Crisis, EU Subsidies and Agribusiness Market Power," Testimony to the Senate Standing Committee on Agriculture and Forestry, Ottawa, Ontario, 2/17/2000, http://www.nfu.ca/feb17-brief.htm. A broadside on the human rights effects of the WTO agreement is IATP and 3D3, "Planting the Rights Seed," March 2005.

183. William R. Cline, "Trading Up: Trade Policy and Global Poverty," *CGD Brief*, 2(4/2) (2003).

184. World Bank, "Agricultural Trade Reforms."

185. Ibid.

186. Eduardo Porter, "Ending Aid to Rich Farmers May Hurt the Poor One," *New York Times,* 12/18/2005, 4.

187. Peter Mandelson, "EU Agriculture and the World Trade Talks," speech at the National Farmer's Union (NFU) Annual Conference, 2/27/2006, Birmingham, http://europa .eu.int/comm/commission_barroso/mandelson/speeches_articles/mandelson_ sptemplate.cfm?LangId=EN&temp=sppm084_en, last searched 4/27/2006.

188. Peter Mandelson, "EU Trade Policy after Hong Kong," speech at Haus der Deutchen Wirtschaft, 1/23/2006, Berlin, http://europa.eu.int/comm/commission_ barroso/mandelson/speeches_articles/mandelson_sptemplate.cfm?LangId = EN& temp = sppm078_en, last searched 4/26/2006.

189. Just as Europe had a wide range of nontrade concerns for subsidizing agriculture, many other countries have put forth a wide range of arguments for maintaining or abolishing agricultural subsidies, including food security (a variant of the right to food). For an overview, see "Non-Trade Concerns: Agriculture Can Serve Many Purposes," http://www.wto.org/english/tratop_e/agric_e/negs_bkgrnd17_agri_e.htm, last searched 5/04/2006.

190. Aaronson reviewed the consultation Web sites and could find no public consultation focused on human rights broadly construed or specific human rights such as labor rights or access to food. See http://trade-info.cec.eu.int/civilsoc/meetlist.cfm, last searched 12/14/2006. They have focused on related topics such as health, aid and development, and sustainability.

191. "MEPs Evaluate EU Actions on Human Rights in the World," http://www. europarl.europa.eu/news/expert/infopress_page/015-8235-138-05-20-902-20060512IPR 08070-18-05-2006-2006-true/default_en.htm; and European Parliament Resolution on the Annual Report on Human Rights in the World 2005 and the EU's Policy on the Matter, (2005/2203(INI), 5/18/2006, at http://www.europarl.europa.eu/ sides/getDoc.do?pubRef=-//EP//TEXT+TA+P6-TA-2006-0220+0+DOC+XML+ V0//EN&language=EN, both last searched 7/18/2006.

6. The United States: At Cross Purposes–Americans at the Intersection of Trade and Human Rights

1. Spanish explorers first discovered cacao when they conquered Mexico in 1521. Europeans set up colonial plantations for growing cacao and sugar in Africa. Cacao is still harvested, fermented, dried, cleaned, and roasted – mostly by hand – on similar plantations today. "All About Chocolate," http://www.fieldmuseum.org/ chocolate/history_intro3.html. Also see Sudarsan Gahavan and Sumana Chatterjee, "Why Slavery Still Exists: Those along the Chocolate Chain Put the Blame on Someone Else," at http://vision.ucsd.edu/~kbranson/stopchocolateslavery/atasteofslavery. html. In 2000, the Department of State concluded that some 15,000 children were sold into forced labor on cocoa, cotton, and coffee plantations in the Ivory Coast from countries such as Mali. The State Department reported on this problem in the Ivory Coast in 2000, http://www.globalexchange.org/campaigns/fairtrade/cocoa/ usStateDept022301.html, last searched 6/12/2006; Humphrey Hawksley, "Mali's Children in Chocolate Slavery," 4/12/2001, http://news.bbc.co.uk/1/hi/world/Africa/ 1272522.stm; and Sudarsan Gahavan and Sumana Chatterjee, "A Taste of Slavery,"

6/24/2001, http://vision.ucsd.edu/~kbranson/stopchocolateslavery/atasteofslavery.html both last searched 6/12/2006.

2. Congressman Engel proposed House Amendment 142 to HR 2330 in the 107th Congress. The House approved the bill by recorded vote: 291–115. See http://thomas. loc.gov/cgi-bin/bdquery/z?d107:HZ00142, last searched 6/14/2006.

3. Interview with Peter Leon, legislative director for Congressman Eliot Engel (D-NY), 6/14/2006. Senator Harkin developed the legislation that mandated that the Department of Labor report on the worst forms of child labor. He has ensured appropriations and programs are in place to combat child labor, and he developed the legislation to approve the international treaty banning child labor. http://harkin.senate.gov/issues/issues.cfm?t=2, last searched 6/12/2006.

4. "The Protocol for the Growing and Processing of Cocoa Beans and Their Derivative Products in a Manner that Complies with ILO Convention 182 Concerning the Prohibition and Immediate Action for the Elimination of the Worst Forms of Child Labor," also known as the Harkin–Engel Protocol, is available at http://www.nca-cma.org and http://www.responsiblecocoa.com/responsible/. The industry agreed to take specific steps to eliminate the worst forms of child labor. The Protocol was signed by Larry Graham, president of the Chocolate Manufacturers Association, and William Guyton, president of the World Cocoa Federation, on September 19, 2001. It was witnessed by Congressman Engel and Senators Harkin and Herbert Kohl, the ambassador of the Ivory Coast, as well as representatives from the ILO, the General Secretary of the International Union of Food Agricultural, Hotel, Restaurant, Catering, Tobacco and Allied Workers Associations (IUF); as additional witnesses were NGO representatives from Free the Slaves, the National Consumers League, and the Child Labor Coalition. The chief executives of several major chocolate companies wrote that they endorsed the protocol, as did the Association of the Chocolate, Biscuit and Confectionary Industries of the European Union. http://www.caobisco.com, last searched 6/14/2006.

5. If the companies had to have their chocolate labeled, that could lead consumers to become more aware of the conditions in which chocolate is produced; and some consumers may have boycotted chocolate products, chocolatiers or cacao traders.

6. After an in-depth investigation of conditions of cacao plantations in Ivory Coast in 2006, BBC reporter Humphrey Hawksley found little evidence that industry efforts were changing farm conditions and concluded: "No one is in charge of the efforts put in place under the Cocoa Protocol. There's no place the buck stops. In the cocoa belt, it's only a short drive to find children working with machetes amid some of the worst poverty anywhere in the world." Aaronson telephone interview with Hawksley, 2/23/2007.

7. However, some NGOs condemned the protocol because they thought it could not effectively tackle problems of child labor in cocoa production. For example, one NGO, the International Labor Rights Fund, filed suit against Nestle, ADM, and Cargill for falsely claiming that they were addressing the problem of forced child labor on farms producing cocoa. Other NGOs such as Global Exchange called on consumers to purchase only fair-trade chocolate. Under California's unfair business practice law, firms can be sued for false or misleading statements. The suit had not been decided as of June 2006. http://www.laborrights.org/projects/childlab/cocoa.htm, last searched 6/14/2006. On pushing for fair-trade chocolate, see http://www.

globalexchange.org/campaigns/fairtrade/cocoa/ and http://www.baido.org/topics/
environment/2002/tfusa_berkeley_coffee.php, all last searched 6/14/2006.

8. According to Senator Harkin's Web site, some positive steps have been taken to address the worst forms of child labor in cocoa growing. These include the creation of the International Cocoa Initiative Foundation, which is now beginning to form partnerships with NGOs to provide social protection programs in West Africa. The countries have also initiated small pilot projects that will be used to develop a child labor monitoring system. Although the July 1, 2005, deadline was not fully met, the cocoa industry representatives assured Senator Harkin and Representative Engel that they remained fully committed to achieving a certification system, which can be expanded across the cocoa-growing areas of West Africa and will cover 50% of the cocoa-growing areas of Ivory Coast and Ghana within three years. Nonetheless the two officials issued a press release, where Congressman Engel stressed, "I am calling on the CHOCOLATE industry to do the right thing. If they do not, legislation might be needed to end this evil practice." Press release, "For Valentines Day: Engel and Harkin Warn Americans That Holiday Chocolate Is Made by Child Slaves," 2/14/2005, http://www.house.gov/apps/list/press/ny17_engel/pr021405.html, last searched 6/26/06.

9. International Cocoa Organization, "Protocole for the Growing and Processing. . . ." 8/11/2001, at http://www.worldcocoafoundation.org/Labour/Child/Initiative/pr_06_04.asp

10. U.S. Agency for International Development and U.S. Department of Labor, "Child Labor in the Cocoa Section of West Africa: Sustainable Tree Crops Program" and "International Institute of Tropical Agriculture: A Synthesis of Findings in Cameroon, Cote D'Ivoire, Ghana and Nigeria," 8/2002. For examples of actions taken in the Ivory Coast, see Republic of Côte D'Ivoire, "Snapshot on Remediation Activities," 5/2006, http://www.cacao.ci/. The government of Ghana has developed a draft plan to protect children, prevent child trafficking, teach labor inspectors, and ensure that children are in school and not working. See ICI Newsletter, Issue No. 4, April/May 2006.

11. The labor advisory committees weigh the impact of a proposed trade agreement on labor rights. Moreover, in accordance with Executive Order 13126 and GSA Federal Acquisition Regulations, ILAB maintains a *list of products* that are believed to have been made using forced or indentured child labor. http://www.dol.gov/ilab/regs/eo13126/main.htm. Pursuant to section 2102(c) of the Trade Act of 2002, the president is also required to prepare several reports to Congress related to new free trade agreements. Among these reports are a United States Employment Impact Review, Labor Rights Report, and Laws Governing Exploitative Child Labor Report. The Department of Labor, in consultation with other federal agencies, has been delegated the responsibility for preparing these three reports. http://www.dol.gov/ILAB/media/reports/flt/main.htm; and http://www.dol.gov/ILAB/media/reports/usfta/main.htm, both last searched 6/26/2006/. U.S. policymakers also do an environmental review of trade agreements.

12. At its 2006 trade policy review, the U.S. government reported to the WTO that with trade policy tools, U.S. policymakers prod the rest of the world "to value freedom, transparency, accountability and openness." "This broad objective is accompanied by a range of policy priorities including . . . enhancing transparency, the avoidance of regulatory measures as a means to advantage domestic producers . . . and the continued

incorporation of government procurement, labour, and environmental issues into future U.S. trade agreements." WT/TPR/S/160, 14, 34.

13. We note that although the UDHR does not directly refer to IPR, it gives people the rights to protect the products/processes/ideas that they have created. The UDHR also grants everyone the right to participate and benefit from science, arts, and culture. Thus, there is tension between the creators of information, the users of information and those people that ensure the use and diffusion of information within the UDHR. Scholars disagree as to whether intellectual property rights are human rights. According to scholar Peter Drahos, they are universally recognized rights but not universal human rights. But U.S. policymakers see protecting these rights as essential to development. Dr. Peter Drahos, "The Universality of Intellectual Property Rights: Origins and Development," prepared for the Panel Discussion on Intellectual Property and Human Rights, Geneva, 11/9/1998, www.wipo.int/tk/en/hr/paneldiscussion/papers/index.html, last searched 7/20/2006. On the U.S. view of IPR, see "Focus on Intellectual Property Rights," http://usinfo.state.gov/products/pubs/intelprp/guide.htm; http://usinfo.state.gov/products/pubs/intelprp/approach.htm, all last searched 7/20/2006.

14. John Gerald Ruggie, "American Exceptionalism, Exemptionalism and Global Governance." This chapter was published in Michael Ignatieff, *American Exceptionalism and Human Rights* (Princeton: Princeton University Press, 2005).

15. Thomas K. McCraw, ed., *Creating Modern Capitalism: How Entrepreneurs, Companies, and Countries Triumphed in Three Industrial Revolutions* (Cambridge, MA: Harvard University Press, 1997), p. 348.

16. NA, "Us versus Us, American Values Divide as well as Define the Country," *The Economist*, 11/6/2003, http://www.economist.com/surveys/printerfriendly.cfm?story_id=2172019; and "The Last, Best Hope of Earth?" *The Economist*, 11/06/2003, http://www.economist.com/surveys/printerfriendly.cfm?story_id=2172153, both last searched 4/18/2006. According to a 1997 poll by Peter D. Hart Associates focused on human rights, 61% of Americans polled think that the United States is one of the best countries at safeguarding human rights. But only 32% of those polled were familiar with the Universal Declaration of Human Rights. The Peter D. Hart poll of 1,004 respondents was conducted on 11/3–4/1997, http://www1.umn.edu/humanrts/edumat/adultsur.htm, last searched 6/11/2006.

17. According to the human rights scholar David Forsythe, "Americans generally see themselves as an exceptionally good people who have compiled an enviable record of protecting personal freedom. This national self-image affects the American world view. Since the time of George Washington, and despite certain traditions of isolationism and non-alignment, the United States has professed to want to teach the rest of the world about democracy and freedom." David P. Forsythe, "U.S. Foreign Policy and Enlarging the Democratic Community," *Human Rights Quarterly* 22(4) (2000), 988–1010. Also see Thomas G. Weiss, Margaret E. Crahan, and John Goering, *Wars on Terrorism and Iraq: Human Rights, Unilateralism, and U.S. Foreign Policy* (New York: Routledge, 2004).

18. Yale Law School Dean Koh notes that the Senate has been traditionally reluctant to ratify human rights treaties despite drafting those treaties. Harold Hongju Koh, "How Is International Human Rights Law Enforced," *Indiana Law Journal* 74 (1999),

1412. In the United States the process toward ratification begins when the president endorses the document by signing it. It is then submitted to the Senate, along with any administration recommendations. The Senate Foreign Relations Committee first considers the convention, conducting hearings to monitor public reaction. The Foreign Relations Committee may then recommend the convention to the Senate, possibly with reservations or qualifications. Such reservations are often based on the need to enact new legislation in order to conform to a convention. However, the federal system of the U.S. government gives individual states, not the national government, the right to make law in many areas such as criminal and family law. Next the full Senate considers the convention. Finally, if the Senate approves the convention, the president formally notifies the UN that the United States has ratified and thus become a state party to the convention. The United States and Somalia are the only countries that have not ratified the Convention on the Rights of the Child. The United States is also one of only a handful of countries that have not ratified the Convention on the Elimination of All Forms of Discrimination against Women. Finally, the United States has not ratified the International Covenant on Economic, Social and Cultural Rights or the American Convention on Human Rights.

19. Thalif Deen, "U.S. Under Fire for Labor Rights Abuses," 3/17/2006. The article reports that ICFTU Secretary General Guy Ryder noted that "the credibility of the United States . . . is severely damaged by the lack of protection for working people . . . within its own borders." Also see Thomas Kent, "Putin Challenges U.S. on Human Rights," 6/2/2006, http://www.forbes.com/home/feeds/ap/2006/06/02/ap2790746.html; "Human Rights Record of the United States in 2004," http://english.people.com.cn, 200503/03/eng20050303_175406.html, both last searched 2/28/2006. On rejection of the U.S. model, see Ronald Asmus, Philip P. Everts, and Pierangelo Isernia, "Across the Atlantic and the Political Aisle: The Double Divide in U.S.-European Relations," *Transatlantic Trends* 2004, http://www.compagnia.torino.it/English/comunicazioni/pdf/GMF%20Trends%202004.pdf, last searched 6/24/2006; Andrew Kohut and Bruce Stokes, "Two Americas, One American: The Differences That Divide Us Are Much Smaller Than Those That Set Us Apart from the Rest of the World," 6/6/2006, http://pewresearch.org/obdeck/?ObDeckID=29; "The Problem of American Exceptionalism: Our Values and Attitudes May Be Misunderstood but They Have Consequences on the World Scene," http://pewresearch.org/obdeck/?ObDeckID=23, both last searched 6/26/2006.

20. Brian Knowlton, "The U.S. Image Abroad: Even China's Is Better," *International Herald Tribune*, 6/24/2005; see the surveys at the Pew Global Attitudes Project, http://pewglobal.org/reports/display.php?ReportID=252, last searched 6/24/2006. On attitudes toward the role of government, see Kohut and Stokes, "Two Americas, One American." Americans are skeptical that large state bureaucracies can and should deliver public goods such as education or health care.

21. Amnesty International United States of America, http://web.amnesty.org/web/web.nsf/print/&A350B3812B2715680256FF0003B7FA6, last searched 4/18/2006; http://www.amnestyusa.org/countries/usa/document.do?id=ar&yr=2005; and http://www.amnestyusa.org/us/index.do, both last searched 6/14/2006.

22. Human Rights Watch, "World Report 2005, United States," at http://www.hrw.org, last searched 5/16/2006.

23. The National Health Interview Survey at www.cdc.gov/nchs/about/major/nhis/ released200606.htm#1. Also see http://www.merck.com/cr/enabling_access/developed_ world/in_the_us/home.html, both searched 6/26/2006/. Statistics on educational attainment (for 2004) also show significant disparities between minorities and white. While some 85.8% of all white non-Hispanic Americans and 80.6% of all non-Hispanic African Americans graduated high school only 58.4% of Hispanics did so. Some 27.7% of non-Hispanic whites, but only 17.6% of non-Hispanic blacks and only 12.1% of Hispanics graduated college in 2004.

24. For example in 1789, Congress passed the Alien Tort Claims Act, which provides federal courts with jurisdiction over violations of the "law of nations."

25. United States Institute of Peace, Special Report, "U.S. Human Rights Policy: A 20-Year Assessment," 6/16/1999; and John Parker, "A Nation Apart," *The Economist*, http://www.economist.com/surveys/printerfriendly.cfm?story_id=2172066, last searched 6/12/2006.

26. U.S. Human Rights and Democracy Strategy: Supporting Human Rights and Democracy: The U.S. Record 2005–2006, at www.state.gov/g/drl/rls/shrd/ 2005/63942.htm: and "Fact Sheet: Supporting Human Rights and Democracy," which argues that human rights is a cornerstone of U.S. foreign policy, www.state.gov/g/drl/rls/64132.htm, both last searched 4/10/2006. President Bush said, "Freedom by its nature must be chosen and defended by citizens." In FY 2005, the State Department reported that the United States budgeted $1.4 billion for human rights and democracy programming. For a scholarly criticism of the U.S. commitment, see Jan Hancock, "Understanding Universal Human Rights Discourse in Times of Exception," ISA Conference, 3/23/2006; in possession of author.

27. Human rights policymakers direct much of their human rights assistance toward projects that advance rights essential to democracy and good governance, projects that expand religious freedom and those that promote labor rights. http://www.state .gov/g/drl/; http://www.state.gov/g/drl/c7607.htm (on programs); http://www.state .gov/g/drl/c10790.htm; http://www.state.gov/g/drl/lbr/; www.state.gov/g/drl/irf/; and http://www.usaid.gov. For an example of U.S. human rights priorities see the Middle East Partnership Initiative, at http://mepi.state.gov/c10120.htm, all searched 6/21/2006.

28. The value of trade in goods and services (imports and exports) was 31.5% of GDP in 2004. Economic Report of the President, 2005, pp. 34–35; and 2005 Trade Policy Agenda, p. 5. Figures updated for June 2006, http://www.census.gov/foreign-trade/Press-Release/current_press_release/exh1.txt, last searched 6/21/2006.

29. On an overview of U.S. trade policies and practices, see WTO Trade Policy Review, WT/TPR/S/160, 24. The report notes close to 38% of all tariff items entered the Untied States duty free. Also see ICFTU, "Internationally Recognized Core Labour Standards in the United States: Report for the WTO General Council Review of the Trade Policies of the United States," 3/13–15, 2006, p. 2, http://www.icftu.org. On criticism of U.S. agricultural policies, see Todd Moss and Alicia Bannon, "Africa and the Battle over Agricultural Protectionism," http://www.cgdev.org/doc/expert %20pages/moss/Moss.pdf, both last searched 6/10/2006.

30. On U.S. development of the GATT/WTO, see Susan Aaronson, *Trade and the American Dream*. On U.S. influence on the WTO see Sylvia Ostry, "China and the WTO: The Transparency Issue," *UCLA Journal of International and Foreign Affairs* 3(1) (1998), 3–11.

31. WT/TPR/S/160, 13.

32. William H. Cooper, "Free Trade Agreements: Impact on U.S. Trade and Implications for U.S. Trade Policy," RL31356, 4/19/2006, CRS-4. On aggressive unilateralism, see Jagdish Bhagwati and Hugh T. Patrick, eds., *Aggressive Unilateralism: America's 301 Trade Policy and the World Trading System* (Ann Arbor: University of Michigan Press, 1990).

33. WTO/TPR/S/160, 14; and WTO/TPR/G/160, 11.

34. WT/TPR/S/160, vii, and "Concluding Remarks by the Chairperson," 3/22–24/2006. The Brazilian government report was refreshing in that it also blamed its trade problems on its own bad policies. Brazilian Report on Trade Barriers by Roberto Abdenur," pp. 9 and 11, http://www.brasilemb.org/trade_investment/barr_intro2005.pdf, last searched 5/30/2006.

35. Press Release, House Committee on Ways and Means, http://waysandmeans .house.gov/News.asp?FormMode=print&ID=434.

36. Robert McMahan, "The Rise in Bilateral Free Trade Agreements," Council on Foreign Relations, 6/13/2006, http://www.cfr.org/publication/10890/rise_ in_bilateral_free_trade_agreements.html; and Congressional Budget Office, CBO, "The Pros and Cons of Pursuing Free Trade Agreements," 7/31/2003, http://www.cbo .gov/showdoc.cfm?index=4458&sequence=0, both last searched 6/15/2006. Also see WTO Consultative Board, "The Future," 19. South Africa's former trade minister, Alex Erwin on p. 22. The WTO Consultative Board noted that many of these FTAs have "non-trade" objectives, including "one-sided provisions on IPR," and could be designed as "templates" for new demands in the WTO – an oblique criticism of the United States.

37. Evan Davis, "The Death of the WTO's Doha Talks," news.bbc.co.uk/2/hi/ business/5215318.stm; BBC, "Leaders Cling to Trade Talk Hopes," news.bbc.co.uk/ 2/hi/business/5213728.stm; WTO Talks, India Not to Budge from Its Stand Says Nath," http://www.zeenews.com/znnew/articles.asp?aid=311354&ssid=50&sid=BUS; Isabel Goncalves, "African Reaction to WTO Collapse Mixed," http://www.ibtimes. com/articles/20060725/africa-wto-tarriffs-subsidies.htm; and Reuters, "U.S. Says EU Statement on WTO Talks Failure 'False'," http://www.redorbit.com/news/general/ 586569/us_says_eu_statement_on_wto_talks_failure_false/index.html; and on restarting, see WTO, "Lamy Asks for Support on Final Stretch of Negotiations," 3/23/2007, http://www.wto.org/english/news_e/sppl_e/sppl57_e.htm last searched 4/1/2007.

38. The United States reports these duty-free benefits apply to some 85% of the products in the U.S. tariff schedule. WTO/TPR/S/160, 33, 34 On the belief that trade is more powerful than aid, see *Economic Report of the President*, 2005, p. 165. The United States also allows products of the U.S. insular possessions, freely associated states such as Micronesia, and the West Bank and Gaza unilateral tariff preference treatment.

39. The United States determines GSP country eligibility based on income and specific conditions such as compliance with labor rights, help in the war on terrorism, and protecting IPR. A country can be graduated from GSP when a country reaches the per capita income cutoff or when a total value of a product it exports to the United States reaches a specific cutoff threshold. Communist countries do not receive benefits.

40. 2005 Trade Policy Agenda, p. 274; and Fact Sheet, Coalition for GSP, http://www.tradepartnership.com, last searched 6/6/2006. Some countries lost GSP

eligibility when they became members of the European Union (for example, Hungary and Poland). Bahrain and Barbados were graduated from GSP on January 1, 2006.

41. "Grassley Reluctant to Take Up GSP Renewal, Ties It to Doha Talks," 2/17/2006; "Grassley Warns Brazil, India on GSP; Stops Short of Predicting Graduation," _Inside U.S. Trade_, 2/17/2006; and "Schwab Says GSP Review will Consider Limits on India, Brazil," _Inside U.S. Trade_, 8/1/2006. In 2005, 22.3% of India's exports, 14.9% of Brazil's exports, 36% of Croatia's exports, and 17.4% of South Africa's exports to the United States were based on using GSP. "The US Generalized System of Preferences Program: An Update," http://www.tradepartnership.com.

42. 2005 Trade Policy Agenda, pp. 277–281.

43. On the most recent budget, see http://www.usaid.gov/policy/budget/cbj2007/si/trade.html. The funds directed toward labor rights have been significantly reduced in recent years. See Kim Elliott, "A Better Way Forward on Trade and Labor Rights," 3/29/2007, at http://www.cgdev.org/content/publications/detail/13380. Some members of Congress have introduced legislation to improve coordination of trade policy and trade capacity building. See http://thomas.loc.gov/cgi-bin/cpquery/?&sid= cp109UC8hl&refer=&r_n=hr486.109&db_id=109&item=&sel=TOC_152896&

44. WT/TPR/S/160, 13–15.

45. Richard F. Grimmet, "Foreign Policy Roles of the President and Congress," CRS Report, 6/1/1999, http://usinfo.state.gov/usa/infousa/politics/pres/fpolicy.htm. In 1986, Congress enacted comprehensive sanctions against South Africa over the veto of President Reagan.

46. http://www.ustr.gov/Who_We_Are/Mission_of_the_USTR.html

47. Five members from each house are formally appointed under the statute as official congressional advisors on trade policy. USTR also provides detailed briefings on a regular basis for the Congressional Oversight Group (which includes members from a broad range of committees, not just the trade writing committees [Senate Finance and House Ways and Means]), http://www.ustr.gov/Who_We_Are/Mission_of_the_USTR.html. On public hearings, see http://www.ustr.gov/outreach/transcripts/index.htm and 2005 Trade Policy Agenda, p. 289. http://www.ustr.gov/Document_Library/Reports_ Publications/2005/2005_Trade_Policy_Agenda/Section_Index.html?ht=.

48. For information on what other U.S. government agencies do on trade, see http:// www.ustr.gov/Who_We_Are/USTR's_Relationship_with_Other_Government_Agencies .html, last searched 5/20/2006.

49. Transparency is very important to the working of the U.S. government. U.S. law mandates that "interested persons, including foreigners, can petition for the issuance, amendment or repeal of a rule." Federal government agencies must respond to all such petitions. Under the Congressional Review Act, Congress may overturn a rule, or such rules may be judicially reviewed. 5 USC 801 et seq, in WT/TPR/S/160, 50. Also see 2005 Trade Policy Agenda, p. 284, and notices on http://www.ustr.gov/ Document_Library/Federal_Register_Notices/2006/March/Section_Index.html, last searched 5/22/2006.

50. Consists of political appointees at the level of deputy U.S. trade representative or under secretary.

51. These executives, who are generally political appointees, also make decisions on cross-cutting trade issues that can affect national security.

52. Advisors on the ACTPN are vetted by the White House Office of Personnel.

53. The policy advisory committees are appointed by the USTR alone or in conjunction with other Cabinet officers. USTR solely manages the Intergovernmental Policy Advisory Committee (IGPAC). The others are the Agricultural Policy Advisory Committee (APAC), Labor Advisory Committee (LAC), and Trade and Environment Policy Advisory Committee (TEPAC). Each committee provides advice based on the perspective of its specific area. According to USTR, representatives are appointed jointly by USTR and the Secretaries of Commerce and Agriculture, respectively. Each sectoral or technical committee represents a specific sector or commodity group (such as textiles or dairy products) and provides specific technical advice concerning the effect that trade policy decisions may have on its sector, http://www.ustr.gov/Who_We_Are/Mission_of_the_USTR.html. GAO recently criticized the process, noting that policymakers marginalize labor and environmental groups; and the process doesn't adequately cover broad based trade issues that don't fit in neat sectoral or issue boxes. GAO, "International Trade: Advisory Committee System Should be Updated to Better Serve U.S. Policy Needs," GAO-02-876, p. 2–6.

54. USTR asserts that recommendations for candidates for committee membership are collected from a number of sources, including members of Congress, associations and organizations, publications, and other individuals who have demonstrated an interest or expertise in U.S. trade policy. Membership selection is based on qualifications, geography, and the needs of the specific committee. Members pay for their own travel and other related expenses and must obtain a security clearance, http://www.ustr.gov/Who_We_Are/Mission_of_the_USTR.html. For a broader discussion of these issues, see Aaronson, *Redefining*, 43–45.

55. For example, the IPR advisory committee includes representatives of law firms, associations, and companies and not scientists, drug consumers, or file sharers. GAO-04-912, p. 14–15.

56. For example, to ensure that it obtains objective advice on public health questions, USTR recently noted "we are seeking...qualified applicants from the public health and health care communities to serve on the Industry Trade Advisory Committee on Chemicals, Pharmaceuticals, Health Science Products and Services and the Industry Trade Advisory Committee on Intellectual Property." USTR, "Facts on the Doha Round: United States Leadership in Providing Access to Medicines," http://www.ustr.gov. This open call for advisors resulted from a lawsuit by public health officials demanding to have their views represented on six international trade advisory committees. "Federal Court to Decide on Future of Public Health Lawsuit," *Inside U.S. Trade*, 4/28/2006, p. 13.

57. USTR must submit an authorizing bill for negotiations and an implementing bill. Congress has ninety days to vote up or down on an implementing bill (for example, to approve a trade agreement) or sixty days if the bill does not propose changes to tariff schedules and the revenue they provide. Michael J. Glennon, Thomas M. Franck, and Robert C. Cassidy, Jr., *United States Foreign Relations Law: Documents and Sources, International Economic Regulation*, Vol. 4 (London: Oceana, 1984), p. 40–45.

58. Not surprisingly, these limitations have led some trade agreement critics to argue that the fast-track process is flawed and undemocratic. For suggestions, see Aaronson, *Redefining*, pp. 15–25; and Bruce Stokes and Pat Choate, *Democratizing U.S. Trade Policy* (Washington, DC: Council on Foreign Relations, 2001).

59. GAO, Report to the Chairman, Committee on Ways and Means, U.S. House, "International Trade: Improvements Needed to Track and Archive Trade Agreements," GAO/NSIAD-00-24, 12/14/1999, pp. 1–15 and 26–28.

60. Rules include technical regulations and sanitary and phytosanitary measures. Information about rulemaking is online at http://www.gpoaccess.gov/fr/index.html and http://www.gpoaccess.gov/cfr/index.html. Also see WTO/TPR/G/160, p. 49.

61. Under the Trade Act of 2002, the Department of Labor prepares three reports: the U.S. Employment Impact Review, the Labor Rights Report which examines labor rights abroad, and the laws governing exploitative child labor. See www.dol.gov/ilab/media/reports/usfta.main.htm.

62. Aaronson, *Taking Trade to the Streets*, pp. 32–33 and 35–49.

63. Sandra Polaski, "Cambodia Blazes a New Path to Economic Growth and Job Creation," Trade, Equity and Development Project, No. 51, Oct. 2004, pp. 16–17. The two countries could develop this special arrangement because Cambodia was not yet a member of the WTO, and textiles were subject to specific quotas under temporary WTO rules. Polaski, an expert on labor rights, believes the agreement worked because it created a positive incentive that operated prospectively after Cambodia demonstrated improvements in labor standards. http://www.ustr.gov/Document_Library/Press_Releases/2002/January/US-Cambodian_Textile_Agreement_Links_Increasing_Trade_with_Improving_Workers'_Rights.html

64. Labor rights advocates, development officials, and scholars view the project as successful. Because the project generated information for market actors, companies were able to choose factories and make sourcing decisions based on information about workplace conditions generated by the ILO. Workers' rights improved, although Cambodia continued to have some labor rights problems. Sandra Polaski, "Cambodia Blazes"; Regina Abrami, "Worker Rights and Global Trade: The U.S.-Cambodia Bilateral Textile Trade Agreement" (Harvard Business School, Case Study No-9-703-034, 2004); and Kevin Kolben, "The New Politics of Linkage: India's Opposition to the Workers Rights Clause," *Indiana Journal of Global Legal Studies* 13(1) (2006), 35. USTR has reported that the United States will continue to model how Cambodia follows through on its commitments to funding the ILO monitoring project and whether labor rights continue to improve. On the role of the World Bank and on U.S. monitoring, see 2005 Trade Policy Agenda, p. 239.

65. On the ILO program, see http://www.betterfactories.org/ILO/default.aspx?z=1&c=1; http://www.betterfactories.org/ILO/faq.aspx?z=9&c=1. On outside perspectives, see Elizabeth Becker, "Labor Standards Help Cambodia Keep Customers," *New York Times*, 5/11/2005, http://www.iht.com/articles/2005/05/10/business/textile.php; and Sandra Polaski, "Combining Global and Local Forces: The Case of Labor Rights in Cambodia," *World Development*, 5/1/2006, at http://www.carnegieendowment.org/publications/index.cfm?fa=view&id=18544&prog=zgp&proj=zt The U.S. government wrote in 2006 that the Cambodian government selectively enforces labor rights. "Most Cambodian workers were subsistence rice farmers, and although there was an expanding service sector, most urban workers were engaged in small scale commerce, self employed skilled labor, or unskilled day labor. Only a small fraction (estimated at less than 1 percent) of the labor force was unionized, and the nascent trade union movement was weak but growing stronger. Unions suffered from a lack of resources, training, and experience. Unions were concentrated in the garment and

footwear industries, where approximately 40 to 50 percent of the 333,144 workers were union members. . . . Enforcement of the right of association and freedom from antiunion discrimination was poor. The government's enforcement efforts were further hampered by a lack of political will and by confused financial and political relationships with employers and union leaders. The government also suffered from a lack of resources, including trained, experienced labor inspectors, in part because it did not pay staff adequate salaries. The law prohibits forced or compulsory labor, including forced labor by children, but the government did not enforce its provisions adequately." U.S. Department of State 2006 Report on Country Human Rights Practices, 2006, Cambodia at http://www.state.gov/g/drl/rls/hrrpt/2006/78769.htm

66. The Comprehensive Anti-Apartheid Act of 1986 (PL 99-440) was signed 10/2/1986. States and local governments as well as universities played a major role in the antiapartheid movement that led to the sanctions. See Robert K. Massie, *Loosing the Bonds: The United States and South Africa in the Apartheid Years* (New York: Doubleday, 1997).

67. International Religious Freedom Act of 1998 (H.R. 2431) and its amendment of 1999 (PL 106–55), http://www.uscirf.gov/about/authorizinglegislation.html, last searched 6/06/2006.

68. The executive order cited "continuing concern about the presence and activities of certain terrorist groups, including Hamas and Palestinian Islamic Jihad, and the prevalence of human rights violations, including slavery, restrictions on religious freedom, and restrictions on political freedom." In October 2002, President Bush stated that "[b]ecause the actions and policies of the Government of Sudan continue to pose an unusual and extraordinary threat to the national security and foreign policy of the United States, the national emergency declared on November 3, 1997, and the measures adopted on that date to deal with that emergency must continue in effect beyond November 3, 2002," http://www.whitehouse.gov/news/releases/2004/09/20040909-10. The Sudan Peace Act, signed into law by President Bush, outlined stiff sanctions, ranging from a downgrading of diplomatic relations to a UN arms embargo, which could have been imposed if the Sudanese government negotiated in bad faith with rebel forces, primarily the SPLA, html://www.eia.doe.gov/emeu/cabs/sanction.html, both last searched 6/10/2006.

69. Message to Congress, 5/23/2001, http://www.presidency.ucsb.edu/ws/print.php?pid =61407; and http://www.treas.gov/offices/enforcement/ofac/legal/eo/diamond_eo.pdf.

70. The Cuban Liberty and Democracy Solidarity Act (PL 104-114); the Iran and Libya Sanctions Act of 1996 (PL 104172). See Grimmet, "Foreign Policy Roles," p. 15, footnotes 51 and 52.

71. The text of the Burmese Freedom and Democracy Act is at http://www.thomas.gov/cgi-bin/query/D?c108:1:./temp/~mdbseIWWS1; for a contrary view, see David I. Steinberg, "Burma: Feel-Good U.S. Sanctions Wrongheaded," *Yaleglobal*, 5/19/2004, http://yaleglobal.yale.edu/display.article?id=3901.

72. Vladimir N. Pregelj, CRS Issue Brief, "IB93107: Normal Trade Relations (Most-Favored Nation) Policy of the United States," p. 8. Although the president was required to replace the term "most-favored nation" in 1998, the MFN term is used internationally and in U.S. trade agreements.

73. Pregelj, "Normal," p. 3. The decision included Czechoslovakia, a member of the WTO (see Chapter 1).

74. Pregelj, "Normal," p. 4. The president's waiver authority and the existing waivers are renewed annually in midyear; and the country has concluded a trade agreement with the United States providing for reciprocal MFN treatment, and the agreement is approved by joint resolution enacted under a specific fast-track procedure. The president's report can be disapproved by a fast-track enactment of a joint resolution.

75. For example, in October 1982, Congress suspended Poland's MFN status after the Polish government took steps to repress dissent. The most controversial issue related to U.S. MFN treatment has been U.S. policy toward China. Members of Congress were particularly concerned about Chinese treatment of political dissidents and minorities and China's suppression of worker rights. However, after years of debate, Congress granted China permanent normal trade relations status on December 27, 2001. http://www.usembassy-china.org.cn/econ/grants1227.html, last searched 7/20/2006.

76. Committee on Ways and Means, Subcommittee on Trade, "To Explore Permanent Normal Trade Relations for Russia," 4/11/2002; and "Vietnam PNTR Could Be Delayed over Religious Freedom Questions," *Inside U.S. Trade*, 7/21/2006, 1, 14.

77. Statement of Congressman Chris Smith, "Congressional-Executive Commission on China Hearing on Combating Human Trafficking in China: Domestic and International Efforts," 3/6/2006. The Global Online Freedom Act of 2006 (H.R. 4780) attempts to establish minimum corporate standards for online freedom and prohibits U.S. businesses from hosting an e-mail server or search engine (services trade) within countries that systematically restrict internet freedom, http://www.cecc.gov/pages/hearings/2006/20060306/ChrisSmith.php?PHPSESSID=1580a13cf3bd746981f 8762e44c3b165. The bill is available at http://www.govtrack.us/congress/billtext.xpd?bill=h109-4780, both last searched 6/12/2006.

78. NA, "Hot Topic: Will the New Congress Shift Gears on Free Trade?," *Wall Street Journal*, 11/18/2006, A7; Alan Beattie, "Transcript: Susan Schwab Interview," *Financial Times*, 11/17/2006, http://www.ft.com/cms/s/3e115144-7613-11db-8284-0000779e2340.html; Sebastian Mallaby: "Breaking the Trade Deadlock: Opposing Parties Can Join Forces," *Washington Post*, 11/20/2006, A17.

79. Some prominent House Republicans expressed support for the Democrats' proposals. The Democrats would also like to see programs to cushion workers from trade related job losses, health insurance, pension portability, retraining programs, wage insurance and an expansion of the patchwork of unemployment insurance programs. The Democrats rejected an earlier compromise proposal from the administration, which attempted to reference ILO standards while preventing the United States from taking on any trade obligations with respect to the ILO. Martin Vaughan, "Rangel Plan Might Be Only the Start of Talks," *Congress Daily*, 3/28/2007; Steven Pearlstein, "A Grand Bargain to Rescue Trade Policy," *Washington Post*, 3/28/2007, D1; Doug Palmer, "Bush Tells Congress He Will Sign Panama Trade Pact", Reuters, 3/30/2007, http://www.reuters.com/article/politicsNews/idUSN3028576420070330, last searched 4/1/2007. Update as of June, NA, "FTA Template Eludes Conclusion as Levin Seeks to Sway Labor," *Inside U.S. Trade*, 6/15/2007.

80. The ILO Declaration says all members "have an obligation arising from the very fact of membership in the Organization to respect, to promote and to realize" core labor rights. http://www.ilo.org/dyn/declaris/DECLARATIONWEB.INDEXPAGE

81. If the parties could not agree, they could appoint a panel to review cases on issues such as minimum wages, health and safety, and child labor. According to Kimberley

Elliott and Richard Freeman, allegations of forced labor and discrimination are evaluated by a panel of independent experts. It also included the possibility of fines for child labor and other major labor issues. See Elliott and Freeman, *Can Labor Standards*, p. 86. The Congressional Research Service concluded that the NAALC has had positive effects on labor rights in Mexico. It has put pressure on Mexico to enforce its own labor law, permitting a small but growing number of workers the right to organize and bargain collectively; it has led to greater scrutiny of that country's labor law enforcement; and it has led to a reduction of workplace injuries, which suggests better enforcement. Mary Jane Bolle, "NAFTA Labor Side Agreement: Lessons for the Worker Rights and Fast-Track Debate," CRS Report for Congress 97–861E, 12/12/1997, pp. 11–13. For an alternative perspective, see Analysis: the NAALC, www.duke.edu/web/pps114/policy2003/2f/index6a.html.

82. John J. Sweeney, President, AFL-CIO, Testimony on the Jordan Free Trade Agreement, Senate Finance Committee, 3/20/2001, 2–3.

83. Statements by members of Congress on the Jordan-U.S. Free Trade Agreement, http://www.jordanembassyus.org/new/aboutjordan/uj3.shtml#back, last searched 7/30/2006.

84. Grassley noted that former USTR Charlene Barshefsky testified that the labor and environment provisions in the Jordan FTA "while restating the existing commitment of both countries to environmental protection and the ILO's [International Labor Organization] core labor standards, neither imposes new standards nor bars change or reform of national laws as each country sees fit." Ambassador Michael Smith, former Deputy United States Trade Representative and the first American Ambassador to the General Agreement on Tariffs and Trade, testified that "Articles 5 and 6 [of the Jordan FTA] as written are largely fluff, open to widely differing (even if plausible) interpretations and, as such, causes for possible unfortunate differences between Jordan and the United States in the years ahead as the agreement is implemented. Articles 5 and 6 do not advance the 'cause' of either international environmental or labor affairs and add only confusion to what should be a straightforward free trade agreement. Indeed, the only result I can foresee is countries adopting lower environmental and labor standards for fear of themselves being unable to effectively enforce higher standards – hardly a desired result." U.S. Department of State, "Senator Opposes," http://canberra.usembassy.gov/hyper/2002/0924/epf211.htm

85. Pier, "Workers' Rights Provisions," footnotes. 69–70.

86. Elliott and Freeman, *Can Labor Standards*, 88–89; and Destler, *American Trade Politics*, 270, 340–342.

87. Marwan Muasher, Ambassador of the Hashemite Kingdom of Jordan to the United States of America, to the Honorable Robert B. Zoellick, 7/23/2001, and Ambassador Robert B. Zoellick, U.S. Trade Representative, United States of America, to His Excellency Marwan Muasher, Ambassador of the Hashemite Kingdom of Jordan to the United States, 7/23/2001, copies in possession of author.

88. House Report 107–176-Part 1-"United States-Jordan Free Trade Area Implementation Act, VII. Additional Views." Some 13 Democrats expressed this view. See Secthttp://thomas.loc.gov/cgi-bin/cpquery/?&dbname=cp107&sid=cp107gre9Q&refer=&r_n=hr176p1.107&item=&sel=TOC_53714&

89. This means no member's name was recorded as they voted. This gave individual members cover for their votes.

90. Section 2102 (a) Trade Negotiating Objectives of the Bipartisan Trade Promotion Authority Act of 2002. The overall U.S. labor rights negotiating objectives are to "promote respect for worker rights and the rights of children consistent with core labor standards of the ILO . . . and an understanding of the relationship between trade and worker rights; to seek provisions in trade agreements under which parties to these agreements strive to ensure that they do not weaken or reduce the protections afforded in domestic environmental and labor laws as an encouragement for trade; . . . and to promote universal ratification and full compliance with ILO Convention No. 182 . . . " on the prohibition of child labor. As of June 2007, the United States does not promote the same rights as the core ILO labor standards. The United States does not include nondiscrimination in employment.

91. Section 2102, (b) (11) Principal Trade Negotiating Objectives.

92. Section 2102, (c) Promotion of Certain Priorities.

93. In response, USTR set up a new office of labor affairs. That office works closely with officials from the State Department, the Labor Department, and the U.S. Agency for International Development to help countries with which the United States is negotiating (or has negotiated) trade agreements to improve labor rights laws and enforcement. The two-person office oversees and negotiates labor provisions in multilateral, regional, and bilateral free trade agreements, formulates recommendations concerning countries' adherence to workers' rights provisions of U.S. trade preference programs, and develops U.S. positions on the relationship between trade and labor in the International Labor Organization, World Trade Organization, Organization for Economic Cooperation and Development, Inter-American Conference of Ministers of Labor, and other relevant international bodies, http://www.ustr.gov/Who_We_Are/Bios/Lewis_Karesh.html, last searched 6/06/2006.

94. For a good overview, see I. M. Destler and Peter J. Balint, *The New Politics of American Trade: Trade Labor and the Environment Policy Analyses in International Economics* 58, (Washington, DC: IIE, 1999).

95. "U.S. Chamber Welcomes U.S.-Jordan Free Trade Agreement But Opposes Non-Trade Provisions" 10/25/2000. The Chamber, the world's largest business federation representing more than 3 million businesses, does not believe it is appropriate to try and address social and labor issues in trade agreements. http://www.uschamber.com/ press/releases/2000/October/00-185.htm. Other influential business associations were not as adamant that these were nontrade issues. The Business Roundtable appeared to accept the link. See Business Roundtable, TPA Letter to House of Representatives, 12/3/2001, at www.businessroundtable.org/taskforces/taskforce/document.as . . . ; The National Association of Manufacturers said they were open to "dialogue" on linking trade and labor. Keith Koffler, "Business Officials to Fight Labor, Enviro Trade Sanctions," *National Journal's Congress Daily*, 2/16/2001http://www.ilwu19.com/ rustyhook/archives/spring2001/labor.htm

96. Human Rights Watch Briefing Paper, "Labor Rights and Trade: Guidance for the United States in Trade Accord Negotiations, 2002, at hrw.org/press/2002/laborrights-bck.htm; and Testimony of John J. Sweeney, President, American Federation of Labor and Congress of Industrial Organizations on the Jordan Free Trade Agreement, 3/20/2001.

97. NA, "Globalization: What Americans Are Worried About," *Business Week*, 4/24/2000, p. 4. This poll of 1,024 Americans found some 75% think trade agreements should

prevent unfair competition by countries that violate workers rights; 77% thought these trade agreements should prevent the loss of U.S. jobs, and 79% thought Congress should only give China permanent access to the U.S. markets when it agrees to meet human rights and labor standards. A more recent 2004 PIPA/Knowledge Networks poll found that nine in ten favor incorporating labor and environmental standards into trade agreements. "Majority of Americans Disapproves of U.S. Government Approach to Trade: Wants More Efforts to Mitigate Effects on Workers, Environment," 1/22/2004, http://worldpublicopinion.org/pipa/articles/btglobalizationtradera/81.php?nid=&id=&pnt=81&lb=btgl, last searched 6/2/2006.

98. Steven Kull, "Mexican, U.S. Publics Strongly Support Labor and Environmental Standards in Trade Agreements," 7/20/2005, http://worldpublicopinion.org/pipa/articles/brlatinamericara/73.php?nid=&id=&pnt=73&lb=btgl . . .

99. As Carol Pier of Human Rights Watch has noted, the decision to limit the labor rights provisions subject to binding dispute settlement is suggested by the Bipartisan Trade Promotion Act. Carol Pier, "Workers' Rights Provisions in Fast Track Authority, 1974–2007, A Historical Perspective and Current Analysis," 13 *Indiana Journal of Global Legal Studies* 77 (2006), 5. Pier notes that TPA could either "give rise to enforceable workers' rights protections or . . . preclude this possibility."

100. Labor Advisory Committee for Trade Negotiations and Trade Policy, "The U.S.-Singapore Free Trade Agreement," 2/28/2003, 6, 16.

101. William B. Clatanoff, Assistant U.S. Trade Representative for Labor, to George Becker, Chair, Labor Advisory, and Response to Labor Advisory Committee Report on the Proposed Chile and Singapore FTAs, no date, 2–3, www.ustr.gov/assets/Trade_Agreements/Bilateral/Singapore_FTA/Reports/asset_upload_file763_3221.pdf, last searched 7/30/2006.

102. Report of the Labor Advisory Committee for Trade Negotiations and Trade Policy, Chile, 2/28/2003, 16; Australia, 3/12/2004, 14; Central America, 3/19/2004, 15; Morocco, 4/6/2004, 9; Dominican Republic, 4/22/2004, 7; Bahrain, 7/14/2004, 8; Oman, Peru, 2/1/2006, 12. It is interesting to note that the membership of the LAC went from 58 in 2004 to 28 (26 from unions and 2 from academia). These reports are all available at the http://www.ustr.gov/Trade_Sectors/Labor/Section_Index.html and for individual trade agreements, and labor reports at each trade agreement's Web page linkable from http://www.ustr.gov/Trade_Agreements/Bilateral/Section_Index.html

103. Human Rights Watch argued that the existing dispute settlement mechanisms have often failed to address allegations made in complaints and, in some cases, have issued reports lacking findings of fact; and ministerial consultations, often recommended by National Administrative Offices, have resulted in agreements that provide little possibility for resolving problems identified in complaints. The Jordan FTA, for its part, relies exclusively on the trading partners' political will to enforce the accord's labor rights commitments, thereby compromising the implementation of those commitments, http://hrw.org/press/2002/10/laborrights-bck.htm, last searched 6/06/2006.

104. USTR, "Morocco FTA Leads to Progress on Labor Reform, Cooperative Approach Produces Real Results," 6/23/2004.

105. "USTR Cool to Finance Labor Amendment to Oman Draft FTA Bill," *Inside U.S. Trade*, 5/19/2006, pp. 1 and 19; "USTR Cites Oman Labor Rights Move in Advance of House Vote on FTA," *Inside U.S. Trade*, 7/14/2006, 9; and http://www.thomas.gov/cgi-bin/bdquery/z?d109:HR05684:@@@X. USTR Press Release, "Status of Oman

Labor Commitments," 7/2006, http://www.ustr.gov/assets/Document_Library/Fact_Sheets/2006/asset_upload_file562_9641.pdf

106. Steven Greenhouse and Michael Barbaro, "An Ugly Side of Free Trade: Sweatshops in Jordan," *New York Times*, 5/3/2006; "Jordan Curbing Abuse of Workers: Minister," *The Peninsula*, http://www.thepeninsulaqatar.com/Display_news.asp?section=World_News&subsection=Gulf%2C+Middle+East+%26+Africa&month=June2006&file=World_News2006061844959.xml and "USTR Cool to Finance Labor Amendment to Oman Draft FTA Bill," *Inside U.S. Trade*, 5/19/2006, pp. 1–2.

107. Interview with Kimberley Ann Elliott, Institute for International Economics, 6/3/2006; Kimberley Ann Elliott, "A Better Way Forward on Trade and Labor Standards," 3/29/2007, http://www.cgdev.org/content/publications/detail/13380; and "U.S. Budget Proposal Shortchanges Labor Rights," http://hrw.org/English/docs/2004/02/04/usint7268.htm, last searched 6/7/2006.

108. For a good assessment of the problems of U.S. capacity building, see GAO, "Foreign Assistance: U.S. Trade Capacity Building Extensive, but Its Effectiveness Has Yet to Be Evaluated," GAO-05–150, 2/2005. No congressional committee has direct responsibility to fund capacity building. In June 2006, Congressman Jim Kolbe proposed gathering trade-capacity-building funds, scattered throughout the U.S. government, into a new account to provide an incentive to countries to enter into new trade agreements. "Needs and Solutions: Trade Capacity Building in Sub-Saharan Africa," 3/17/2006, summary at http://www.carnegieendowment.org/events/index.cfm?fa=eventDetail&id=865&&prog=zgp&proj=zted, Committee on Appropriations, Subcommittee on Foreign Operations and export Financing, 5/19/2006, http://appropriations.house.gov/index.cfm?fuseAction=PressRelease . . . , both last searched 6/7/2006. On the new fund, see "House Appropriations Approves New Trade Capacity Fund for 2007," *Inside U.S. Trade*, 5/26/2006, p. 11. Kolbe's plan would take money from funds in USAID and the Department of State, not USTR.

109. Thus, USAID agreed to purchase and install computers and provide training to manage trade data in the CAFTA countries. The U.S. Department of Labor contributed to projects to strengthen labor relations. The Humane Society of the United States committed to provide assistance to broaden outreach to civil society and agreed to provide workshops in administrative procedures. And the Worldwide Responsible Apparel Production certification program agreed to train governments, manufacturers, and civil society leaders in factory compliance and labor inspection. See Tratado de Libre Commercio Entre Centroamericay Estados Unidos, "Conceptual Proposal for a National Action Plan: Costa Rica," http://www.ustr.gov/assets/Trade_Agreements/Bilateral/CAFTA/asset_upload_file310_3357.pdf; and "Strengthening Democracy, Promoting Prosperity: A Partnership to Build Capacity in Costa Rica, El Salvador, Honduras, Guatemala and Nicaraugua," http://www.ustr.gov/assets/Trade_Agreements/Bilateral/CAFTA/asset_upload_file445_3363.pdf, both last searched 5/27/2006.

110. Lance Compa and Jeffrey S. Vogt, "Labor Rights in the Generalized System of Preferences: A 20-Year Review," *Comparative Labor Law & Policy Journal* 22(199) (2001), 5 and 7.

111. Laura M. Baughman and Justin D. Hoffman, "Written Statement of the Coalition for GSP to the Committee on Ways and Means," U.S. House, 2/15/2006,

http://www.tradepartnership.com, last searched 6/06/2006; and interview with Laura Baughman, president of the Trade Partnership, 6/8/2006. The GSP program affects some 140 countries, but they comprise a small percentage of U.S. imports. Only 10% of total imports from developing countries benefit from GSP. But many countries rely on this program for market access for their exports. And many U.S. firms are dependent on key products imported under GSP, such as ferroalloys used in steel or spices used in food products.

112. 2005 Trade Policy Agenda, p. 239; and http://a257.g.akamaitech.net/7/257/2422/14mar20010800/edocket.access.gpo.gov/2004/04-8203.htm, last searched 6/06/2006. On April 12, 2004, USTR announced it was reviewing Bangladesh's GSP privileges, because Bangladesh had not implemented long-standing commitments to the United States to allow its national labor law to be applied in its export processing zones. In 1999, the AFL-CIO filed a petition seeking withdrawal or suspension of GSP benefits for Bangladesh. USTR accepted the petition for review, sought public comment on the petition, including whether withdrawal or suspension of benefits is warranted, and conducted a public hearing. In Bangladesh, unions are very corrupt, and the government has sought to establish new mechanisms for workers to organize collectively, http://www.thedailystar.net/2005/07/25/d5072501085.htm.

113. Scholars Kim Elliot and Richard Freeman found relatively higher success rates when human rights groups were involved in the petition. More democratic countries tend to be more amenable to improving workers' rights. Countries that are more trade dependent on the United States tend to be more willing to work toward change. Finally, their assessment suggests that it is easier to improve minimum wages and safety rather than long-standing practices such as child or forced labor. Elliott and Freeman, *Can Labor Standards*, pp. 76–78, quotation on p. 78, also see p. 84.

114. Compa and Vogt, "Labor Rights in the GSP," pp. 14, 49, 57. As examples of inconsistent application of labor rights GSP criteria, they cite Chile, Malaysia, Indonesia, and Pakistan.

115. For example, the Mexican government has requested consultations on labor rights affecting migrant workers at one of the largest egg farms in Maine, as well as on the rights of workers to organize at a California solar energy panel manufacturer. See Public Submission 9501; 9801; 9804 at http://www.dol.gov/ilab/programs/nao/status.htm#iib4; http://www.dol.gov/ilab/programs/coopact/sectcoopact.htm; and http://www.dol.gov/ilab/programs/coopact/sectcoopact.htm#iii, last searched 6/05/2006.

116. Mexico NAO Submission 2003–1 (North Carolina) was filed by the Farmworker Justice Fund, Inc., and Mexico's Independent Agricultural Workers Central (CIOAC), http://www.dol.gov/ilab/programs/nao/status.htm#iib4.

117. U.S.-Australia Free Trade Agreement, Report of the Labor Advisory Committee for Trade Negotiations and Trade Policy, 3/12/2005, pp. 4–5. U.S. workers are obtaining fewer benefits such as pensions and healthcare. Policymakers have not adequately funded programs for worker retraining.

118. ICFTU, "Internationally Recognised Core Labour Standards," pp. 1–7, 11, 18–19. The ICFTU noted that only 12.5% of the U.S. labor force is unionized. The United States has also some problems of forced labor, prison labor, and trafficking in women. Wage inequalities between men and women and between different ethnic groups still exist.

119. As of 2006, most Republican members of Congress probably would accept a definition of internationally accepted labor rights that means adherence to the four fundamental rights outlined in the ILO Declaration on Fundamental Principles and Rights at Work (freedom of association, recognition of the right to collective bargaining, effective abolition of child labor, and the elimination of discrimination in respect of employment and occupation). But they claim they will not accept an approach to linking trade and labor standards that binds the United States to adhere to ILO Conventions that Congress has not agreed to or which subjects the United States to binding dispute settlement under the agreement.

120. On Malaysia, Eileen Ng, "Anti Free Trade Alliance Demands End to talks on U.S.-Malaysia Pact," Associated Press, 10/30/2006; "Disagreements between US Malaysia on Free Trade Pact," http://today.reuters.com/news/articlenews.aspx?type=politicsNews&storyID= 2006-11-01T052250Z_01_SP305837_RTRUKOC_0_US-TRADE-USA-MALAYSIA.xml&WTmodLoc= PolNewsHome_C2_politicsNews-6;
For another example (South Africa), see Michael Hamlyn, "U.S. all or nothing position derails trade talks," *Business Report*, 11/16/2006, http://www.bilaterals.org/article.php3?id_article=6489; all last searched 11/20/2006.

121. The South Koreans have joined with North Korea in creating a free trade zone (Kaesong). Many U.S. policymakers were reluctant to include the Kaesong free trade zone in its negotiations with South Korea. Some labor and human rights advocates have argued that the North Korean regime exploits its workers in Kaesong. South Korean officials and some other analysts respond by saying that conditions in Kaesong are far better than those in the rest of North Korea. However, North Korea does not meet internationally recognized core labor standards; its workers are not permitted their rights to associate, organize, and bargain collectively. In addition, the North Korean government retains a large share of the money paid to each North Korean worker. Suk Kim, "The Korea–U.S. Free Trade Agreement, the Kaesong Industrial Complex, and U.S.–Korea Relations," *Japan Focus, An Asia-Pacific ejournal* at http://www.japanfocus.org/products/details/2345; and Kelly Olsen, "South Korea, U.S. Try to Save Trade Deal," *Sacramento Bee*, 4/1/2007, at http://dwb.sacbee.com/content/business/24hr_business/story/3589711p-12853210c.html, last searched 4/1/2007. Bloomberg reports that the two sides agreed to discuss goods made there "at a later stage." The Korean daily *Chosun Ilbo* indicated that the Korean trade minister and president said that Kaesong products would in principle be eligible for treatment as South Korean, under a provision in the FTA for an 'outward processing zone'. However, the deputy US Trade Representative Karan Bhatia insisted that there was nothing in the FTA that would "allow goods processed or made in North Korea to enter the US." NA, "U.S. and South Korea Conclude Free Trade Agreement," *Bridges Weekly Trade Digest*, Vol. 11, No. 12, 4/4/2007, at http://www.ictsd.org/weekly/07-04-04/story1.htm

122. Michael Doyle, "Misquoting Madison," http://www.legalaffairs.org/issues/July-August-2002/scene_doyle_julaug2002.msp, last searched 7/26/2006.

123. Communication from the United States on Article X of GATT 1994, G/C/W/384, 6/7/2002; and Robert B. Zoellick, "Free Trade and the Hemispheric Hope," 5/7/2001.

124. UNDP, Human Development Report, 2002, *Deepening Democracy in a Fragmented World*, 2–4, http://hdr.undp.org/reports/global/2002/en/, last searched 8/1/2006.

125. For an archival history of these perceptions and how they led to the development of the ITO and the GATT, see Aaronson, *Trade and the American Dream*, 20–40. Reflecting

that concern, in 1944, President Roosevelt sent William H. Culbertson to conduct a fact-finding tour of North Africa and the Middle East to investigate the degree to which British governmental agencies were trying to control trade. Culbertson concluded that "the American government must lend affirmative support sufficient to create conditions of equality in the face of policies now pursued by other major powers." Randall Bennett Woods, *A Changing of the Guard: Anglo-American Relations 1941–1946* (Chapel Hill: University of North Carolina Press, 1990), 189–190.

126. House Special Committee on Post-war Economic Policy and Planning, *Eighth Report Pursuant to H.R. 60: A Resolution Authorizing the Continuation of the Special Committee on Post-War Economic Policy and Planning, Economic Reconstruction in Europe,* 79th Congress 11/12/1945, 3–9.

127. Aaronson, *Trade and the American Dream,* pp. 82–83. Article X (GATT 1994) says "laws, regulations, judicial decisions and administrative rulings of general application, made effective by any contracting party ... shall be published promptly in such a manner as to enable governments and traders to become acquainted with them. Agreements affecting international trade policy ... shall also be published.... Each contracting party shall administer in a uniform, impartial and reasonable manner all its laws, regulations, decisions and rulings of the kind described in paragraph 1 of this article." WTO, "Article X of GATT 1994-Scope and Application, Note by the Secretariat," TN/1/12/2005.

128. Sylvia Ostry, "China and the WTO: The Transparency Issue," *UCLA Journal of International and Foreign Affairs* 3(1) (1998), 5, 9–10. Dr. Ostry notes that the United States demanded rules for publication and administration of trade regulations designed to limit the room for administrative discretion (distrusted by the Americans after their experience with King George). She concludes that with these provisions, the United States exported its approach to due process, legalization, and transparency into the world trading system.

129. Overview of Trade Facilitation Work in 2002 and Communication from the United States on Article X of GATT 1994, G/C/W/384, 6/7/2002. Other countries commenting on GATT Article X were the European Community, Japan, Korea, and Canada. http://www.wto.org/english/tratop_e/tradfa_e/tradfa_e.htm and http://www.wto.org/english/tratop_e/tradefa_e/tradfa_overview2002_.

130. Congress first made transparency a principal trade negotiating objective in the 1988 trade bill and again in the 2002 Bipartisan Trade Promotion Authority Act. The Omnibus Trade and Competitiveness Act of 1988 (PL 100-418), Section (a) (3), "The principal negotiating objective of the United States regarding transparency is to obtain broad application of the principle of transparency and clarification of the costs and benefits of open trade policy actions through the observance of open and equitable procedures in trade matters by Contracting Parties to the GATT."

131. Bipartisan Trade Promotion Authority, Sec. 2102, (b) 5. at http://www.sice.oas.org/trade/tradeact/act7.asp

132. Bipartisan Trade Promotion Act, Sec. 2102 (8) (A).

133. Bipartisan Trade Promotion Act, Sec. 2102 (11) (G).

134. http://www.ustr.gov/Trade_Agreements/Bilateral/Section_Index.html; and http://search.crownpeak.com/cpt_search/result_1?account=1003&q=transparency+chapters&submit.x=0&submit.y=0.

135. For example, see Chapter 20 of the Australia/U.S. FTA, http://www.dfat.gov.au/trade/negotiations/us_fta/final-text/chapter_20.html; or Chapter 17 of U.S./Bahrain, and Section 19 of U.S./Peru. at www.ustr.gov/Trade_Agreements/Bilateral

136. www.cec.org/jpac

137. www.cec.org/citizen/index.cfm?varlan-english and Bringing the Facts to Light, A Guide to Articles 14 and 15 of the North American Agreement on Environmental Cooperation, at www.cec.org.

138. Laura Silvan, "10 Years of NAFTA Commission on Environmental Cooperation in Mexico: Resolving Environmental Problems and Fostering Citizen Participation," IRC Strategic Dialogue No. 1, 12/13/2004, www.irc-online.org/content/dialogue/2004/01.vp1.php, last searched 8/3/2006.

139. According to President George W. Bush, "open trade . . . spurs the process of economic and legal reform. And open trade reinforces the habits of liberty that sustain democracy over the long term." U.S. Trade Representative Robert Zoellick quoted Bush in Testimony to the Senate Finance Committee, "America's Trade Policy Agenda," 3/5/2003.

140. On the Middle East, see Ambassador Robert B. Zoellick, "Global Trade and the Middle East: Reawakening a Vibrant Past," World Economic Forum, Jordan, 6/23/2003 and Statement of Ambassador Peter F. Algeier, Acting U.S. Trade Representative, before the Senate Finance Committee, 4/13/2005, 6–8. On Central America, see Ambassador Robert B. Zoellick, op-ed, "A Free Trade Boost for Our Hemisphere," *Wall Street Journal*, 11/17/2003, and Ambassador Robert B. Zoellick, "The Route From Miami to Economic Freedom," op-ed published in *Financial Times*, 12/9/2003.

141. CAFTA provides a good example of public concerns about trade agreements. http://www.cispes.org/english/Campaign_Against_CAFTA_FTAA/DR_CAFTA_0503.pdf.

142. See Final Environmental Review of the Agreement on the Establishment of a Free Trade Area between the Government of the United States and the Government of the Hashemite Kingdom of Jordan, no date, 14; and Interim Environmental Review, U.S./Panama Free Trade Agreement, June 2004, 8, both at www.ustr.gov.

143. USTR press release, "U.S. to Seek Input on Environmental Trade Effects," 9/09/2003, www.ustr.gov.

144. Ambassador Peter F. Allgeier, Acting U.S. Trade Representative, US-CAFTA-DR, Testimony before the Senate Finance Committee, 4/13/2005, at http://72.14.209.104/search?q=cache:Z686HdpyT48J:www.senate.gov/~finance/hearings/testimony/2005test/patesto41205.pdf+Max+Baucus+public+participation,+CAFTA&hl=en&gl=us&ct=clnk&cd=15&client=firefox-a

145. UN Development Programme, United Nations Environment Programme, World Bank and the World Resources Institute, "World Resources, 2002–2004: Decisions for Balance, Voice and Power," Chapter 3, 11, 48. The Rio Declaration on the Environment asserted that "environmental issues are best handled with the participation of all concerned citizens. States shall facilitate and encourage public awareness and participation by making information widely available." The Rio Declaration on the Environment was adopted by 178 nations in June 1992, Rio de Janeiro, United Nations Conference on Environment and Development.

146. Report of the Trade and Environment Policy Advisory Committee (TEPAC) 7/14/2004. 7.

147. Interview with Mark Linscott, Assistant USTR for the Environment, and Jennifer Prescott, Deputy Assistant USTR for the Environment, 8/1/2006.

148. See Articles 19.3 and 19.4 U.S. Chile FTA, http://www.ustr.gov/Trade_Agreements/Bilateral/Chile_FTA/Final_Texts/Section_Index.html

149. USTR, "Participation, Empowerment, Partnership: Seeking Sustainable Results through US Trade Capacity Building," 12/2005, 5, at www.ustr.gov. USTR officials gave frequent public presentations about public participation. See Global Alliance for Human Sustainable Development, Human Society International, and Cedarena, "Environmental Perspectives on DR-CAFTA, University of Costa Rica, 8/31/2004, and Tatiana Gutierrez Wa-chong, "Invertiran millones En Proyectos de Cooperacion Ambiental," *La Prensa*, 8/31/2004. Information provided by Mara Burr, Deputy Assistant USTR, e-mail 8/4/2006.

150. Senator Max Baucus, "Looking Forward on Trade – The Agenda for 2005, Remarks to the Global Business Dialogue," 7/13/2004; at http://www.senate.gov/~finance/press/Bpress/2004press/prb071304.pdf

151. Part of the Agreement's work program is to build capacity to promote public participation in environmental decisionmaking. The agreement was negotiated by the Department of State. Environmental Cooperation Agreement, 2/18/2005, http://www.state.gov/g/oes/rls/or/42423.htm; www.state.gov/g/oes/rls/or/2006/67395.htm. Also see U.S. Central America Dominican Republic Sign Environment Pacts, usinfo.state.gov/wh/archive/2005/feb/18–537689.html. The Council met for the first time on May 24, 2006.

152. Communiqué of the Environmental Affairs Council of the Dominican Republic-Central America-United States Free Trade Agreement, 5/24/2006, at www.state.gov/g/oes/rls/or/2006/67395.htm

153. E-mail, Mara Burr, Deputy Assistant USTR for the Environment, 8/4/2006.

154. Interview with Mark Linscott and Jennifer Prescott, 8/2/2006. On Baucus pressure, see letter from Max Baucus, James M. Jeffords, Jeff Bingaman, and Ron Wyden to Ambassador Rob Portman, 11/10/2005. The writers noted, "We applaud your oft-stated eagerness to work with both sides of the aisle to rebuild the trade consensus. Including the same robust environmental provisions that were included in DR-CAFTA is an excellent step in that direction. For the Peru agreement, see http://www.ustr.gov/Trade_Agreements/Bilateral/Peru_TPA/Section_Index.html; for Colombia FTA, see http://www.ustr.gov/Trade_Agreements/Bilateral/Colombia_FTA/Section_Index.html.

155. http://www.ustr.gov/Trade_Agreements/Bilateral/Colombia_FTA/Draft_Text/Section_Index.html, 18.3.

156. www.ustr.gov/trade_agreements/bilateral/Peru, Chapter 18.

157. TEPAC, "The U.S. – Bahrain Free Trade Agreement," 8. See Attachment 1, Separate Statement of TEPAC members Rhoda H. Kapartkin, Consumers Union, William A. Butler, Audubon Naturalist Society, Daniel Magraw, Center for International Environmental Law, and Durwood Zaelke, Center for Governance and Sustainable Development.

158. Report of the Trade and Environment Policy Advisory Committee (TEPAC), "The U.S. Oman Free Trade Agreement, 6–10; Attachment 1, 3–4. http://www.ustr.gov/Trade_Agreements/Bilateral/Oman/Section_Index.html

159. The U.S. Environmental Protection Agency announced a grant competition won by the Environmental Law Institute for a grant to train Moroccan NGOs and the Moroccan Department of Environment to build capacity to protect their environment and enhance their environmental enforcement regimes. But the grant did not delineate that the recipient must teach Moroccans how to participate in environmental

decision-making. http://www.epa.gov/oia/grants/morocco/trade/index.html#I, last searched 8/7/2006. ELI has significant expertise in political participation, see http://www.elistore.org/reports_list.asp?topic = Public_Participation. USTR officials told us they plan to do something similar in Bahrain and Oman. E-mail Jennifer Prescott to Susan Aaronson, 8/7/2006.

160. MCOT News, "PM Calls for More Public Participation in FTA Deals," http://www.bilaterals.org/article.php3?id_article=953&var_recherchublic+information, last searched 8/3/2006. Meanwhile, EPA is reviewing its public participation efforts.

161. Robert B. Zoellick, "Trade Health and Africa's Future," *Journal of Commerce*, 6/30/2003, http://www.ustr.gov/Document_Library/Op-eds/2003/Trade,_health,_Africa's_future.html?ht=. The article was also written by Jacob Nkate, Botswana's minister of trade and industry, and Raymond Gilmarti, CEO of Merck, a major U.S. drugmaker.

162. Rafael Pastor, "The Impact of Free Trade Agreements on Intellectual Property Standards in a Post TRIPS World," 4/2/2006, http://www.bilaterals.org/article.php3?id_article=4311, last searched 5/20/2006; and NA, "Patently Problematic," *The Economist*, 9/14/2002, http://www.economist.com/science/displayStory.cfm?story_id=1325219.

163. See, as example, "Civil Society Report on Intellectual Property, Innovation and Health," http://www.policynetwork.net/main/index.php; and Commission on Public Health, Innovation and Intellectual Property Rights, "Public Health, Innovation, and Intellectual Property Rights," 4/3/2006, http://www.who.int/intellectualproperty/documents/thereport/en/index.html, both searched 5/18/2006; and "How Poor Countries Can Avoid the Wrongs of Intellectual Property Rights," *The Economist*, 9/14/2002, http://www.economist.com/science/displaystory.cfm?story_id+1325360. For a scholarly overview of these issues, see Carsten Fink and Keith E. Maskus, *Intellectual Property and Development: Lessons From Recent Economic Research* (Washington, DC: World Bank and Oxford University Press, 2005), pp. 1–13. In September 2002, an international study group warned that IPR systems may introduce distortions that are detrimental to development. For example, in many developing countries, domestic industries profit by copying rather than innovating; thus, IPR protection does not help them. The study group concluded that industrialized countries should pay more attention to reconciling their commercial self-interest with the need to reduce poverty in developing countries, which is in everybody's interest. Commission on Intellectual Property Rights, "Integrating Intellectual Property Rights and Development Policy: Report of the Commission," London, 9/2002, p. 3.

164. World Bank, "Global Economic Prospects and the Developing Countries," 2002, 137.

165. ACT UP says it is a group of people united in their anger about AIDS, at http://www.actupny.org/reports/tsunami.html. Jamie Love is the Director of Consumer Project on Technology (CP-Tech), http://www.cptech.org/jamie/; CPATH at http://www.cpath.org/. On Oxfam, see *Rigged Rules*, 209–210. And Oxfam Briefing Note, "Undermining Access to Medicines: Comparison of Five US FTA's," 6/16/2004.

166. Davinia Ovett, "Making Trade Policies More Accountable and Human Rights-Consistent: An NGO Perspective of Using Human Rights Instruments in the Case of Access to Medicines," forthcoming in Benedek *et al.*, eds., *Economic Globalization and Human Rights* (New York: Cambridge University Press, 2006), at http://www.3dthree.org/en/page.php?IDpage=13, last searched 8/06/2006.

167. Susan K. Sell, "HIV/AIDS Drugs: The Politics of Access, Paper Prepared for workshop on 'The policy and Politics of HIV/AIDS,'" 5/5/2006, at www.wws.princeton.edu/pai/SSell%20HIV%20AIDS%20Drugs.doc, last searched 7/30/2006.

168. This term comes from author Ted C. Fishman, who uses the term to describe China's approach to manufacturing. Ted Fishman, "Manufaketure," http://www.engin.brown.edu/courses/en100/IP/manuFAKEture.html, last searched 5/20/2006.

169. For example, on April 4, 2006, the chairmen of three House committees warned the Bush administration not to yield to Brazilian and Indian demands to amend TRIPS rules to require that patent applicants disclose the source of genetic materials such as plant life and traditional knowledge. "House Chairmen Warn USTR against Patent Changes in Doha Round," *Inside U.S. Trade*, 4/14/2006, p. 7.

170. Ibid.

171. Press release, "Commerce Secretary Carlos Gutierrez Unveils Initiatives to Fight Intellectual Property Theft," 9/21/2005, http://www.commerce.gov/opa/press/Secretary_Gutierrez/2005_Releases/September/09-21-05%20IPR%20initiatives.htm. Virginia Brown Keyder has an interesting scholarly take on this. See Virginia Brown Keyder, "From Information to Property and Back Again," *Information and Communications Technology Law* 14(3) (October 2005), 299-312.

172. The U.S. Department of Commerce reported that, in 2005, intellectual property theft cost U.S. businesses an estimated $250 billion per year and 750,000 jobs. In 2004, the White House initiated a new program, Strategy Targeting Organized Piracy (STOP! Initiative). The program brings together USTR and the Departments of Commerce, Homeland Security, State, and Justice, Economic Report of the President, 2005, p. 226.

173. Section 2012. (b)(4).

174. USTR, "Intellectual Property Solutions to Public Health Issues," http://www.ustr.gov/Trade_Sectors/Intellectual_Property/Public_Health/Section_Index.html?ht=, last searched 7/30/06. Quote from Paragraph 6 of the Doha Declaration on the Trips Agreement and Public Health, IP/C/W/358, 7/9/2002.

175. Press Release, "U.S. Announces Interim Plan to Help Poor Countries Fight HIV/AIDS and Other Health Crises," 12/20/2002, at http://canberra.usembassy.gov/hyper/2002/1223/epf105.htm, last searched 4/01/2007

176. United States Welcomes Negotiations Leading to Positive Outcome on Enhancing Access to Medicines," 12/06/2005, http://www.ustr.gov/Document_Library/Press_Releases/2005/December/United_States_Welcomes_Negotiations_Leading_to_Positive_Outcome_on_Enhancing_Access_to_Medicines.htmlwww.ustr.gov/document_library/Press_Releases/2005/December; last searched 4/1/2007.

177. USTR, "Fact Sheet on Access to Medicines," 7/09/2004, www.ustr.gov.

178. U.S. persons refer to the language in the Special 301 legislation as well as the language in trade promotion authority.

179. For example, on January 17, 2006, the United States requested that individuals provide information on countries that deny adequate and effective protection of intellectual property rights. *Federal Register* 71(10), 1/17/2006, 2611.

180. USTR, 2005, "Special 301 Report: Executive Summary," at http://www.ustr.gov. One study found that pharmaceutical firms have a strong influence on which countries get placed on the Watch List. M. Asif Ismail, "Drug Makers' Trade Group Makes the Industry's Priorities U.S. Trade Policy," Center for Public Integrity.

http://www.bilaterals.org/article.php3?id_article=2233. However, the United State must rely on industry groups for such information.

181. GAO 04-912, 10-11. China, Paraguay, and the Ukraine have spent time as Priority Foreign Countries but are no longer because they are subject to monitoring under separate agreements. The United States has placed other countries such as Egypt, the European Union, Israel, Korea, and Russia on the Priority Watch List or on the Watch List. The report also includes a section praising those countries that work to improve their IPR enforcement. USTR, "U.S. Government Praises Philippines for Improved IPR Enforcement: Ranking on Annual Report Lowered," http://www.ustr.gov/Document_Library/Press_Releases/2006/February/US_Government_Praises_Philippines_for_Improved_IPR_Enforcement.html, last searched 4/1/2007.

182. GAO-04-912, 25.

183. GAO-04-912, 12, 13. The USTR also reviews IPR enforcement in countries that receive benefits from other trade preference programs, such as the Andean Trade Preference Act or the Africa Growth and Opportunity Act, AGOA. But the United States has used this leverage to prod Colombia to ensure the legitimate use and licensing of software and pressed Mauritius to resolve some ongoing trade mark issues.

184. Report of the Industry Function Advisory Committee on Intellectual Property Rights for Trade Policy Matters (IFAC-3), "The U.S.-Morocco Free Trade Agreement, The Intellectual Property Provisions," 4/6/2004, at www.ustr.gov/bilaterals, 3, 4.

185. The United States has also negotiated some twenty-five IPR specific agreements with countries that are not members of the WTO or as part of broader bilateral agreements. GAO-04-912, 13, 14; and USTR, Special 301 Report 2005.

186. USTR, "Fact Sheet on Access to Medicines, 7/09/2004.

187. Pastor, "The Impact," pp. 11–15

188. Human Development Report 2005, p. 137.

189. UN News Center, "UN Human Rights Expert Urges Peru, US to Protect Health in Any Trade Deal," 7/7/2004, at www.bilaterals.org/article.php3?id_aricle=274&var+recherche; last searched 7/30/2006.

190. Health GAP, "Policy Brief: Response to USTR Fact Sheet on CAFTA and Access to Medicines," 3/16/2005, at www.healthgap.org., last searched 8/2/2006. The law allowed generic manufacturers to obtain market registration without repeating the clinical tests conducted by brand-name manufacturers.

191. U.S. Morocco Free Trade Agreement: Access to Medicines, 7/19/2004, www.ustr.gov/document_library/fact_sheets/2004/US-Moroc; last searched 8/7/2006.

192. USTR, "Pharmaceuticals and the US-Thailand Free Trade Agreement," Trade Facts, 1/2006, www.ustr.gov.; and USTR, "Fact Sheet on Access to Medicines," 7/9/2004, www.ustr.gov/document_library/fact_sheets/2004/fact_sheet_on_Access_to_Med; 4/11/2006.

193. See, as an example, "Understandings Regarding Certain Public Health Measures," Colombia, http://www.ustr.gov/Trade_Agreements/Bilateral/Colombia_FTA/Draft_Text/Section_Index.html, last searched 8/7/2006.

194. For example in its report on CAFTA, this advisory committee noted, "the alarming increase in the international trade in counterfeit pharmaceutical products is raising public health concerns." Report of the Industry Trade Advisory Committee on Intellectual Property Rights (ITAC-3), The U.S.-Central American Free

Trade Agreement, 3/12/2004, http://www.ustr.gov/assets/Trade_Agreements/Bilateral/ CAFTA/CAFTA_Reports/asset_upload_file571-5945.pdf. ITACs have different numbers because the U.S. Government reorganized the advisory committee structure.

195. Report of the Industry Trade Advisory Committee on Intellectual Property Rights (ITAC-15), The U.S.-Peru Trade Promotion Agreement, 2/1/2006, at www.ustr.gov/ bilaterals/peru, 5–7, 16.

196. "Letter from 90 NGOs to U.S. Trade Representative Robert Zoellick, at www.cptech.org/ip/health/trade/ngos05272004.html, last searched 8/07/2006. Also See Marilyn Chase and Sarah Lueck, "In New Trade Pacts, U.S. Seeks to Limit Reach of Generic Drugs," *Wall Street Journal*, 7/6/2004, A1 at http://lists.essential.org/ pipermail/ip-health/2004-July/006664.html, last searched 8/2/2006.

197. Elizabeth Becker and Robert Pear, "Trade Pact May Undercut Inexpensive Drug Imports," *New York Times*, 7/12/2004, at http://query.nytimes.com/gst/fullpage. html?sec=health&res=9A03E0D9113BF931A25754C0A9629C8B63, last searched 4/1/2007.

198. According to the Forum on Trade and Democracy, in 2004–2005, state legislatures introduced 600 bills and resolutions to manage drug costs. Many of the proposals are based on private-sector bargaining practices. Among the popular state initiatives are: pharmaceutical benefit management rules, which increase transparency and accountability of companies that manage drug purchases for the state; and drug import programs, which help consumers to gain access to FDA-approved drugs that are sold at a lower cost in Canada and Europe. http://www.forumdemocracy .net/trade_topics/drug_purchasing/prescription_drugs1.html, last searched 8/02/2006.

199. House Ways and Means Committee Staff, "A New Trade Policy for America," 3/29/2007, at http://waysandmeans.house.gov/media/pdf/NewTradePolicy.pdf.

200. Intergovernmental Policy Advisory Committee, "The U.S. Australia Free Trade Agreement," 3/12/2004, at www.ustr.gov/bilaterals/australia.

201. Rahm Emmanuel, Charles B. Rangel, and Pete Stark to Ambassador Rob Portman, 10/7/2005, http://www.house.gov/stark/news/letters.htm, last searched 7/30/2006. The members noted that "Guatemala, which has the largest number of people infected with HIV/AIDS in Central America, was forced to repeal a law protecting its ability to access life saving pharmaceuticals in order to comply with its CAFTA commitments . . . Congress has consistently directed the Administration to negotiate trade policies that protect public health. However, our current system shuts out the very voices that would ensure the realization of those goals." In 2002, GAO found that "new stakeholders in the trade process, such as public health . . . have limited or no participation in the formal committee system." See James L. Nash, "Congressmen Seek Higher Public Health Profile in Trade Negotiations," 10/13/2005, www.occupational hazards.com/articles/14156.

202. CPATH, "Notes From Meetings of Public Health Organizations and Office of the US Trade Representative," 6/12/2006, at http://www.cpath.org/public-health- representation.htm

203. In its 2007 Trade Policy Agenda, USTR is still very focused on IPR enforcement and shows little flexibility on this issue. http://www.ustr.gov/assets/Document_ Library/Reports_Publications/2007/2007_Trade_Policy_Agenda/asset_upload_file278- 10622.pdf

204. Bush on poverty in Kathern McConnell, "Free Trade Essential for Global Poverty Reduction, Bush Says," 6/15/2006, http://www.usembassy.org.uk/trade474.html, last searched 6/21/2006. Bush also quoted in Susan Ariel Aaronson, *Redefining the Terms of Trade Policymaking* (Washington, DC: NPA, 2001), p. 1.

205. On the GAO, see "Congressmen Seek," and Intergovernmental Policy Advisory Committee, "The US-Peru Trade Promotion Agreement," 7–12.

206. In 1630, Clergyman John Winthrop called on the Puritan colonists of New England to make their new colony in Massachusetts Bay as a city set on a hill which cannot be hid. The city would be watched by the world. The idea that America should be a beacon or light onto the world was accepted by leaders from Abraham Lincoln to Ronald Reagan. However, according to Andrew Kohut and Bruce Stokes, "nothing is more vexing to foreigners than Americans' belief that America is a shining city on a hill – a place . . . where a better way of life exists." Kohut and Stokes, "The Problem of American Exceptionalism."

207. James M. McPherson, "For a Vast Future." Also "Lincoln and the Millennium," Jefferson Lecture, http://www.neh.gov/whoweare/mcpherson/speech.html, last searched 6/24/2006.

208. Nick Wadhams, "U.N. Says Human Rights Violators Cite U.S.," *Washington Post*, 10/24/2006, A4.

7. Conclusion

1. "So You Want to Buy Prescription Drugs in Canada," PBS Frontline, www.pbs.org/pages/frontline/shows/other/etc/so.html. \ , last searched 7/2/2006. Reimportation of prescription drugs by anyone other than the drug's manufacturer is a violation of federal law, but the USG rarely enforces these provisions regarding personal use. The FDA argues it may not be safe to buy drugs from foreign pharmacies, which are not subject to the agency's jurisdiction and could be counterfeit or adulterated. U.S. spending on drugs increased 19% in 2002, whereas other health costs rose 12%. Many states are working on drug import programs to gain access to FDA approved drugs that are sold at a lower cost in Canada and Europe. In 2003, Congress authorized the FDA to allow wholesale imports if the FDA certifies that these imports are safe and reduce the cost of drugs, but the FDA has yet to issue such regulations. http://www.forumdemocracy.net/trade_topics/drug_purchasing/prescription_drugs1.html and http://www.retiredamericans.org/ht/d/Releases/cat_id/511/pid/368, all last searched 4/6/2007.

2. Bill Hogan, "Bus Stop: Why were FDA Agents Searching Our Bags," 6/2004, at http://www.aarp.org/bulletin/prescription/a2004-06-10-busstop.html?print=yes, last searched 7/2/2006.

3. Ibid.

4. In 2003, Congress passed a law revising the Medicare prescription drug program to provide some prescription drug coverage, but that program does not benefit all needy Americans. However, officials at Medicare can't negotiate lower drug prices with either domestic or foreign drug manufacturers. The U.S. pharmaceutical market is unique because the government funds much of the research for drugs, but doesn't cover the cost of drugs. http://www.retiredamericans.org/ht/d/Releases/cat_id/512/pid/369, last searched 7/6/2006.

5. Seniors and those with disabilities often pay out of pocket because they have acute and chronic illnesses and are less likely to have insurance coverage. Many retirees no longer have health benefits. Outpatient prescription drugs are not covered by Medicare.

6. Roger Pilon, "CATO Policy Analysis: Drug Reimportation: The Remarket Solution," No. 521, 8/4/2004.

7. U.S. policymakers argue that because they can't ensure the safety of imported drugs, it does not make sense to count on imports to reduce the price of medications. Rich Weiss, "Two Reports Fault Drug Importation: Government Studies Cite as Concerns Cost of Setting up Program, Safety," *Washington Post*, 12/22/2004, at http://www.washingtonpost.com/wp-dyn/articles/A17702-2004Dec21.html. On the U.S. position, see William K. Hubbard, Associate Commissioner for Policy and Planning, FDA, to Robert P. Lombardi, Esq., The Kullman Firm, 2/12/2003, at www.fda.gov/ora/import/kullman.htm.

    The United States has also placed strict conditions in its FTAs regarding how these drug purchasing programs may operate. As a result, some state government officials fear that America's FTA partners could challenge the operations of state pharmaceutical benefit cost management programs in a trade dispute. Several governors wrote to Ambassador Rob Portman, former U.S. Trade Representative, noting that certain trade agreements "could be used to prevent the reimportation of U.S. pharmaceuticals into our country." Governor Christine Gregoire to Ambassador Rob Portman, 3/13/2006, at www.ustr.gov, last searched 7/2/2006.

8. The drugs cannot be resold. See smart-drugs.net/fda.html, last searched 7/6/2006.

9. Omer Farooq, "Suicide Spree on India's Farms," *BBC News*, 6/3/2004; news.bbc .co/uk/2/hi/south_asia/3769981.stm; Zubair Ahmed, "Debt Drives Indian Farmers to Suicide," *BBC News*, 5/1/2006, news.bbc.co.uk/2/low/business/4954426 .stm; "India Tries to Stem Farmers' Suicides," 6/30/2006, http://english.aljazeera.net/ NR/exeres/7CCF8C5A-A146-48BC-8992-A2A029C10CC3.htm; and *Frontline*, "Seeds of Suicide,' http://www.pbs.org/frontlineworld/rough/2005/07/seeds_of_suicid.html, all searched 7/5/2006.

10. "Farmers Suicide: The Government has Identified 31 Districts in the 4 States," Jansmacharnet, 7/1/2006, http://www.jansamachar.net/display.php3?id=&num= 5312&lang=English, last searched 7/5/2006.

11. Ashling O'Connor, "Debt-hit farmers flock to suicide," *The Australian*, 7/4/06, www.theaustralian.news.com.au/story/0,20867,19672510-2703,00.html, last searched 7/5/06. Critics of the Indian government's policy say that agriculture is driven by subsidies rather than strategic investments. India invests about 0.5 percent of its agricultural GDP in agricultural research, compared with 0.7 percent in developing countries and 2 to 3% in the developed world, according to a report by the International Food Policy Research Institute.

12. Interview with Sachin Chaturvedi, Research and Information Systems for Developing Countries, Delhi, India, April 10, 2006; interview with Dr. Bose, economist, Communist Party of India, New Delhi, India, April 11, 2006; interview with Dr. Biswajit Dhar, professor and head of WTO Studies Program, Indian Institute of Foreign Trade, New Delhi, India, April 14, 2006; and interview with Dr. Sharma, Indian Human Rights Commission, New Delhi, India, April, 2006.UNDP, "Trade on Human Terms: Transforming Trade for Human Development in Asia and the Pacific," July 2006, at http://www.undprcc.lk/rdhr2006/index.asp; 60l last searched 7/5/2006.

13. Ernst-Ulrich Petersmann, "Time for Integrating Human Rights into the Law of World-wide Organizations: Lessons for European Integration Law for Global Integration Law," 17, 26.
14. UNDP, "Human Development Report 2005," 118–122, quote on 119.
15. 3D3, "Planting the Rights Seed: A Human Rights Perspective on Agriculture Trade and the WTO," Backgrounder No. 1, 3/2005, 4.
16. Commission on Human Rights, "Economic, Social and Cultural Rights: The Right to Food: Report Submitted by the Special Rapporteur on the Right to Food, Jean Ziegler, in accordance with Commission on Human Rights Resolution 2003/25, E/Cn.42004/10, 2/9/2004, 6–8.
17. The Indian government develops trade positions to guarantee the right to food of the Indian people. http://www.wto.org/english/res_e/booksp_e/casestudies_e/case15_e.htm
18. UNDP, "Human Development Report 2000, 84.
19. Bruce Stokes, "Germany Stalled," *National Journal*, 7/15/2006, 38–42.
20. Between 31 March 2003 and 14 March 2006, 69 WTO members submitted 69 initial offers on services:

> Albania; Argentina; Australia; Bahrain; Barbados; Brazil; Brunei Darussalam; Bulgaria; Canada; Chile; China; Chinese, Taipei; Colombia; Costa Rica; Croatia; Cuba; Czech Republic; Dominica; Dominican Republic; El Salvador; Egypt; European Communities and its member states; Fiji; Former Yugoslav Republic of Macedonia (FYROM); Gabon; Grenada; Guatemala; Guyana; Honduras; Hong Kong, China; Iceland; India; Indonesia; Israel; Jamaica; Japan; Jordan; Kenya; Korea; Liechtenstein; Macao, China; Malaysia; Mauritius; Mexico; Morocco; New Zealand; Nicaragua; Norway; Oman; Pakistan; Panama; Paraguay; Peru; Philippines; Poland; Qatar; Saint Kitts and Nevis; Saint Lucia; Saint Vincent & the Grenadines; South Africa; Senegal; Singapore; Slovak Republic; Slovenia; Sri Lanka; Suriname; Switzerland; Thailand; Trinidad and Tobago; Tunisia; Turkey; United Arab Emirates; United States; Uruguay. http://www.wto.org/english/tratop_e/serv_e/s_negs_e.htm. .For a good overview of how countries have dealt with services negotiations, see WTO, "Managing the Challenges of WTO Participation: Case Studies," at http://www.wto.org/english/res_e/booksp_e/casestudies_e/casestudies_e.htm, all last searched 7/12/2006.

21. See Human Development Report, 2002, Appendix, 1.1, "Gauging Governance: Measures of Democracy and Political and Civil Rights," 36–37. A critical take on this report is NA, "A Democratic 21st Century? Signals from the United Nation's Human Development Report, 2002, Review Article," *Governance and Development Review*, www.ids.ac.uk/gdr/reviews/review-11.html, last searched 8/15/2006.
22. Dani Rodrik, "Trade Policy Reform as Institutional Reform," August 2000 paper, 18, at http://ksghome.harvard.edu/~drodrik/Reform.pdf, last searched 7/27/2006.
23. Daniel A. Farber, "Rights as Signals," 40–41.
24. See discussion in Chapter 1.
25. Foreign Investment Advisory Services, "Cambodia: Corporate Social Responsibility in the Apparel Sector and Potential Implications for Other Industry Sectors," April, 2005. http://www.ifc.org/ifcext/economics.nsf/AttachmentsByTitle/CSR-Cambodia+Final+FIAS+Report+April+19.pdf/$FILE/Cambodia+Final+FIAS+Report+April+19.pdf, last searched 8/31/2006.
26. UNDP, *Human Development Report 2005*, 10.

27. The poll findings were drawn from the 2005 Globe Scan Report on Issues and Reputation, based on a global poll of citizens across 20 countries conducted between June and August 2005 by research institutes in each participating country. See "20 Nation Poll Finds Strong Global Consensus: Support for Free Market System, But Also More Regulation of Large Companies," www.worldpublicopinion.org/pipa/articles/ btglobalizationtradera/154.php?nid = &id = &pnt = 154&lb = btgl,   last   searched 7/26/2006.

28. This builds on the SAARC Human Resource Development Center, "Training Course on Good Governance," 2004, at http://www.shrdc-isb.org.pk/Training/ 05.GoodGovernance.pdf, last searched 8/31/2006

29. ILO, Bureau of Multinational Enterprises, "Labour and Social Issues Relating to Export Processing Zones," Geneva, 1998. For example, the WTO allows members to put in place export processing zones (EPZs) to attract foreign investment and stimulate trade. Developing country policymakers have often exempted firms in these zones from certain fiscal or financial regulations and others do not require firms in their EPZs to comply with labor laws. As a result, workers in these EPZs often toil in substandard conditions and have little recourse to improve such conditions. Some employers ignore minimum wage regulations, fail to give workers written contracts of employment specifying the hours of work, wages, and other entitlements, or provide decent working conditions.

30. The UN Commission on Human Rights adopted a resolution on April 20, 2005 (by a vote of 49 to 3 with 1 abstention) requesting "the Secretary-General to appoint a special representative on the issue of human rights and transnational corporations and other business enterprises ... with the following mandate: (a) To identify and clarify standards of corporate responsibility and accountability for transnational corporations and other business enterprises with regard to human rights; (b) To elaborate on the role of States in effectively regulating and adjudicating the role of transnational corporations and other business enterprises with regard to human rights, including through international cooperation; (c) To research and clarify the implications for transnational corporations and other business enterprises of concepts such as "complicity" and "sphere of influence"; (d) To develop materials and methodologies for undertaking human rights impact assessments of the activities of transnational corporations and other business enterprises; and (e) To compile a compendium of best practices of States and transnational corporations and other business enterprises ... " http://www.business-humanrights.org/Categories/UNintlorgs/ UNintergovernmentalorgs/UN/UNSpecialRepresentativeonbusinesshumanrights, last searched 7/12/06. Ruggie has developed an interim report and asked for a one year extension. See http://www.business-humanrights.org/Documents/Ruggie HRC2007; and http://www.unhchr.ch/huricane/huricane.nsf/view01/ 19207DD921EE5D22C12572AC00702E2C?opendocument,   both   last   searched   4/1/ 2007.

31. China provides a good example of this dilemma. Several U.S. and European companies power the Internet in China and several of these companies complied with Chinese government demands that they restrict Internet sites (undermining freedom of information) and report on bloggers who criticize official Chinese government policy. U.S. and EU legislators have proposed policies to help companies avoid these problems. and the

EU Parliament "welcomed" a draft law designed to regulate the activities of Internet companies when operating in repressive countries – the Global Online Freedom Act (GOFA) – that has been introduced in the U.S. Congress. http://www.business-humanrights.org/Links/Repository/929033

32. On CSR, see David Vogel, *The Market for Virtue: The Potential and Limits of Corporate Social Responsibility* (Washington, DC: Brookings: 2005); S. Prakash Sethi, *Setting Global Standards: Guidelines for Creating Codes of Conduct in Multinational Corporations* (Hoboken, NJ, Wiley, 2003); Susan Ariel Aaronson, "Minding Our Business: What the United States Government Has Done and Can Do to Ensure that U.S. Multinationals Act Responsibly in Foreign Markets," *Journal of Business Ethics* 59 (2005), 175–198; and Susan Ariel Aaronson and James Reeves, *Corporate Responsibility in the Global Village* (Washington, DC: NPA, 2001).

33. For example, the Dutch government pushed the OECD to develop a paper on this relationship, OECD Secretariat, "Informing Consumers of CSR in International Trade," 6/28/2006, in author's possession. The Dutch government organized a workshop on these issues in Rotterdam on September 26, 2006.

34. For example, some European governments including Belgium want ILO conventions to be included as selection criteria for the awarding of public contracts. Some provinces of Italy use SA 800 certifications to award public procurement. In 2001 the Danish Parliament passed an act which enables public authorities to stipulate certain social obligations in relation to enterprises that either provide services for the public authority or are receiving grants from the public authority. europa.eu.int/comm/employment_social/emplweb/csr-matrix/csr_topic_allcountries_en.cfm?field=14

35. According to an ILO report, eco and social labeling programs may improve social or environmental conditions and raise funds for educational and rehabilitation programs. They may build consensus on social and environmental objectives. But they may also cause developing country firms that can't comply to go bankrupt and jobs, particularly developing country jobs, to disappear.

36. WTO Analytical Index; Technical Barriers to Trade: Agreement on Technical Barriers to Trade, /www.wto.org/english/res_e/booksp_e/analytic_index_e/tbt_01_e.htm#top. Currently, WTO rules state "In conformity with Article 2.9 of the Agreement, Members are obliged to notify all mandatory labeling requirements that are not based substantially on a relevant international standard and that may have a significant effect on the trade of other Members. . . . When assessing the significance of the effect on trade of technical regulations, the Member concerned should take into consideration such elements as the value or other importance of imports in respect of the importing and/or exporting Members concerned, whether from other Members individually or collectively, the potential growth of such imports, and difficulties for producers in other Members to comply with the proposed technical regulations. The concept of a significant effect on trade of other Members should include both import-enhancing and import-reducing effects on the trade of other Members, as long as such effects are significant."

37. Editorial, "A Dangerous Job in Colombia," *New York Times*, 7/12/2006, A22.

38. Brazil's National Action Plan for Human Rights, available online in English: http://www.ohchr.org/english/countries/coop/brazil.htm. Also, see UNDP, "Human Development Report 2000," 118.

39. http://www.humanrightsimpact.org/about-the-database/, last searched 7/27/2006.
40. See, for example, Lael Brainard, ed., "Security by Other Means: Foreign Assistance, Global Poverty and American Leadership," Executive Summary in possession of author, see, http://www.brookings.edu/global/security_chapters.htm, last searched 7/26/2006.
41. See, for example, "Secretary-General Says High Level Political Attention Has Been Diverted From Key Challenges of Sustainable Development," press release SG/SM/9280, 4/28/2004 at www.un.org/news/Press/docs/2004/sgsm9280.doc.htm; Jean-Pierre Chauffour, Senior Economist and Representative to the WTO, "Institutional Accountability in pro-Human Rights-Growth Policies: The IMF Perspective,"7/21/2005, at http://www.ohchr.org/english/issues/poverty/docs/3sfMrChauffourIMF.pdf; Dani Kaufmann, "Human Rights and Governance: The Empirical Challenge," 15–16; and UNDP, "Trade on Human Terms: Transforming Trade for Human Development in Asia and the Pacific," July 2006, at http://www.undprcc.lk/rdhr2006/index.asp, 15, all last searched 7/5/06.
42. We are heartened that some policymakers are beginning to think along these lines. In a public letter to the WTO's trade ministers, published on July 26, 2006, WTO Director General Pascal Lamy noted, "I ask you to look at the big picture . . . and consider those living in poverty who saw in these negotiations a hope for a better life . . . The WTO has the possibility to contribute to making this world fairer and more stable. Please think about that."Pascal Lamy: What Now, Trade Ministers?" *International Herald Tribune*, 7/27/2007, http://www.iht.com/articles/2006/07/27/opinion/edlamy.php, last searched 7/27/2007.

Index